Ethics at the Edges of Life

Books by Paul Ramsey

The Ethics of Fetal Research
The Patient as Person: Explorations in Medical Ethics
Fabricated Man: The Ethics of Genetic Control
The Just War: Force and Political Responsibility
Deeds and Rules in Christian Ethics
Who Speaks for the Church? A Critique of the 1966 Geneva Conference on Church and Society
Nine Modern Moralists
Christian Ethics and the Sit-In
War and the Christian Conscience: How Shall Modern War be Conducted Justly?
Basic Christian Ethics

Edited by Paul Ramsey

(with John F. Wilson) *The Study of Religion in Colleges and Universities*
(with Gene H. Outka) *Norm and Context in Christian Ethics*
Religion: Humanistic Scholarship in America
Freedom of the Will (by Jonathan Edwards)
Faith and Ethics: The Theology of H. Richard Niebuhr

Ethics at the Edges of Life

Medical and Legal Intersections

The Bampton Lectures in America

Paul Ramsey

New Haven and London Yale University Press

1978

Designed by John O. C. McCrillis
and set in Times Roman type.
Printed in the United States of America by
Vail-Ballou Press, Inc., Binghamton, N.Y.

Published in Great Britain, Europe, Africa, and Asia (except Japan) by Yale University Press, Ltd., London. Distributed in Latin America by Kaiman & Polon, Inc., New York City; in Australia and New Zealand by Book & Film Services, Artarmon, N.S.W., Australia; and in Japan by Harper & Row, Publishers, Tokyo Office.

Library of Congress Cataloging in Publication Data

Ramsey, Paul.
Ethnics at the edges of life.

Includes index.
1. Medical ethics. 2. Life and death, Power over.
3. Medical laws and legislation—United States.
4. Christian ethics. 5. Medical policy—United States. I. Title.
R724.R3 174'.2 77-76308
ISBN 0-300-02137-2
ISBN 0-300-02141-0 pbk.

To
my grandson
Joshua Warren Wood IV

Oh horrible sophistry, spreading microscopically and telescopically abroad in folio upon folio and which qualitatively speaking produces nothing, but certainly fools men into giving up a simple and profoundly passionate admiration and wonder of things which is the motive power of ethics.

Søren Kierkegaard, *Journals*

It happened that a fire broke out backstage in a theater. The clown came out to inform the public. They thought it was a jest and applauded. He repeated his warning, they shouted even louder. So I think the world will come to an end amid general applause from all the wits, who believe that it is a joke.

Søren Kierkegaard, *Either/Or*

Contents

Preface

In November 1975, I gave the Bampton Lectures in America at Columbia University. The Bampton Lectures were founded on a bequest of Ada Byron Bampton Tremaine in 1928, who designated a course of lectures, to be given periodically, "of a theologic nature, similar to the 'Bampton Lectures' in the University of Oxford, England, founded by John Bampton, Canon of Salisbury." The Bampton Lectures at Oxford have been given for many, many decades; they are the most honored lectures in theology at Oxford.

Of the lectures given on the Bampton endowment in America, Arnold J. Toynbee's in 1948 were the first to be published. Subsequent Bampton Lecturers in America include C. H. Dodd, Lewis Mumford, James B. Conant, John Baillie, Eric L. Mascall, Paul Tillich, Northrop Frye, Fred Hoyle, Alasdair MacIntyre, Paul Ricoeur, Jacob Bronowski. For me to be added to such a list of distinguished intellectuals was a great, if undeserved, honor.

The committee that extended the invitation to me consisted of James A. Martin, Jr., chairman of the Department of Religion at Columbia University; William Theodore de Bary, Horace Walpole Carpenter Professor of Oriental Studies, provost of the university, and vice-president for academic affairs; J. Paul Martin, director of the Center for Religion and Life; and Roger L. Shinn, dean of graduate studies, Union Theological Seminary. William J. McGill, president of Columbia University, signaled the importance of this lectureship to the university community by his warm, not routinely official, introduction of me at the first of my four Bampton Lectures.

I am deeply grateful for the formal honor of being the 1975 Bampton Lecturer but even more for the cordiality these individuals extended to me, for the response of faculty and students, and for the opportunity to participate on this occasion in a medical ethics seminar at the Columbia College of Physicians and Surgeons and in a panel on "Death as the Ethical Problem for the Professions" at one of the regular meetings in which, uniquely, the faculty and students of Columbia maintain a continuing discussion of general, humanistic education.

The present volume is a revision and extension of my Bampton Lectures. Chapters 4 and 7, " 'Euthanasia' and Dying Well Enough" and "In the Matter of *Quinlan,*" were originally the first lecture. Chapter 2, on abortion and the problem of conscientious refusal, was the second lecture. The fourth and final lecture, on the benign neglect of defective newborns, is extended here into two chapters and also into the analysis of principles at other points as well. Entirely omitted is the third of the four Bampton Lectures, entitled "The Continuing Story of Fetal Research Ethics," which was an analysis of the moral reasoning in the report on this question by the National Commission for the Protection of Human Subjects in Biomedical and Behavioral Research. That lecture plus a full scale case study of the decision-making process that went on in the National Commission's deliberations will be incorporated in a revised and enlarged—and, I think, definitive—edition of my book *The Ethics of Fetal Research.*

Since I undertook to revise and extend the Bampton Lectures rather than quickly publish them in a slender volume as delivered, it then seemed logical for me to take up adjacent issues in additional chapters. Besides the issue of institutional and individual conscience clauses in the matter of abortion, the *Edelin* case intruded as well as *Planned Parenthood* v. *Danforth,* the most important United States Supreme Court decision since 1973 affecting our practice in regard to the first of life. Chapters on these cases are added to comprise part 1. Then there were certain sequelae to the *Quinlan* case—as well as positions announced since I first addressed the issue of neglecting to treat defective newborns—that seemed to me to demand equal attention. These chapters are added to complete Part Two on medical, ethical and legal intersections at the last of life.

This makes for some imbalance between part 1, "The First of Life" (three chapters), and part 2, "The Last of Life" (six chapters). If such an observation occurs to anyone, he or she will have stepped within the ambit of one theme this volume will argue. As a society we are already beginning to believe that decision not to treat defective newborns is a "first of life" issue. I locate that as a "last of life" problem—hence the observed imbalance. While there may be some meaning in speaking of the "untimely" death of the young, I see no conclusive reason for saying that six months of babyhood or two years of infancy are of less ultimate worth than sixty years of manhood or womanhood. I know the greater *worths* the latter have, but not the greater worth. Respect for life and the protection of life in our medical, ethical, and legal traditions do not vary according to duration, achievement, or productivity. As the author of Ecclesiastes observed, we are all soon off to the dead. Vanity of vanities, all is vanity, he said; I say, equality.

I do not decide the question whether there are nonreligious warrants for such a view. Indeed, I venture to believe that there may be a truly *humanistic* ethics which acknowledges the awesome claims and entitlements of another human life simply because he or she is a human being. Where I would be inclined to say the "sanctity" of human life, the reader may choose rather to say the "dignity" of human life. There may be vector convergence between religious ethics and humanistic ethics, so long as the value of *human* life is not allowed to acquire a generic meaning—species life, familial life, social life—which obliterates the individual who (the religious say) is still our neighbor whatever may be his or her condition or achievement or duration or productivity.

It is in this context that I do not hesitate to write as a Christian ethicist. No more did I hesitate in my first major book on medical ethics to invoke ultimate appeal to scripture or theology and to warrants such as righteousness, faithfulness, canons of loyalty, the awesome sanctity of a human life, humankind in the image of God, holy ground, *hesed* (steadfast covenant love), agape (or "charity"), as these standards are understood in the religions of our culture, Judaism and Christianity. I do not hesitate to employ the norms of past Christian medical ethics, even while proposing their radical revision in the present volume.

The physicians, lawyers, ethicists, and—most of all—the ordinary concerned citizens to whom I address my analysis and argument need in no way be offended by the religious warrants that are decisive for me. Such a person can read with a view to showing that there is a nonreligious replacement for "my neighbor as holy ground" that still sustains an inviolable human dignity. It is not so much that I grant this may be true as that I am myself profoundly uninterested in finding out whether it is or not. That would be such a reader's business if—as I suppose—there may be a real convergence of religious and truly humanistic views of the worth and inviolability of a human life.

It is true that I do ask something of such a reader. There are pages, passages, and a few entire sections where religious justifications are explicitly invoked and *explained.* Indeed there are one or two places where such a reader—if he reads on and does not skip—would be drawn into intra-Christian debate over the meanings to be prolonged from "our" religious ethics. At these points, an open-minded reader can persist for insight and read as if he is inquiring into a conversation overheard.

I go too far in apology. Such a reader will not find most of the following analysis to be parochially limited to a religious outlook. This is true for two reasons. In the first place, the Judeo-Christian tradition decisively influenced the origin and shape of medical ethics down to our own times. Unless an author absurdly proposes an entirely new ethics, he is bound to use ethical principles derived from our past religious culture. In short, medical ethics nearly to date is a concrete case of Christian "casuistry"—that is, it consists of the outlooks of the predominant Western religion *brought down to cases* and used to determine their resolution. This is the sense in which professional medical ethics is only a special case of a more general ethics. As Sir Patrick Devlin said of lifelong marriage as the ideal or norm in Western civilization, it got there because it was Christian; it cannot be eliminated without bringing the whole house down. Whether medical ethics needs religious foundation, and whether it will be misshapen without it, awaits demonstration—or, more likely, the test of time. I do not undertake to argue the point. The humanist no more than I should want our opposite positions tested at such fateful costs. I do say, however, that the notion that an individual human life is absolutely unique, inviolable, irreplaceable, noninterchangeable, not substitutable, and not meldable with other lives is a notion that exists in our civilization because it is Christian; and that idea is so fundamental in the edifice of Western law and morals that it cannot be removed without bringing the whole house down.

In the second place, whether our moral outlooks are inspired by a humanistic vision of life or by a religious perspective, there may be a convergence between these points of departure on the plane of special moral problems. We may reasonably hope, and we need to search, for a fruitful meeting between various ultimate "good reasons" put forward in support of moral judgments as we move into the area of the specific dilemmas taken up in this volume, such as euthanasia, the treatment of defective newborns, the protection of an effective liberty of conscience in regard to abortion, spousal or parental participation in an abortion decision, and a physician's standard of care for a possibly viable infant "delivered" by abortion. In our pluralistic society, reasonable ethical discourse is still possible on these questions. My experience is that "unbelievers" often understand better than some of my fellow "believers" that religious warrants need not be silenced in order to engage in fruitful moral discourse about urgent common problems. Besides, everyone has an ultimate and no one leaves behind his unargued viewpoints when entering a rational argument.

The integrated theme of this volume is to direct attention to medical, ethical, and legal intersections at the edges of life, in the first and at the last of it. This does not mean that we begin with ethical analysis and then later on take up briefly the question of professional practice and the formulation of public medical policy, or that we secondarily come to the law on these questions. Each chapter is concerned with medicine, ethics, law, and with medical and public policy. Passages or chapters that open with an attempt to reason morally concerning right and wrong do not end, and would be incomplete, without examining relevant laws or court decisions that make policy. Passages or chapters that open with questions of law or public policy set by law do not end, and would be incomplete, without the interlaced or concluding ethical evaluation. The decision of the Supreme Court of New Jersey in the *Quinlan* case, the Fourteenth Amendment rights of defective newborn infants, the "conscience clauses" in the United States Code and in state statutes, the Supreme Court's landmark decision in *Planned Parenthood* v. *Danforth,* and California's National Death Act are some of the public policies framed by law taken up for detailed analysis. Integrated with these are the views of and relevant arguments among theologians and ethicists on the issues in question. Throughout the concern is with medical ethics *and* legal or public policy; with the processes of public policymaking and the ethical ingredient in policy formation.

Therefore when I directly undertake legal analysis I mean at the same time to engage in ethical assessment of a court's or of the law's reasoning. I mean also to hold up these legal processes and the law's final authorization of important national policies as mirrors in which we can see reflected the state of moral questions as these are perceived today—mirrors in which powerful trends in the ethos of contemporary society can be clearly seen. Social and institutional criticism is the aim: an ethical assessment of the discourse going on concerning issues of medical practice and public policy. The reader is also invited to join me in wrestling with the question of how, if at all, morality influences public policy, and to join me (so far as the reader agrees with my critique) in searching for institutions and decision-making processes that may incarnate a somewhat higher level of public moral discourse and reasoning.

Individual chapters in this volume have been read and criticized by Professor John A. Robertson, University of Wisconsin Law School; Professor Yale Kamisar, University of Michigan Law School; Professor Walter Murphy, my colleague at Princeton, whose specialty in our Department of Politics is constitutional law; and J. Warren Wood III, Secretary and Counsel of the Robert Wood Johnson Foundation. I have profited from their comments. I learned also from One Unnamed, Blessed be He, the anonymous reader of an earlier manuscript for the Press. The reader's scrutiny went far beyond the call of duty or the fee he was paid, and I learned a great deal at that point in the production of the present volume. No doubt, flaws in my argument might have been corrected and clarity of statement improved if there had been time for me to seek other readers as well—especially comments from ethicists whose writings I have submitted to critical analysis. But then, gentle reader, you would have been forced to wait another year before seeing this book in print. Let me simply say—possibly over the objection of my editor, Jane Isay, at the Yale University Press—that I regard publication as only another form of communication. One reaches a larger audience, but the printed word is only a little less perishable than good conversation. I do not write for ages to come. That reminds me: to Jane Isay and Helena Bentz Dorrance—my friendly irritants, companions in arms, editors par excellence, whom I warmly embrace ambivalently—thanks are due. Both confidence and criticism they extended; without them this volume might not have been, or would have been of far less merit than it now perhaps can claim. Mrs. Doris Nystrom and Mrs. Phyllis Durepos did the typing: bravo!

This volume, then, invites participation at one stage in an ongoing discussion of some contemporary issues in ethics, in medical and public policy, which I believe to be important for the moral history of humankind, both in this country and in the world at large. The volume is addressed to lawyers, to physicians, to ethicists of any persuasion, to the religious, and above all to the general reader who needs to hear those others talk. If someone in one or another of those categories is offended when the address seems to be to someone else, I am sorry, but still I must say that all must be addressed, and we must address one another across those boundaries if there is to be any healing word spoken or heard by anyone.

This book—my last in medical ethics—is dedicated to my grandson. Whoever he may be in future years, wherever he may be in time's devolutions, whatever he may think, I hope he grasps the distance to be gained by a human being—from the most pressing, critically urgent problems or from the somber themes on all these pages—only by the irony and the humor of the quotations from Kierkegaard which I place at the first or else by the thoughts of Plato and St. Augustine at the end.

Princeton, New Jersey
June 27, 1977

PAUL RAMSEY

PART ONE

The First of Life

1

The Supreme Court's Bicentennial Abortion Decision: Can the 1973 Abortion Decisions be Justly Hedged?

On July 1, 1976 the United States Supreme Court gave us its bicentennial abortion decision. The next day it announced its ruling on the constitutionality of capital punishment. In the matter of the death penalty, the several opinions of the justices depended heavily on the fact that numerous state legislatures had recently adopted revised provisions for capital punishment. This fact, they argued, demonstrates that capital punishment is not widely regarded as per se "cruel and unusual punishment." [1] In the abortion decision,[2] however, the Court extended its use of "substantive due process" reasoning to overrule the judgment of the legislature of the state of Missouri in a statute [3] carefully crafted to mesh with the parameters of the Court's 1973 decisions.[4]

1. *Woodson* v. *North Carolina*, 428 U.S. 280 (1976); excerpt and analysis in *The New York Times*, July 3, 1976.

2. *Planned Parenthood* v. *Danforth*, 428 U.S. 52 (1976). Justice Blackmun delivered the opinion of the Court, in which Justices Brennan, Stewart, Marshall, and Powell joined. Justice Stevens joined also in part but dissented in parts joined by Chief Justice Burger and Justices White and Rehnquist. Justice Stewart filed a concurring opinion in which Justice Powell joined. Justice White filed an opinion concurring in part and dissenting in part, in which Chief Justice Burger and Justice Rehnquist joined. Justice Stevens filed an opinion concurring in part and dissenting in part. These divisions as well as the substance of the opinions to be examined below demonstrate that the citizens and legislatures of the several states should continue to exercise their constitutional function in enacting legislation that will test the meaning and limits of *Wade and Bolton*. Indeed, as we will see, the Court practically invites this.

3. H.C.S. House Bill no. 1211, appended to the *Planned Parenthood* v. *Danforth* decision.

4. *Roe* v. *Wade*, 410 U.S. 113 (1973), and *Doe* v. *Bolton*, 410 U.S. 179 (1973). Historically the phrase "due process of law" that appears in the Fifth and Fourteenth amendments to the U.S. Constitution referred solely to procedures, to the notion that government could not move against a citizen without observing traditional procedures—in the judicial process, for example, indictment by grand jury and trial by jury. Beginning in the 1850s, however, a very different idea began to grow onto the

The landmark abortion decision of the Supreme Court was sparsely, and for that reason alone misleadingly, reported by even our best newspapers. Often it was portrayed as a "victory" for unlimited abortion, calling for decent silence from those opposed to its arguments. I propose to analyze the arguments as well as the rulings of the Court and the concurring and dissenting opinions, quoting extensively from what the justices said. This is not only proper; it is a civic duty—if ever a greater measure of reason is to be introduced into advocacy. The Court would simply issue *rulings* if it did not intend its written *opinions* to be taken seriously.

My purpose is to use this decision as a magnifying glass held up to the moral fabric of this nation, through which we can see clearly what is happening (or what *has* happened) to us as a people. From this

---

older notion. This new concept implied that there were certain things that government could not do to a citizen *regardless* of procedural niceties.

The principal context in which this new doctrine developed was that of protection of private property. Thus Chief Justice Roger Brooke Taney invoked it in the Dred Scott case, 19 How. 393 (1857), to place the slaveholder's right to property in the slave over the slave's right to liberty or even to access to the federal courts to determine which right should prevail. It was not, however, until the generation after the Civil War that substantive due process became firmly embedded in American constitutional law.

The most important substantive right protected was one intimately connected with industrialization and commerce—freedom of contract. This right modern jurisprudential jargon might call one of the "penumbral" inferences from the right to hold property. Speaking for the Supreme Court in 1905, Justice Rufus Peckham could correctly hold that in terms of substantive due process state efforts to establish maximum working hours were an abridgement of the sacred rights of both worker and owner to negotiate as equals; so the regulations constituted "mere meddlesome interferences with the rights of the individual . . ." (*Lochner* v. *New York,* 198 U.S. 45). Two decades later, George Sutherland, again speaking for the Court, summed up the rule regarding a manager's and a worker's right to agree on less than the minimum wage: "Freedom of contract is, nevertheless, the general rule and restraint the exception; and the exercise of legislative authority to abridge it can be justified only by the existence of exceptional circumstances" (*Adkins* v. *Children's Hospital,* 261 U.S. 525 [1923]).

It was this doctrine that the Nine Old Men used to strike down "progressive" state legislation. The enactment of a federal income tax by the U.S. Congress (i.e., by proper procedural due process) did not withstand constitutional scrutiny in face of the Court's "substantive due process" (*Pollock* v. *Farmer's Loan and Trust Co.,* 157 U.S. 429, rehearing, 158 U.S. 601 [1895]). This can only be read as the Court's legislation of its own policy wisdom in place of the deliberations and law of the Congress. After the great battle between FDR and the Court over the constitutionality of New Deal legislation, the justices began denouncing substantive due process; and, in

perspective Justice Blackmun's opinion for the Court manifests who and where we are; the dissent manifests what might have been; and the vacancy that remains points to tasks of recovery yet to come. The Court is not to be blamed; it shares with many the pity that needs to be cried over Jerusalem.

We went on that week to a glorious celebration of our Declaration of Independence. In that spirit it can be suggested that he remains a slave who is unwilling to dissent from the "hierarchical magisterium" of the judicial branch of government. Indeed, the claim must surely be made that, as with the church, no hierarchical magisterium can function properly and wisely without vocal—if measured—dissent. Better decisions should come from those who, by office and calling, speak for us and for the Constitution as a living document that binds

---

economic regulation at least, the Court has abandoned the doctrine. But beginning in the 1920s, the justices—prodded by Holmes and Brandeis and later by Stone and Cardozo and Hughes—began to admit that the logic of substantive due process would include certain other fundamental rights such as those protected by the First Amendment. Thus these were included in the rights that the due process clause of the Fourteenth Amendment guarded against state encroachment. Later, of course, liberal judges found that the due process clause was a shorthand way of saying that states had to respect most of the rights listed in or implied by the Bill of Rights.

As late as 1963, however, the Court purported to sound the death knell for the doctrine of substantive due process. In *Ferguson* v. *Skrupa,* 372 U.S. 726, 730, Mr. Justice Black's opinion for the Court said: "We have returned to the original constitutional position that courts do not substitute their social and economic beliefs for the judgment of legislative bodies, who are elected to pass laws." Barely two years later, however, the right of privacy received the blessing of substantive due process (*Griswold* v. *Connecticut,* 381 U.S. 479 [1965]).

In incorporating provisions of the Bill of Rights into the Fourteenth Amendment's due process clause, including the "penumbral" right of privacy, the justices have obviously been applying a rebaptized version of substantive due process. For ideological rather than logical reasons, however, they become incensed when someone points out that they are still following the doctrine forcefully rejected in *Skrupa.* In *Wade,* only Mr. Justice Stewart, concurring, was forthright on this point—and plunged ahead. Stewart wrote: "As so understood, *Griswold* stands as one in a long line of pre-*Skrupa* cases [i.e., cases protecting property from the reach of legislation] decided under the doctrine of substantive due process, and I now accept it as such."

In this chapter we examine yet another case in which the Court substitutes its social and medical beliefs for the judgment of the Missouri legislators, who were elected to pass laws. "The competing arguments on these issues [spousal and parental consent] make it clear . . . that the Court is acting very much like a legislative body by arguing what is best for society, rather than what is constitutionally required" (George J. Annas, "Abortion and the Supreme Court: Round Two," *Hastings Center Report* 6, no. 5 [October 1976] : 16).

us together as one people. A fair comment on the Court's decision cannot fail to note commendable clarifications and interpretations of the law which might not have been forthcoming had the challenged statute never been enacted by the state of Missouri. That same process must continue through statutes enacted in any or all of the states.

A Definition of Viability

The Missouri statute defined viability as "that stage of fetal development when the life of the unborn child may be continued indefinitely outside the womb by natural or artificial life-supportive systems." That definition was upheld. In doing so, however, the Court observed that "it is not the proper function of the legislature *or the courts* to *place* viability" (italics added). Placing or locating viability is not the same as defining viability, whose location is then left to the discretion or reasonable medical judgment of physicians. The constitutionality of the Missouri definition had been challenged because it conflicted with the measure of trimesters used in *Wade*. The Court therefore drew back from the latter. Physicians are generally agreed, I gather, that the Court's use of trimester language and its location of viability at twenty-eight or even twenty-four weeks were "bad medicine" and bad fetal physiology, even in 1973.

The Missouri definition was also challenged because of its use of the expression "continued *indefinitely* outside the womb" (italics added). Here the Court observed that, if anything, the statute's words "continued indefinitely" favor rather than disfavor physicians' judgments, since "arguably, the point when life can be 'continued indefinitely outside the womb' " by natural or artificial life-supportive systems "may well occur later in pregnancy than the point where the fetus is 'potentially able to live outside the mother's womb' " (the language of *Wade*).

In his concurring opinion, Justice Stewart (joined by Justice Powell) observed that "the critical consideration is that the statutory definition has almost no operative significance"; it merely requires the physician to *certify* that the fetus to be aborted is not viable; he saw no "chilling" effect.

But a statutory definition may have more "operative significance" than Stewart and Powell suppose—even when not combined with its displacement of trimester language from center stage. The justices may not realize the lacunae and the confusion left by *Wade* in the public's mind and in physicians' practice. Here it is pertinent to quote from a statement issued by the executive board of the prestigious American College of Obstetricians and Gynecologists:

> The College further recognizes that the United States Supreme Court and the several states have never clarified the issues raised by the delivery of live infants, whether previable or viable, resulting from legal abortion procedures. This lack of clarification places physicians in legal jeopardy. The College recognizes that issues of life and death are properly the province of courts and legislatures, but the College asserts also that if the state's compelling interest in the quality of medical care of its citizens is to be served, the laws must be clear on the issues at stake.[5]

Not unnaturally, the Court supposed that "issues of life and death" are covered constitutionally by the Fourteenth Amendment (where also it found the woman's right of privacy, on which was grounded her and her physician's liberty to abort) and—as we shall see—also covered by the existing criminal law of the states.

Nevertheless, by upholding Missouri's definition of viability, the Court has helped to clear up confusion left by *Wade* concerning the state's continuing and undiminished interest in the protection of a possibly viable infant. Another "operative significance" or side effect of the definition of viability may be a greater understanding that a woman's lawful right to an abortion means no more than her right to have her pregnancy terminated; and it in no way means her right to

5. "Some Ethical Considerations on Abortion," approved by the executive board of the American College of Obstetricians and Gynecologists, October 27, 1975, as amended December 12, 1975. The above quotation follows a noteworthy statement of professional ethics in the practice of medicine by fellows of the college, who have "traditionally been responsible for the welfare of the pregnant woman *and her fetus*. . . . The College affirms that the resolution of such conflict [in cases justifying induced abortion] in no way implies that the physician has an adversary relationship towards the fetus, and therefore, the physician does not view the destruction of the fetus as the primary purpose for abortion. The College consequently recognizes *a continuing obligation on the part of the physician towards the survival of a possibly viable fetus* where this obligation can be discharged without additional hazard to the health of the mother" (italics added). That is as clear a statement as could be made of the fact that, in medical ethics, abortion is a severance procedure (a termination of *pregnancy*) and that a woman has no fundamental need for or right to a dead fetus although its death may often be tragically unavoidable.

have the procedure produce a dead baby. To my amazement, in discussion groups throughout this land, I have found that many people suppose that the moral and legal issues this raises can be settled by asking abortion counselors to tell us what women expect. That would imply an extension of a woman's right over her body and control over her reproductive capacities that, until now, everyone should have known to be unlawful [6] and wholly immoral.

The Woman's Written Consent

The Missouri statute required, even in the case of an abortion during the first twelve weeks of pregnancy, that the woman certify in writing her consent to the procedure and "that her consent is informed and freely given and is not the result of coercion." That was challenged as "overboard and vague" and in conflict with *Bolton*'s prohibition of layers of state regulation between a woman and her physician in first trimester abortions. The Supreme Court upheld the provision. Precisely because a decision to abort is an important and often stressful one, a state may act to insure a woman's awareness of the decision and its significance by requiring prior written consent.

The noteworthy aspect of the Court's decision on this point is that in so ruling it did not ask whether consents required in Missouri do or do not single out the abortion procedure. It did not require that abortion consents be the same as in the case of all other operative procedures. To the contrary, the Court said, "We see no constitutional defect in requiring [prior written consent, certified to be informed and uncoerced] only for some types of surgery as, for example, an intracardiac procedure, or where the surgical risk is elevated above a specified mortality rate, or, *for that matter, for abortions*" (italics added).

6. In granting the physician-appellants "standing" to challenge the constitutionality of Missouri's statute, the Court agreed with them that if, for example, the definition of viability threatened them, "they should not be required to await and undergo a criminal prosecution as the sole means of seeking relief." But at that point (in note 2), the Court observed: "This is not so, however, with respect to § 7 of the Act pertaining to state wardship of a live born infant" resulting from an abortion. Indeed, the physician-appellants did not contend that this section of the act threatened to incriminate them. That section abrogated maternal and paternal rights (if the husband consented to the abortion) and declared a "live born infant" following an abortion procedure to be "an abandoned ward of the state." That withstood constitutional scrutiny. Below we shall consider a similar bill recently enacted by the California legislature.

The Spouse's Consent

Here we reach the first point of disagreement among the justices. The Missouri statute required prior written consent of the spouse of the woman seeking an abortion during the first twelve weeks of pregnancy, unless "the abortion is certified by a licensed physician to be necessary to preserve the life of the mother." In *Wade* and *Bolton* the Court had reserved opinion on the question of spousal consent. Now *Planned Parenthood* v. *Danforth* holds a requirement to be unconstitutional.

Here, too, we reach a point where the Court's reasoning mirrors the present moral fabric of our society and the assumptions concerning the nature of the community of marriage prevalent today. Attorney General John C. Danforth rested his case for the people of Missouri on the state's long-standing interest in "marriage as an institution, the nature of which places limitations on the absolute individualism of its members." The physician-appellants, Danforth said in his brief, "see marriage as the cohabitation of two individuals, each of whom possesses separate *individual* rights which may be in conflict. . . . Abortion is a purely personal right of the woman, and the *status of marriage* can place no limitations on personal rights" (italics added). Here was a conflict of world views, between the state's claimed interest in *the bond* of marriage, and marriage as a contract between individuals who remain as atomistic as before. In support of a state's legitimate interest in "marriage as an institution," a number of other "joint consent" requirements were cited in Missouri law and in the laws of other states: joint consent to allow the adoption of a child born out of wedlock; joint consent to artificial insemination and as a condition for the legitimacy of children so conceived; spousal consent for voluntary sterilization. Indeed, it is hard to see why the Court's reasoning in striking down spousal consent to abortion should not also undermine some or all of the other joint consent requirements; all are blanket spousal (or natural father) consent requirements.

However, the Court sided with the physician-appellants, who argued that this provision was obviously designed to afford the husband the right unilaterally to prevent or veto an abortion; and moreover whether or not he was the father of the fetus. Perhaps that was the right ruling to hand down, given the present realities of marriage and the prevalent understanding of the marriage covenant. Still, we may ask why there was not (except in note 11 of the opinion) a shadow of the suggestion (as in the case of parental consent, discussed below) that a softer claim in behalf of a husband might withstand constitutional scrutiny—insuring, for example, that he be informed and that he be given an opportunity for consultation in a matter of such possible importance to him and to the marriage. Instead, the Court simply *praised* mutual agreement as the *ideal* for marriage.

A discerning reader of the Court's opinion cannot fail to notice—on first reading, and before getting to the dissent—the oddity of the majority's reason for finding no room for spousal consent. The state cannot "*delegate* to a spouse a veto power which the state itself is absolutely and totally prohibited from exercising during the first trimester of pregnancy" ((italics added). The state has "no constitutional authority to *give* the spouse unilaterally the ability to prohibit the wife from terminating her pregnancy when the State itself lacks that right" (italics added). Noting that "no marriage may be viewed as harmonious or successful if the marriage partners are fundamentally divided on so important and vital an issue," the Court pointed out that "*giving* the husband a veto power exercisable for any reason whatsoever or for no reason at all" (italics added) was unlikely to foster "mutuality of decisions vital to the marriage relation . . . even if the State had the ability to *delegate* to the husband a power it itself could not exercise" (italics added).[7]

In short, the husband was construed as entirely a "delegate" of the state. In *Wade* and *Bolton* the Court acknowledged or recognized a woman's right to private decision making with her physician, free from state constraints during the first twelve weeks of pregnancy. A right said to be *hers* was described, circumscribed, legitimated, and given effect in a legal decision. A newly recognized right was protected. She was "given" or "delegated" nothing—except from a narrowly positivistic and indefensible view of the law.

When, however, a claim to spousal rights was made, such rights

7. At this point the reader should note the "logic" which the Court must now follow—so long as the right to abortion remains an absolute not to be accommodated to other rights, roles, and relations. Having rested *Wade* upon the state's powerlessness to intervene between a woman and her physician, the Court seems now impelled to find "state action" abounding almost everywhere. Thus, as we shall see in chapter 2, "conscience clauses" (enacted by proper procedural due process of Congress or the states) are likely to fall rapidly before the doctrine that the state cannot delegate to consciences a power it, the state, does not have.

(the Court said) would have to be "given" or "delegated" to a husband from some nonexistent fund of state powers. None was *acknowledged* to belong to a spouse because of his role and relationship in marriage as an institution or covenant, in which the partners might not remain individuals alone, with none of their former rights or expectations "alienated" to the marriage bond. May not a spouse intervene in unilateral marital decisions when the state cannot? Was not construing a husband to be no more than a state agency the reason the majority of the Court found no basis for suggesting that a husband may have *some* legally protectable right to participate in an abortion decision even in a less-than-ideal marriage?

Perhaps no decisive objection can be lodged against the Court's *practical* wisdom when it recognized that a woman who obtains an abortion without the approval of her husband is also "acting unilaterally," but that "since it is the woman who physically bears the child and who is the more directly and immediately affected by the pregnancy, *as between the two the balance weighs in her favor*" (italics added). That, indeed, is a paramount reason for not allowing blanket spousal veto; and that was facially or literally, the statute before the Court. Also, the Court was making law for a world of broken-down marriages—or as Christians say, for a fallen world. So it could not mandate the ideal. But these considerations also imply that there might be a more nuanced adjudication of rights in a bent and conflicted world. It is to be hoped that state legislatures will not be deterred, by the present flat rejection of spousal rights, from enacting more nuanced statutes, and that there will be a legal passageway for such statutes to come before the Supreme Court for review (as was invited by the Court in declaring blanket parental veto to be unconstitutional).

Philosophically, we need to go deeper than the surface, practical level (which itself may have been sufficient ground for the ruling) and get at the contemporary understanding of marriage that was reflected in the Court's opinion. I have already spoken of the spouse's having only such rights and privileges or responsibilities as the state "gives" him in the matter of abortion. However, there is more to be said. Seemingly gone from our law is any notion of the marriage bond or the state's long-standing interest in "marriage as an institution." In marriage today, the woman remains *la femme seule*. The husband remains *l'homme seul*.

I add here (in connection with the next ruling) that in the family, children are *les enfants seuls* —to be protected as separate entities by a possible *future* decision of the Supreme Court from some of the consequences of an abortion decision made *without* the knowledge of or possible guidance from the best state agency yet devised to do that—parents. Young women's interests as *les enfants seuls* is the Court's focus of attention, not the state's interest in the parental-filial or family bond as such.

Likewise, Missouri's interest in the marriage bond was no longer acknowledged when the Court flatly ruled out its requirement of spousal consent. A spouse was treated as if he were still *l'homme seul,* and not *le mari.* This is the devastating consequence of atomistic individualism, mentioned by Danforth in his brief as a viewpoint the state of Missouri had no interest in promoting.

Evidence of this philosophy is already manifest in the rapid movement in recent years to divorce by "mutual agreement," to the exclusion of any operationally effective state interest in the bond of marriage. Who can deny that more frequently than not it is the husband who simply says "I divorce thee" (as in traditionally Islamic lands) when he testifies that the marriage is "irreconcilable." The state's sole remaining concern is the children, whose interests despairing domestic court judges do their best patchwork job to protect—often in the face of a father with additional children from a second marriage to support. Perhaps it is the fate of all the industrialized, urbanized, secular societies to *complete* the movement from status to contract in *every* human relation.[8] One can only regret the fact that the Court found no way (perhaps it could not) to lend support to the "holding action" of the people of Missouri—against the day when may come in God's time a sea-change in the silent moral assumptions of people generally, who now live under conditions (some law-made) that daily assault the moral fabric remaining in our society and impair the *humanum* of humankind.

Some readers may well protest that I am exaggerating the philosophical and societal assumptions that undergirded the Court's opinion

8. Only not quite *complete* that movement, since where only contractual relations are the web of life there is anarchy, no society. There will remain the naked power of government over an aggregation of individuals, and the accoutrements of power—including that of the hierarchical magisterium of a Supreme Court that sometimes respects the moral fabric of our society, sometimes not, and whose rulings all fear to reverse.

in *Planned Parenthood,* following the "substantive due process" reasoning and the judicial activism that led it, in *Wade* and *Bolton,* to take from the people the power to determine the limits of protectable human community at the first of life.[9] The Court's assumptions in its Bicentennial abortion decision are essentially those of Rousseau—that upon entering every relation a human individual remains as free as before, that no one can or should will today what he shall will tomorrow. Individuals remain atoms, none bound; moments of decision remain atoms, none binding or continuous in force. At least, not so far as appeal may be made to the state's interest.

Those societal and philosophical assumptions stem from and are expressed in an extreme notion of the right of privacy that in recent years has raced throughout American law. Rousseau's notion of freedom is at the heart of our current view of privacy. His contrasting notion of self-enslavement has become our notion of all societal and intersubjective bonding. The state's interest in radical individualism, instead of in marriage as a limiting bond of indefeasible responsibility (with rights and dues pertaining thereto), is expressed even in one of the earliest and most eloquent expressions of the right of privacy:

> We deal with a right of privacy older than the Bill of Rights—older than our political system, older than our school system. Marriage is a coming together for better or for worse, hopefully enduring, and intimate to the degree of being sacred. It is an association that promotes a way of life, not causes; a harmony in living, not political faiths; a bilateral loyalty, not commercial or social projects.[10]

That statement from *Griswold* may have been needed to nullify Connecticut's law against the use of contraceptives, with its threat of state inspectors in the marriage chamber. Still it says more than was necessary and jettisons a view of marriage that is also older than the Bill of Rights, older than our political system. Marriage is not yet a

9. *Vide* the decisive defeat of liberalized abortion by popular vote in both Michigan and North Dakota (culturally diverse states) shortly before the 1973 decisions; and see also my testimony before the Senate subcommittee considering proposed constitutional amendments, "Protecting the Unborn," *Commonweal* May 31, 1973, pp. 308–14.

10. *Griswold* v. *Connecticut,* 381 U.S. 479, 486 (1965), quoted in the *Planned Parenthood* decision, note 10.

mere "association," a "harmony of living" only, a "coming together, hopefully enduring, and intimate to the degree of being sacred." Every marriage in the eyes of the law is entered by parties who—before a civil magistrate and even for the seventh time—promise one another a permanent union, "till death us do part."

It is also still assumed that the parties convey to one another—in the language of an earlier age—rights to acts of loving sexual intercourse that nourish and strengthen the marriage union. The married do not retain *absolute* rights over their own bodies or in that respect remain as free as before. Of course, they should work out the manner and time and circumstances as a harmonious expression of their bilateral loyalty to one another, and doubtless when that conveyal is unilaterally withdrawn the marriage is at an end. However, given consensual divorce, we are no longer likely to have divorce proceedings that will say that such a unilateral decision to withhold bodily intercourse is a violation of the just expectations of one's partner in marriage. In any case, the privacy of those communications in marriage free from state intrusion, and not the privacy of individuals in indeterminate association, would have been an equally firm foundation for the *Griswold* ruling.

Moreover, *Eisenstadt* [11] could have taken the marriage union to be in some sense an "independent entity" in the eyes of the law, since a cognizable relation needing privacy and protection need not have "a mind and heart of its own." Here again we can discern the omnivorous influence of a personalistic, individualistic notion of privacy. Nothing, it would appear, that has not a mind or heart of its own seems to qualify as matter in whose protection, and protection from state intrusion, the state has an interest. Surely it was not necessary for the Court to say, in that case, that "if the right of privacy means anything, it is the right of the individual . . . to be free from unwarranted government instrusion into matters so fundamentally affecting a person as the decision whether to bear or beget a child." Likewise it was

11. *Eisenstadt* v. *Baird,* 405 U.S. 453: "The marital couple is not an independent entity with a mind and heart of its own, but an association of two individuals each with a separate intellectual and emotional makeup. If the right of privacy means anything, it is the right of the *individual,* married or single, to be free from unwarranted government intrusion into matters so fundamentally affecting a person as the decision whether to bear or beget a child" (Blackmun's emphasis in the present opinion, note 11).

unnecessary for the Court in its present decision to underline the word *individual.* Cannot there be a right of privacy within marriage as an institution, a right of a marriage's privacy? Or, if the language of rights is inappropriate to use, can we not say simply that marriage should be free from heavy-handed state intrusion? And that the state has an interest in protecting the marriage bond? Still, if a corporation can be deemed to be a "person" in the eyes of the law and be treated as if it had a mind and heart of its own, I don't see why marriage cannot be similarly understood. The sole obstacle to such a conception—and one that erodes the view of marriage which shaped our law—is our current atomistic individualistic notion of privacy.

Finally—and to return to what philosophically was at stake in spousal consent—it has been the law's assumption that marriage entails the conveyal to one's partner of access to the possibility of having children of one's own. Reproductive capabilities are not withheld, as may rightfully be done so long as persons remain *la femme seule* or *l'homme seul.* These powers are given over not so much to the other party as to the marriage union itself. Nonetheless, as *Eisenstadt* maintained, the two individuals remain individuals—each with a "separate intellect and emotional makeup." That is their actuality as persons; and respect for the irreducible and irreplaceable otherness of one's partner has always been the ideal in marriage. From the pinnacle of their personhood and in mutual respect for the other's individual privacy, presumably a couple ideally makes joint decisions concerning the timing of procreation and the number or spacing of children to be conceived. Still, "separate intellect and emotional makeup" is not the matter of marriage; that does not define the "specific difference" between marriage and any other relationship in which there also should be genuine respect for the distance, the inviolability, the privacy, and the dignity of another individual. Mutual bodily lovemaking and access to the possibility of a fruit of that union are the constituent elements of marriage; these are its specific differences from all other interpersonal relations.[12] That understanding is still extant, as the

12. Statutory law at some future date may attempt to give legal backing to marriage agreements in which the parties have *expressly excluded* having children. It is difficult to say *how* the law could do this, in an age when marriages in general have ceased to be enforceable and divorce is granted on grounds of irreconcilability. It is enough to say here that if and when that happens, marriage will have become—what it now is not—a contract in which the parties draw up the stipulations; and the

people of Missouri said through their representatives in the legislature; and it shall remain so even though, given consensual divorce, the law may no longer state that unilateral withholding of access to progeny of the marriage is a violation of a natural right in marriage and of the legitimate expectations of either party within the union.

Most of the foregoing points were grasped and forcefully expressed

---

law of domestic relations will presumably be taught in law schools as the second semester of the law of contracts. To understand what was at stake in the question of spousal consent in *Planned Parenthood* v. *Danforth* it is sufficient to ask, What now is the law's understanding of marriages from which having children has *not* been expressly excluded by the "contracting" parties? What still is the meaning of the role and relationship into which they are presumed by the law to have entered? I suppose the legal way of asking these questions is: What is the common-law meaning of marriage? In that, Missouri by statute expressed a long-standing state interest.

The foregoing is also background for saying that only by a category-mistake, with consequent other definitional confusions, could a state give legal status to homosexual *marriages.* Something of the same confusion would result—with consequent weakening of the moral fabric of our society—from defining marriage as "taking one another for a while." To say this is *not* to say in either case that the state has any interest in intruding upon such informal relationships between consenting adults, be they transient or enduring in intention. Holding fixed the meaning of *contract* (i.e., an arrangement conditionally entered into whose nature is entirely a creation of the parties), I also do not exclude the possibility that the state could be persuaded that that some sorts of contracts between homosexuals, or contracts between heterosexual partners specifically limited in duration and by other conditions, are of such importance in themselves and to others that the state should require fiduciary loyalty of the contracting parties and enforce the contract by penalizing the offending party by fines or imprisonment. But since even marriages are no longer enforceable, it is hard to imagine the state taking an interest in such purely private arrangements. Since "privacy" has so far eroded the meaning of marriage, it has destroyed the social worth of its simulations as well. Can there be a status symbol where there is no status? Perhaps to gain favorable tax status? Then "marriage" will have become what Marx said that it was: a bourgeois commercial arrangement. (For a proposal for "marriage" contracts limited as to time, see Paul Ramsey, "Marriage Law and Biblical Covenant," in *Religion and the Public Order 1963,* ed. Donald A. Giannella [Chicago: University of Chicago Press, 1964], pp. 41–77.)

In any case, a category-mistake is still a category-mistake. A relation having constituent elements which the law simply recognizes ought not to be interchanged with relations whose constituent elements are altogether the creation of the autonomous wills of the contracting parties. A relation *entered* is not the same as a relation *made up.* These are distinctions in kind, not of degree only. Clear thinking calls for us not to imagine that using the term "marriage" provides a real bridge between the two. Lapses in language usage lead rather to mistakes in thought. Such a slippage in language (or category-mistake) led *Griswold* to define marriage as an "association," a "harmony," a "coming together . . . intimate to the degree of being sacred"—a definition consistent with its individualistic notion of privacy.

in the dissenting opinion in *Planned Parenthood* written by Justice White, joined by Chief Justice Burger and Justice Rehnquist.[13] The dissenters began by saying that "the task of policing [the] limitation on state police power is and will be a continuing venture in substantive due process" begun by *Wade*. But even accepting the *Wade* decision they saw no reason for invalidating five of the provisions of the Missouri statute.

To any reasonable mind, it seems to me, the dissent destroyed the argument about the state *delegating* to a spouse a right it did not have. The issue is not that he was delegated "the power to vindicate the State's interest in the future of the fetus." Instead, the issue should be seen to be one of *"recognizing that the husband has an interest of his own* in the life of the fetus which should not be extinguished by the unilateral decision of the wife" (italics added). The question was whether to give effect to that recognizable right. A mother's interest in deciding whether or not to terminate her pregnancy "outweighs the State's interest in the potential life of the fetus" during the first twelve weeks of pregnancy. But it does not logically follow that "the husband's interest is also outweighed" or that his right "may not be protected by the state." "A father's interest in having a child—perhaps his only child—may be unmatched by any other interest in his life." Thus with the concurring opinion of Justices Stewart and Powell, the three dissenters elevated the issue into one of conflict of rights. The dissent did not venture to decide (as did the Court and also the Stewart / Powell concurrence) which of these rights or interests outweighs the other. "These are matters which a State should be able to decide free from the suffocating power of the federal judge, purporting to act in the name of the Constitution."

Justice Blackmun, speaking for the Court, makes reference to "the dissenting opinion of our Brother White." His comment clearly is in no way pertinent to the main thrust of the dissenters' argument (or to

13. Justice Stewart, joined by Justice Powell, in his concurring opinion said only that "whether the State may constitutionally recognize and give effect to a right on [a husband's] part to participate in the decision to abort a jointly conceived child . . . seems to me a rather more difficult problem than the Court acknowledges." That statement elevates the problem into a conflict of *rights*, and it softens the claim of spousal right to one of participation in the decision. Thus the reasoning of the concurring opinion was different in important respects from that of the Court's opinion. But, having said so, Stewart and Powell agreed on balance with the Court's ruling. Still, their reasoning invites a more nuanced statute from Missouri.

a ruling that might have been forthcoming if a majority had joined them). Their argument led straight to the conclusion that in a genuine conflict of recognizable rights and interests the Court's judgment ought not to be presumed better than that of a state legislature. Instead of addressing this issue, Brother Blackmun reminded Brother White that the section in dispute between them "does much more than insure that the husband *participate in the decision* whether his wife should have an abortion."

It is important, here, that it was Blackmun, speaking for the Court, who raised the softer claim of the spouse's *participation.* Thus, it is to be hoped that state legislatures will take this to be an invitation to formulate different statutes that cannot be construed to mean blanket spousal veto but that insure spousal foreknowledge and participation in abortion as a marital decision. It is also to be hoped that legislatures will not be barred from doing so by the fact that judges in state and district courts may routinely read and apply *Planned Parenthood* v. *Danforth.*

Another important reason we need more nuanced statutes (however complex the task of legislative draftmanship) is that in such conflicts of recognizable rights it is not only the husband's interest that need to be given some effect. The wife also may need protection from undue pressure from her spouse to have an abortion. Is prior written consent certifying that her decision is informed and uncoerced likely to be sufficient? May not state legislatures endeavor to enter this entanglement of needs and rights if the Court can enter it and decide the issue one way?

Parental Consent

The Missouri statute required the consent of one parent or person in loco parentis to a first trimester abortion of an unmarried girl under eighteen years of age unless the abortion was certified by a licensed physician to be necessary in order to preserve the life of the mother. Attorney General Danforth in his brief contended that this was "a reasonable means of furthering the State's long-standing interest in protecting minors, supporting parents in the discharge of their responsibilities and promoting the stability of the family unit." He cited Missouri laws "replete with provisions" reflecting these combined state interests. The Court ruled this requirement also to be unconstitutional.

It said, "the State may not impose a blanket provision"; and it used precisely the same reasoning in this instance as when it struck down the spousal consent requirement. "Just as with the requirement of consent from the spouse, so here, the State does not have the constitutional authority to *give* a third party an absolute, and possibly arbitrary, veto . . ." (italics added).

In reference to the state's interest in "safeguarding the family unit," the Court said two things. (1) It equalized parental interest and the minor's interest, and atomized the family bond. "Any independent interest the parent may have in the termination of the minor daughter's pregnancy is no more weighty than the right of privacy of the competent minor mature enough to have become pregnant." Apart from distributing the family bond to individuals *seuls* having possibly conflicting and equally weighty interests or rights, that seems a strange definition of maturity! (2) The Court disagreed with and supplanted the state legislature's judgment concerning what will actually serve to strengthen the family unity. (That is called "substantive due process" with consequent judicial activism.)

At the end, however, the Court suggested a better understanding of maturity. "We emphasize," it said, "that our holding that [this section] is invalid does not suggest that every minor, regardless of age or maturity, may give effective consent for termination of her pregnancy." That practically invites the Missouri legislature to bring forward another statute that may orchestrate parental direction and guidance with a minor's consent but which does not make parental consent an absolute prerequisite. We shall return to this point in connection with the Massachusetts decision handed down on the same day.

The Stewart / Powell concurring opinion stressed the alternative of a possibly constitutional parental consent or parental participation provision. It stressed that the constitutional deficiency of the Missouri statute lay strictly in its "imposition of an absolute limitation on a minor's right to obtain an abortion." If the Court were presented with "a provision requiring parental consent or consultation in most cases," and allowing for judicial resolution of any disagreement between parent and minor, or for judicial determination that the minor is mature enough to give an informed consent without parental concurrence, such a statute would present "materially different constitutional issue[s]." Justices Stewart and Powell also emphasized that "there can be little doubt that the State furthers a constitutional end by encouraging an unmarried pregnant minor to seek the help and advice of her parents in making the very important decision whether or not to bear a child." Finally they brought up a point that was part of Missouri's brief and not mentioned in Blackmun's opinion (which does cite the ten- and eleven-year-old cases)—namely, that "it seems unlikely that [a minor] will obtain adequate counsel and support from the attending physician at an abortion clinic. . . ." The Court seems to assume throughout that the minor girl will have a personal physician.

The three dissenting justices again homed in on the notion of the state having no constitutional authority to "give" a parent rights it does not have. They criticize the Court's opinion for rejecting the notion that "the *State* has an interest in strengthening the family unit," and for its individualistic concept of a parent's "independent interest." The purpose of Missouri's parental consent requirement was "not merely to vindicate any interest of the parent or of the State." That purpose was rather to vindicate the very right given effect by *Wade*—namely, the right of the pregnant woman to decide "whether *or not* to terminate her pregnancy" (the dissent's emphasis).

Since, however, the Court had not actually rejected the notion that "the State has an interest in strengthening the family unit," the disagreement in practical outcome lies elsewhere. The dissenters respected "the traditional way by which States have sought to protect children from their own immature and improvident decisions." In contrast, the majority of the Court preempted that judgment and itself determined what would or would not strengthen the family unit or protect minors from improvident decisions. Of course, the Court's distribution of equal and independent interests lay beneath its resort to substantive due process.

Justice Stevens devoted almost the entirety of his "partly" dissenting opinion to argument in favor of Missouri's parental consent requirement. (That adds up to four Justices who would have upheld.) It is true that Stevens interpreted the Missouri provision broadly to mean parental participation and advice. Nevertheless, his arguments in favor of that construction and in favor of upholding are worthy of note. Since "the Court recognizes that the State may insist that the decision not be made without the benefit of medical advice," and "since the most serious consequences of the decision are not medical in character," Stevens saw no reason why a state could not with equal legitimacy insist that there be other appropriate counsel as well. There is, indeed, a logical issue here. The requirement of a physician's concurrence and a requirement of parental concurrence both facially grant blanket vetos. The Court must have thought physicians as a class would be permissive and parents adamant as a class. But if physicians are always permissive and never veto or refuse their concurrence, then *Wade* inaugurated a national medical policy of abortion upon request. That is the popular understanding, but the Court did not say that—as Burger expressly pointed out in his concurrence. Its notion was that medical judgment in consultation with women seeking abortions be freed from state intrusion for the first twelve weeks of pregnancy. This is expressed verbally in the requirement that a woman's decision not be made without benefit of medical advice and consent.[14] Why,

14. See pp. 58–61 below. Here I may draw attention to an additional odd result of *Planned Parenthood.* It seems obvious that *Wade* directly and immediately withdrew from states as *parens patriae* any power to deny abortions to female wards. Yet this conclusion—in Connecticut, at least—was drawn instead from *Planned Parenthood.* That state's Department of Children and Youth Services had denied the operation to eleven teenagers. The Legal Aid Society of Hartford County sued in their behalf; the United States District Court ordered the abortions. The decision of the justices was based on *Planned Parenthood*'s denial that real parents have any say in the abortion decisions of their teenage daughters because the state has no say. Thus, what the state cannot do as parens patriae in the case of minors who are wards of the state followed from what parents cannot do in Missouri in the case of their children, which followed from what the state cannot do (see *Wade*) (*New York Times,* October 3, 1976). Moreover the court in the Connecticut case did not wait for the outcome of the remanded Massachusetts cases to determine to what extent parents as such may still remain the court's model for parens partiae.

It is not irrelevant to add that in upholding a constitutional right to give one's children a religious education (*Pierce* v. *Society of Sisters,* 268 U.S. 510 [1925]), the United States Supreme Court said, "Those who nurture [the child] and direct his destiny have the right, coupled with the high duty, to recognize and prepare him for [religious and moral] obligations." When now a most serious moral decision comes into view, parents are stripped of the right and high duty to direct a child's destiny in that matter—unless the outcome in Massachusetts and the fate of more nuanced statutes from Missouri and other states prove to be different from *Planned Parenthood,* or unless this decision is reversed. Indeed, a contradiction at the very heart of the legal notion of privacy can be demonstrated by the words of one of its most stalwart proponents. Concurring in *Bolton,* Justice Douglas listed among the elements of privacy: "freedom of choice, . . . respecting marriage, divorce, procreation, contraception, and *the education and upbringing of children*" (italics added). If the latter belongs to parents' right of privacy, then *Planned Parenthood* makes clear that privacies conflict. That called for adjudication, not the annulment of one by the other.

then, may not parental counsel be freed from state interference by exactly the same sort of requirement? Why is the one a blanket veto power and the other not? Or better, why is one potential veto constitutionally permissible and the other not? The only answer I can think of is that the Court wanted minor women to be able to run from their family unit as readily as they can run from one doctor to another; to choose her "parents" (her principal counselors) as freely as she chooses a physician. Again, the family unit was atomized.

Justice Stevens also criticized the Court's opinion for assuming that "every parent-child relationship is either (a) so perfect that communication and accord will take place routinely or (b) so imperfect that the absence of communication reflects the child's correct prediction that the parent will exercise his or her veto arbitrarily to further a selfish interest rather than the child's interest." In between those two extremes, there is the pedagogical and indeed constraining function of the law to promote the stability of the family unit. Stevens saw no reason why a state legislature may not, in their wisdom or lack of it, impose "a parental consent requirement as an appropriate method of giving the parents an opportunity to foster [a minor's] welfare by helping a pregnant distressed child to make and implement a correct decision." The state has an interest in that—not in "the impact the parental consent requirement may have on the total number of abortions that may take place."

Here, implicitly, is a new note—namely, that such required parental involvement may have either no impact or a restraining impact, or for that matter it may serve to increase the number of abortions sought by minors. Indeed, another reason for statutes more nuanced than the one before the Court is that minor women may need some protection (if such can be devised) from parents who insist they abort. A young woman's certification that she was not coerced may often need backing by her (and the general public's) awareness that, in the last resort, a court stands ready to protect her from some modern parents.

Finally, Stevens criticized the Court for its assumption that "the capacity to conceive a child and the judgment of the physician are the only constitutionally permissible yardsticks for determining whether a young woman can independently make the abortion decision." He doubted the Court's "empirical judgment." Even if the Court were correct, Stevens said, in its judgment concerning a young woman's privacy and the advent of her competence to use it wisely, the states have traditionally selected a chronological age as a standard; and he saw no sufficient grounds in the nature of an abortion decision to preempt states' rights to do the same in that case also.[15]

A full and fair appraisal of the Court's ruling against Missouri's parental consent requirement cannot be made without reference to two Massachusetts cases joined and decided the same day *Planned Parenthood* v. *Danforth* was handed down.[16] These cases were class actions—on one side, an uncertain number of "Mary Moes," pregnant minors wishing to terminate their pregnancies, and on the other side, Jane Hunerwadel, a parent of an unmarried female of childbearing age. They came to court, each petitioning for justice for themselves and those similarly situated under a 1974 Massachusetts statute which states: "If the mother is less than eighteen years of age and has not married, the consent of both the mother and her parents is required. If one or both of the mother's parents refuse such consent, consent may be obtained by order of a judge of the superior court for good cause shown, after such hearing as he deems necessary." That is the act's central section.

Thus, the issue of parental consent seemed squarely joined, but in a context that allowed prompt appeal beyond parental refusal of consent. The "Mary Moes" wanted the act declared unconstitutional for reasons remarkably similar to those we have reviewed in the Court's opinion in *Planned Parenthood* v. *Danforth*. Mrs. Hunerwadel, however, asked only that the district court "refrain from deciding any issue in this case" because the act "was susceptible of a construction by the state courts that would avoid or modify any alleged federal constitutional question." That was the way the Supreme Court went, as we shall see. So we do not yet have a definitive ruling, nor do we know what room will be found for guaranteeing parental involvement in the abortion decision of a minor child or for promoting the stability of the family.

The district court had declared the act to be unconstitutional in a

15. Eighteen years does seem unwise, though the age a state picks should be deemed constitutional. Just as eighteen is too old an age in our society to light upon in defining "statutory rape," so also legislators could recognize the generally greater maturity of young women today in enacting statutes protecting them within the family unit in the matter of abortion. Many states have the category of "mature minor" (see below).

16. *Bellotti* v. *Baird,* 428 U.S. 132 (1976).

two-to-one decision,[17] for reasons that are by now familiar to the reader. The act gave parents not only consultative rights but a veto; in this case it gave parents *or a court* the veto: ". . . the minor's consent *must* be supplemented *in every case,* either by the consent of both parents, or by a court order." So far as parental consent was concerned, the issue came down to the question of whether "parents possess, apart from right to counsel and guide, *competing* rights of their own" (italics added). Concerning the provision for resort to court orders, the district court held that the state cannot control a minor's abortion decision in the first trimester *any more* than it can control that of an adult. If that ruling had been upheld by the U.S. Supreme Court, along with the district court's view of "competing rights" and parental "veto," any parental "right to counsel and guide" would also have been given no effect. We would have been left with an astonishing and indefensible understanding of the state's interest in protecting minors and of the role of law in directing society to a common good.

The Supreme Court did not so rule—Justice Blackmun again delivering the opinion for the Court. It vacated the district court's ruling of unconstitutionality and remanded the case to Massachusetts for further interpretation of the statute. Thus the Supreme Court did not face squarely the issue of a constitutionally permissible parental consent requirement qualified as in the Massachusetts statute. In a sense the issue was avoided—but in an entirely proper judicial manner, one which (we shall see) the dissenters in *Planned Parenthood* v. *Danforth* appealed to in their opinion on a provision of the Missouri statute we have yet to discuss.

Upon appeal from the district court, the Supreme Court was confronted by adversaries who gave widely divergent interpretations of the meaning and effects of the Massachusetts law, which need not be rehearsed here. The Court, therefore, needed to "go no further than the claim that the District Court should have abstained pending a construction of the statute by the Massachusetts courts." There was prima facie reason to believe that adoption by the Massachusetts courts of the appellants' interpretation would "at least materially change the nature of the problem." "It is sufficient that the statute is susceptible of [that] interpretation . . . and we so find, and that

17. *Baird* v. *Bellotti,* 393 F. Supp. 847 (D. Mass. 1975).

such an interpretation would avoid or substantially modify the federal constitutional challenge to the statute, as it clearly would. Indeed, in the absence of authoritative construction, it is impossible to define precisely the constitutional question presented." So the district court erred in not certifying to the Supreme Judicial Court of Massachusetts appropriate questions concerning the meaning of the statute and the procedures it imposes.

The Court said much the same thing concerning another relevant matter that had arisen. The state of Massachusetts enacted, subsequent to the district court's opinion, a statute governing the consent of minors undergoing other medical procedures. Any distinction between those procedures and abortion was challenged before the Supreme Court. Concerning that, the Court said that "the constitutional issue cannot now be defined . . . for the degree of distinction between the consent procedure for abortion and the consent for other medical procedures cannot be established until the nature of the consent required for abortion is established." The Court did point out, however, that "as we hold today in *Planned Parenthood* . . . not all distinction between abortion and other procedures is forbidden." Finally, the Court expressed confidence that "in the light of our disapproval of a 'parental veto' today in *Planned Parenthood,* . . . the lower Massachusetts courts, if called upon to enforce the statute pending interpretation by the Supreme Judicial Court, will not impose this most serious barrier."

So that is where we are at the moment of this writing. The Supreme Court never issues promissory notes. Nevertheless—and because hope springs eternal—it may be worthwhile to summarize the construction of the Massachusetts act which, the Court said, would clearly avoid or modify any constitutional challenge to the statute. By that favorable construction: parental consent may not be refused on the basis of concerns exclusively of the parent; sections of the statute other than the one quoted above insured that it preserves the "mature minor" rule in Massachusetts, under which a child determined by a court to be capable of giving informed consent will be allowed to do so; a "mature minor" could obtain such a court certification *regardless* of whether the parents had been consulted or had withheld consent; the procedures involved would be speedy and nonburdensome and would ensure anonymity; and, finally, a judge of the superior court could permit an abortion without parental consent for a minor incapable of rendering informed consent, for "good cause shown." On that view, the statute "prefers" parental consultation and consent. Such a statute, the Court said at the conclusion of the foregoing summary, "as thus read, would be fundamentally different from a statute that creates a 'parental veto.' " No promissory notes, as I said.

Again this is where we are in the people's effort, through their representatives, to contain the adverse impact of the 1973 abortion decisions upon the family unit. After these decisions, the predominance of those seeking abortions switched from married to unmarried women, a large proportion of whom are teenagers. Strange that the hierarchical judicial magisterium has come to have such power over our lives and over the basic human community from which all government arises; strange that courts have begun to believe that the primary rights of the family have to be "delegated" or "given" from a fund of state powers already declared to be deposited nowhere. Nevertheless, there is hope—in the diversity of opinions the justices expressed and which we have reviewed; in the cogency and force of the argument of the dissent, joined in this instance by Justice Stevens; in the closeness of state legislators to the actualities that families must endure; in the legislature's lack of immunity from arousable public opinion; and in the degree to which the Court's opinion invites the states to frame more nuanced statutes that may yet pass constitutional scrutiny. Eternal vigilance is the price public conscience must pay for law that sustains and does not further erode the moral fabric of this nation. In this context, the medical profession needs to realize that insofar as abortion becomes a matter of "family practice," the solution it offers, while arguably helpful individual case by individual case, also tends to produce more cases to be given the same treatment.

Saline Amniocentesis

The Missouri statute prohibited abortion by withdrawal of amniotic fluid and injection of "a saline or other fluid" into the sac *after* the first twelve weeks of pregnancy. Here we have an attempt by that state to fence *Wade* by availing itself of that decision's provision that in midsemester abortions (unlike the first twelve weeks) the state "may, if it chooses, regulate the abortion procedure in ways that are reasonably related to maternal health." The Court, however, ruled that an "outright legislative prohibition of saline" is unconstitutional because it is not a "reasonable" prohibition due to the unavailability of the preferred procedure (prostaglandin injection) in Missouri at the time of the trial and of the appeals. Straightaway one may ask, How else than by an "outright" (or a "flat") prohibition was the state going to protect maternal health if the legislature judged (as did the district court following factual evidence) that both prostaglandin injection and mechanical means of abortion were safer than saline in midsemester abortions?

The Court argued that the words "saline or other fluid" were ambiguous enough to include "the intra-amniotic injection of prostaglandin itself" (one method of its administration) and to prohibit future possible abortion procedures. It pointed to "the anomaly" of prohibiting one method and not also others that are "many times more likely to result in maternal death." [18] The ruling turned, however, neither on vagueness nor argument. It rested rather on the Court's own findings as to the facts, which it presumed to substitute for the findings of fact at all stages below, where the matter had been more fully investigated and argued. That is to say, the Court's ruling rested on its belief that, during the period of time relevant to its decision, 70 percent of midsemester abortions in the United States were by saline injection and that the availability of prostaglandin technique was especially limited in Missouri. It concluded that the Missouri statute was an unreasonable and arbitrary regulation "*designed* to inhibit, and having the effect of inhibiting, the vast majority of abortions after the first 12 weeks" (italics added). One may ask whether it is not unusual, not to say unjudicial, for the Supreme Court to presume "bad faith" on the legislature's part in enacting this provision? As we shall see, there was another and quite different reading of its "designs."

Justice White's dissenting opinion, joined by Burger and Rehnquist, came down most forcefully against this overruling and the design ascribed to the legislature. The dissent asserted that the majority re-

18. The Court also brought up an "argument" that no student of elementary logic would invoke, namely, that "the maternal mortality rate in childbirth does, indeed, exceed the mortality where saline amniocentesis is used." On that score, if the state has an overriding interest in protecting the health of its female citizens it ought to prohibit *pregnancy*, or make abortion compulsory because most methods are "safer" than continuing a pregnancy.

lied (a) on the testimony of one doctor and (b) on citation of *another* case,[19] in which "a different court concluded that the record in its case showed the prostaglandin method to be unavailable in *another* State—Kentucky—*two years ago*" (italics added). On the positive side, the dissent itself cited one doctor who in the record "quite sensibly testified that if the saline method were banned, hospitals would quickly shift to the prostaglandin method," and it cited the chief of obstetrics at Yale University, who suggested that "physicians should be liable for malpractice if they choose saline over prostaglandin after having been given all the facts on both methods."

Justice White affirmed that "without such evidence [of unavailability] and without any factual finding [to that effect] by the court below, this Court cannot properly strike down a statute passed by one of the States. Of course, there is no burden on a State to establish the constitutionality of one of its laws. . . . I am not yet prepared to accept the notion that normal rules of law, procedure, and constitu-

19. *Wolfe* v. *Schroering*, 388 F. Supp. 631 (W. D. Ky. 1974), modified, 541 F.2d 523 (6th Cir. 1976). Round and round the precedent-setting goes. The United States Court of Appeals for the Sixth District "stayed deciding the appeal [from the Kentucky case] on October 31, 1975, pending the Supreme Court decision in *Planned Parenthood*." Citing *Planned Parenthood*, the appellate court upheld the lower court in declaring unconstitutional the provision in Kentucky's statute prohibiting the saline method of abortion. But that ruling by the district court for the western district of Kentucky had in turn already been cited by the lower court in *Planned Parenthood* as its chief authority for ruling unconstitutional Missouri's statute prohibiting the saline method!

In the Kentucky case, the United States Court of Appeals for the Sixth District also followed *Planned Parenthood* in *upholding* the woman's written consent (also a twenty-four hour waiting period) and in *striking down* spousal or parental consent. The state, the appellate court reasoned, "cannot constitutionally authorize spouses, parents or guardians to 'veto,' for no reason or an impermissible reason, *to wit*, other than protecting maternal health, such as [impermissibly] protecting an unrecognized interest in fetal life." Here was an additional stress. Since the state's interest in the potentiality of life begins only at viability, a husband's interest can also only begin at that point. He can have no more interest than the state; his possible "agency" begins precisely where the state's agency begins! *Wolfe* v. *Schroering* goes on to say, "We refrain from deciding whether a more narrowly drafted requirement of spousal consent, permitting the husband father to 'veto' a post-viability abortion not necessary 'for the preservation of the life or health of the mother,' would pass constitutional muster in light of the recognizable [i.e., the state's recognized] post-viability interest in fetal life." The court also observed that such a statute would be redundant since Kentucky already has a statute prohibiting postviability abortions as invited by *Wade*. This opinion comes up again, in chapter 2, in connection with the conscience clauses.

tional adjudication suddenly become irrelevant because a case touches on the subject of abortion."

Justice White's dissenting opinion gave the favorable reading of the legislature's "designs." In any event, he wrote, "the point of [this section] is to change the practice under which most abortions are performed under the saline amniocentesis method and to make the safer prostaglandin method generally available." That would be desirable; or, at least, the legislature could so view it. "That should conclude our inquiry, unless we purport to be not only the country's continuous constitutional convention but also its *ex officio* medical board."

Justice Steward, joined by Justice Powell, in his concurring opinion, however, stated simply that he agreed fully with Justice Stevens on the unconstitutionality of a prohibition of the saline method. That was the concurring part of Justice Stevens's opinion (by far the larger part was dissent from the Court's overruling of the parental consent requirement). Stevens agreed with the Court's basis for its decision in its finding of facts. Not unimportantly however, he wanted to point out that, in his view, "the United States Constitution would not prevent the State legislature from outlawing the one [procedure] it found to be the less safe even though its conclusion might not reflect a unanimous consensus of informed medical opinion."

May it be presumed from their silence on the point, that Justices Stewart and Powell agreed with the Court's imputing to the Missouri legislature a design to prevent post-twelve-week abortions rather than the intent to protect maternal health? Perhaps not, since we ought to think the best of everyone. But then the Court should have thought better of the state legislators.

It is appropriate at this place to introduce a different perspective on the issue—one that should come up in future efforts to humanize medical practice again up to the level, say, of the medical ethics expressed in the 1975 statement of the executive board of the American College of Obstetricians and Gynecologists.[20]

The point is that use of prostaglandin is also *better for the fetus*. Prostaglandin and saline both produce "labor," but saline first scorches and destroys the unborn life. The widening use of the prostaglandin method is liable to make more visibly evident the fact that abor-

20. See p. 7 and n. 5 above.

tion is a "severance procedure," by producing a not insignificant number (one is significant enough) of possibly viable infants from late abortions.

The medical ethical question (and the moral issue for any human being) is whether prostaglandin should be the preferred procedure *also* for this reason. The American College of Obstetricians and Gynecologists stated that its fellows have "traditionally been responsible for the welfare of the pregnant woman and her fetus." It acknowledged the legal and ethical incongruity or conflict of responsibilities introduced where there is justification for inducing abortion. Still it concluded that "the physician does not view the destruction of the fetus as the primary purpose of abortion." It further concluded that "the College consequently recognizes a continuing obligation on the part of the physician towards the survival of a possibly viable fetus where this obligation can be discharged without additional hazard to the health of the mother."

That wording should be carefully noted. The moral issue for a physician (and for anyone involved in abortion—the woman, abortion counselors, etc.) is, Does that continuing obligation "reach back" to include a possibly viable fetus *in utero* and not only a possibly viable abortus? Does it reach back as an obligation bearing upon the choice among alternative abortion procedures? The answer seems obvious if that obligation toward the welfare of the fetus "can be discharged without additional hazard to the health of the mother." Even if—in a suppositive case contrary to fact—prostaglandin afforded *no greater* benefit to the welfare of the mother than alternative procedures, the answer to the ethical question of its preferred use should certainly be the same.

The *legal* question is similar, although the answer is constitutionally in grave doubt. Why may not conscientious legislators advance these considerations *also* as good reasons for prohibiting saline abortion in mid-pregnancy? The legal problem, of course, arises from the "bad medicine" of *Wade*'s trimester language, with the rulings affixed thereto, and from the Court's steadfast refusal to acknowledge the correct grey area of "possible viability." In the 1973 abortion decisions the Court allowed that after the first twelve weeks the state "may, if it chooses, regulate the abortion procedure in ways that are reasonably related to maternal health." The American College states that medical ethics requires physicians, even in an abortion procedure, to recognize their continuing obligation toward the survival of a possibly viable fetus "where this obligation can be discharged without additional hazard to the health of the mother." That already is significantly different language with different impacts on practice. The Court has now ruled unconstitutional the effort of one state legislature to give effect to the plain language of *Wade* concerning the protection of maternal health. It seems unlikely, then, that the Court will allow reference to be made to the welfare of the fetus when maternal life and health are not a competing interest.

However, there is at least a small opening to be discerned, beginning with language elsewhere in *Wade* and joined by the constitutional permissibility of the *definition* of "viability" in *Planned Parenthood* v. *Danforth.* In *Wade,* the Court recognized a growing state interest in "protecting the potentiality of human life" alongside its interest in protecting the health of the pregnant woman. These are "separate and distinct" interests. Insuring a woman's health becomes after twelve weeks an interest to which the state can begin to give effect. Meantime, the other interest is also growing "in substantiality as the woman approaches term"—not exactly in tandem, however. Still there comes an indeterminate point during pregnancy when each becomes "compelling"—one from twelve weeks, the other later. What is the latter point? Notably, *Wade* does *not* say from twenty-four weeks. Here the Court did not use trimester language.[21] It said instead that the "compelling" point is at "viability."

Thereupon *Wade* pronounced: "If the State is interested in protecting fetal life after viability, it may go so far as to proscribe abortion

21. Our courts do seem laggard in understanding where viability may now be placed by an acceptable constitutional definition of it. They still often say twenty-eight weeks or possibly twenty-four! Our National Commission, however, located a category of "possibly viable infants" of between twenty and twenty-four weeks gestational age and between five hundred and 600 grams in weight (*Research on the Fetus,* Report and Recommendations of the National Commission for the Protection of Human Subjects of Biomedical and Behavioral Research, DHEW Publication no. [OS] 76–127, 1975). These standards were accepted by the Secretary of HEW (*Federal Register* 40, no. 154 [August 8, 1975]: 33552). If we really mean to protect possibly viable infants, we shall have to begin to promote their survival upon a provisional estimate of twenty weeks gestational age of fetuses in utero and five hundred gram weight for live-born abortuses—until such judgments are revised in the light of signs of evident nonviability.

during that period except when it is necessary to preserve the life and health of the mother." Some "pro-life" people unaccustomed to reading legal decisions have regarded the hypothetical "if" and "may" as expressions of the Court's callousness toward unborn life even late in pregnancy. That is not correct. It is rather an open invitation to the states to fill the vacancy left by the effect of *Wade* in striking down both the long-standing and the newly enacted state laws governing abortion.

Again, I think, language is important. *Wade* did not say that the state may give effect to its compelling interest in potential human life provided there remains a reasonable relation to maternal health. That was its language for an earlier span of time (from twelve weeks until, presumably, viability) when the interest in maternal health alone could be given effect. Nor did *Wade* say, in the words of the American College, that the state's interest in potential life may be given effect provided that it can be discharged "without additional hazard to the health of the mother." It said rather, "except when [abortion] is necessary to preserve the life and health of the mother." "Necessary to preserve" seems a significantly stronger statement than "no additional hazard," although I allow that the expressions overlap to define a grey area in which a physician's discretion must come into play. Still, both legally and morally, it would seem, a fellow of the college could fulfill his responsibility both to the welfare of the pregnant woman and to her fetus in some abortions.

Right ethical reasoning cannot be kept from reaching back and affecting a physician's choice of an abortion procedure in borderline cases, or even his choice to correct for his possible error in estimating gestational age or for his ignorance of the strength or weakness of a particular fetus until it is delivered. Logically, the answer to the legal question must be the same. I suggest that any reasonable person must conclude that if a state can "go so far as to proscribe" abortion after viability, it may, if it chooses, prohibit saline abortion, or in some manner favor prostaglandins, in order also to give effect to its compelling interest in the potentiality of life from some point in midsemester abortions—unless, for example, the physician certifies that there is reasonable certainty that the fetus is nonviable. The choice of prostaglandin over saline rarely (almost certainly never) imposes any additional hazard to the welfare of the mother. If there are such cases, the physician could be required and allowed to so certify.

Among an indeterminate number of other possible statutes that the people of the United States should construct in order justly to hedge the 1973 abortion decisions, this is a modest suggestion concerning choice of modes of abortion that seek to protect potential human life. The Court in its present decision left standing a provision of the Missouri law which reads: "No abortion not necessary to preserve the life or health of the mother shall be performed unless the attending physician first certifies with reasonable medical certainty that the fetus is not viable." In view of this, a parallel statute might be promptly enacted to read: No abortion shall be performed by saline amniocentesis unless. . . .[22]

If the Missouri legislature had explicitly stated its compelling interest in potential human life without diminishing its interest in the welfare of the pregnant woman (and without placing its interest in potential life to be operative from twelve weeks), the Supreme Court could hardly have said nay to this without lawmaking that would clearly surpass *Wade*. Some such legislative attempt would have had the further benefit of perhaps raising the moral level of medical practice—which, it cannot be denied, often falls far short of the medical ethics recalled to mind by the statement of the American College of

22. LeRoy Walters, Director of the Center for Bioethics, Kennedy Institute, at Georgetown University, put the argument as follows: "Let us suppose that at seven and one half months of pregnancy immediate termination is medically indicated. Let us suppose, further, that two alternative methods of delivery exist, one of which increases the chances of infant survival but entails higher risk to the the pregnant woman, the other of which decreases both the risk to the woman and the probability of infant survival. In my view, the law should not require moral heroism of the pregnant woman in this case by asking her to place her own life at higher risk for the sake of the viable fetus, just as the law should not *require* parents to rescue their children from burning buildings. If the above example is changed, however, to pose a choice between two alternative methods of termination, one of which has a lower risk for *both* pregnant woman and fetus, then the legislature could appropriately decide that the rights of a clearly viable fetus are sufficiently strong to justify requiring use of the safer method. . . ."

Walters applies the same reasoning to the "possibly viable infant" of twenty to twenty-eight weeks gestational age. "If a method of abortion became available which demonstrably entails lower risks both to the pregnant woman and to the fetus (possibly prostaglandins), then assuming the general availability of the safer technique, the legislature might wish to require the use of that technique in abortions beyond the nineteenth week of gestation (except in cases where use of the technique is medically counter-indicated). The dual justification for such a requirement would be the enhancement of maternal health and the protection of fetuses which may have crossed the viability threshold" ("The Unwanted Child: Caring for the Fetus Born Alive after an Abortion," *Hastings Center Report* 6, no. 5 [October 1976] : 14–15).

Obstetricians and Gynecologists. In any case, carefully drafted legislative trials of many sorts are only ways of finding out what the law means or what the Court means (or intends to mean). Such efforts are always constitutionally in order. They serve to teach the Court what it should teach this nation, at least in the sense of enabling it to refine the meaning and application of its rulings and possibly to modify them. Our Constitution and the federal system do not work merely by decisions from on high, people being only compliant.

Some degree of reaching back, in the alternatives among abortion procedures, to give effect to the state's interest in potential human life would seem to be entirely constitutional—until one reads what the Court said about the remaining provision of the Missouri statute significant enough to discuss here.

Standard of Care

The statute further provided:

> No person who performs or induces an abortion shall fail to exercise that degree of professional skill, care and diligence to preserve the life and health of the fetus which such person would be required to exercise to preserve the life and health of any fetus intended to be born and not aborted. Any physician or person assisting in the abortion who shall fail to take such measures to encourage or to sustain the life of the child, and the death of the child results, shall be deemed guilty of manslaughter.[23]

Before going on, a reader may profitably give himself a little test. Reread those two sentences. Does the second say anything more or other than the first? The first, of course, expresses the positive duty of a physician, and the second describes his failure—adding, of course, a criminal category. Reread the two sentences again. Is not the same thing said in two different ways? Also, taking both sentences together, is not the obligation expressed in that paragraph precisely the medical ethics in the statement of the College of Obstetricians and Gynecologists which we have been considering?

Here the Court agreed with the district court, holding the first sen-

23. This was the sole provision, out of sixteen sections of the Missouri law, that the district court held to be unconstitutional.

tence to be "unconstitutionally overboard because it failed to exclude from its reach the stage of pregnancy prior to viability," and because the first sentence reads "fetus" while the second reads "child." That meant that the first sentence reached back in establishing a standard of care (or at least was vague about how far back); the second did not.

Attorney General Danforth had argued that the first sentence states a standard of care while the second describes the circumstances when that standard applies. Despite its use of the term *fetus,* the first sentence, he said, has no application until a live birth occurs. He further argued that *nothing* in the legislative history of this section supported the view that the first sentence was intended to have any effect other than the second was intended to have. Finally, he pleaded that *if* the Court agreed with the unanimous opinion of the district court not to take into account the legislature's debates, and if it deemed his construction to be a "sophisticated" one, and if it was therefore inclined to declare the first sentence facially unconstitutional, the Court should leave the second sentence standing under the act's "severability" provision.

The Court held that the section "must stand or fall as a unit. Its provisions are inextricably bound together." The criminal category imposed by the second sentence and its use of the word *child* simply do not modify the duty imposed by the previous sentence—and that "impermissibly requires the physician to preserve the life and health of the fetus, whatever the stage of pregnancy."

Before consulting other opinions filed, one has reason to wonder how a state legislature in the fourth year of our era A.W. (after *Wade*) could possibly have imagined they could get away with *that* interpretation. Earlier the Court ascribed to the legislators a disingenuous "design" to prohibit all post-twelve-week abortions; now it seemed to impute stupidity to them. A fair comment, however, must allow that the first sentence is vague about whether that standard of care need be applied only after the stage of viability.[24] We need also to ask

24. Still, we can ask whether the states may take into account the degree of unremovable uncertainty and the fallibility of physicians' judgments about viability in setting a standard of care that aims to give effect to its compelling interest in potential human life. The Supreme Court seems inflexibly discognizant of grey area or borderline problems. Unless states can enter this area to protect possibly viable human life, the criminal law will eventually become by no means so sturdy a protection as the Court seems to believe it is.

whether the Court does not often or ordinarily take into account the legislative history of statutes in assessing their constitutionality.

In any case I must say that it is a pity that the Court did not invoke the "severability" provision of the act, as Danforth urged, and declare only the first sentence to be unconstitutional. Those two provisions—if such they were—are not "inextricably bound together" if the first is not there. By striking down the entire section, the Court left a gap in our law that the state legislature attempted to fill; or at least it left standing a popular misunderstanding of the law when presented with an opportunity to correct it.

The reason the Court seemed serenely unconcerned with these consequences of its ruling are important to note. It remarked almost in passing, that "a physician's or other person's criminal failure to protect a live born infant surely will be subject to prosecution in Missouri under the State's criminal statutes." In short, the entire section seemed constitutionally redundant to the Court. To which a proper citizen's response is, Has the Court never heard of the Edelin case and of the viewpoint widely expressed by some of the most liberal and informed opinion in this country to the effect that, even *supposing* the physician in that case did what he was accused of doing in an abortion procedure, he should not be declared guilty or punished *retroactively* for an action not clearly criminal when done at the conclusion of an abortion procedure? Has the Court also not heard of the announced practice of medical neglect of defective newborns by physicians who, because their patients are babies and are defective and a burden to parents and to society, do not seem to believe that their practice is or may well be deemed to be "negligent manslaughter"? Has the Court not noted the petition for clarification of the responsibilities of physicians from the prestigious American College of Obstetricians and Gynecologists? There seems to be an amazing insularity on the part of the Court, which imperially does not hesitate to strike down laws enacted by those less insulated. Redundant laws may sometimes be needed. Missouri should promptly reenact the same statute or one quite like it, without the first sentence, and find out what then the Court will say.

In doing so, Missouri (or any other state) should retain one important element from the first sentence. Although flawed by its use of the word *fetus,* that provision contained the standard of care to be legally and morally imposed, in the words "exercise that degree of professional skill, care and diligence to preserve the life and health . . . which such person would be required to exercise to preserve the life and health of any . . . intended to be born. . . ." That was the substantive standard of care imposed by the words *such measures* in the second sentence. The standard is *equal care*.

Precisely that standard was recently enacted by the California legislature and signed into law by Governor Brown in September 1976. Assembly Bill no. 2346 adding sec. 25955.9 to the Health and Safety Code of California provides that "the rights to medical care [are] the same for an infant prematurely born alive in the course of an abortion as for a premature infant of similar medical status who is born spontaneously." A fetus would be considered a live-born person if, outside the womb, it manifests a sustained heart beat, umbilical pulsation, spontaneous respiration, and movement of voluntary muscles. Given those manifestations of life, who would say that morally or legally a physician's standard of care should be different because the live-born person resulted from premature birth or from spontaneous or induced abortion? The cases are similar in all morally relevant respects. Whether our law of negligent or reckless homicide will be weakened by the 1973 abortion decisions depends very much upon the outcome of any constitutional challenge to the California law.

Postponing a bit longer a look at the dissenting opinion on the standard-of-care provision in the Missouri statute, sound ethical reasoning may be advanced and the proper legal standard may be clarified by a brief parenthetical analysis of an earlier version of the California statute, corrected before passage. The penultimate version read:

> Whenever an abortion procedure results in a live-born person, the physician or physicians performing the abortion procedure shall take all reasonable steps, *except extraordinary means,* in accordance with good medical practice, to preserve the life and health of the live-born person. Nothing in this subdivision shall be construed as requiring a physician to give higher priority for life-saving medical treatment of the live-born person than to the mother.[25] [Italics added]

25. Assembly Bill no. 2346, California Legislature, 1975–76 Regular Session, as amended in assembly through January 5, 1976.

I have emphasized the questionable stipulation in the proposed statute; those words highlight the merit of the first sentence of the Missouri provision when viewed as setting a standard of care for the "possibly viable infant" in utero or ex utero. For, surely, an ethical physician should treat one preemie the same as any other, whether delivered into his hands by induced abortion or by spontaneous abortion / premature birth. Such infants are equally fragile and—if deemed to be possibly viable—equally deserve *extraordinary* care; but the proposed California statute seemed to exclude that in the case of action to preserve the life and health of a live-born person following induced abortion. Surely the legislature meant to say all along what it finally enacted in a statute requiring that the same care should be taken of live-born persons having similar medical status—whether "wanted" or "unwanted." If "unusual" efforts are exerted following premature birth or spontaneous abortion, the same efforts should be made in behalf of a live-born "abortus" (unless, *in either case,* there are medical counterindications).[26]

26. LeRoy Walters (in "The Unwanted Child," p. 14) presented written testimony on the California bill. He proposed that "the legislature adopt a formal-equality principle: All newborn infants should be treated equally, without regard to the circumstances of their delivery. . . . If a hospital's neonatal intensive care unit would normally attempt to save the life of a spontaneously delivered infant of the same health status, age, and weight, then the equality principle would require identical treatment of the hysterotomy survivor. . . . The formal-equality principle does not specify what treatment should be given. . . . It merely requires that this infant receive the same treatment as a similar, spontaneously delivered infant." This standard of care "does not recommend compensatory, especially vigorous, or maximal treatment for the survivors of abortion. A simple equality of treatment is enough." Nor would the principle entail omitting extraordinary measures, if needed. Again, simple equality of treatment is the measure. On the other hand, "if the mother or both parents request that the surviving infant be allowed to die, this request should be denied if it conflicts with the equality principle." In short, abortion has nothing at all to do with the rights of a live-born person, and laws may have to be passed to make that clear.

Extrapolating from studies limited to New York State and City, Walters estimates that, in the nation as a whole, there may have been 84 live deliveries following saline abortions in 1974, 25 live deliveries following hysterotomies, and 87 following prostaglandin abortions—a total of 196 nationwide. He acknowledges the weak data base and the tentativity of these projections; and, of course, he knows that physician discretion would in many of these cases correctly judge the infants to be unsalvageable and that many may not medically qualify as live-born persons under our negligent manslaughter statutes.

Still, "we have to set aside as irrelevant the fact that such births are rare," as Sissela Bok writes in the same symposium on the statute. "This fact does not eliminate the moral dilemma which exists whether there is one victim or ten thousand."

The sentence in the Missouri statute which we are discussing, when viewed as setting a standard for medical care, would clearly require a physician to exercise *that degree* of professional skill, care, and diligence to preserve the life and health of the live-born individual following abortion which such a physician would be required to exercise in the case of any possibly viable infant intended to be born and not aborted.[27] The first sentence of the Missouri statute ought to be revised, as I have just done in a paraphrase of its first sentence, and promptly reenacted. The constitutionally fatal word was *fetus*. Viewed as setting a standard of care, to which the next sentence gives effect, the first sentence is by no means a "sophisticated" or tendentious requirement. When articulated, it instead simply expresses the common moral intuition that "similar cases are to be treated similarly" by anyone wishing to do the right thing—induced abortion notwithstanding. To fulfill that continuing obligation may require "extraordinary means."

Of course, such a revised statute might not be wise even if it proved constitutional. It might not be wise for this reason alone: it could be counterproductive, by encouraging physicians to choose methods of abortion that most certainly will destroy fetal life in midpregnancy. The standard of care would have to be coupled with a prohibition, for example, of saline abortions in midpregnancy. That, in turn, seems likely to pass constitutional scrutiny only if the Court recognizes a grey area of possible and uncertain viability, and if it can be convinced that there is a *state* interest in giving effect to possible fetal viability, not just a medical ethical obligation.

We can now rapidly conclude by looking at what the dissent said about the points made by the Court. The three dissenting justices

---

Bok agreed with Walters's equality principle, although she recommended that a time limit after which elective abortion is prohibited would be better than statutory standards of care. Moreover, Bok stressed a point that needs to prevail in public consciousness—namely, that "while a woman does have a right to an abortion in the sense of the termination of pregnancy, she does not have a right to the death of the fetus" ("The Unwanted Child," pp. 10–15).

27. In connection with the issues to be raised in chapters 5 and 6, below, it should be observed that neither statute says anything about whether the live-born person was born defective or not. And in striking down the Missouri statute the Court suggested that it was redundant; all questions about a legal obligation to preserve the lives of possibly viable infants are already—the Court supposed everybody knew—covered by the criminal law.

read that first sentence to set a standard of care, with the meaning I have just tried to clarify. "If this section is read in any way other than through a microscope," Justice White wrote, "it is plainly intended to require that, where a 'fetus . . . [may have] the capability of meaningful life outside the mother's womb' [citing *Wade*], the abortion be handled in a way which is designed to preserve that life notwithstanding the mother's desire to terminate it."

Indeed, "even looked at through a microscope the statute seems to go no further. It requires a physician to exercise '*that* degree of professional skill . . . to preserve the fetus' which he would be required to exercise if the mother wanted a live child" (the dissent's emphasis). Then the dissent, rather cunningly I think, supported that reading by pointing out that during an abortion performed when there is no chance of fetal viability outside the womb, the physician would be at liberty to exercise no care or skill at all to preserve the life of the fetus "no matter what the mother desires." It is possible fetal viability that counts, not the initiation of an abortion procedure or the woman's expectations. I may add that in a similar case of premature delivery of a clearly nonviable baby where birth and long life had been in view, the physician would similarly be at liberty to exercise no care or skill at all to preserve that baby's life—again, "no matter what" the mother (and the physician) desires or what she had hoped.

Plainly, the statute was intended "to operate only in the grey area after the fetus *might* be viable but while the physician is still unable to certify 'with reasonable certainty that the fetus is not viable.' "[28] Because the dissent recognized there to be such a "grey area" in the nature of fetal development and in the uncertainty and fallibility of physicians' judgments, and only because it did so, the dissenting justices would have upheld the statute. To the extent of such a "grey area" and only to that extent, I judge, the dissenters would have given legal effect to a physician's obligation reaching back to a "possibly viable infant." Because the majority did not recognize such a grey area, and only because it did not do so, the Court struck down the statute; and for the same reason it would permit no legal formulation of a physician's obligation to choose an appropriate abortion method for a possibly viable infant—encompassing the time, however brief, before

28. Here the dissent cites the undisputed section of the Missouri statute *prohibiting* abortion without such certification except to promote the mother's life and safety.

the physician can certify with reasonable certainty that the fetus is not viable. That was "bad medicine," bad law, and at this point a touching faith in the omnicompetence of physicians' judgments or in the uniformly high level of their ethical practice.

"Incredibly," the dissenting opinion goes on to say, "the Court reads the statute to require 'the physician to preserve the life and health of the fetus, whatever the stage of pregnancy.' " Or, as I said above, the Court imputed stupidity to the state legislators. In more restrained language, the dissent says only that the Court thereby attributed to the Missouri legislature "the strange intention of passing a statute with absolutely no chance of surviving constitutional challenge under *Roe* v. *Wade.*"

The question whether a constitutional provision of state law is severable from an unconstitutional provision was, in the dissenters' opinion, "*entirely* a question of the intent of the state legislature." "At worst," that first sentence was ambiguous. Therefore, the dissent would have ruled that the district court erred in deciding the constitutional question: it should have abstained "until a construction may be had from the state courts." "Under no circumstances," said the dissent, should the Court have declared that section of the Missouri statute unconstitutional 'at this point'—before hearing that state's courts' construction of its meaning and effects. Interestingly enough, this was precisely the way the Court—that same day—dealt with the Massachusetts statute providing for parental consent. To abstain or not to abstain, that is the question; and again, it seems, the Court does whichever it pleases.

Finally, the dissenting opinion drops a footnote which, to my amazement and delight, reads as follows:

> The majority's construction of state law is, of course, not binding on the Missouri courts. If they should disagree with the majority's reading of state law on one or both of the points treated by the majority, the State could validly enforce the relevant parts of the statute—at least against all those people not parties to this case.

I like that. The state of Missouri may have some recourse besides drafting a new statute and waiting to see. That's what we need—a little judicial rebellion among the followship.

If the opinion dissenting from the Court's Bicentennial abortion decision does not, in future years, come to be regarded as one of the great dissents in the history of the United States Supreme Court, then our children and our children's children will not even have been cognizant of the fact that they have journeyed on into the setting sun of Western law and morality, not seeing the shadows. We may even now be living "between the evenings" (a beautiful—and, I believe, Jewish—expression for "twilight"). That's the sum of it.

2

Abortion after the Law

Conscience and Its Problems

In November 1974, Dr. Bernard N. Nathanson published a brief article in the *New England Journal of Medicine* entitled "Deeper into Abortion." [1] I read the article as a recantation of very many—not all—of Dr. Nathanson's activities over the past six or seven years. Since nobody writes "retractions" these days, he is all the more to be honored for his candor.

In early 1969 Nathanson and a group of "equally concerned and indignant citizens" organized the National Association for the Repeal of Abortion Laws (now—same acronym—the National Abortion Rights Action League). The group was "outspokenly militant," "enlisted the woman's movement and the Protestant clergy into [their] ranks," "used every device available to political-action groups such as pamphleteering, public demonstrations, exploitation of the media and lobbying. . . ." Nathanson tells of one occasion on which his three-year-old son proudly carried a placard urging legalized abortion. Success came when Governor Nelson Rockefeller signed into law the New York State Abortion Statute of 1970.

But that was not the end of Nathanson's pilgrimage. "Our next goal," he tells us, "was to assure . . . that low cost, safe and humane abortions were available to all. . . ." So the Center for Reproductive

1. Bernard N. Nathanson, "Deeper into Abortion," the *New England Journal of Medicine* 291, no. 22 (November 28, 1974) : 1189–90. Dr. Nathanson is now associate attending physician at New York Hospital and chief of ob-gyn at St. Luke's Hospital in New York City. Unfootnoted quotations to follow are from this article. For an update on Nathanson's opinions, see Norma Rosen, "Between Guilt and Gratification," *New York Times Magazine*, April 17, 1977. Ms. Rosen elicited responses from other physicians about their feelings by framing questions like those Nathanson had put to himself. One such inquiry was: "What about those who feel we are losing commitment to human seed?" Any reader can see the astonishing bias in such a formulation, and its complete misrepresentation of Nathanson's views.

and Sexual Health was established: "the first—and largest—abortion clinic in the Western world." By February 1972 the center had performed 60,000 abortions with no maternal deaths—a record of which, on that score, Dr. Nathanson is justifiably proud. Moreover, let us be clear, he still believes there should be no laws prohibiting abortion.

Even "A Form of Human Life" an Issue for Conscience

Yet after a year and a half as director of the largest abortion clinic in the Western world, Nathanson resigned because he was "deeply troubled by [his] own increasing certainty that [he] had in fact presided over 60,000 deaths." The fetus is as alive as anyone who "flunks" the Harvard criteria for a physician's declaration that a terminal patient has died. Still Nathanson claims only that human life is a "continuous spectrum" along which we designate "bands" by the words *embryo, fetus, infant, child, adolescent,* and *adult*. He does not speak of the fetus as a "person," or as a congener equal to the rest of us. He had presided over 60,000 deaths of "a form of human life." Still—remembering his no-holds-barred militancy—Nathanson writes:

> Somewhere in the vast philosophic plateau between the two implacably opposed camps—past the slogans, past the pamphlets, past even the demonstrations and the legislative threats—lies the infinitely agonizing truth. We are taking life, and the deliberate taking of life, even of a special order and under special circumstances, is an inexpressibly serious matter.

I must say that Dr. Nathanson cops out to some degree when he lays upon women alone the responsibility for creating a wholly new attitude toward the "inexpressibly serious matter" of abortion; and when the only recommendation he comes up with is that something needs to be done about "the narrow partisanship of committed young women who have had abortions . . . who typically staff the counselor ranks of hospitals and clinics now."

"Certainly, the medical profession itself cannot shoulder the burden in this matter," Nathanson writes. He has two reasons for that opinion: the first a good reason, the second questionable. First, a decision to abort seldom today needs to be made on medical grounds.

As another physician has written, "Abortion is no more purely a medical problem just because the physician wields the curette than chemical warfare is purely a problem for pilots because they press the lever releasing the chemical." [2] The second reason for placing on women alone the burden for creating a new climate of opinion regarding abortion is that the Supreme Court's phrase "between a woman and her physician" is "an empty one since the physician is only the instrument of her decision, and has no special knowledge of the moral dilemma or the ethical agony involved in the decision."

That the physician qua physician has no special moral wisdom on this or any other nonmedical dilemma, we may agree; but not that a physician is "only the instrument" of his patients' decisions. I see no reason at all to regard physicians and nurses in the ob-gyn service simply as "animated tools"—which was Aristotle's definition of a slave. They, too, have consciences; theirs are moral or medical-moral decisions. Nathanson manifested this, of course, by writing his article; and its publication in a prestigious medical journal constituted a call to his fellow professionals to give second thought—and deeper thought—to the "infinitely agonizing" issues raised by our widening practice of abortion. There is, therefore, no reason for the penultimate word in the following sentence to be *her:* "The din that has arisen in our land has already created an atmosphere in which it is difficult, if not impossible, for the individual to see the issues clearly and to reach an understanding free from the taint of the last shibboleth that was screamed in her ear." Since his article's publication, I venture to say that Dr. Nathanson has been much in demand on the lecture circuit—as anyone would be who managed today to say something sensible on this subject. His call is clear: "The issue is human life, and it deserves the reverent stillness and ineffably grave thought appropriate to it." ". . . there is a danger that society will lose a certain moral tension that has been a vital part of its fabric, . . . [and that we will] permit ourselves to sink to the debased level of utilitarian semiconsciousness."

Nathanson's article gives us an excellent start in addressing the topic "Abortion after the Law." The legal wars and disputes are over

2. E. Fuller Torrey, ed., *Ethical Issues in Medicine* (Boston: Little, Brown and Co., 1968), p. viii. Cf. p. 77: "Abortion is a medical issue only because it is the doctor who wields the necessary instrument."

in the sense that the legality of abortion has been sweepingly settled for our whole nation. What now? What are the opportunities and perils or problems ahead?

An Opportune Moment for Moral Dialogue

I shall speak mainly of perils and problems ahead, if we are to avoid further descent into technological barbarism. But first, mention should be made of the opportunities that could be seized. Now that abortion is no longer a criminal offense, the religious communities could draw closer together in making explicit what they mean to teach about the preciousness of unborn life.

In the first place, church and synagogue can be seen to be closer together now than when, during the legal wars, Jewish teaching was libeled by identification with the view of modernity that there is protectable human life only after birth. I began this chapter with the views of Dr. Nathanson because he expressed—knowingly or not—the traditional Jewish account of the fetus. Prenatally, it is only a "form of human life." I wanted to indicate that problems of conscience in the matter of abortion do not surface only among those who believe that from conception a developing embryo—or the fetus from some point in its uterine gestation—is a protectable "person." Public discussion of the morality of abortion is not set on edge simply because a large number of people in the United States hold the traditional Christian viewpoint that—granting some variation over the centuries as to where to draw the line—*never* located the emergence of the human person at birth. Even so, I wanted to signalize that a problem of conscience still remains.

Technically, it is true that in Jewish teaching there is individual human life only after the head or the greater portion of the fetus has passed through the birth canal. But it is superficial to contrast Jewish teaching with Christian opinion just because that is the traditional Jewish definition of when human life *begins*. The Jewish reverence for what the Supreme Court called "the potentiality of life" is well expressed by the teaching that one should violate the most holy days—the Sabbath and Yom Kippur—to save a fetus, which is only potentially a human being. One violates for him this Sabbath so that he will remain alive to observe many Sabbaths.[3] So from different definitional premises, a wide range of Jewish opinion is operationally very similar to that of traditional Roman Catholicism—namely, that abortion is justified only to save the mother's life. Jewish ethics simply did not have to distinguish whether the death of a fetus was brought about directly or indirectly, since the fetus and mother are not believed to have *equal* title to life. In Jewish ethics one may directly destroy fetal life in a necessary abortion, while in traditional Catholic ethics even a necessary abortion must be indirectly intended. This single distinction between orthodox Jewish thought and orthodox Christian thought is seldom correctly explained; even Catholics often say that their church

3. *b Yoma 85b;* David Feldman, *Contraception and Jewish Law* (New York: New York University Press, 1968), p. 264. Concerning craniotomy (which Catholic teaching had difficulty "resolving" as a case of "indirect" therapeutic abortion) Jewish teaching was simply: "If a woman is in hard travail, one cuts up the child within her womb and extracts it member by member because her life has priority over it; but if the greater part of it was already born, it may not be touched, since one does not set aside one life for the sake of another" (*Mishnah, Oholot* 7 : 6; see Immanuel Jakobovits, *Jewish Medical Ethics* [New York: Block Publishing Company, 1959, 1975], p. 184; also Feldman, p. 275).

Nevertheless, the life of the unborn child was precious, next only to the mother's life. "There are three [persons] who drive away the Shekhima from the world, making it impossible for the Holy One, blessed be He, to fix His abode in the universe and causing prayer to be unanswered: . . . [The third is] he who causes the fetus to be destroyed in the womb, for he destroys the Artifice of the Holy One, blessed be He, and His workmanship . . . [F]or these abominations the Spirit of Holiness weeps . . ." (*Zohar, Shemot* 3b).

Indeed it appears that Jewish ethics gives justification for craniotomy (direct abortion) more readily than it finds justification for abortion in cases where it is not the *fetus* who is pursuing the mother's life but some medical condition instead. The pursuer doctrine applied to the abortion issue was a distinct departure by Maimonides. Either mother or fetus can be "pursuer," "aggressor," in case the other must die; or rather, the mother is pursued "from Heaven"; and one may intervene to save her by acting directly against the fetus, if need be, since it is only a form of human life. When, however, the life-threatening situation in pregnancy emanates from causes *other* than the fetus, those causes must themselves be attacked, not the unborn child. "It follows that we may not induce abortion . . . to save her from a disease deriving from other 'fevers' . . . in the sixth month of her pregnancy . . . for only the pursuer may be killed in self-defense or for defense of another . . . but this fetus is no pursuer. . . . We must save her by other treatments" (R. Issac Lampronti, *Pahad Yitzhak,* s.v. n'falim.) If those other treatments fail, and only if they fail, this "stringent" position might allow the adoption of another rule, one which "coincides with a leniency in the Catholic position," namely, *indirect* abortion (Feldman, p. 282). See Feldman, pp. 275–84 for a discussion of the pursuer doctrine.

opposes "therapeutic" abortion when the meaning is "direct" therapeutic abortion.

In the second place, with the end of our legal quarrels, the short-lived apostasy of most Protestant churches from the common Christian tradition concerning the sanctity of unborn life could now be ended. We can return to an ecumenical concern for what Christianity may have to say to its constituencies and to the world at large about the morality (not the legality) of abortion. This will be the case if we are more concerned about what the church has to say to the modern world than about what the modern world says the church should say. Time was, when we Protestants bemoaned the fact that the Pope's pronouncement of the dogma of the Virgin Mary's bodily assumption into heaven threw another roadblock in front of the coming unification of Christianity. Yet we have not hesitated to do with alacrity the same thing in the matter of the morality of abortion.

My own church's statement of social principles reads as follows (now that we can strike out the call for decriminalizing abortion):

> Our belief in the sanctity of unborn human life makes us reluctant to approve abortion. But we are equally bound to respect the sacredness of the life and well-being of the mother, for whom devastating damage may result from an unacceptable pregnancy. In continuity with past Christian teachings, we recognize tragic conflicts of life with life that may justify abortion. We call all Christians to a searching and prayerful inquiry into the sorts of conditions that may warrant abortion.[4]

That is not a bad beginning if the churches mean to address an independent witness to the modern world. It should mean, for example, that the question, When does protectable human life begin? is one that must more urgently be raised and answered in a Christian moral context, now that it seems pointless to raise that question in a legal context.

In sum, with the Court having rightly or wrongly settled the legal issue, the Protestant and Catholic churches and the synagogue need no longer confuse the legal questions with the moral. That is an opportunity to be seized.

I want, however, to address myself to the perils and the pressures

4. Sec. 72(d), 1972 Statement of Social Principles, United Methodist Church.

that hospitals, physicians, and nurses must face today if they wish to give effective expression to their professional, moral, or religious conscience in the matter of abortion.

The problem of conscientious refusal to perform elective abortions or to participate in such procedures can quickly be introduced by several illustrations drawn from the testimony of record in a trial challenging the conscience clause of the state of Kentucky:

> If the X hospital were forced, that is, the Board of Trustees were forced by law to carry out abortion, they would have to decide whether to operate as a hospital or give the hospital up and sell it to somebody else. Some of the members of the Board of Trustees have spoken to me about that particular problem. . . .[5]

> I might give you just a couple of cases. This one happened in one of the Midwestern states . . . a hospital whose Board of Trustees had o.k.'d abortions. Here's a lady, divorced or widowed nurse, several small children to support, chief nurse in the operating room, excellent track record, apparently earning a reasonable salary and needed that to care for her family. They began to do abortions. She refused to be part of what she called killing babies. There were other nurses in the theater; she didn't have to be involved. Two weeks after the abortions started, . . . suddenly a great deal of fault was found with what had previously been exemplary performance in her job; she was transferred to night duty on the psych ward. I think it speaks for itself. There was no way that this woman could retaliate. . . .
>
> Let me just give you one more example. . . . This one lad who had 3.9 out of a possible 4.0 average in premed at Notre Dame University. Now Notre Dame last year was rated number eight among all the universities in terms of excellence. And high among its departments is its premed. So this person, by that standard an exceptional guy, and he was . . . a very well balanced young man. He had applied to a variety of medical schools and he told us this story. I am free to tell you the university he came from because it might give you a clue as to his opposition to abortion. I won't tell you which of the ivy league schools he

5. Testimony of Dr. Herringer, *Wolfe* v. *Schroering*, 388 F. Supp. 613 (W.D. Ky. 1974).

> went to for his interviews. He said, "In 30 minutes the person who interviewed me asked me seven different times, in one way or another, my opinion on abortion; would I participate and so forth." He said, "When I left that interview my knees were jelly." He said, "No way am I going to get into that school unless I would have perjured myself repeatedly." Now . . . [there is] just no way you could say that that boy was rejected from that school because of his pro-life proclivities. They would have found another reason, as you know.[6]

The wave of the future seems clear to me if there is not a profound change of moral opinion in our nation. The three-judge district court in *Wolfe* v. *Schroering,* which heard the comprehensive abortion statute of Kentucky challenged on constitutional grounds, handed down its decision on November 19, 1974. In that decision, the district court struck down Kentucky's institutional conscience clause. Despite the fact that the statute included a severability clause, the court went further and *invalidated Kentucky's individual conscience clause,* which had not even been challenged. Appeal from this decision was argued before the Sixth Circuit on October 16, 1975.[7] In that appeal,

6. Testimony of Dr. Wilke, *Wolfe* v. *Schroering,* 388 F. Supp. 613 (W.D. Ky. 1974). The thesis of this chapter is not an *induction* from these cases, or from additional illustrations to be introduced later. It rather draws support from the reader's experience, knowledge, or wisdom about what is required to prevent discrimination on ground of race, sex, or ethnic or religious background in any institutional setting, which is always facially deniable.

7. See below pp. 75–76 for a discussion on the long-delayed opinion of the U.S. Court of Appeals for the Sixth Circuit in the *Schroering* case, upon appeal from Kentucky. The appeals court's ruling and opinion [541 F.2d 523 (6th Cir. 1976)] upsets my "wave of the future" prediction above—provided a decision still to come from the United States Supreme Court is in accord with the sound legal, medical, and moral reasoning by which the appeals court reversed the Kentucky court and upheld that state's conscience clauses.

The case involved a *public* hospital, but that was not the chief reason the Kentucky court struck down that state's institutional conscience clause in 1974 (now reversed). The matter was taken up in terms of the section of the statute not requiring hospitals (sic) to perform abortions, with its antidiscrimination clause for hospitals that choose not to perform abortions. The court held the conscience clause (1) unconstitutional in itself because it singled out abortions, thereby treating the abortion process differently from other medical procedures; and (2) unconstitutional in relation to sec. 6 (2) of the statute requiring that abortions be performed in a hospital. The latter, standing alone, was not "tainted with unconstitutional effects," but, by itself, the former was. The state could not subtly discourage the performance of abora brief *amici curiae* on behalf of Kentucky Registered Nurses was entered, in an attempt to save the individual conscience clause even if the institutional conscience clause failed.

Before going further into conscience and its plight in the United States, we can gain a certain distance and a needed perspective on the dimensions of the problem we are addressing by briefly considering the state of affairs in Great Britain—another modern industrial nation and the seat of our liberties. This will be to emulate the prophet Amos, who first drew attention to something gone awry in neighboring foreign lands before espying like transgressions in Judah or Israel. So let us go abroad for a moment.

THE NULLITY OF THE CONSCIENCE CLAUSE IN GREAT BRITAIN

The abortion act of 1967 in Great Britain reads, in its crucial first section, as follows:

> A person shall not be guilty of an offense under the law relating to abortion when a pregnancy is terminated by a registered medical practitioner if two registered medical practitioners are of the opinion, formed in good faith—
>
> (a) that the continuation of the pregnancy would involve risks to the life of the pregnant woman, or of injury to the physical or mental health of the pregnant woman or any existing children of her family, greater than if the pregnancy were terminated; [8] or

tions by providing that hospitals that do not allow abortions may not be discriminated against when no such provision exists for hospitals which *do* perform abortions. These grounds suggested ways in which the legislature of Kentucky could have reframed its statute and enacted a conscience clause that would pass constitutional scrutiny. Still, one cannot fail to ponder the moral condition of a society whose courts proceed to set precedents that weaken actual cases of conscience under color of granting equal status to claims of conscientious objection to *other medical procedures* no one has ever conscientiously objected to, and under color of protecting hospitals that do abortions—which no one discriminates against.

8. In arriving at this opinion "account may be taken of the woman's actual or reasonably foreseeable environment" (sec. 2). T. N. A. Jeffcoate deems provision (a), above, to be "beyond rational interpretation"; it means that "doctors are now being asked to decide whether the physical and mental benefits of performing an operation on one person are less than the nebulous ones to which a third person, such as a step-son aged fifteen, might be exposed by having a half-brother" (since the regulations define "children of the family" to mean natural, adopted, foster, or step-children up to age sixteen). (*Morals and Medicine* [London: British Broadcast-

(b) that there is a substantial risk that if the child were born it would suffer from such physical or mental abnormalities as to be seriously handicapped.

Notice should be taken of the fact that (a) and (b) simply state when abortion shall *not* be regarded as an offense under the law. That negative language decriminalizes abortion under the stated conditions. It places abortion under those circumstances in the area of liberties which, while not prohibited by law, receive no encouragement from the law. The 1967 abortion act may be compared with the Feversham Committee's recommendation that artificial insemination from donors be free from legal restriction or the Wolfendon Report's advocacy that homosexual acts in private between consenting adults be removed from the category of legal offenses. So consenting women and medical practitioners shall not be regarded as guilty of an offense under the law relating to abortion when a pregnancy is terminated under the stated conditions. The fact that the 1967 abortion act merely permits and does not encourage abortion is sustained by the conscience clause, which reads: "No person shall be under any duty, whether by contract or by any statutory or other legal requirement, to participate in any treatment authorized by this Act to which he has a conscientious objection." [9]

Since Great Britain beat the United States by five years in liberalizing abortion (I cringe at the necessity of that debased usage of the word *liberal*), we can look to the British experience to see something of the future to which we are coming. The lengthy "Report of the Committee on the Working of the Abortion Act," headed by the Hon. Mrs. Justice Lane, was issued in April 1974. The Lane Report generally approves the working of the 1967 regulations. It pointed out that (as I have suggested) the act "did not cast upon hospitals or doctors any specific duty to provide for or perform abortions; it modi-

---

ing Corporation, 1970; New York: Oxford University Press, 1971], p. 34). This is a clear case of "social utilitarianism" melding lives together in search of the greatest total good. The irony is that the calculus "greater than," etc., was introduced into the British law to put some limit upon or to indicate a measure for medical judgments when they launch upon the chartless ocean of "foreseeable environmental" threats to the mental health of a woman and her existing children.

9. Sec. 4 (1). That liberty is limited, it is true, by the next subsection which makes it a "duty to participate in treatment which is necessary to save the life or prevent the grave permanent injury to the physical or mental health of a pregnant woman."

fied the previous law as to abortion by providing that it is not an offense to terminate a pregnancy on the grounds set out. . . ." Nevertheless, the Lane Report found there to be cast upon the National Health Service a "positive responsibility to provide for abortion" under those permitted conditions.[10] Here then is the contradiction: How can this affirmative obligation be cast upon the health service while still retaining *effective* provision for "conscientious objection" (which the Lane Report still endorses)? [11]

The answer must be that a general obligation to provide abortion services cannot be made consistent with freedom of conscientious refusal. Upon the issuance of the Lane Report, the *British Medical Journal* [12] promptly called for the removal of liberty of conscience. "A conscience clause was manifestly essential when the Act came in," it editorialized, "since many gynecologists had sincere moral or ethical objections to abortion on some of the grounds introduced by the new Act." But "seven years later the situation has changed." Nullification of the conscience clause can be effected administratively, without new legislation, the editorial observed, quoting with approval a statement elsewhere in the Lane Report: "It is inevitable that the health authorities should prefer the appointment to certain posts of those who see abortion as properly part of clinical gynecological practice." We in the United States should note especially the editorial's none too subtle suggestion about how to avoid a law protecting individual conscience and the Lane Report's prediction of its inevitable nullification in practice.

In short, professional judgment or conscience contrary to abortion will be squeezed out. The medical and nursing professions will be reshaped to conform. Only those already in ob-gyn practice will be protected by the conscience clause; but over the course of time they will pass from the human scene. If a conscience clause is still on the books, that will protect a Dr. Nathanson who, already in the service, develops a left-handed conscience about what he has been doing. But no young person will be appointed as a nurse or intern in ob-gyn, or be graduated "properly" trained, who already has such a conscience.

Witness three examples measured by the British experience:

10. "Report of the Committee on the Working of the Abortion Act." (London: Her Majesty's Stationery Office, 1974), par. 398.

11. Ibid., pars. 360–61.

12. April 13, 1974.

A young physician. The Supreme Court decision in 1973 came at a point in my residency training in obstetrics and gynecology where I was two and one-half years into a three and one-half year program. For the first six months following that decision I worked either directly in the ——— Clinic itself or at X Hospital. However, for the last six months of my training, beginning in July 1973, I was asked to complete my training at Y Hospital where abortions were now being performed on demand. For all intents and purposes, I could have finished my training at X Hospital where adequate gynecological training in gynecologic surgery was available. However I was told that I would have to complete my training at Y Hospital under the senior gynecologic surgeons who were present only at the Y Hospital. Only later did I find out that other residents have completed their training at X Hospital under the junior gynecologic surgeons. At this point, I had only six months remaining in my training. However, I decided that I could not work in a hospital that did abortions. I was assured by the faculty that I would not have to either participate or assist in the performance of abortions. However, knowing how residency staffs operate, it is not unusual for a resident to take a vacation or become ill or have to take a leave of absence for a brief period of time in which I perhaps might have to participate even if it were just preoperatively in working up such patients. However, my conscientious objection went much deeper than that and it involved the essential support of an institution which was involved in these kinds of killing operations. Since the ——— Clinic did not comply with my request to finish the residency at X Hospital, I felt forced to resign my position there. Incidentally, I am also a conscientious objector to the service in the Armed Forces on similar reasons. My in-depth reasons in regard to these conscientious objections certainly go much deeper than that and involve my view of Christianity and what that means to my involvement in life.[13]

A nurse anesthetist in New York City. This young nurse was still receiving her training in anesthesiology. When abortion became law in New York, she voiced her opposition and refused to give anesthesia to abortion patients. As a result, she was not assigned

13. This case I obtained directly from the young physician in question, whom I know and trust.

to any patients. . . . Without experience she would not be permitted to graduate. She went to her superior and requested patients other than abortion patients. The superior said, "You want work, we'll give you work." She was then scheduled to work twelve hours a day, every day of the week. She worked this schedule for three months without a day off. Finally she capitulated and began to give anesthesia to abortion patients. Her last case was to assist with a hysterotomy abortion. She was ordered to give a dose of morphine to the mother that was known to be lethal to the baby she carried. She refused to do this, but she did administer the anesthesia. Upon the delivery of a four pound baby, dead from the overdose, she left the operating room vomiting. Since that time she has suffered from insomnia and is having great difficulty in functioning as a professional nurse.[14]

A young student nurse at a hospital in Cincinnati. At first she could see no harm in abortion, but as her knowledge grew, her opinion changed. She made the grave error of sending a letter

14. This and the following example, and other cases to be introduced later in this chapter, I vouch for because I know the proxy who communicated with me. For many readers this will seem to be an insufficient data base, and possibly biased. The National Federation of Catholic Physicians' Guilds appointed an ad-hoc committee on medical school discrimination. It studied the problem by distributing a questionnaire to medical schools. Nothing proved, nothing disproved, is a fair reading of the report (*Linacre Quarterly,* February 1976).

Please note, however, that the chief points to be demonstrated are the extraordinary pressure placed upon individual conscientious refusals (because ob-gyn and allied services must run a "tight ship") and the complexity of the problem of making the conscience clause *effective.* See also note 6, above.

For several years I have lectured, in an undergraduate course at Princeton, on the problem of conscientious refusal on the part of medical personnel. Two years ago one of my students—a top-flight student, a devout Christian (not a Catholic) who brought his well-formed conscience to the course—was asked in his medical school interview (at a leading Eastern medical school) what his opinion was on abortion. Having been properly briefed, the student demanded to know why the interviewer asked that question. The reply was, "Oh, we just want to see how applicants can handle a question."

On January 24, 1977, Senator Richard S. Schweiker (R-Pa.) introduced bill S.784, "Unbiased Consideration of Applicants to Medical Schools." The bill would bolster the conscience clauses by prohibiting the "questioning, verbally or in writing, [of] any individual who is applying for admission as a student about his or her views on abortion or sterilization," or any discrimination based on "religious beliefs or moral convictions" or for conscientious nonparticipation following admission. S.784 is unlikely to get through Congress; in my judgment, we shall have to wait for the disposition of the conscience clauses by the courts.

describing abortion procedures and voicing her opposition to them to the *Cincinnati Enquirer*. The paper published the letter. Within two weeks of its publication she was called before the director of nurses and the chief of obstetrics and gynecology. She was severely reprimanded and debased. She was called unfeeling and unwomanly. Finally she was expelled for academic incompetency (strangely enough, she was carrying a B average). Fortunately she was accepted by a Catholic hospital in Chicago and graduated with honors. However, it cost her parents $2,000 and the girl a year of time and a year's salary which would not have been expended if she had graduated from her original school.

Of course, there was a flurry of protests in Great Britain against the implications of the Lane Report. Norman St. John-Stevas, M.P., wrote that "the most sinister feature of the report is its unproved assertion that the provision of abortion is now a duty under the national health service. . . . [That assumption] needs vigorous rebuttal since its acceptance would nullify the effect of the conscience clause. . . ." The correspondence column of the *British Medical Journal* was filled with other letters—pro and con, some irate, some sad, some apprehensive—concerning the future of gynecological departments in Great Britain if the Lane Report were to be accepted by the government. Mainly there was the concern that a young nurse or doctor would have no prospect of specializing in ob-gyn if he or she strongly believed, for professional, medical, or moral reasons, that abortions permitted by the 1967 act are wrong.

An article in the *Times* [15] reports the following: A Member of Parliament, Mr. Rossi, wrote to Mrs. Barbara Castle, minister in charge of the Department of Health and Social Services (DHSS), in behalf of a constituent who had been refused employment as a gynecological consultant. He asked for a list of hospitals at which his constituent might be sure there would be no obstacle in his path if he chose to exercise the rights guaranteed medical practitioners by Parliament in 1967. A Dr. David Owen replied for Mrs. Castle. He pointed out that although the Lane committee found that doctors with conscientious objection to abortion felt there was discrimination against them, the committee also thought it inevitable that health authorities would prefer to appoint doctors prepared to carry out abortions where this is an

15. Ronald Butt, "Abortion: The Dangerous Pressure on Doctors," the *Times* (London), January 30, 1975.

integral part of the service. Dr. Owen continued: "As I see it, the statutory 'conscience clause' . . . preserves the rights of established staff not to take part in certain procedures . . . but it does not touch on the position of staff not established but simply seeking appointment." The right place for the reference to the need to carry out abortions is in the job description or interview; and if a candidate accepts this, it "would be inappropriate to question him on his religious or personal beliefs." So ruled the DHSS of the United Kingdom. There the conscience clause has served as a temporary expedient to smooth the path of transition from one ethics to another. The young doctor in this case decided to emigrate. To where, I do not know.

In a letter addressed to all regional medical officers in Great Britain, the chief medical officer of DHSS advised:

> Where it can be established after consultation with the relevant specialist advisers that there is a demand which cannot be met and where patient care would suffer if a doctor appointed to a particular vacancy did not feel able, on grounds of conscience, to be involved in, or advise on, the termination of pregnancy it may be stated that the post includes duty to advise on, undertake, or participate in termination of pregnancy. As you will appreciate, the question may arise not only for posts in obstetrics and gynaecology, but also in anaesthetics and psychiatry.

That statement makes it clear that, despite and contrary to the wording of the abortion act, Great Britain has by administrative decision instated a policy of abortion on demand, and that more than one sort of medical consultant is now required to acquiesce.

The chief medical officer went on to say:

> The Advisory Appointments Committee will wish to be satisfied that applicants are in all respects fitted and prepared to carry out the full range of duties which they might be required to perform if appointed. In doing so, inquiries about duties that relate to termination of pregnancy should be confined to professional intention, and should not extend to questions about candidates' personal beliefs.

Ponder the distinction made by that last sentence. From the perspective of past Christian ethics, it must be said that only the most degenerate forms of Lutheranism set such a gulf between "the Kingdom of God inwardly" (personal, conscientious beliefs) and one's official or professional intention to perform certain outward behaviors in obedience to the "princes" of this world. So far as I know, the Church of England has not protested.

In Great Britain, at least, the conscience clause has been interpreted so as to reshape the morality of a major part of the medical and nursing professions and, in the final analysis, to make it quite impossible for a new attitude toward the taking of life (which deserves "reverent stillness and ineffably grave thought"—Nathanson) ever to rise again from the ashes or to gain footing in the ob-gyn service. Has not the National Health Service sunk to "the debased level of utilitarian semiconsciousness" in the enforcement of morals at the point of employment?

Did the 1973 Abortion Decisions Cast upon the Medical Profession a Duty to Perform Abortions?

There can be no more important point to make clear in the reader's, and in the public's, mind than the fact that both Great Britain and the United States began with quite similar law on the matter of abortion. In 1967 an act of Parliament and in 1973 the United States Supreme Court's decisions *placed abortion in an area of liberties.* Neither nation established such a "right" to abortion that would entail an impelling duty on the part of members of the medical profession generally to provide such services or an obligation on the part of interns or nurses to participate in such procedures.

Only three Justices—Justice Douglas, with his reference to a woman's "preferred life style" (concurring in *Doe* v. *Bolton*),[16] and Justices White and Rehnquist, dissenting in that case—were of the opinion that the Court on January 22, 1973, gave women a constitutional right to abortion upon their own request. Mr. Chief Justice Burger, concurring in *Bolton,* specifically stated that, "Plainly, the Court today rejects any claim that the Constitution requires abortion on demand." His view was that the Court's decisions simply liberated "carefully deliberated *medical* judgments relating to life and health" (italics added). The abortion decisions may reveal on the part of the Court a naive faith in physicians and an insensitivity to the social

16. *Doe* v. *Bolton,* 410 U.S. 179 (1973).

pressures and pecuniary temptations about to be released upon them. Still, as a matter of law Justice Burger's reading seems plainly correct.

If there is any hope that conscientious professional judgment is not to be overwhelmed by pressures to conform, it is of first importance that we correctly understand the Supreme Court's opinions. Mr. Justice Blackmun, speaking for the Court in *Roe* v. *Wade* [17] and in *Bolton,* did not make hospitals, physicians, or nurses "state agencies." Nor did he command them to insure a woman's constitutional "right" to abortion. The Court did not speak of a woman's constitutional right to an abortion on demand, or (more mildly) on request to a hospital or physician. Indeed, the Court specifically rejected, on the one side, amicus curiae opinions advising the Court to declare abortion a constitutional right, and on the other side, amicus curiae opinions petitioning it to declare the unborn child a person whose life was fully protected by the Fourteenth Amendment. The Court ruled instead that the *state* has no power to say or do anything about the matter of abortion for the first trimester. It vacated state power. That, I suggest, placed abortion during that period in an area of liberties, quite analogous to the British act in 1967. That liberty, of course, will be protected; but if there is no constitutional right to abortion, there can be no correlative legal duties cast upon hospitals, physicians, or nurses. All, including the pregnant woman, are in an area of liberty of conscience and action. All, except the state, are left to say yes or no.

Looking more closely at the text, I do not find that Justice Blackmun, when writing the Court's opinion in both *Roe* v. *Wade* and *Doe* v. *Bolton,* ever used the phrase "between the woman and her physician" when he vacated state power. The emphasis was placed, of course, on the woman's right of privacy; but within that, the emphasis fell on the medical judgment of her physician. *Wade* specifically rejects the claim that the woman's right or the privacy involved is absolute. ". . . It is not clear to us that the claim asserted by some *amici* that one has an unlimited right to do with one's body as one pleases bears a close relation to the right of privacy previously articulated in the Court's decisions." A woman's right of privacy prevails over *state* regulation or prohibition for the first trimester, after which state interest begins to grow. Nothing is said about that right of pri-

17. *Roe* v. *Wade,* 410 U.S. 113 (1973).

vacy prevailing over the professional judgment or conscientious objections of others not the state. In order to distinguish this case from *Griswold,* Blackmun reached back to the beginning of pregnancy: "The pregnant woman cannot be isolated in her privacy. She carries an embryo and, later, a fetus. . . . The situation therefore is inherently different from marital intimacy, or bedroom possession of obscene material, or marriage, or procreation, or education. . . ."

Confusion has arisen in public understanding because of the mistaken assumption that where there is no state interest there is a *right* with correlative duties on the part of others and a claim to be served with state assistance. However, nothing in what the Court said about the state's interest (beginning at the end of twelve weeks) entails that *before that* the woman's privacy remains sole in the sense that a physician simply has to act according to her commands. Indeed, summarizing in *Wade,* Justice Blackmun wrote, "For the stage prior to approximately the end of the first trimester, the abortion decision and its effectuation must be left to the medical judgment of the pregnant woman's attending physician." In *Bolton* we read him agreeing with the district court that "the medical judgment may be exercised in the light of all factors—physical, emotional, psychological, familial, and the woman's age—relevant to the well-being of the patient. Here the Court added the notation that "this allows the attending physician the room he needs to make his best medical judgment. And it is room that operates for the benefit, not the disadvantage, of the pregnant woman." Then, as is well known, Justice Blackmun searched for the point or points at which "the woman's privacy is no longer sole" in another sense—i.e., where there comes to be a state interest in protecting her health or a potential human life, or both, and when these interests may be deemed compelling.

Clearly, the law of *Wade-Bolton* permitted subsequent decisions to say that a woman at no time in pregnancy is "isolated in her privacy"—*isolated* in the sense of without spouse or parents. *Planned Parenthood* did not take that possible route. We have already dissected that opinion's astonishing connection of spouse and parents with "state action" so the Court could find a constitutional issue.

In any case, according to the law of *Wade-Bolton,* a professional medical judgment during the first trimester was not rendered of no account by liberating abortion decisions. Physicians were not turned into mere instruments of women's wishes. An affirmative duty was not cast upon medical professionals to perform all abortions—or some, or for that matter *any*—requested of them if in a physician's judgment there were no medical reasons for abortion in the cases presented to him. Medical judgment was liberated for the first trimester; it was not constrained by the Court's decision; it was not made captive to a woman's decision. The constraints come from elsewhere.

Conscience clauses in the United States are entirely consistent, even supportive, of the law of *Wade* and *Bolton*. The codes to be considered in the next section are in general consistent with placing abortion in an area of liberties. The situation was similar in Great Britain in 1967.

Conscience Clauses in the United States

Since liberalized abortion was brought about in the United States by judicial decision, there is under our system no national abortion act, as in Great Britain, containing a conscience clause. But legislation in the United States and in at least thirty-three states contain conscience clauses. We need next to examine representative examples of these provisions. The ultimate question we should have in mind is whether these provisions are apt to protect the freedom of conscience of medical personnel, or whether the conscience of the profession is going to be thoroughly reshaped to accord with the "conscience of the laws" on abortion, mistakenly interpreted.

The federal Conscience Clause Act [18] ties its protection to "any grant, contract, loan or loan guarantee" under various federal funding sources: e.g., the Public Health Service Act, the Community Mental Health Centers Act, the Developmental Disabilities Services and Facilities Construction Act. It provides that the receipt of such grants, etc., does not authorize "any court or any public official or other public authority" to require "any individual or entity" to act in furtherance of a sterilization or abortion procedure. The individual may not be coerced into cooperation "if his performance or assistance in the performance of such procedure or abortion would be contrary to his religious beliefs or moral convictions." The "entity" may not be required to make its facilities available "if the performance of such procedure or abortion in such facilities is prohibited by the entity on

18. 42 U.S.C. 300 a-7.

the basis of religious beliefs or moral convictions." Here, at the federal level, we have both an individual and an "institutional" conscience clause, and this is not limited to religious objection. Nor may any entity that does not itself invoke the institutional conscience clause be penalized by courts or funding agencies for failure to provide personnel where to do so would be "contrary to the religious beliefs or moral convictions of such personnel."

At the same time, the federal Conscience Clause Act provides that entities in receipt of federal grants, etc., may not discriminate against individuals because of conscience. It does this *evenhandedly*. No entity may discriminate in the employment, promotion, or termination of employment of any physician or health care personnel, or discriminate in the extension of staff or other privileges to any physician or other health care personnel "because he performed or assisted in a lawful sterilization procedure or abortion" or "because he refused to perform or assist in the performance of such a procedure or abortion on the grounds that his performance or assistance in the performance of the procedure or abortion would be contrary to his religious beliefs or moral convictions, or because of his religious beliefs or moral convictions respecting sterilization procedures or abortions."

Turning to state legislation, the following are representative characteristics or provisions with which these laws attempt to protect conscience in the ineffably serious matter of abortion.

Evenhandedness. Some of the state statutes are explicitly as evenhanded as the United States Code; others are impliedly so. The Kentucky Revised Statute sec. 313.800, para. 11(c), defines it to be unlawful discriminatory practice for "any public or private agency, including a medical, nursing or other school to deny admission to, impose any burdens in terms of conditions of employment upon, or otherwise discriminate against any applicant for admission thereto or any physician, nurse, staff member, student or employee thereof, on account of the *willingness* or *refusal* of such applicant, physician, nurse, staff member, student or employee to perform or participate in abortion or sterilization by reason of objection thereto on moral, religious or professional grounds, or because of any statement or other manifestation of attitude by such person with respect to abortion or sterilization if that health care institution is not operated exclusively for the purpose of performing abortions or sterilizations" (italics added). The California Health and Safety Code sec. 25955 states that "no . . . employee or person with staff privileges in a hospital, facility or clinic shall be subject to any penalty or discipline by reason of his refusal to participate in an abortion." It then goes on to say: "No such employee of a hospital, facility or clinic which does not permit the performance of abortions, or person with staff privileges therein, shall be subject to any penalty or discipline on account of such person's participation in the performance of an abortion in other than such hospital, facility or clinic." Likewise, Michigan Compiled Laws sec. 331.555, § 5, provides that "a hospital, clinic, institution, teaching institution, or other medical facility which elects to refuse to allow abortions to be performed on its premises shall not deny staff privileges or employment to a person [or discriminate against its staff members or other employees] for the sole reason that that person previously participated in, or expressed a willingness to participate in a termination of pregnancy." Those sorts of provisions permit the exercise of both institutional conscience and individual conscience either way.

Public hospitals. Many of the statutes extend an "institution" conscience clause to public hospitals and public medical and nursing schools as well as to private ones; likewise, nonsectarian private hospitals, medical schools, and nursing schools come under the clause no less than those having denominational religious sponsorship. The Ohio Revised Code sec. 4731.91 in parallel paragraphs expressly provides first that "no private hospital, private hospital director or governing board of a private hospital is required to permit an abortion," and "no public hospital, public hospital director or governing board of a public hospital is required to permit an abortion." The legislation of other states implicitly does the same by the use of the indefinite article or other expressions encompassing all entities. Thus, Michigan Compiled Laws sec. 331.551, § 1: "*A* hospital, clinic, institution or other medical facility shall not be required . . ." (italics added). Tennessee Code sec. 39-304: "*No* hospital shall be required to permit abortions to be performed therein" (italics added). Florida Statutes sec. 458.22(5): "Nothing in this section shall require *any* hospital or *any* person to participate in the termination of a pregnancy . . ." (italics added). Only the California Health and Safety Code sec.

25955(c) limits the institutional conscience clause and the protection of the hospital administrators and board members to the sectarian religious hospitals in that state: "Nothing in this chapter shall require a nonprofit hospital or other facility or clinic which is organized or operated by a religious corporation or other religious organization, . . ." that paragraph reads.

Professional conscience. The grounds for objection to performing an abortion or for conscientious willingness to do so, on the part of individuals or institutions, are variously described as "professional, ethical, moral, or religious"; "moral, religious, or professional"; or with the word *professional* omitted, "moral, ethical, or religious"; "moral or religious"; or simply "contrary to the conscience or religious beliefs of any person." [19]

Before trying to show that we are entering—irreversibly, I believe—into a situation altogether different from that contemplated by these statutes, let me briefly comment both on the significance of some of the terms used in the legislation we have just reviewed, and on the protections intended (and needed).

First, in our law there is no distinction drawn between religious reasons and "ethical, moral" reasons for conscientious objection. In *United States* v. *Seeger,*[20] on the matter of conscientious objection to participation in war, Mr. Justice Clark for the Court held that the test determining whether a belief or conviction is "religious" was "whether a given belief that is sincere and meaningful occupies a place in the life of the possessor parallel to that filled by the orthodox belief in God of one who clearly qualifies for the exemption." He echoed the words of Judge Irving R. Kaufman in the lower court: [21] In today's "skeptical generation . . . the stern and moral voice of conscience occupies the hallowed place in the hearts and minds of men which was traditionally reserved for the commandments of God." Therefore, one can deduce that ethical and moral reasons are as much grounds for objection to participation in abortion procedures as are religious reasons. All are protected by the statutes we have reviewed.

19. These quotes are, in order of citation, from Mich. Comp. Laws sec. 331.552, § 2; Ky. Rev. Stat. sec. 311.800, § 11; Cal. Health and Safety Code sec. 25955(a) and (b); Fla. Stat. sec. 458.22(5), Mass. Gen. Laws chap. 122, sec. 121, and R.I. Laws sec. 23-16-10.1; and N.Y. Civ. Rights Law (Consol.) sec. 79-i(1).

20. 380 U.S. 163 (1965).

21. 326 F.2d 846 (2d Cir. 1964).

That means, second, that if we are to enact or maintain institutional conscience clauses they should not be limited to entities "organized or operated by a religious corporation or other religious organization" (Cal. Health and Safety Code sec. 25955[c]). The United States Code and the codes of other states ought not to go the way of California. Today, when the Chase Manhattan Bank is a "corporate citizen" and many of us, especially youth, are concerned that there be great "corporate responsibility" in the matter of investments in South Africa, for example, we ought to be just as concerned about the corporate responsibility of private nonprofit hospitals. A member of the board of directors and the administrator of a private entity have their consciences, too; and those persons ought to be protected from the enforcement of morals as much as any persons connected with, say, a Catholic, Jewish, or Lutheran hospital or service.

Whether a hospital chooses as an entity to provide "liberal" abortion service or not to do so, upon all alike is then cast the burden of insuring liberty of individual conscience contrary to one or the other institutional conscience. In the present climate, where the demand is strong upon *medical* institutions to provide an essentially *social* service, we may have to strike a compromise and require public hospitals to make provision for abortion practice. But whatever our personal opinions on the morality of abortion may be, we should not as a nation choose a course of action or legislation by which every private hospital becomes in effect a public one, or is construed as a "state agency," and sectarian hospitals or services become the "Amish" of future ob-gyn practice. No more should the consciences of ob-gyn personnel in all nonreligious private hospitals be reduced to ineffectuality or driven to "Lutheran" inwardness because of the absence of effective institutional conscience clauses; nor should the consciences of hospital policy makers, administrators, physicians, and nurses be forced to become everywhere the "animated tools" of patient desires.

Third, the ethical or moral reasons for refusal cannot be separated from the *professional* judgments of medical personnel, just as ethical objection cannot be distinguished from religious objection. In the matter of abortion, perhaps uniquely, physicians and nurses make *medical-moral* judgments, not *separate* medical and moral judgments that may or may not converge. That follows from the special responsibility that flows from possessing special knowledge, and from medical ethics which views the fetus and the mother both as patients—as the American College of Obstetricians and Gynecologists recently restated. While good medicine may not always be good morals, this is apt to be the case or be believed to be the case—either way—in the matter of abortion. We should, therefore, approve the wording of sec. 331.552, § 2, of the Michigan Compiled Laws, which states that any physician or any nurse, medical student, student nurse, or other employee of a medical facility where abortion is performed "who states an objection to abortion on *professional, ethical, moral, or religious grounds* may not be required to participate" (italics added). And this refusal shall not result in "any disciplinary or discriminatory action . . . against the person."[22]

Dr. Nathanson wrote, in the article cited above, that "there are seldom any purely medical indications for abortion." The implication is that there *are* rare cases in which abortion is medically indicated. A physician who believes *that* is making what I call a medical-moral judgment; he might say it is simply his *professional* reason for refusing to do most of the sorts of abortions performed today. Is not that professional conscience to be protected? Does it not fall within the area of liberties that was allowed when Justice Blackmun wrote that during the first trimester "the abortion decision and its effectuation must be left to the medical judgment of the pregnant woman's attending physician"? If not, then, physicians and nurses already established in ob-gyn practice may have to hide behind refusal on moral grounds, much as young men who held moral objection to participation in war were often forced to hide behind appeals to "religious" objections.

Moreover, the medical or nursing student while still in training is in a much more profound dilemma of conscience. Student doctors and nurses may be forced into learning situations or training procedures that they regard as in themselves violations of their professional and moral integrity, if to graduate they must participate in abortions for which they believe there are no medical indications or moral justification.

Fourth and finally, individual conscience clauses are going to prove worthless unless (a) institutional conscience clauses are effective and (b) there is "affirmative action" to insure that institutions in no way discriminate against conscientious objection to participation or co-

22. Kentucky Senate Bill 259 (1974), creating sec. 311.800 of the Kentucky Revised Statutes, uses similar language in secs. 11(1) and 11(2c).

operation in abortion. This is simply to say that a moral person needs social space. Individual conscience needs *Lebensraum* even though we Americans are self-confident individualists who do not think so.

I insert here three final examples to show the complexity of insuring, within a closely cooperating medical team, a genuine possibility of effective conscientious refusals.

> *A hospital intake worker.* She was required to interview incoming patients, many of whom were seeking abortions. She also had to handle the bottles that contained the fetuses, although this task was taken from her when she complained. She had to talk at various times with the girls who were getting abortions, while they were on her floor. She had to take orders from the doctors who were performing the abortions. Finally, she had to fill out the final forms for release and put down information about the abortion.
>
> She complained time and again about all this involvement. She asked the hospital to switch her. They could have, and they did have other positions in the hospital. Although they made various promises, they never switched her to a position where she would not have been involved with abortions.
>
> Finally she quit and applied for unemployment compensation. Meanwhile she was looking for another job but she was having a hard time because of the reason she left her first employment. The State Administration for Unemployment granted her the compensation, ruling initially that she had quit with justification. The hospital then appealed the case. Attorney X represented the woman and subpoenaed all sorts of people and records from the hospital. The hospital finally decided that it would be best not to fight and acquiesced to the decision of the unemployment bureau.
>
> *The head nurse on a gynecological ward for over 10 years.* Since the abortion decision of 1973, large numbers of saline abortions have been performed in her hospital. The saline was injected in the operating room and the patients were then transfered to her ward where the nurses delivered the dead fetuses in the room. She recounted many situations horrifying to her. Buckets of formalin were kept in rooms for aborting mothers because of the macerated condition of most of the aborted fetuses. After an in-

cident in which this nurse *believed* she saw a doctor drown a baby in formalin, she personally removed all the buckets and required that those physicians or nurses who needed them must ask for them. She also questioned the validity of the consent to this procedure as most of the girls who came to her ward thought the abortion was over with the injection of the saline. They did not know they had to go through labor and delivery. Those girls who were conscious at the time of delivery—and most of them were—were often shocked at the size of the fetus and many expressed regret. The entire staff with the exception of one part-time nurse was extremely upset about having to assist and deliver these saline abortions.

The hospital in a written directive stated that henceforth the saline would be injected in the treatment room on this gynecological ward and the head nurse was expected to staff this treatment room for these procedures. The head nurse discussed this with the other nurses and all, with the exception noted above, refused to have anything to do with injecting the saline. The head nurse returned in writing the staff's response and received in return a written note to the effect that those members of the staff, herself included, could look for jobs elsewhere. At this point, the nurse was given, by a counselor she went to, copies of the ——— state conscience clause and the federal conscience clause. The administration was informed that if they did indeed fire these nurses, they would be acting in violation of both state and federal law. To our knowledge the hospital withdrew the demand to perform saline abortions on this ward. However, they are still done in the operating room and sent to this ward for delivery.

Nurses who are inadvertently involved, particularly in late trimester abortions. This situation is usually not an intentional transgression by the hospital or physician, but often the nurse is the only one available. In both saline and prostaglandin abortions, the time lapse between injection and delivery can vary widely. What is the nurse to do, particularly on the evening and night shifts when she may very well be the only one there? Many nurses have expressed extreme distress and have said, "What could I do? I could not leave this woman when she was crying in pain, or her bed was wet with blood and amniotic fluid, or the baby was already in the bed." The supervisor might have tried to handle this situation for them if they had made known their objections, but many times the supervisor was busy elsewhere. Out of sympathy for the distressed woman the nurses would care for her despite their own feelings; however, many of them suffered from guilt later for having done even this much. This is obviously not a malicious violation of the nurses freedom of conscience but it is a fairly typical situation and one which frequently develops around the country.

The foregoing cases demonstrate, of course, that there are difficult administrative problems in implementing the conscience clauses. Still, moral persons need social space. Otherwise, outward behavior and job descriptions will drive professional, moral, and religious ideals or beliefs into irrelevant inwardness, and personal integrity will be destroyed. We have seen how this happened under the directives of the National Health Service in Great Britain. Unless we in the United States can find a truly pluralistic and personalistic (not individualistic) solution to the problems of professional conscience in the matter of abortion, there will be good moral reason for many people to oppose the present movement toward the adoption of a national health plan.

Individual conscience clauses in legal statutes are going to prove worthless, I said above, unless effective means are found to enforce them at the point of admission to medical or nursing school, at all points during the required training, as they relate to qualifications for graduation, and at the point of admission to internship or employment by hospitals. Without effective enforcement, indeed without means to ferret out discrimination, the conscience clauses are nugatory. But I suggest that liberty of conscience is at least as important as freedom from discrimination for reason of race or sex. Moreover, today, abortion is the issue of conscience; tomorrow the scene shifts to the special care nursery and the issue will be the liberty of professional, moral, and religious objection to the neglect of defective newborns.

I further suggest that conscience clauses are null and void unless the Department of Health, Education, and Welfare requires hospitals and medical and nursing schools to demonstrate affirmatively that their admissions, hiring, and promotion policies are nondiscriminatory, as is now required in the case of the hiring of women and members of minorities to university faculties or the guaranteeing of the availability of credit cards or bank loans to women regardless of marital status. Who reading these pages expects conscience clauses in medical matters to obtain such backing? Yet only so could we learn which is the good conscience that drives out the bad in the ob-gyn service, just as we already know in some cases which is the most money that lures away from the less within that service.

Meanwhile, a campaign has begun to cast upon hospitals, doctors, and nurses the specific duty to perform abortions. The Alan Guttmacher Institute (a division of Planned Parenthood Federation of America) recently issued a report entitled *Provisional Estimates of Abortion Need and Services in the Year Following the 1973 Supreme Court Decision.*[23] The upshot is, not unexpectedly, that services are lacking or insufficient. In the report, *need* means "felt need" or "manifested need," and to measure that for the country as a whole requires a base line. The base line used in the report to estimate "need" was the number of abortions performed among New York City residents in 1971 (used as the high estimate) and among California residents in 1973 (used as the low estimate).

Please note that the estimate of need based on New York City figures was drawn from that period of time when Dr. Bernard Nathanson was head of the largest abortion clinic in the world. He now has voiced professional, medical, and moral objection to that practice which the Alan Guttmacher Institute would now cast upon the medical and nursing profession as a specific duty. If this is allowed to happen and if conscience clauses fall or are not made effective, then there can be no hope for the wholly new attitude toward the "inexpressibly serious matter" of abortion for which Nathanson called. I can think of no better cause for Dr. Nathanson—with his former militancy—and all of us to embrace than actualizing and defending

23. Christopher Tietze, M.D., principle investigator, et al. The Alan Guttmacher Institute, 515 Madison Avenue, New York (1975). See also Jane E. Brody's report, *The New York Times,* October 7, 1975; and Terri Schultz's article, "Though Legal, Abortions Are NOT Always Available," *The New York Times,* January 2, 1977, sec. 4.

liberty of conscience among the medical personnel in ob-gyn and allied services.

The New Jersey Supreme Court's Institutional Conscience Clause Decision

When I first learned about the rather swift nullification of Great Britain's conscience clause by administrative interpretation, I supposed that was mainly a result of the pressure for conformity in a national health service. Because our federal system permits variation by states, because there is greater religious and moral pluralism in the United States, and because "social" medicine had not proceeded so far, I reasoned that the process would be slower in this country; that there would be time for more considered opinion to form from the contending forces of a morally divided nation, with perhaps a different outcome. I hoped against hope, and against my own moral reason, that while this nation could not endure half slave and half free, it could endure in conflicted conscience half abortionist and half antiabortionist in insitutional accommodations. In any case, the idea that the issue can be confined to the inner forum of conscience is a mirage of atomistic individualism and of the "liberal" mind.

I did not reckon with the capacity of an imperial judiciary using substantive due process in a fashion that would outrage liberals if the protection of property were still the issue to be decided by courts instead of by bodies elected to pass laws. I also did not reckon with the capacity of courts to find "state action"; and in the matter of abortion to find that since the *state* has no power to intervene in early abortions no one else has. It is not unlikely, I now see, that the Supreme Court may claim to be a national medical policy board. The United States may move more rapidly than Britain did. It is not too farfetched to imagine that a time will come when the only persons not construed to be state delegates will be medical doctors and nurses who are willing behaviorally to cooperate in abortion requests. Many of these will cabin their contrary professional judgment and conscience.

The Supreme Court will soon decide whether Congress may prohibit federal funds from being used to pay for abortions. Also, it is reported, the Court will soon decide whether *public* hospitals may decline to offer elective abortion services.[24] The Supreme Court may or may not soon reach into the matter of private, nonsectarian hospitals; it may or may not declare unconstitutional the legislation by Congress and the states which sought to protect by institutional conscience clauses the freedom of such hospitals and clinics to determine their own medical policy. There are cases in the courts, at state and appellate levels, that have gone against a state's institutional conscience clause as well as against the individual conscience clause. An extensive notion of "state action" may possibly nullify the conscience clauses under the United States judicial system more rapidly than the administrative regulations sent down by the National Health Service in Great Britain. For if an absolute right to abortion is assumed, state action must be found to reside in every contrary claimant—else, under our system, there is no constitutional question.

The Supreme Court's decision in *Planned Parenthood* v. *Danforth* is not encouraging. Still our examination of the Court's decision in that case should have sharpened the vision of any reader of the New Jersey Supreme Court's decision that *requires* all private nonsectarian hospitals or clinics to offer elective abortion services despite plain words of the legislature's institutional conscience clause. The crux of this decision is the same—I must say—totalitarian reasoning: where the state is powerless, no one else—no spouse, no parent, no "entity," no board of directors of a private hospital—has any liberty or indepent role to play. The Supreme Court of the United States may decide whether it will continue in this direction before these words can be read.

On November 17, 1976, Chief Justice Richard J. Hughes speaking for the court handed down its decision six to one in the case involving several plaintiffs against the Bridgeton Hospital Association, Newcomb Hospital, and Salem County Hospital for their failure to provide elective abortions.[25]

I go at once to the crux of the court's decision. It did in no way connect its decision with federal funds going to these private hospitals. As we have seen, the federal conscience clause is regularly attached to funding bills to break the connection, in the minds of some, that

24. Terri Schultz, "Though Legal, Abortions Are NOT Always Available," the *New York Times,* January 2, 1977, sec. 4.

25. *Doe* v. *Bridgeton Hospital Assn.,* 71 N.J. 478, 366 A. 2d 641 (1976).

a private medical center is transformed into a public or quasi-public institution because of the tax money it receives. If it is not the acceptance of public money that turns a private entity into an agent of the state, what then can be the reasoning? The astonishing answer to that question must be simply that the state legislature's enactment of a law stating that "No hospital shall be required . . ." transformed all private hospitals or clinics, whose freedom was supposed to be protected by that statute, into state agencies that cannot be so protected. Since the state—the argument runs—itself has no power to intervene between a woman and her physician's medical decision during the first trimester of pregnancy, no private institutions can be delegated such power. Such a delegation or transfer of power was attempted by the legislature in its institutional conscience clause; for the court to have decided in favor of the hospital plaintiffs would have been a similar act of state delegation.

That clearly means a pipeline of power, with rights flowing in one direction only, from the state to private entities. The powerlessness of the state renders private entities equally powerless. No freedoms inhering in lesser corporations or associations are there simply to be recognized and given effect by the legislature or by the court; those rights are wholly derivative from the power of the state—which has none in the matter of abortion. There exists no reservoir of state power on which the New Jersey state legislature or the court could draw in creating and conferring upon the governing boards of private health-care facilities a right of refusal for conscientious or professional medical reasons. Makers of hospital policy are, thus, creatures of the state—following the Supreme Court's *Wade-Bolton* regime which simply declared the state to be powerless. To use a religious analogy, if there is no treasury of the merits of the saints on which the official church draws to forgive sins, no one else can forgive sins; and the attempt of, say, Protestant churches to assure individuals or groups that they can forgive sins fails because the official church has no treasured-up competence from which to convey to them such power of forgiveness.

Thus the New Jersey Supreme Court made itself the state's community and private hospital board. This it did, oddly, by saying that such boards of directors are as powerless to set hospital policy as itself or the legislature. So an act of the legislature designed to preserve a freedom residing in private hospitals was construed itself to be "state action" assigning to them freedoms the state does not have. One powerless entity, the state, creates another powerless entity, private hospitals.

That was the "argument." Then the court addressed itself to the plain language of the New Jersey conscience clause: "No hospital shall be required. . . ." "We do not construe the statute," it pronounced, "to be applicable to *non-sectarian* non-profit hospitals" (italics added). In other words, in order to avoid declaring the institutional conscience clause to be facially unconstitutional, the court chose rather to say that the words of the statute meant something other than what they plainly said. That is, the court ruled that the legislature really had in mind what the court itself knew to be wisest and best—namely, that only sectarian religious hospitals are free to refuse to institute liberal abortion services. So in this case the statutory language "No hospital" meant "No sectarian hospital"; just as in the *Seeger* case, the Supreme Court declared that the Congress did not mean to require "duties to a Supreme Being superior to all others" when it said it meant exactly that. A strange reversal is taking place in the matter of conscientious objection: in the matter of abortion, the claim must be narrowly sectarian; in the matter of engaging in warfare "religion" encompasses any personally decisive conscientious objection.

We saw that *Planned Parenthood* did not object to a state legislature singling out a given medical procedure—even abortion—for special treatment. The New Jersey Supreme Court did not follow this latitude. Instead, it singled out abortion as the one form of health care to be forced on all private hospitals. It did not hesitate to do this even when presented with evidence that there were hospitals thirty miles away that afforded the women plaintiffs effective access to their "right" to an abortion. Logically, the decision would have been the same even if the alternative services had been available a block away. Forced private institutional abortion is the issue—not freedom. By ruling that community hospitals possess no more policy-making power than the legislature (even when the legislature tried to say otherwise), the New Jersey Supreme Court seized the role of local hospital boards of directors in determining medical policy. The reader should note that the impulse behind all this is that, in order for there to be a constitutional question in any action following *Wade-Bolton,* the courts must find improper "state agency."

That was the crux of the decision. However, another matter of law was invoked: the "innkeepers law." Inns hold themselves out to provide food and lodging for travelers. They have one purpose only, and like the telephone company they may be required to make their services available without discrimination. But both are unlike hospitals or clinics, which offer a variety of health services. Some hospitals provide sorts of services that others do not, though all relate to health care. A plurality and diversity in hospitals is needed to meet the manifest medical needs of the entire population. The services offered must, of course, be extended without arbitrary discrimination. But not every service need be deemed a medical one; and even so, not every medical service need be extended by every hospital and clinic. Even if there is a general right to health care, no one presumes that this requires every hospital everywhere to provide every form of service. In order to find support for its decision in the "innkeepers law," the New Jersey Supreme Court singled out one particular form of health care and declared that to be constitutive of every "inn." If such a construction of the medical profession is allowed to stand, then an *essential* ingredient of every physician's and nurse's job description must also be the provision of abortion services. As with the inn, so with innkeepers. Logically and practically, individual conscience clauses protecting medical professionals stand or fall with the institutional conscience clause. The job description of a medical entity, its performance required by law, cannot be different from the description of its personnel's professional duties—at least, not for long.

However, the decision of the United States Court of Appeals in *Wolfe* v. *Schroering*[26] was an encouraging one. This court's opinion is a good one to place alongside New Jersey's. It also expresses the sort of social and legal compromise that needs to be made in regard to public and private hospitals if we are going to continue to value not only the freedom of religious or sectarian institutions but the freedom of nonsectarian "lesser corporations," associations, and institutions in our society. The appeals court focused on the fact that the hospital in question was a *public* hospital, and it ruled constitutional the pro-

26. *Wolfe* v. *Schroering* 388 F. Supp. 613 (1974), modified, 541 F. 2d 523 (6th Cir. 1976). See n. 7, above, and also chap. 1, n. 20, with its textual reference.

vision "No hospital shall . . ." by construing it to apply to *private* hospitals, notably not "sectarian" hospitals alone. The opinion states: "We are of the view that the conscience clause may constitutionally permit 'private' hospitals and health care facilities and physicians and nurses and employees to refuse to perform or participate in performing abortions for 'ethical, moral, and religious or professional reasons.' " Its reasoning about public hospitals as well was nuanced in a way that physicians and administrators should endorse: "We express no opinion as to under what circumstances a public hospital may refuse to perform abortions for non-ethical reasons, such as lack of personnel or facilities or of specialization in non-obstetrical and non-surgical fields. . . . In other words, we do not require all public hospitals to perform abortions; we simply hold that the state cannot constitutionally authorize public hospitals to refuse to perform abortions for 'ethical' reasons." Public hospitals, thus, are "state actors"; but that casts upon them no duty to provide one or another medical service. The court went on to say that "a more narrowly drafted 'conscience' clause, however, would presumably be constitutional if limited to permitting public hospitals to refuse to allow post-viability abortions for the 'ethical' . . . interest in the potentiality of human life . . . except where it is necessary, in appropriate medical judgment, for the preservation of the life and health of the mother." The court concluded, "we thus sustain the invalidation of the conscience clause as applied to public hospitals, and construe the district court opinion as not invalidating the conscience clause as applied to private hospitals. . . ."

On June 27, 1977, the Supreme Court refused to review, and thus left in effect, the decision of the New Jersey Supreme Court in *Bridgeton*, the conscience clause case.[27] Thus the Court reached the end of its October 1976 term without directly confronting the constitutional issues being raised concerning the institutional and individual conscience clauses. Moreover, at the time of this writing, there is no record of an appeal from the decision of the court of appeals in *Schroering*.

However, the Court's opinion in *Poelker* v. *Doe*,[28] handed down

27. The *New York Times*, June 28, 1977.

28. *Poelker* v. *Doe*, no. 75-442, 45 LW (June 21, 1977), pp. 4794–97. Related cases handed down the same day were *Beal* v. *Doe*, no. 75-554, 45 LW, pp. 4781–87 and *Maher* v. *Roe*, no. 75-1440, 45 LW, pp. 4787–94. The Court ruled in these cases

on June 20, 1977, took a surprising turn that has important bearing on the policies of *public* hospitals in the matter of abortion. This needs to be noted here and compared with the appeals court decision in *Schroering* before concluding our account of legal developments so far.

In a class action Jane Doe challenged both a "policy directive" of the mayor and the director of Health and Hospitals of Saint Louis, and the longstanding staffing practice at Starkloff, one of the municipal hospitals in that city. The policy and the practice prohibited the performance of abortions in the city hospitals except when there was a threat of grave physiological injury or death to the mother. Justice Powell delivered the opinion of the Court, which was a brief one in this case. The mayor's *personal* opinions and the fact that the physicians and medical students at Starkloff's ob-gyn clinic are drawn from the faculty and students at the Saint Louis University School of Medicine, a Jesuit-operated institution opposed to abortion, were not matters for review. The policy directive governing city hospitals, along with city hospital practice derivative from that, was the target challenged. The Court found "no constitutional violation by the city of St. Louis in electing, as a policy choice, to provide publicly financed hospital services for childbirth without providing corresponding services for nontherapeutic abortions." It pointed out that the mayor is a public official, responsible to the people of Saint Louis, whose policies are subject to public debate and approval at the polls. Citing the Court's opinion in *Maher*—which found no constitutional fault if a state, pursuant of democratic processes, expresses by its use of medicaid funds, a public-policy preference for normal childbirth—*Poelker* simply extended that ruling to municipalities as well.

Thus, the Court did not adopt the *Schroering* ruling that a public hospital is a state agency that cannot (except for "nonethical" reasons) constitutionally fail to provide elective abortions. It did not restrict this policy choice to *private* hospitals and clinics. Nor did the Court suggest, as did *Schroering,* that since hospitals are not required to provide every medical service, a public hospital might refuse to perform abortions for "nonethical reasons." Also unlike *Schroering,*

---

that states may or may not use medicaid funds to pay for elective abortions. The shock waves that followed these decisions were due at least in part to the fact that the media had for four years joined advocates such as Planned Parenthood and the American Civil Liberties Union in systematically misinterpreting *Wade* and *Bolton.*

the Court did not advise a more narrowly drawn policy for public hospitals, prohibiting only *postviability* abortions "for the 'ethical' . . . interest in the potentiality of life . . . except for the preservation of the life and health of the mother." I conclude from this brief systematic comparison that the Court's opinion in *Poelker* must be based either (a) on a sharp distinction between an "ethical" and a "public-policy" reason or (b) on there being a public-policy interest or preference *before* viability that a state or municipality may choose or not choose to express pursuant to democratic processes.

The latter is the Court's opinion, whatever it philosophically may think about (a) above. To substantiate this, we have to go to *Maher* (as the Court did), and the reader may also want to read *Beal,* handed down on the same day. The challenge in *Maher* v. *Roe* was brought by Susan Roe when she failed to secure a physician's certification that abortion was "medically necessary" in her case, which was required by Connecticut in order for the procedure to be paid for by medicaid funds. Justice Powell's decision for the Court (six to three) need not have surprised anyone who ever read *Wade* and *Bolton* with care. In addition to the interpretation of the 1973 decisions given above, one need only reflect that to locate *compelling* state interest at viability, in possibly prohibiting abortion, in no way entails that a state does not have some less significant interests before that point in pregnancy, if in the pursuit of these interests the state does not *prohibit* abortion. Abortion was placed in an area of liberties; and all subsequent efforts to veto that have been struck down. In *Maher* the Court reached quite different questions—namely, whether the state must remain neutral between abortion and childbirth, and whether the use of public funds is a reasonable way to encourage whichever of these two outcomes it favors as a matter of public policy.

The district court [29] had held that "abortion and childbirth . . . are simply two alternative medical methods of dealing with pregnancy," that the state can have no *fiscal* interest since "abortion is the least expensive medical response to pregnancy," that it cannot justify its refusal to pay for one of these procedures because "it *morally* opposes such expenditure of money," that it cannot *discourage* women from choosing an abortion, that to do so by medicaid regulations discriminates against a class of the indigent.

We cannot take up here all the points made by Justice Powell for

29. 408 F. Supp. 660.

the Court. Some, however, must be mentioned because of their bearing on the issues dealt with in this volume. Chief of these is Powell's assertion that "the District Court [mis]read our decisions in *Roe* v. *Wade* . . . as establishing a fundamental *right* to abortion and therefore concluded that nothing less than a *compelling* state interest would justify Connecticut's different treatment of abortion and childbirth" (italics added). Arguing that *Maher* constitutes "no retreat from *Roe* or the cases applying it," Powell writes that "there is a basic difference between direct state interference with a protected activity and state encouragement of an alternative activity with legislative policy." Connecticut could not "penalize" a woman who had an abortion by refusing her medicaid payments; it cannot prohibit abortion before viability; it cannot grant spouses or parents or anyone the power to interpose an "absolute obstacle" to the woman's decision. But all this "implies no limitation on the authority of a State to make a *value judgment* favoring childbirth over abortion, and to implement that judgment by the allocation of public funds" (italics added). To protect freedom to travel does not mean the government must pay for it. To prohibit states from forbidding the maintenance of private schools [30] does not mean that such schools must, as a matter of equal protection, receive state aid. In any case, *Roe* v. *Wade* was distinguished from previous "privacy" cases because the woman is never alone during pregnancy: She "carries an embryo," the Court said, "and, later, a fetus, if one accepts the medical definitions of the developing young in the human uterus." There may then be a state interest, even a significant state interest in potential life throughout pregnancy growing in substantiality as the woman approaches term; that interest becomes "compelling" at viability.[31] Finally, "when an issue involves policy choices as sensitive as those implicated by public funding of nontherapeutic abortions, the appropriate forum for their resolution in a democracy is the legislative." The states are free to pay for one or both ways of dealing with pregnancy.

There is not space here, nor would it be pertinent, for me to go

30. *Pierce* v. *Society of Sisters,* 268 U.S. 510 (1925).

31. For the first time in the line of decisions dealing with abortion, certainly with great frequency for the first time, the opinions in these three related cases all use trimester language—i.e., "end of second trimester" or "third trimester"—approximately to locate viability. The Court seems to be learning less and less about medicine.

into the many important legal and moral issues raised by the present decisions, or to study fully the Court's reasoning or the arguments of concurring and dissenting opinions.[32] I have said just enough to indicate what the law of the land now is with regard to the range and limits of public policy in the matter of abortion. This is important for anyone who may wish to forecast whether the conscience clauses will pass constitutional scrutiny, or even whether the Court now need reach the issue. The law of *Beal, Maher,* and *Poelker* is important also for anyone who asks whether the fabric of our law has not been altered in unnecessary ways under the weight of the misconstrual of *Wade-Bolton* by the courts themselves or at least by interpretations of those cases—interpretations that now have been laid to rest by the Court itself. Looking back, this question can be asked of *Planned Parenthood.* It comes up again in connection with the manslaughter law applied in the *Edelin* case, to be considered in the next chapter, and in connection with legislative efforts to set a standard of medical care for the fetus—even before viability, if legislation proposes to do that.

Postscript for "the Religious"

The title of the final section of this chapter is intended to convey a certain irony. At least, the expression "the religious" is used with double entendre. First, there is the ordinary meaning of being a religious person with consciously held beliefs and corresponding moral outlook. Such persons are often highly aware of serious issues of conscience that may arise in connection with their participation in activities or pursuits that are necessarily collective and in which the joint actors do not share the same relevant judgments concerning right and wrong. There is a long tradition of discussion, among religious ethicists, of the problem of "cooperation" in wrong doing—when this may be excusable or when it is not. I shall analyze some of the contemporary Roman Catholic discussion of cooperation in a pluralistic society.

32. In *Poelker*—the city hospital casė—the crux of the disagreement between Powell's opinion for the Court and Brennan's dissent seems to me to be whether the state has any less than "compelling" interest in potential life, and whether it has such less-than-compelling interest *before* viability. Brennan writes, for example, that "expressing a preference for normal childbirth" does not satisfy the standard of "compelling" interest. The Court never said it did.

Other readers of this volume may wish to skip to the next chapter. I urge them not to do so, since there is a second sense in my use of the word *religious*. Most readers may belong to this group. I term them the *Seeger* "religious" people. To paraphrase words from the Court's decision in that case, questions of conscience are pertinent, even in a pluralistic society and in a skeptical generation, to those for whom "the stern and moral voice of conscience occupies the place in the hearts and minds of men which was traditionally reserved for the commandments of God." There may be a commonality between the explicitly religious and the *Seeger* religious. For it may be that the latter hold a moral belief in the matter of abortion "that is sincere and meaningful [and] occupies a place in the life of the possessor parallel to that filled by the orthodox [Jewish or Christian] belief . . . of one who clearly qualifies for the exemption" from participating in an abortion procedure or in a hospital's adoption of an elective abortion policy. The *Seeger* religious should perhaps speak of the problem now to be examined as that of "collaboration." The flavor of that word will help anyone to step into the issues at stake in "cooperation."

One may admire the "personalistic" expression of contemporary individualism that governs in "Catholic Hospital Ethics: The Report of the Commission on Ethical and Religious Directives for Catholic Hospitals of the Catholic Theological Society of America." [33] The commission acknowledged the "conscience demands" of the "corporate moral person," the Catholic hospital. Reacting overmuch to a

33. *Linacre Quarterly* 39, no. 4 (November 1972) : 246–68. I should make clear that *Catholic Hospital Ethics* is on the whole a conservative document. It calls for making "discreet adaptation to the contemporary situation (which is the question of 'cooperation')." The specific targets mentioned are sterilization, donor insemination, "insemination that is totally artificial," masturbation as a means of obtaining seminal analysis. The report calls for directives not codes, principles not prescriptions, for less stress on direct / indirect action as a physical structure, for "a Christian theology of moral law"; and for greater recognition that some past teachings are in doubt and that health services commonly accepted in the medical world are, "at least in some cases, not morally harmful according to the judgment of many prudent men." While the report appeals to religious liberty as basis for saying that pluralism can be "acknowledged in principle as a *normative* context" (italics added), it nevertheless says that "today's situation of pluralism . . . urges us to support certain standards more strongly than others lest our fundamental moral values . . . be lost." Hence "the establishment of an institutional code . . . is fully warranted in reference to abortion. . . . The fact that society is abandoning other means of protecting life itself in its earliest stages of development makes even more urgent a general but clear and firm policy of exclusion of abortion on the part of Catholic health institutions."

Catholic hospital remaining an "ecclesiastical moral person" only, with vertical responsibilities solely within the body of the church, the commission recognized that the Catholic hospital is "no longer a religious island," "this health facility is becoming a quasi-public, pluralistic institution with multiple social and moral accountability." On these grounds, it called for a model of "horizontal accountability" in understanding "the Catholic hospital-as-moral-person." So far so good, at the level of generality—though even at that level I had supposed the church knew more about the meaning of horizontal accountability than about pluralistic liberty within its walls.

At the level of practical application,

> the critical question is whether the exercise of religious liberty should be limited also by the fact of administering or seeking treatment in a Catholic hospital. From the hospital's perspective the issue is whether it can allow a course of action dictated by the conscience of the patient, or of both the patient and the physician, both contrary to the professed institutional code (or institutional "conscience") of the hospital. If the hospital invariably insists on the execution of its moral norms, it will presumably be acting according to its own moral standards, but it may also be disproportionately infringing on the rights of other people in our society.

Then the commission gives a "for instance": "It may be necessary to permit a procedure in a Catholic hospital which is the community's only health facility, while the same action would not have to be admitted in a Catholic hospital located in a large metropolitan area where other facilities are available."

The theologians did not mean that to be policy in regard to abortion. Still that seems a strange understanding of "the health care apostolate" or of how to "minister, in the name of Christ, to the needs of today's mankind." The theologians would in principle turn Catholic hospitals into public entities and abolish the institutional conscience clause even before the states or our courts do.[34] At the same time, they

34. *Taylor* v. *St. Vincent's Hospital*, 369 F. Supp. 948 (D. Mont. 1973), aff'd 523 F. 2d 75 (9th Cir. 1975), cert. denied, 424 U.S. 948 (1976). The details of this case are significant. James and Glorida Taylor of Billings, Montana, were expecting their second child, to be delivered by caesarian section. Mrs. Taylor requested tubal ligation at the time of delivery. St. Vincent's Hospital—the one hospital in Billings

would manufacture problems of *Lebensraum* for individual Christian professional conscience on the part of interns and nurses practicing even within Catholic hospitals.

On both points, the United States Code and some of the state laws protecting institutional conscience (while requiring nondiscrimination *either way* against individuals for their actions or advocacy elsewhere) are a better way to adjudicate conflicts of conscience in a pluralistic society. The United States Code, as we have seen, is verbally evenhanded, prohibiting discrimination regardless of institutional policy against persons who either performed or assisted in the performance of an abortion or who *refused* to perform or assist in such procedure. Michigan Compiled Laws sec. 331.555, § 5, also, for example, prohibits any entity that refuses to allow abortions to be performed on its premises from denying staff privileges or employment to any person "solely for the reason that that person previously participated in, or expressed a willingness to participate in a termination of pregnancy." Surely a physician should be willing to abide by the institutional conscience expressed in the bylaws of a hospital where he has staff privileges. That institutional conscience need not be atomized in order to prove nondiscriminatory.

At the same time and by way of contrast we need to note the California Health and Safety Code sec. 2595(a), which, while giving stautory protection to individual conscience, goes on to state that "no provision of this chapter prohibits any hospital, facility, or clinic which permits the performance of abortion from inquiring whether an employee or prospective employee would advance a moral, ethical or religious basis for refusal to participate in an abortion before hiring or assigning such a person. . . ." Herein, along with California's

with maternity services—refused because of its long-standing moral policy prohibiting contraceptive sterilization. The Montana court granted an injunction against the hospital and the operation was performed. The legal issue, however, proceeded through channels. The Church Amendment—the federal institutional and individual conscience clause—was enacted by Congress. Whereupon the Montana court revised its opinion, holding that as a result of the Church Amendment the concept of state action was inapplicable and the hospital was free to prohibit the disputed procedure. No mention was made of the fact that St. Vincent's is run by a Roman Catholic order, or of the fact that it offered medical services to an entire area, or of public funds (if any) or tax exemptions. The United States Court of Appeals for the Ninth Circuit affirmed that decision, and the Supreme Court denied certification. (*The New York Times*, March 2, 1976.)

limitation of the institutional conscience clause to sectarian entities, we see the wave of the future that threatens to overwhelm the ob-gyn profession and render it of one mind. Meantime, the theologians seem to want the institutional conscience of Catholic entities to become more and more like a banner unfurled, while the practice of physicians and patients on their premises conflicts. There must be something wrong with a proposed hospital ethics which in California would in principle mean that a Catholic or other religious hospital should as an entity cooperate with the *person* of a physician performing forbidden actions (how can abortion long be excluded?) on its premises, and which allows nurses also to cooperate (thus placing some individual consciences under unavoidable systemic pressure), while any other entity permitting the performance of sterilization or abortion may discriminate at the point of employment against those persons who have professional, religious, or moral objection to participation in that entity's announced practice.

Realistically, it is quite impossible to understand the ease with which the Commission of Catholic Theologians defended a view of moral agency which without significant alteration also could entail giving up the *Lebensraum* that remains for professional medical conscience against our current abortion practice. It will be small consolation for Chrisitian interns and nurses to be reminded that they are cooperating not with *acts* of sterilization or abortion but with *persons* who do them. If room for institutional conscience is not preserved, these will be equivocal excuses—like saying go ahead if you have an aged grandmother or five children to support and need the job, or if you do not "formally" consent to the rightfulness of your part of the procedure.

I have studied and studied Charles Curran's chapter "Cooperation in a Pluralistic Society" [35] and still cannot comprehend the reasoning in it. The distinction between the *person* and his *acts,* and between cooperating with him as a person and cooperating with wrongful actions, in the theologians' critique of past Catholic hospital practice reduces the issues involved to cooperation between two Cartesian "mental substances"—their actions belonging to the realm of matter,

35. Charles Curran, *Ongoing Revision: Studies in Moral Theology* (Notre Dame, Indiana: Fides Publishers, Inc., 1975), pp. 210–28.

"extended" and societal substance.[36] Curran appears to go further. His image seems to be that of two zombies thinking about cooperating with one another. He distinguishes not only between the person and his acts, but also—within the person—between support of his evil will and cooperation with him in his subjective belief that his will and acts are not evil. So here we have three foci: the person as a repository of invincible ignorance, the person as formally willing an action, and the action put forth. By these segmentations, the moral question of cooperation or conscientious noncooperation in evildoing or even with evildoers is to all effects abolished, because it is driven even deeper into subjectivity where an arbitrary liberty of the person, who actually is doing no evil, could be upheld by another, even cherished by him. An affirmative obligation to cooperate in wrong actions and with erroneous wills is thus derived from the meaning of cooperation with other *persons*.

Curran achieved this result by wrapping a very old wineskin around some heady new wine. In a morally pluralistic society, Curran writes, "even in accord with the older [Catholic] understanding it is impossible to speak about the bad will of the primary agent"; "there can be no formal cooperation when the individual does not have a bad will"; sincere "invincible ignorance" is widespread today.[37] In a morally pluralistic society there can be no formal cooperation with—or culpable, immediate material influence on—the bad will of primary agents where, on widely controverted issues, there rarely are subjectively bad wills. Such wills are most rare. So also bad moral actions are most rare (since little, if anything, is intrinsically evil). This does not solve the moral problem of cooperation in evildoing; it dissolves that problem. It does not solve the problem of cooperation with evildoers (with *persons* who mean evil); it dissolves that problem, too. Indeed, one need not have waited to situate the issue in a morally pluralistic society. Most people in all ages act *sub specie boni*. In any case, the issue to which past discussions of cooperation

36. On this anthropology, we may ask, what has happened to the teaching about the virtues of the moral agent and, correlated with that, his acts? In cooperating with the person, how can one avoid willing and influencing and signaling support of his vices as a person no less than of a vice's aptitude for exercise in corresponding actions?

37. Op. cit., p. 220.

and conscientious refusal to cooperate were addressed had to do with what *the cooperator* understood *himself* to be doing and was actually doing or influencing in the moral order—not first of all what the primary agent thought *he* was doing. That issue still remains with us, despite all attempts to dissolve it.

Curran also supports his view of rather indifferent cooperation with well-meaning people in a pluralistic society by analogy with the Catholic church's recent teaching on religious liberty. Linking the issue of cooperation with those teachings on religious liberty has the effect of elevating the claims of cooperation ascribed to a primary moral agent to the status of a right, and it tends also to aggravate the predicament of institutional and individual cooperators because of an implied duty to do so. Doubtless it is correct to advise someone to follow even an erring conscience, or to speak in some sense of the "right" of a person having an erring conscience to do so. That may well be *his* duty. But when the issue of cooperation is brought up, subjective conscience becomes largely a matter of excusability and the right of a primary agent to follow his conscience *elsewhere*. That should entail no sense of obligation (as ordinarily is the case with "rights") to promote his doing so. And, I repeat, the institutional or individual cooperators should first of all be concerned with what *they* are doing in the moral order or believe they should be doing. They have their consciences, too—else there is no issue, there is no *conflict* of consciences. That issue has been dissolved, not solved.

Curran calls his reader's attention, it is true, to the *dissimilarities* between religious liberty and the matter of cooperation with someone believed to be doing moral wrong. In the case of respecting, even upholding in the social order, the religious liberty of another, *there is no concurrence in the act of another person*. Also, religious liberty concerns the relationship of *government* to the individual and to diverse religious groups, *not* the relationship of one individual to another. Finally, religious liberty is not exactly the same as all other kinds of liberty.[38] This third dissimilarity is vague, but the first two

38. Ibid., p. 218–19. It is quite impossible to argue that unnecessary abortions do not seriously injure the common good, since that practice says that some lives do not count or count less in the commonality. Here pointing to a generally valid distinction between *sin* and *crime* or between morality and public policy or law is not pertinent. Religious ethicists taking that tack should read Baruch Brody's chapter "Abortion and the Law," in his *Abortion and the Sanctity of Life* (Cambridge, Mass.: MIT

are precise—and sufficient to show that cooperation remains a serious moral question both for institutions and for individuals. Neither the old wineskin of "invincible error" nor the new wineskin or religious liberty can entirely encompass the serious moral question cooperators must raise, and neither can change the taste of vinegar.

Curran, however, gives no effect to the dissimilarities to which he drew attention. He uses the analogy of religious liberty, he asserts, because "in both cases the dignity of the human person to act with responsible freedom must be taken into account." [39] That, too, is vague, until its skeleton is filled in by an *anthropology* that segments subjectivity, will, and act in *moral agency*. Perhaps enough has been said about the nature of moral agency. Even if Curran's was a correct analysis of the human action of a wrongdoer—or one to be used in certain contexts for other purposes—it in no way helps with the problem that a cooperator in believed-evil has on his hands. Not unless he thinks that he, too, is a zombie or a Cartesian "mental substance." In that case, all along he had no problem.[40]

Press, 1975), pp. 42–63. In regard to *life* as with *slavery,* we cannot say, as Justice Roger B. Taney is reported to have said about his decision in *Dred Scott,* "Anyone who has moral objection to slavery doesn't have to own one" (Kenneth D. Vanderhoet, "Euthanasia: Fetal-NeoNatal-Infanticide," *Bioethics Northwest* no. 1 [Winter 1976] : 4). In matters so basic as slavery and the taking of life, one who believes either to be wrong cannot fail to advocate public and legal policy prohibiting such actions. As the grounds for conscientious refusal to cooperate are similarly strong, we likewise need to insure systematic protection of the right so to refuse.

39. Op. cit., p. 219.

40. Richard A. McCormick, S.J., holds a sounder view of cooperation in this instance. "If one objects to most abortions being performed in our society as immoral," he asks, "is it morally proper to derive experimental profit from the products of such an abortion system? Is the progress achieved through such experimentation not likely to blunt the sensitivities of Americans to the immorality (injustice) of the procedure that made such advance possible, and thereby entrench attitudes injurious and unjust to nascent life?" McCormick answers: "This is, in my judgment, a serious moral objection to experimentation on the products of most induced abortions (whether the fetus be living or dead, prior to abortion or postabortionally)." Indeed, the moral problem of cooperating in or even benefiting from fetal research, the subjects of which are obtained from our present "abortion system," is made more difficult, not easier to resolve, because ours is a morally pluralistic society. These issues, McCormick writes, are "especially relevant in a society where abortion is widely done and legally protected" ("Experimentation on the Fetus: Policy Proposals," in *Research on the Fetus,* Appendix to Recommendations and Report, National Commission for the Protection of Human Subjects of Biomedical and Behavioral Research, DHEW publication no. (OS) 76-128, part 1, no. 5, p. 5). McCormick's

In regard to recent efforts to revise radically the treatise on cooperation and its problems, I must judge the proposals to be *replacing* ones, supported by inadequate theoretical reasons. On matters of practical application, however, a fair comment must not fail to notice that the theologians' target is mainly contraceptive sterilization or other "offenses" less serious than abortion. Curran, for example, concludes that a Catholic or some other doctor who believes contraceptive sterilization is wrong (or wrong for *this* patient?) "can do such an operation without cooperating with the bad will of the patient because the patient has no bad will in this case. . . . Without unduly sacrificing personal conscience the doctor *could* argue that in this case one is providing a service for which this individual person has a right even though the physician disagrees with the operation from a moral perspective" (italics added). Of course, the doctor *could* argue the other way also, since he is not a mere "conduit or robot who has no freedom in this matter."[41] Since no doubt he is an "immediate cooperator," he *could* refuse. Still, on the other hand, he *could* appeal to the fact of a morally pluralistic society, and *could* perform the sterilization in good conscience for someone who believes it is medically and morally indicated.

Here we are not mainly interested in the question of contraceptive sterilization, and, besides, that is not a frontier of mine as it is for Curran. Could a doctor perform an abortion in similar circumstances? Curran's answer is no. There is a great difference between the two operations: abortion involves (or is conscientiously believed to involve) "harm done to a third, innocent party." It harms the public order, injures the common good by taking life that should count in that common good. "I do not see how," Curran concludes, "the physician could ever perform such an operation except in the most extreme cases," that is, when the physician *himself* judges an abortion to be morally justified and necessary.[42]

Curran's practical applications are the same for hospitals. One

---

reasons for moving from morality to public policy, however, are less adequate than those Curran stated above but did not make determinative even in the matter of cooperation. McCormick writes that "what actions ought to be controlled by policy is determined not merely by the immorality of the action, but beyond this by a *single* criterion: feasibility" (ibid., pp. 1–2, italics added).

41. Curran, op. cit., p. 222.

42. Ibid., pp. 222–23.

could make the case for a Catholic hospital's "right to live by its moral code even in the midst of our pluralistic society"; but he prefers "a more nuanced approach" in the case of sterilization. "The cooperation of the hospital is less proximate than that of the doctor doing the sterilization." If *he* could, *it* surely could allow that operation. Besides, since Catholics have a right to dissent with the church's official teachings on this issue, how can the faithful be denied the right to practice their dissent in a Catholic hospital?[43] Curran does not address the serious logistic problem in any medical service of giving effect to the conscience of nurses or other staff who *dissent from that dissent,* and who *could* decide that they must refuse to cooperate (having a better view, as well they may, of the integrity of the human acts of moral agents, their own and others).[44]

43. Ibid., pp. 224–25.

44. See Vitale H. Paganelli, M.D., "An Update on Sterilization," in *Linacre Quarterly* 44, no. 1 (February 1977) : 12–17. In the same issue (pp. 18–36) Charles Curran published an article entitled "The Catholic Hospital and the Ethical and Religious Directives for Catholic Hospital Facilities." Both articles take into account the fact that, because of the hospital directives and their theological critics, a special review committee of the National Conference of Catholic Bishops sent the issue of contraceptive sterilization to Rome for guidance. On December 4, 1975, Bishop James S. Rausch, current general secretary of the NCCB, distributed that response (dated March 13, 1975) to all the American bishops—Archbishop Joseph Bernardin, president of the NCCB, having on April 14, 1975, already reaffirmed the directives' teaching to be applicable to all Catholic hospitals.

In this most recent article Curran again advances the arguments we have examined above. Some subtle yet significant differences in emphasis, however, should be noticed. (1) There is a fuller showing—quoting responses of various national bishops' conferences to *Humanae Vitae*—that whoever has dissented from the church's teaching on ordinary contraception logically must also dissent from the prohibition of vasectomy and tubal ligation. This, I judge, is a debater's point, designed to set bishops against bishops in their pastoral role and to show that "if one, after prayerful and thoughtful consideration, has already dissented from such teaching, such dissent can continue to be a legitimate option for the loyal Roman Catholic." (2) Expanded reference is made to the grounds for believing that whoever is "invincibly ignorant" (this includes, "the whole sphere of psychological incomprehension, unconscious resistance, invincible prejudices, wishful thinking and affective transferences of every kind") is himself not an evildoer; and, likewise, cooperation with such a person is no problem. Even without these latter-day depth-understandings—and without appeals to a morally pluralistic society—it always made sense to say that (since the human will is oriented toward the good) few if any people in any age or culture do what they believe at the time of action to be wrong or evil. In any case, as I have said, this is *not* the problem of the cooperator who must decide whether he is going to be an accomplice in what *he* believes to be wrongdoing. (3) A new "fall-back" position is advanced—namely, that "in terms of specific content, conclusions and

It has been necessary to stay with sterilization as an illustration for the background to now ask: How can the theoretical inadequacy of Curran's analysis of the morality of cooperation in wrongdoing be kept from having the same practical consequences in the matter of abortion? Generally Curran keeps the issues separate, although there are signs that he may not long be able to do so. He uses that word *could* again in the most forceful statement of his present opinion: "One could argue very strongly in this case that the Catholic hospitals should never cooperate with direct abortion because to do so would bring harm to the innocent human being whom Catholic ethical teaching believes to be present." However, he points to the fact that "even

---

proximate content dispositions," there is no such thing as a distinctively Christian ethics. Even if that were a defensible position (having no other consequence than that the Christian ethicist would have nothing more to do except go into preaching salvation or doing pastoral work in behalf of a truly human morality), it would not be pertinent to the problem we are presently discussing. The "distinctively Christian" has no pertinence at all, unless Curran means to join sectarian Christians (which he does not) who affirm that every specific moral teaching is to be drawn straight out of the Bible or from the tradition of revelation. "Cooperation" concerns generally human morality, "the whole moral law" drawn from moral reason by the Christian no less than by others. I trust Curran does not mean to say, for example, that moral conviction against abortion becomes a matter of distinctive Christian tenets because Christians also hold such views. If so, he anticipates and encourages parochializing this general moral question. Certainly Curran would not say that cooperation in negligent or direct manslaughter in the neonatal nursery can be considered to be an open question because there is no "specifically Christian ethic" on the matter. (4) I find in Curran's present article a greater emphasis on "the limits of dissent"—and good reason for the limitation. "If one emphasizes only the possibility of dissent on specific moral questions," he writes, "then it becomes impossible for the Church or its teachings to take on any incarnational existence, in a given historical time and place." While the historical self-identification and praxis of the church never furnished an absolute criterion of truth, "nonetheless it is the only acceptable norm of the historical community as such." That, I thought, was the kind of *authority* always ascribed to encyclical teachings. Those statements of Curran's go far in the direction of withdrawing criticism of the hospital directives for addressing to institutional policy the teachings which the church proposes to the conscience of individual members. They also undercut any absolute line between pastoral concerns and institutional witness. (5) Finally, Curran seems to backtrack while still emphasizing the *possibility* of dissent. "Perhaps the Congregation [in reaffirming the prohibition of direct sterilization] is merely saying that in its prudential judgment reasons for dissent do not exist in this case," he writes. "Perhaps it would allow for the possibility of dissent but not in such a way that theological dissent becomes a 'theological source' which the faithful might invoke against the authentic magisterium" (n. 31 of article). To allow that dissent is not a "theological source" seems to mean that the teaching remains authoritative for Catholic institutions until it is changed, and authoritative for consciences that are not invincibly ignorant.

on the matter of abortion there can be dissent within the Roman Catholic Church." How then can we not fail to ask this question as well: "Is it possible for the church to operate Catholic hospitals in which Catholics are not able to exercise their right to dissent?" Curran's answer is simply to say that "because of the nature of what is involved I believe even those who dissent should be willing to uphold the right of the majority of Roman Catholics *at the present time* to give this communal witness in our society" (italics added).[45] How better to grease the slippery slope than in the context of a theoretical argument, anthropology, and act-analysis that dissolves the moral problem of cooperation and conscientious refusals to cooperate in evil-doing, especially on the part of (more "remote") institutions?

In the last resort, Curran is prevented from taking the stance of sectarian Christianity (such as the Mennonites' on participation in warfare) by the "important ecclesiological difference" between such a position and that of his own church, which has always "opted for a stance of cooperation with the world even though it recognizes at times it should and must disagree with what is happening in the world." [46] The upshot, however, is failure to locate in the modern world such a time or issue. Instead, cooperation with ethical pluralism becomes the way to cooperate with the world. Moreover, in this collection of essays on "ongoing revision," it is dissent within the church that has come to have the right-making and wrong-making power that was formerly ascribed to the hierarchical magisterium. ". . . The principal theological argument [formerly advanced] for the existence of this [papal] power [to dissolve marriages between baptized and unbaptized persons] is the fact that the pope has exercised such power." [47] Now, the *fact* of dissent in the church (and in society generally) seems to be advanced as a right-making reason simply because it "has exercised such power." But again these are frontiers that are not mine.[48]

45. Ibid., pp. 225–27. I suppose that "at the present time" the church should still give communal witness to the fact that ravaging a virgin is so monstrous a crime that the action of a servant in helping his master to climb over a wall to do that deed is never excusable. Past discussion among moralists about "immediate material cooperation," etc., pivoted around that (seventeenth century) case (Curran, op. cit., pp. 216–17).

46. Ibid., p. 226.

47. Ibid., p. 93.

48. Despite the disclaimer in the last sentence of the above paragraph, I ought with intellectual candor to say that appeals to a *right-making* character *either* of papal statements *or* of dissent within the church seem to me to be as "preposterous"

A final word in behalf of the *Seeger* religious. It will be the most remarkable of doctrines if the Supreme Court—having created the "*Seeger* religious" only a few years ago by interpreting Congress to mean "conscientiousness" by the words "owing duties to a Supreme Being superior to all others"—should now turn around and say that the words "No hospital shall . . ." in federal and state conscience clauses means "No *sectarian* hospital shall be required. . . ." Such "double think" will be noteworthy for ages to come should the Court make law in this fashion with, in addition, a case or cases before it involving statutes (such as the federal conscience clause) that allow institutions or individuals to refuse participation in abortion because such procedures would be contrary to "religious belief" *or* "moral conviction." Such a hypothetical, future decision would say, in effect, that "moral convictions" are "religious" if and only if they are held by explicitly religious institutions or individuals, while *Seeger*

---

as John Bennett's "ecumenical elitism" (as David H. Smith deems that to be in his review of Bennett's *The Radical Imperative,* in *Worldview* 19, no. 6 [November 1976] : 52–54). Neither the magisterium, nor dissent therefrom, nor an ecumenical consensus should serve as an "epistemological principle"—to use Smith's expression. Bennett's theory of ecumenical discussion seems to be that "World Council of Churches or NCC policy statements"—in Smith's words—"may not be absolutely true, but they are more likely to be true than the views of grassroots Christians." I suggest we should ascribe right-making power neither to the views of grassroots Christians nor to anyone else *simpliciter,* as Curran seems to do in his constant reference to present and future dissent within the church. Of course, he never says expressly that dissent is "more likely to be true" (or even "seems likely to win") because it is dissent. Anyway he in the main means "grassroots" moral theologians, vocal intellectuals, and certain powerful, probably secular forces within the church. Among all these competing claims to authority, I know no sound ground on which to stand except Martin Luther's principle: Believe neither pope nor council nor consensus nor dissensus "until [you are] shown by scripture and sound reason." Then everyone refers his considered opinion proleptically to the church to be, in which he too claims to be a servant of the servants of God; and neither a hierarchical magisterium nor dissent from that nor an ecumenical consensus can say him nay. None are "epistemological" authorities; nor is pluralism a normative context. For individually or together we acknowledge no such right-making sources; these are only powerful persuasions that may be wrong. The sole remaining consideration is that—in Smith's words—there is "a side of the Gospel that calls Christian *communities* to social responsibility in some form." The way to that communal witness we ought assiduously to seek, but no one should do so by sacrificing scripture and sound reason, or by deeming the powerful forces of ecumenical consensus or papal statements or dissent within the church to be right making. The need for communal witness, or dissent from past teaching, in no way shows what that social responsibility should be.

affirmed prima facie "moral convictions" to be "religious" when firmly held by the expressly nonreligious. In sum, this would be a tour de force whose sole explanation would be the Court's strenuous construction to protect Seeger's refusal coupled with a similarly strenuous construction to deny protection to conscientious refusals on moral grounds in the case of abortion. I know of no church or religious body or institution which bases its views of the morality of abortion mainly on distinctive "religious belief" or on privileged revelation; the basis claimed for objection is always "moral conviction," whose good reasons are in principle accessible also to the *Seeger* religious.

If the Court mandates that "no hospital" must mean "no *sectarian* hospital," then there will be an impelling social obligation upon Jewish, Methodist, Baptist, Lutheran, and other "sectarian" hospitals sponsored by denominations—which like the Catholics have opted to be of influence in the world and not withdraw into "Amish" enclaves—to abandon the policies allowing elective abortion that now are in effect. For this will be the only way to provide young members of these congregations, as well the *Seeger* religious, who choose to go into medicine, nursing, psychiatry, and anesthesiology in ob-gyn service, the social space moral persons need.

3

The *Edelin* Case

On December 17, 1976, the Supreme Judicial Court of Massachusetts handed down its decision in the case of *Commonwealth* v. *Kenneth Edelin*.[1] Dr. Edelin had been indicted for reckless manslaughter in connection with a hysterotomy abortion on a seventeen-year-old unmarried woman in Boston City Hospital on October 3, 1973. The criminal charge was based on actions alleged to have been performed or omissions in reckless disregard for the life of the child during and following that abortion. Dr. Edelin was not indicted for manslaughter *because* he performed an abortion in late pregnancy. That supposition is a canard given ever more currency by the press, and even by some intellectuals, bent on confusing the public on moral questions. Nor was Dr. Edelin acquitted of "manslaughter by abortion" as Walter Cronkite sensationally and triumphally announced on national television news on the evening of December 17.

A careful analysis of the decision of the Supreme Judicial Court of Massachusetts in the Edelin case, and of the dissent by Chief Justice Hennessey, may be one way for the reader to engage with me in some significant moral reflection. I shall make no comment upon Edelin's guilt or innocence of the offense for which he was legally indicted and has now been acquitted. It is not necessary for anyone to imply that the Scottish verdict of "not proven" might have been better, in order to address the decision of the court in this case with the urgent question whether *the law* of homicide was deformed in any way, or the law's protection of human life weakened in any measure, by the line of reasoning or by elements in the reasoning that reached that verdict of acquittal.

I have but one tentative thesis—namely, the familiar maxim that hard cases can make bad law. And bad morals as well, because of the pedagogical impact of law upon behavior and upon people's concep-

1. OOO Mass. OOO, 359 N.E. 2d 4 (1976).

tions of right and wrong. Any grey area in the fabric of the law—in a matter so fundamental as the protection of life—tempts customary morality into that grey area and renders the fabric of morality correspondingly uncertain. Further specification of the meaning of these preliminary comments must await the opinions' answers to the questions I shall address to them.

The Opinions

Dr. Edelin was convicted of reckless manslaughter by the jury in his trial and sentenced to one year probation by Judge McGuire. Edelin appealed both the judgment and the lower court judge's refusal of a new trial. The supreme judicial court promptly granted the defendant's request for direct appellate review.

All six justices who heard the appeal reversed Edelin's conviction. There the agreement ends. Five of the six justices, while reversing the judgment, entered a verdict of *acquittal;* and for them Justice Kaplan wrote the opinion of the court which ends the case legally. Chief Justice Hennessey would have ordered a *new trial,* while joining in the unanimous opinion of his colleagues that the *conviction* should be reversed. We shall examine his dissent, along with the court's reasoning ("the Kaplan opinion"); that is more important for our purposes than its ruling.

The five justices who agreed to enter a judgment of acquittal (where Chief Justice Hennessey would instead have ordered a new trial) were themselves in major disagreement. The five agreed only that on the point of guilt for "wanton" or "reckless" conduct there was insufficient evidence for the trial judge to permit the case to go to the jury. Three justices (Kaplan, Braucher, and Wilkins) would have both reversed and acquitted for the additional reason that there was insufficient evidence of live birth for the case to be permitted to go to the jury. These two points do not seem separable; indeed, they seem to laymen to be related in specific serial order: live birth; reckless conduct. Justices, judges, and lawyers, however, customarily take difficult points in the reverse order. In this case, the justices assumed live birth in order to get at the conduct issue. If there was insufficient evidence of the defendant's reckless conduct, the live birth issue becomes moot. That is to say, the perhaps more difficult question was rendered moot.

But there was a third reason these three justices would have acquitted: prejudicial divergence between the judge's instructions and the indictment. The three (Kaplan included) did not write a separate opinion; instead Justice Kaplan expressed and clearly demarcated their views in the court's opinion: the judge's instructions were *too broad,* the three justices believed, because the jury was permitted to consider evidence of Dr. Edelin's prenatal conduct. Justice Reardon, joined by Justice Quirico, wrote a concurring opinion, but these two justices criticized the judge's instructions in a manner opposite to the criticism of their colleagues: those instructions, they believed, were *too limiting,* else the judge might without legal flaw have sent the case to the jury to decide about live birth and reckless conduct. The Reardon opinion was that the law of the manslaughter statute encompasses both prenatal and postnatal conduct, while the opinion's view of "the law of the case" (a judge's instructions *determines* "the law of the case") was that this was mistakenly limited to the jury's examination of postnatal conduct alone. Yet another flaw was found in the instructions by Chief Justice Hennessey: the trial judge failed to explain to the jury how to determine facts the defendant might "reasonably" be expected to know. The jury had not been provided a standard by which to judge the reasonableness of Edelin's belief that the fetus was dead, upon which belief he based his conduct.

The decision, then, turned on questions of reckless conduct, live birth, and the trial judge's instructions. The justices' evaluation of these questions, however, went in many directions. To repeat: they unanimously agreed to set aside the verdict of guilty. By five to one they entered a verdict of acquittal; the chief justice would have ordered a new trial. The five justices whose views went to acquittal by the appellate court disagreed themselves about *which* facts (reckless conduct or live birth) were of insufficient evidence to go to a jury, and they also disagreed about *what was wrong* with the trial judge's instructions. Three of these five justices read the instructions to *include* Dr. Edelin's "prenatal" conduct and found that to be the flaw. Two of these five justices read the instructions to *exclude* prenatal conduct and found that to be the flaw. Disagreement about the instructions is the most important aspect of these opinions: it means that the justices could not agree on what *the law* of manslaughter now means in the Commonwealth of Massachusetts! They did not agree about how "the law of the case" (the judge's instruction) was incompatible with the manslaughter statute. No lawyer reading this case can possibly determine how he should now advise a physician who is his client.

A final preliminary comment: it is very rare indeed for an appellate court to enter an acquittal when it reverses a conviction in a trial court. Ordinarily a new trial is ordered. I myself have heard good lawyers remark about the *Edelin* decision, "They retried the case!"—implying that the appellate court usurped the role of the jury as trier of fact. If a judge instructs a jury incorrectly as to law, then a new trial is the usual outcome. I do not pretend to know how an appellate court draws a line between evidence sufficient to go to a jury with proper instructions and evidence insufficient to go to a jury even with proper instructions (i.e., the rare case in which a new trial is *not* ordered). A careful reader of the opinions has good reason to suspect that the supreme judicial court decided to acquit, in part at least, because they could not agree about the instructions that would have been proper for Judge McGuire to give a new jury. When we who are laymen in the law, however, hear lawyers describe the controversies over facts that generally go on in trials, and hear them say, with a pinch of cynicism, that our legal system "lets the jury decide whom to believe," we can only say, "Dr. Edelin must be a lucky man," or "His mother must have loved him very much," or "The angels watched over him," or speak some incantation we civilized people still use to ward off evil spirits from ourselves.

Basic Circumstances

The young woman in this case placed her last menstrual period at a date that would indicate that she was seventeen weeks pregnant. However, Dr. H. R. Holtrop, chief of outpatient ob-gyn service at Boston City Hospital, estimated gestational age to be twenty weeks. He approved saline abortion. Dr. Edelin was asked to carry out the procedure. In the interim before that was attempted, a third-year medical student estimated gestational age to be twenty-four weeks but did not insist on it because of his lack of clinical experience. Junior resident Dr. Enrique Gimenez-Jimeno also estimated twenty-four weeks and recorded a fetal heartbeat. (Dr. Gimenez was later to testify against Dr. Edelin that there was an interval of at least three minutes before he extracted the fetus from the uterus.) With those new estimates before him, Dr. Holtrop reexamined the patient and moved his estimate up from twenty to twenty-one or twenty-two weeks. He used a tape measure rather than his fingers to determine breadth from umbilicus to fundus. Moreover, Dr. Gimenez had not taken the precaution of asking the patient to void her bladder, and this could have distorted his larger estimate. Informed about these divergent estimates, Dr. Edelin did his own measurements and estimated the gestational age to be between twenty and twenty-two weeks.

Saline abortion was twice attempted. From the failure of the first attempt (October 2, 1973), Dr. Edelin surmised that he was dealing with an anterior placenta (this may have influenced the procedure he deemed proper when he later did a hysterotomy abortion). Saline abortion was tried again the following morning by Dr. James F. Penza, associate director of the department and Edelin's supervisor. It had already been agreed that Edelin would proceed to hysterotomy if the second attempt failed.

After the operation the resident pathologist weighed the fetus twice and recorded 600 grams. Following the indictment, however, at an autopsy on February 12, 1974, Dr. George W. Curtis, the medical examiner, found the weight to be 693 grams plus 7 grams for the umbilical cord (1 pound, 8½ ounces total). His opinion was that soaking the fetus for more than four months in formaldin *would not have increased the weight and might have reduced it.* Crown-to-heel length was 33.5 centimeters, and crown-to-rump length 21 centimeters.

The fetal lungs were also examined. The lungs sank in water and had a solid appearance; that indicated, according to the medical examiner, absence of any prior respiratory movement. Later, however, microscopic examination of lung tissue fixed on slides showed partial expansion of some of the alveoli. That suggested respiratory activity but did not determine when or where it had taken place. The medical examiner thought there were three possibilities: the fetus under distress might have sucked amniotic fluid, or taken in room air through the uterine incision, or breathed in air after delivery clear of the uterus.[2] Dr. John F. Ward, a pathologist, testified that the micro-

2. The court remarked after summarizing Dr. Curtis's testimony, "The last might betoken postnatal 'life' in some sense." That sentence is a nice summary of a con-

scopic examination of lung tissue showed that the fetus "did breathe outside the uterus." The court observed that Ward's adoption of the third option was influenced by his skepticism about the first option; in that skepticism, the court found Ward to "stand somewhat apart from other experts." Among witnesses for the commonwealth, Ward placed gestational age at twenty-six weeks, others settled upon twenty-four.

As for Dr. Edelin's conduct during the abortion procedure, a period of three minutes or more was in dispute. Dr. Gimenez testified that he walked into the operating room and saw Dr. Edelin (whose back was turned toward him) making a sweeping motion, evidently detaching the placenta. Then ensued, Gimenez testified, an interval of "at least three minutes" during which Edelin remained motionless, his eyes and those of other members of the operating team fixed on a clock on the wall. The fetus was then taken from the uterus. Edelin tried to determine fetal heartbeat and finding none turned back to his primary patient. On this point, Gimenez's testimony that "the baby was dead," it "had no sign of life such as breathing or movement" supported Edelin; while a *defense* witness said ten seconds (not Edelin's "few" seconds) would be required to reach certainty about the existence of fetal heartbeat.

The commonwealth particularized that the act during the hysterotomy which constituted manslaughter was Dr. Edelin's "waiting three to five minutes after he manually separated the placenta from the uterine wall and before he removed the person from the abdominal cavity of his mother." Edelin's own account of the interval of time was that the sac burst and that he was busy dealing with the spill and grasping the extremities of the fetus to extract it. The court accepted the plausibility of his explanation: "the pause Dr. Gimenez spoke of may well have been the interval of the delay in delivering the fetus that was due to the rupture of the amniotic sac." That was sufficient to rebut proof of intentional neglect or of wanton or reckless conduct.[3]

---

clusion to be supported below: that the court's precaesarian, prehysterotomy interpretation of the law's meaning of "liveborn" combined with the "meaningful life" standard from *Wade* has now been imprinted in the law of homicide. At the moment, I ask the reader to attend mainly to the disputed facts.

3. Whether Dr. Edelin was immobile for those minutes or exceedingly active may be an example of the sort of factual disputes which, my legal counsels tell me, often go to juries to "decide whom to believe."

The Court's Decision

The case before the supreme judicial court fell, in its opinion, in a lacuna between *Wade* and *Bolton* (1973) and the enactment of new comprehensive legislation by the Massachusetts legislature in August 1974.[4] The Supreme Court's January 1973 decisions "rendered inoperative" Massachusetts's criminal abortion statute. That "introduced a new regime" affording only the stated constitutional protections in an abortion action. The Supreme Court had allowed—even invited—the state to promote its "interest in the health of the mother" after the first trimester and / or promote its "interest in the potentiality of human life" after the stage of viability. But on October 3, 1973, when the events of which Edelin was accused occurred, the state had done neither. That left the homicide statutes alone applicable in the case before the appeals court. Moreover, the prosecution had not been so inept as to indict Edelin for abortion or for homicide by abortion.

The *mens rea* ("guilty mind") of manslaughter as charged breaks down into whether Dr. Edelin's conduct was "wanton" and "reckless" and whether he was, at the least, "consciously ignorant" of the fact (i.e., should have been aware) that *this particular* fetus was possibly viable and was liveborn. We shall later examine a mare's nest of questions about how the court dealt with this second question. But first, the components of the decision—and their cogency.

Before going to trial the commonwealth was required to particularize the indictment. An accused may be guilty as charged only if he is charged as guilty; justice to a defendant requires specification of an indictment—in this case, both as to time and place. The state had to particularize not only *when* (the three to five minutes) but also *where* the alleged offense took place. Edelin's defense asked whether "the death of the 'person' referred to in the indictment took place (a) when the fetus was inside the body of the mother? (b) when the fetus was partially expelled or removed from the body of the mother? or (c) when the fetus was totally expelled or removed from the body of the mother?" The commonwealth declined those options as delimited (which was its privilege), refusing to settle for (c). Its re-

4. Mass. Gen. Laws ch. 112, sec. 12H–12R.

sponse was to embrace *both* (b) and (c): the death occurred "when Baby Boy [5] was within the mother, albeit detached from the mother and independent of the mother, and . . . when Baby Boy was partially expelled or removed from the body of the mother." The defense contended that manslaughter could be proved if, but only if, the fetus was born alive completely outside the mother's body and *at that stage* was destroyed by homicidal acts. The prosecution's case may be described, I suppose, as a transitive one: that the fetus became independent of the mother's support system upon the detachment of the placenta, that evidence of expansion of the lungs showed that Baby Boy was "liveborn," not dead, and that Dr. Edelin proceeded recklessly in disregard of available professional knowledge that the fetus might be viable, could be delivered alive, and indeed might be salvageable.

The trial judge instructed the jury on the meaning of a charge of "wanton" and "reckless" conduct. This required proof of "indifference to or disregard of the probable consequences to the rights of others." That was a stronger indictment than "negligence" or even "gross negligence" would have been. He instructed them that the case was "inextricably intertwined" with the *Wade-Bolton* decisions. Those cases had introduced what the supreme judicial court later called a new "dispensation." Finally, he instructed them as to the meaning of manslaughter. That could not be committed on an "unborn person." It required proof of a "person who had been alive outside the body of his or her mother." Transitive descriptions of birth as "the emergence of a new individual from the body of its mother" were set within the language of the law of manslaughter: "born alive and is outside," the judge said; proof was needed beyond a reasonable doubt that the defendant "caused the death of a person who *had been alive outside* the body . . ." (italics added).

That is what I shall call the "born-alive-outside" or the "cargo-transport" language of our law of homicide, now brought into and

5. It is astonishing that liberal intellectuals cringed when they read news reports of such language used during the trial by the prosecution, and how many people rushed to a judgment of bigotry, ignorance, bias, and emotionalism on its part. Are we to say that manslaughter is not possible in the vicinity of an abortion? How else, then, does the state draw up an indictment for manslaughter while impounding the name of the mother?

left unreformulated for a postcaesarian, posthysterotomy era. The supreme judicial court emphasized that language, pointing out that the trial judge's phrases were "cast in the 'past perfect.' "

Taking the evidence in a light most favorable to the commonwealth, the court found nothing of substance in it to permit a submission to a jury of a charge of criminal "recklessness." For—even granting that the fetus may have been alive in the "very narrow sense" that there was "some postnatal gasping of air" as revealed by the microscopic examination of preserved lung tissue, and even granting (as did two justices in the majority, plus the chief justice in dissent) that the evidence on *this* point was sufficient to go to the jury—"nothing of the sort was observable by Dr. Edelin as he carried out the operation," the court declared. "To all appearances the fetus was dead." That seems clearly to be a sound judgment. There was no *mens rea* (guilty mind) involved in the crime for which Edelin was indicted, even if there was evidence enough (as three justices held) to go to the jury on whether an "evil deed" (*actus reus*) was done that day. There can be a *corpus delecti* (in this case, the body of the baby or even the action that killed him) without the intention, recklessness, or negligence sufficient to prove one degree or another of manslaughter.

The words "very narrow sense" and "some postnatal gasping of air," however, should alert the reader to the very broad meaning of live birth the court used in defining the applicable law in this case. (It should be noted that the Kaplan decision spoke not only for the three justices who argued for insufficient evidence of reckless conduct because the judge erroneously included prenatal conduct, but also for the two justices who found insufficient evidence of reckless conduct because the judge limited the jury, they believed, to postnatal conduct.) Here the court criticized Judge McGuire for not discussing the meaning of *alive* when he instructed the jury. He did not specify "how far this connoted an ability to survive, under what conditions, for what *length of time*" to sustain a manslaughter charge (italics added). Moreover, when the judge left it to the jury to determine whether the related concept of "viability" had "any applicability," and when he defined *viability* to mean "the ability to live postnatally," he failed to discuss "what the chances, conditions or *duration* of survival must be" (italics added).

Doubtless the jury needed more instruction on these points. Still the court's decision seems based on too much life expectancy. As I understand it, evidence of a breath of air is not conclusive evidence in a homicide case; neither is brief or long duration of life negatively conclusive. Usually, evidence that the victim was alive shortly before the alleged harm was done is sufficient to maintain the presumption that life continued until the offender acted or omitted to act. In one case, for example, a man poisoned a woman; then, to conceal his crime, he decapitated her. She was alive at the moment of decapitation, and the homicide of which the accused was guilty took place there and then, *not* when he poisoned her—even though she could not be expected to live after the poisoning.[6] Another case held: "It is usually said that the umbilical cord must be severed and an independent circulation established. Ordinarily, if the child has breathed, this would show independent life. But this test is not infallible. Sometimes infants breath before they are delivered, and sometimes they *do not breathe for quite a perceptible period after they are delivered* [and homicide could be committed upon them while their duration of life was indefinite, unascertained]. Generally, however, if respiration is established, that also establishes an independent circulation and independent existence. . . ."[7] The "better opinion," however, is that a child is not fully born until the umbilical cord has been severed, for until then the blood of the child is renovated through the lungs of the mother and its circulation is therefore not independent.[8] Yet the absence of evidence of breathing *supports* a conclusion against a charge of homicide. In one case a woman *confessed* to that crime and led the authorities to the graves of babies she had buried in the basement; but lacking evidence of breathing or other evidence that they were born alive, she was not charged. Yet respiratory activity need not be the only evidence that a child was liveborn in the legal sense; a pulsating umbilical cord is also a fact to be considered; homicide may be done before a liveborn infant breathes. The one thing I do not find in the law of homicide is reference to length or duration of life to come. This is pointed to only in the rule of expediency to protect an ac-

6. *Jackson* v. *Commonwealth,* 100 Ky. 239, 38 S. W. 422, 1091, 18 Ky. L. Rep. 795, 66 Am. St. Rep. 336 (1896).

7. *Morgan* v. *State,* 148 Tenn. 417, 256 S. W. 433 (1923).

8. Tom C. Clark and Thurgood Marshall, *A Treatise on the Law of Crimes,* 6th ed. rev. by Melvin F. Wingersky (Chicago, Illinois: Callagan and Company, 1958), p. 535.

cused—that is, for anyone to be guilty of homicide the victim must die within a year.

Clearly the court's account of the meaning of *liveborn* in the law of manslaughter was affected by its tender, loving care for the *Wade-Bolton* standards on another matter. It even fuzzed its judgment that Dr. Edelin was not guilty of reckless conduct when it rested that judgment on his belief in good faith that the fetus was not viable and was not born alive. To this reader's astonishment, the court also (needlessly) went on to say that "even a three to five minute wait after detachment of the placenta [for which action the court already had sufficient explanation] would not count as recklessness because Dr. Edelin would think it indifferent to the possibility of *meaningful survival*" (italics added). No witness, the court observed, "was prepared to state that this fetus had more than the remotest possibility of *meaningful survival*" (italics added). When before was such language employed in a trial for manslaughter? Clearly, the "caution and circumspection in the interpretation of a criminal statute" which the court used was imported from another department of our law, from the arena of abortion, which even before *Wade-Bolton* was not classed with manslaughter at all but was, rather, a separate legal offense.

Viability

A major question concerning the *Edelin* decision is raised by the court's citation of both *Wade* and *Planned Parenthood* on the matter of "viability."

The statements taken from *Wade* go to the location and definition of viability. The Supreme Court had said that viability is usually placed "at about seven months (28 weeks) but may occur earlier, even at 24 weeks," that it meant that the fetus was "potentially able to live outside the mother's womb, albeit with artificial aid," and that the fetus "presumably had the capability of meaningful life outside the mother's womb." We have already noticed one criticism of the judge's instructions: he did not say what expected length or duration of life constituted viability. Those instructions were flawed for a second reason, as was the judge's conduct of the trial. The court pointed out that "the judge did not bring to bear during the trial (or, for that matter, in his charge to the jury) the Supreme Court's definition of viability in the relevant sense of the point at which the State might, if it chose, constitutionally assert its interest in bringing the fetus to full term." If the words *in the relevant sense* mean anything, presumably they refer to the Supreme Court's reference to twenty-eight or possibly twenty-four weeks and to the fetus's capability of *meaningful* life outside the mother's womb. The trial judge, the court said, should have reined in prosecution witnesses (whose "medical ideas" on the meaning of viability were confused and various) by relating them and channeling them back to the confines of "legal standards." Those legal standards were—one can only suppose—twenty-eight or twenty-four weeks and meaningful life, not simply "the ability to live postnatally."

The court's references to *Planned Parenthood* go the point of a physician's *discretion* in determining viability (see especially note 29 of the opinion). That discretion is without doubt a precious necessity to be preserved. But far more important for the present case was the fact (to which *Edelin* made no reference, or at least made no *use*) that in *Planned Parenthood* the Supreme Court *upheld* Missouri's statutory definition of viability in terms that abandoned the long ago outdated twenty-eight or even twenty-four weeks and the meaningful-life standard enshrined in *Wade*. In upholding the definition of viability in the comprehensive Missouri law, the Supreme Court implicitly criticized itself in *Wade:* "it is not the proper function of the legislature or the courts to place viability." The placement of viability at twenty-eight or twenty-four weeks was an uninformed effort to locate viability, and to that extent did not circumscribe within narrow enough limits the discretion of physicians in determining possible viability. The effect of the "*Wade-Bolton* dispensation" was not to *circumscribe* discretionary decisions during abortions but to *open* them to the possibility of collision with the law of homicide; hence, the present tragic case was at least not discouraged from happening. The provision *upheld* by *Planned Parenthood,* as we saw in chapter 1, defines viability to mean "that stage of fetal development when the life of the unborn child may be continued indefinitely outside the womb by natural or artificial life-supportive systems."

In sum, the *Edelin* decision cited *Wade* to place viability at twenty-eight or twenty-four weeks (hovering in the wings was "meaningful life"), and at the same time it cited *Planned Parenthood* only to enforce the exculpatory force of a physician's discretion in a decision concerning viability. It did not draw attention to the Missouri statutory *definition* of viability upheld by the Supreme Court as among those legal standards the trial judge might have used. Instead the trial judge erred, we are told, because he did not rein in the medical experts for the prosecution and inform his instructions to the jury by the *Wade-Bolton* standards and *Planned Parenthood*'s physician discretion.

Undeniably, in fairness to the accused, it can be argued that the action for which Dr. Edelin was charged fell in the interim between the 1973 abortion decisions and the Missouri case decided in July 1976; and therefore the "new regime" introduced by *Wade* and *Bolton* provided the governing standards. But then, one may ask, what was the force of the supreme judicial court's own citations of *Planned Parenthood*—except that these helped the court reach the conclusion to reverse judgment and enter a verdict of acquittal? To have stressed the Supreme Court's decision to uphold the constitutionality of Missouri statutory *definition* of viability (thus supplanting its own *Wade* standards) would have worked against the reasoning by which the Massachusetts court reached its conclusions. No doubt the Massachusetts court could acquit Dr. Edelin solely on the point of insufficient evidence that the fetus was liveborn (which was *not* the basis of the majority opinion) without leaving an area of uncertainty in and weakening our law of homicide. Insufficient evidence is insufficient evidence. Edelin's acquittal was certainly to be desired, since a physician should not be convicted for conscientious actions (whatever these are) due to a gap the courts themselves opened in our laws protecting human life. Nevertheless, as we have seen, Kaplan's opinion admitted some softness into the law of manslaughter by its references to length of life expectancy qualifying both what was said about "liveborn" *and* what was said about "viability."

On the definition of viability, one may ask in general: Can courts refer to juries as triers of fact and hold trial judges to the factual standards laid down by legitimate public authorities other than the highest court? If so, we should here interject a reference to the definition of viability given by the National Commission for the Protection of Human Subjects in its report on fetal research,[9] accepted and promulgated by the secretary of the Department of Health, Education,

9. *Research on the Fetus,* Report and Recommendations of the National Commission for the Protection of Human Subjects of Biomedical and Behavioral Research, DHEW Publication no. (OS) 76-127, 1975.

and Welfare.[10] The commission defined a category of "possibly viable infants" between twenty and twenty-four weeks gestational age and between five hundred and six hundred grams in weight. (These measurements may be compared with the measurements of Baby Boy disputed in the *Edelin* case.)

I think it would be acknowledged on all sides—by judicial conservatives no less than by judicial activists—that in the growth of the common law or case law, our courts do take cognizance of facts and of authorities for those facts outside courts alone. They need not stand idly by until information gets through to the Supreme Court. Again, of course, whether it would have been fair or just, or *legally* permitted, for the Massachusetts courts to have brought the conclusions of the National Commission (which also postdated the events in question) to bear in the *Edelin* case is an altogether different matter. Still the purpose of summoning expert medical witnesses was to make a fresh determination of the meaning of viability, it would seem. These were witnesses to a factual medical situation which *did* antedate the alledged events of October 3, 1973, and of which, they said, a physician could and should have been aware. Yet the supreme judicial court held the trial judge to *Wade*'s erroneous and long-outdated definition and *within that* to the rule of physician discretion in *Planned Parenthood.*

The facts were knowable. I do not say they were known to Dr. Edelin; he may have been quite guiltless of the mens rea of proceeding wantonly or recklessly toward a possibly viable infant. If the justices of the Supreme Court could be ignorant, so could he have been. Still, the facts were knowable.[11] The background discussion of the National Commission on this point is of the greatest significance. Chairman Kenneth John Ryan, M.D., of the Boston Hospital for

10. *Federal Register* 40, no. 154 (August 8, 1975) : 33552.

11. I, for instance, knew these facts from physicians of my acquaintance who had sufficient authority in these matters to be trusted by a layman. Some of these physicians expressed horror when I showed them the account (published in 1968) of a "perfusion incubator" research trial on a still-living, 26-week, 980-gram abortus. (See Paul Ramsey, *The Patient as Person* [New Haven: Yale University Press, 1970], p. 18.) I had not thought that baby was possibly viable; these physicians said it was and proceeded (in 1968) to push the measurements back. Yet in our late, lamentable abortion "debate," I could not get statements to that effect printed in *Time* magazine. Instead, after telephone interviews which *Time* initiated, someone looked up some very old medical textbook and said I was not an expert.

Women, said at one point: "A fetus can be fragile at 28 weeks." On the other hand, "it might be vigorous at 22 weeks." That went to the point of a physician-researcher's discretion, but also to his or her operational presumption of viability: ". . . when it is presumed to be viable, is fragile, for goodness' sake, do not do anything that is going to harm it." [12]

More to our present point, Chairman Ryan told his fellow commissioners: "If you take practically any medical text on obstetrics, and the common practices in dealing with pregnancies, . . . we have used the 20 weeks and 500 grams as the cut-off point for years, and I can give you any number of texts that have done that." While the general operational category of *viability* was 28, then 26, weeks in the past—he went on to explain—all along "we had used 20 weeks as pushing it back to the point when we considered it *not viable,* and that had existed long before [reports to this commission]." [13]

Therefore, there is ample foundation for the questions I am raising in general and addressing in specific to the *Edelin* decision. Must appellate courts limit trial judges, medical witnesses, and juries to the startlingly uninformed placement of viability that began its course through American law with *Roe* v. *Wade?* Can courts give cognizance to testimony on points of fact or acknowledge other authorities, sometimes public ones, concerning those facts? Must the reference always

12. *Transcript of Fifth Meeting,* April 11–13, 1975, pp. 553. National Technical Information Service, U.S. Department of Commerce, 5285 Port Royal Road, Springfield, Virginia 22151.

13. *Transcript of Sixth Meeting,* April 25–26, p. 160. The British Peel Report in 1972 chose 20 weeks and 300 grams as the point of possible viability. Those medical texts, Ryan said (ibid., p. 126), usually also refer to the fetus as "he." By that was meant "he" as a generic *personal* pronoun, as opposed to "it" (not "he" instead of "he or she"). The fact that only a few years ago our language used to be *unborn baby* instead of *fetus,* and *he* or *she* instead of *it,* is today scarcely remembered. Moreover, the National Commission recently created a new concept—namely, nonviable fetus ex utero. Until now that would have been called a premature *infant.* See John P. Wilson, "Fetal Experimentation: Rights of the Father and Questions of Personhood," *Villanova Law Review* 22, no. 2 (January 1977), pp. 403–17, esp. pp. 405–06; and Dennis J. Horan, "Fetal Experimentation and Federal Regulation, *Villanova Law Review* 22, no. 2 (January 1977), pp. 325–56, esp. pp. 338–40. This novel concept, now for the first time a part of our administrative law, is enough to support one thesis of this volume—namely, that the birth line or viability line is not likely to withstand the currents that today are running against the protection of life in morality and in our law. For, as George Orwell believed, the degradation of *language* is the first sign and cause of a civilization's decline.

be to factual situations already acknowledged by courts above appellate courts or by appellate courts in other jurisdictions? In particular, should a dictum cast off by the Supreme Court in its 1973 *abortion* decision have been allowed to become the legal standard in a *manslaughter* trial?

To reach its conclusion that twenty weeks and five hundred grams was the proper line to draw (to be brought up for possible revision *every year!*), the commission had to set aside the Behrman Report, which recommended twenty-four weeks and six hundred and one grams.[14] To reach that recommendation from a statistical survey, the Behrman Report defined a *reported* viable infant to be one who survived in hospital *or at home for thirty days!* Those that died on the twenty-ninth day, even at home, were declared to have been nonviable all along.[15] If at a given point in time one uses as a numerator the number of people seventy years of age who survive (as it turns out) less than thirty days and as a denominator the number of people of that age, one gets a slim possibility of survival at age seventy, especially in bad weather or during a flu epidemic. There would come an age (say, one hundred) in a given population that everyone in that group would, by definition, be "nonviable."

The importance of introducing this debate behind the national commission's definition of a "possibly viable infant" should be clear. If for *research* purposes an abortus capable of surviving at home for twenty-nine days ought not to be treated as nonviable, should not this and other sound judgments about fetal viability be taken into account by our law of homicide? Yet, as we have seen, the *Edelin* decision faulted the trial judge for not having explained "ability to live postnatally" by instructing the jury on "what the chances, condition or *duration* of survival must be" (italics added), and the *Wade* standard of "meaningful life outside the womb" hovered over the *Edelin* opinion. Even the Missouri statutory definition, "that stage of fetal

14. Richard E. Behrman and Tove S. Rosen, principal investigators, "Report on Viability and Nonviability of the Fetus," *Appendix to Research on the Fetus,* DHEW Publication no. (OS) 76-128, Part I, ch. 12, pp. 1–116.

15. "I think that the non-medical people on the Commission ought to realize that Behrman was talking about babies who went home and survived the newborn period, the first 30 days of life. I cannot call a 29-day-old baby a non-viable fetus ex utero. That is nonsense" (Commissioner Robert E. Cooke, *Transcript of Sixth Meeting,* April 25–26, 1975, p. 144).

development when the life of the unborn child may be continued indefinitely outside the womb," might be construed to invite the same erosion of the meaning of homicide or manslaughter by its use of the word "indefinitely." But that is not so bad as *Edelin*'s "chances, conditions or duration of survival," for *indefinitely* in legal parlance does not have the meaning it has in ordinary speech. *Indefinite* rather means uncertain, not known. Thus a person who was irreparably in the course of dying, whose death indeed was impending, is said to have had "indefinite" survival, when it is a matter of judging as some degree of homicide an intervening act that kills the person. Two moments more survival could be enough to be indefinite, if a person is killed at the penultimate moment of his life. So, also, physicians must make out birth certificates for liveborn infants who nevertheless die in a few minutes (then a certification of death by natural causes is in order). Therefore, the words *continued indefinitely outside the womb* can better be construed as carefully chosen to define viability in language that delineates borders that would allow the law of homicide or manslaughter to be applied without corruption from our law dealing with a medical issue alien to that. I do not read the supreme judicial court to have been that circumspect in its opinion.

The foregoing comments on the meaning of viability adopted into the law governing in the *Edelin* case in no degree weakens or removes what had to be shown. Precisely because this was a manslaughter indictment, the state had the burden of proving not simply that this fetus belonged in a class of "possibly viable" fetuses, or even that it in particular was viable, but that it was actually liveborn. No one can commit homicide on a class.

However, concerning the *law* applicable in a homicide case in connection with an abortion procedure, I am asking an extended question: Cannot courts in the development of case law themselves keep the law of homicide or manslaughter up-to-date with the facts about possible viability, without prejudice to the innocence of a person charged with negligently or recklessly failing to use that available knowledge in the precautions taken in the performance of an abortion? Do not courts regularly do just that sort of thing? Must legislation we waited for—legislation that updates the blunt and inarticulate language of "liveborn outside" in a manslaughter case or, as an alternative, legislation that by a separate statute establishes a standard of care for possibly viable infants?

The *Edelin* decision can be read as a muted call for such legislative steps to be taken. (Again, it may be asked, must courts be so mute when faced with a hard case and when they know, or else are "consciously ignorant," of the need for clearer law?) In reversing and acquitting Dr. Edelin, the court simply observed that the judge should have better articulated the meaning of "viability marking the stage at which a physician would begin to owe a duty to the 'potentiality of human life' inherent in the fetus." That expression from *Wade* and that statement itself suggest that, but for the trial judge's failure, this case might have gone to trial and the decision in it might have constituted a judicial determination of a physician's standard of care for potential human life, for possibly viable infants. At this point, however, the court dropped a significant footnote which, in effect, says that legislation is the only route, and that even a physician's duty arises solely from the positive law.[16]

We therefore may conclude that the ball is thrown to the Massachusetts legislature. The court in this case did not hear—perhaps legally should not have answered—the plea from the American College of Obstetricians and Gynecologists.[17] Still the gap or grey area remains. It is for state legislatures to respond to that plea by enacting into law a standard of care which the profession seems unable to enforce and which the courts either cannot or will not clarify even in the matter of a manslaughter case in connection with an abortion procedure. Yet we have seen the ease with which the United States Supreme Court struck down Missouri's standard of care provision, while the one enacted by California has yet to be tested in the courts. If eternal vigilance is the price of liberty, unfaltering draftsmanship seems the price that must be paid to protect human life—regardless of its state or condition or duration—from all intentional, reckless, or negligent harm. That necessity, I suggest, flows from the penumbral absolutism which has been allowed to surround the "right" to an

16. Note 26 reads: "Of course, *Wade-Bolton* does not itself create any such duty; the time for commencement (after viability) and the nature of the duty are for the State to decide. These are plainly issues for settlement by legislation; on what basis could a judge resolve them? This shows the fancifulness of any idea that during the period between *Wade-Bolton* and the adoption of legislation there could be a valid conviction for manslaughter based on a physician's acts during the prenatal period." Those final words, of course, bring the matter back to the law's precaesarian, prehysterotomy, "outside" language, and to the issue of Dr. Edelin's prenatal conduct, to be discussed below.

17. Quoted and discussed in chap. 1, n. 5 and text, above.

abortion. Lest that right be touched in any way, courts shy away from factually informed interpretations of the law, and legislators shy away from legislation designed to achieve a common good by taking into account the other rights and responsibilities that are at stake as well.

If the trial judge was inarticulate on some points in his instruction of the jury, the court used an unarticulated standard to define *viability* and *born alive*. Its unnuanced and undetailed language speaks of the emergence of a person in the legal sense as if this were a matter of transporting cargo from within a body to an outside space. That, I suggest, is quite inadequate even for natural birth; [18] in any case, more details must be given on which to base evidence of the person's independent life. Such "entirely outside" language (selected for emphasis from the law of manslaughter) seems quite out-of-date in relation to modern medical procedures and technology. I do not deny that the whole fabric of that law is susceptible of sufficient modulation, if courts were willing to give cognizance to new fact-situations. Still, focusing first on one and then on another principal ingredient of the *Edelin* opinions shows that we may have to go to the legislatures (as I have suggested) for homicide or manslaughter statutes that take into account the realities of a caesarian-hysterotomy era and the facts concerning fetal viability. In addition, or instead, we might require "standard of care" statutes in comprehensive regulation of abortion procedures.

We now turn to another chief ingredient on which *Edelin* was based.

Prenatal, Postnatal

The court distinguished severely between Dr. Edelin's "prenatal" conduct and his "postnatal" conduct. Let it be granted at once that a more nuanced concept of liveborn may not have been sufficient to establish wanton or reckless conduct. For no matter where the line is

18. The traditional Jewish view was better than the court's language. It required the passage of the head or only the greater portion of the fetus's body through the birth canal. Perhaps more accurately expressed, after the birth process has begun the fetus is "no longer a dependent part of another's life, but neither is it yet a 'person' in its own right; it enjoys the transitional status of a separate entity but not an independent life" (David Feldman, *Contraception and Jewish Law* (New York: New York University Press, 1968), p. 265. Compare options (b) and (c) of the particulars in *Edelin*, above, which the prosecution refused to separate.

to be drawn on live birth in an abortion situation, the evidence may not have been sufficient to go to a jury on a charge of reckless manslaughter. The decisive element needed to sustain such a charge was evidence of Dr. Edelin's *quo animo* either prenatally or postnatally: that is, whether or not he believed in good faith that the fetus was not viable at the time of the operation and that it was not liveborn. His belief does not seem palpably unreasonable; and, as the court pointed out, reckless manslaughter cannot be supported by proof merely of a *mistake in judgment.* ". . . [C]riminal recklessness is not in the picture if one starts with an understanding of Dr. Edelin's belief and judgment as to viability." (He testified to his personal scruple against aborting a viable fetus.)

I do not know how the accused would have fared if the charge had been negligent manslaughter. More helpful than that distinction (which was not pertinent to this case) would now be some clear analysis by legal scholars of how appellate courts decide, without themselves retrying the case, between entering a verdict of acquittal and ordering a new trial.

Here our concern is to point out that in assessing Dr. Edelin's prenatal and postnatal conduct the court went entirely overboard for entirely inarticulate "outside" language. One reason it did so is noteworthy. The court read the judge's charge in that direction in order to "keep it within constitutional bounds." For, the court observed, "if acts of a defendant during the prenatal period could ever be availed of in obtaining a conviction of manslaughter, that was a legal impossibility in the circumstances of this case after the *Wade-Bolton* decisions." Is this not a case, then, of bending the requirements for a manslaughter conviction to fit legally permitted abortion, instead of coordinating the law of manslaughter with permitted abortion? We saw that, in striking down Missouri's standard of care, in *Planned Parenthood,* the Supreme Court observed that the law of homicide was still in force. There Missouri's use of the word *fetus* inadmissably reached back into the stage entirely "inside" (to use the language of *Edelin*), and by Missouri's likely inadvertent use of that word the Court said that the state reached back into the period before viability as well. When *Edelin* bluntly appeals to the *Wade-Bolton* dispensation and correctly states that to promote the state's interest "in the potentiality of life" would require "tailored legislation," the reader may rightly protest that the state's interest in the present case was not in the potentiality of life (referred to in the abortion decisions) but in the (alleged) actuality of it. The promotion of the latter interest requires more up-to-date and tailored interpretation by courts or legislatures as to the meaning of homicide or manslaughter, as this applies to present conditions at life's beginning.

Alternatively or additionally, provisions could be enacted, in state legislation concerning abortion, that would exhibit society's interest in protecting the life of potentially viable infants and would prevent hard cases from arising in the grey area between abortion and homicide or manslaughter—since it is such cases which threaten to produce case law that would weaken the protection of life from criminally negligent or reckless harm. Consider the following sort of possible legislation, which can be framed from one point in the *Edelin* case.

The court rightly held Dr. Edelin to the established procedures for hysterotomy—which procedures were the undisputed standard practice at Boston City Hospital. That protocol called for detachment of the placenta as the first surgical move after completion of the uterine incision, with subsequent peeling of the amniotic sac. There was testimony for the prosecution that "a reverse procedure, resembling caesarian section . . . was possible and might have been preferable, especially with a fetus of the gestational age approximating that present here: this procedure would involve first breaching the amniotic sac and removing the fetus, then separating the placenta." Such a procedure seems obviously designed to enhance the chance of saving the fetus's life if the fetus is possibly viable.

An ethical physician would (on the facts I am supposing) do that, provided there was no added risk to the life or health of the mother. Such a procedure seems to be called for by the tradition of professional ethics expressed by the statement of the American College of Obstetricians and Gynecologists. But not every physician is so inclined, and the profession seems unable to hold its members to that bracing standard of care for both mother and fetus, nor does it seem able to establish that alternative abortion procedure as the standard for medical practice. If there is no deleterious impact on the life or health of the mother, that seems one way to manifest that abortion in mid or late pregnancy can be and should be a severance procedure, the termination of a woman's *pregnancy,* not the destruction of a possibly viable infant.

I am supposing, therefore, several things which, I think, are factual statements: the *Wade* regime opened up a hole in the medical-moral responsibility of two patients, thus creating a grey area of uncertainty; the medical profession alone cannot close that gap; physicians are vulnerable to prosecution; the language of the law of homicide or manslaughter was honed under no-longer-existing medical circumstance; and, finally, the absolute status accorded one right under the *Wade* regime, along with our courts' inflexible followship, continues to hold open that gap, even to enlarge it, eroding other extant rights and the rights of others, even the right to life of the possibly viable patient, by bending the law of manslaughter under that regime.

One helpful development would be case decisions that would no longer hold (as did *Edelin*) that, to sustain a manslaughter conviction, the conduct to be brought under scrutiny for its lawfulness cannot encompass conduct before "the birth of the fetus through its complete delivery clear of the mother's body"; or, if the common law cannot be that far updated and if to do so would be unjust to defendants, there might be legislation updating our law of homicide and manslaughter which would take into account that in modern medicine birth no longer means what it once did. That would be to bring this department of law into the postcaesarian, posthysterotomy era. *Edelin*'s interpretation of *Wade* pushed the law back into antiquity.

The alternative to developments in the law of homicide or manslaughter would be for legislatures to achieve the same ends by statutes governing the practice of abortion and clearly falling within the *Wade-Bolton* dispensation. At stake is the protection of every possibly viable infant, not simply the state's interest in "the potentiality of human life" after viablility is reached (if the reader makes any distinction between these two ways of stating the point).

Suppose then, I ask, a state legislature wanted to insure the protection of the life of possibly viable fetuses while their mothers are undergoing hysterotomy abortions. Could it go so far as to encourage the alternative procedure referred to and preferred by prosecution witnesses in *Edelin?* Could it move to impel the acceptance of that as standard medical practice? Could it mandate a procedure safer for the fetus in mid- or late-pregnancy abortions, unless the physician certifies that he varied from it in order to promote the life or health of the woman?

There is no good reason why such legislation, if carefully drawn, cannot pass constitutional scrutiny. After all, the states have been told they may even go so far as to *prohibit* abortion to promote their interest in the potentiality of life after viability. The standard of a statute's reasonable relation to promoting the life and health of the mother applied to an earlier stage of pregnancy, from approximately the beginning of the second trimester to viability. I assume, of course, that the courts would not allow the prohibition of postviability abortions in instances where the life and health of the mother could not be insured; similarly, any prohibition of a procedure in hysterotomy abortion that aims better to promote the life and health of a possibly viable fetus must not be binding if a physician certifies that the procedure used was necessary to insure, or was less hazardous to, the mother's life and health.[19] Within that limit, insuring *equal* treatment and care, I see no good reason why this could not be deemed constitutional legislation.

But ours is not an era of good reasons in medical ethics or in law, so far as the abortion absolute is concerned. The Supreme Court in *Planned Parenthood,* we saw, readily struck down Missouri's standard of care provision even though the objectionable sentence was severable from the other that spoke only of the viable infant, and it also struck down Missouri's effort to prohibit saline abortions that are more unsafe for the woman than alternative methods. At least, this was the legislature's finding of fact about saline, upon expert testimony; and the Court is not supposed to substitute its policy wisdom or its judgment of fact for that of a legislature unless there is a clearly constitutional issue. In the light of this recent record, it is difficult to believe that legislation concerning a hysterotomy procedure to be generally followed in mid- or late-pregnancy abortions after possible viability (to promote the state's interest in the potentiality of human

19. My assumption would exclude, to take an extreme example, making the incision a small one for cosmetic purposes, so the woman would look as good as before in a bathing suit, at the cost of greater danger to the fetus. I frame this supposition not to make an outrageous suggestion, but because Dr. Edelin made a small incision which (as I read the case) he did because he had reason to believe he was dealing with an anterior placenta. This in turn led to the need for the actions he testified he was engaged in during three- to five-minute delay in removing the fetus from the uterus. There would have to be expert testimony on the question whether the hysterotomy procedure preferred by certain medical witnesses (because it is more likely to promote the life of the fetus) would be *equally* protective of the life and health of the mother in the kind of case Dr. Edelin believed he was dealing with.

life) will not suffer a similar fate, even if that legislation allows exception to be made when, in the physician's judgment, the mother's interests come genuinely into conflict.

What is called for is a sea change in the moral opinion in this nation—a sea change manifested, for example, by numerous legislatures simultaneously passing standard-of-care legislation, returning again and again to the drafting boards; governors (unlike Governor Carey of New York) willing to sign such legislation to send a message to Washington even in face of *Planned Parenthood;* and courts willing to press to the limit, and beyond, the apparent contours of the *Wade-Bolton* regime, testing every borderline where our law may not be settled.

To judge whether there is realistic ground for hope for any such thing, one must also take into account the fact that there are a number of physicians who, far from wanting the grey area in the law's protection cleared up, would want that grey area expanded. Some physicians endorse placing in the private realm—between family and physician—the choice of giving or refusing care to defective newborns; and they advocate the withdrawal of the law of negligent manslaughter from these cases as well. That issue will be examined in a later chapter. So far, the announcement of this practice of neglect has been met with a mainly complacent, not to say compliant, public response, and by a willingness among intellectuals to discuss the "proposed policy" in a manner that suggests all human feeling has been lost.

The Concurring Opinion

Justice Reardon, joined by Justice Quirico, concurred with the court's result but dissented in part. They agreed that, on the basis of the instructions given, there was not sufficient evidence to permit the case to go to the jury on the question of whether the defendant was guilty of wanton or reckless conduct resulting in a death. In his concurring opinion, Justice Reardon disagreed, however, on the point of evidence sufficient for a jury trial of the question whether there was a live birth; but he would not have directed a verdict of acquittal on the third cardinal issue, namely prejudicial divergence between the accusation as specified by the commonwealth and the judge's instructions. Indeed, he seems to criticize the judge's instruction in a direction opposite from the other three justices (among them Kaplan for the court). A fair reading of the concurring opinion suggests that, without the constraints imposed by the trial judge, the jury need not have excluded what the court called Dr. Edelin's prenatal conduct in reaching a verdict upon the recklessness of which he was accused. It is exceedingly important, therefore, for us to examine the concurring opinion for its partial dissent, and not for completeness' sake alone.

Quoting portions of the charge, Reardon affirms that "no jury under any plain understanding of the English language" could conclude they could bring in a verdict of guilty unless (a) "there had been a live birth of a child outside the body of the mother" and (b) "*subsequently* there were wanton or reckless acts of the defendant." Moreover, the defense had taken no exception to the judge's instructions. Nevertheless Reardon wrote, "I am in agreement with the principal opinion that the evidence of the defendant's postnatal actions was not sufficient to permit such a finding." [20] That is to say, it was not sufficient within the framework of the judge's demarcation of postnatal from prenatal conduct.

Thus, the concurring opinion was constrained, as the jury was, by the judge's "limiting instructions." "I am further of the belief that had the jury not been bound by the limiting instructions," Reardon writes, "it would have been open to them to consider the defendant's prenatal conduct in determining whether his [Dr. Edelin's] conduct was wanton or reckless." Nothing was presented to the jury to indicate that the defendant "at any time felt the slightest concern whether his operation would produce a live birth." There was expert testimony that "removing the placenta in the fashion which occurred in this case was similar to 'cutting the air hose on a salvage diver' and there was medical testimony that death might well follow. It is incontroverted that the treatment accorded to this fetus was not that to be expected when a live birth was desired. In fact, all prenatal conduct [excluded by the judge's instructions] of the defendant was based on the

20. Here the concurring opinion expressly said it reached no judgment about whether the evidence was sufficient to permit a finding of negligence since that was not the indictment. ". . . a jury might properly have found that the extremely brief examination of the child when delivered was not consonant with the care which should have been accorded it. A cursory examination of the anterior chest wall, for a period of three to five seconds only, appears to have been the sole effort by the defendant to determine if life had been produced."

proposition that live birth was not desired." The concurring opinion, as I read it, says that had the judge's instructions *not* erroneously excluded the physician's prenatal actions, the evidence concerning those actions and the physician's attitude might have been submitted to the jury, without legal flaw, to apply the legal meaning of reckless manslaughter.

Here Justice Reardon inserted into the opinions one of only two substantive references to *Planned Parenthood*.[21] This one was on the question of viability. Missouri's standard-of-care provision to protect "the potentiality of human life" was declared unconstitutional, according to the concurring opinion, *only* because (in the words of Justice Blackmun) that section of the statute did not "specify that such care need be taken only *after* the stage of viability has been reached." The flaw in that state's effort to give legal effect to its "compelling interest" in potential human life was not simply its use of the word *fetus*. The statute's unconstitutional aspect was that it failed to exclude reaching back before viability. Since in the *Edelin* case evidence that the fetus was viable was at least sufficient to go to a jury, Reardon concluded: "I see nothing in the *Planned Parenthood* case which inhibits the State from testing the defendant's prenatal conduct in these circumstances in a determination whether his actions were wanton and reckless, *and in my judgment the jury might have so charged*" (italics added). Since the jury was not so charged, the indictment for reckless manslaughter should not have been submitted to them.

Thus, the two justices in *Edelin* who concurred in the judgment would, *without* the judge's "limiting instructions," have in principle allowed a jury to reach back *before natality* (in the legal sense). Their grounds for doing so was that within the *Wade-Bolton* regime, as the Missouri case made clear, there is nothing *unconstitutional* about holding a physician to the highest standards of care, after the stage of viability, for a death that may result upon delivery. If the jury had been so charged, the jury might have assessed whether, in the facts of this case, Dr. Edelin proceeded recklessly in face of the possibility that there were two patients whose welfare came under his care. For the court's opinion to have been that of the two concurring justices in a reckless manslaughter case in abutment with an abortion might have

21. The other is to be found in Chief Justice Hennessey's partly concurring, partly dissenting opinion (below).

been a regrettable outcome, even wrong. But then, in another sense, hard cases make bad law. This only emphasizes again, and from the other side, the fact that *Edelin* did little, if anything, to clear up the grey area. One thing is certain: physicians doing mid-pregnancy or late abortions would be badly advised if they concluded from press reports that *Edelin* drew entirely safe lines between manslaughter and abortion. For with a different charge to the jury, these two justices might well have joined Chief Justice Hennessey in his partial dissent; three to three could have been the outcome in my reckoning of the positions and arguments. This demonstrates the main conclusion to be drawn from these opinions: The Supreme Judicial Court of Massachusetts does not know what the *law* of manslaughter now means; therefore it could not agree on better instructions to be given at a new trial; therefore their only out was to enter a judgment of acquittal.

Then the concurring opinion turned to the matter of a live birth; they believed there was enough evidence of that to go to the jury. We need not rehearse that evidence: body weight, fetal age, respiration. The supreme judicial court itself need not weigh the evidence pro and con, said Justice Reardon. "There was evidence which would permit either an affirmative or negative conclusion on the question, and there was therefore a jury question." The jury "could properly have concluded that a child had achieved life."

Since the prosecution can offer additional particularization of an indictment at any point before the case goes to the jury, the concurring opinion found that the defendant's case had not been prejudiced by any variance. Indeed, it held that there was no significant waffling or variance between the indictment as amply specified and the judge's charge. Certain statements offered by the prosecution in support of this point, and included in the Reardon opinion, are worth pondering. On October 15, 1974, the commonwealth apprised the defendant in writing that it "maintains that the victim in this case was a child detached from his mother . . . [T]he legality of the termination of pregnancy is not an issue. . . . What is at issue is the defendant's additional act, unnecessary to and no part of an abortion, of killing the child, detached from his mother." Prior to opening, the prosecutor said: "I don't want to take my brother by surprise, there will be evidence of breathing." In his opening statement to the jury, he said: "There will be evidence that at the time that this particular male child was detached from the mother and no longer dependent on the mother that the male child would have lived outside the mother." [22]

Here I can only observe that in permitting the jury to determine the matter of live birth, these two justices would also have permitted them to determine, within the framework of a judge's instruction as to law, the meaning of *detached* from his mother, *no longer dependent on* his mother, and the truth of the disputed fact of breathing and the contention that if Dr. Edelin's "wait" had not caused its death the male child "would have lived" outside the mother. Facially, that seems to offer some hope that the common law might be flexible enough to revise the cargo-transport language for *placing* "live birth" and so would helpfully draw a finer line between possible manslaughter and abortion which sometimes need be only a severance procedure terminating a woman's pregnancy.

Additional Views of Three Justices

Incorporated into the Kaplan's opinion for the court was the view of the three justices (Kaplan, Braucher, and Wilkins) who would have gone further than the court by reversing and acquitting *also* because there was insufficient evidence of live birth to go to a jury and because there was prejudicial divergence between the accusation as defined by the commonwealth and the trial judge's instructions. I find this part of the opinion to be in many ways a cleaner and more straightforward analysis.

Here we find the harshest condemnation of the prosecution. "The Commonwealth's original submission that the manslaughter statute should be read to cover the destruction in utero of a 'detached' fetus," these justices say, "amounted merely to a misguided attempt, despite *Wade-Bolton,* to reconstitute the old criminal abortion statute under the guise of manslaughter."

That, of course, was many people's view of Dr. Edelin's indictment

22. Chief Justice Hennessey also agreed with the Reardon opinion that there was no prejudicial variance. Requests by the defense for more specificity Hennessey took to be efforts to obtain admissions from the commonwealth that would support pretrial motions for dismissal. That "effort of counsel was commendable, but it should not result later in a dismissal on variance grounds simply because the defendant did not achieve the results he had hoped for from his attempts to bind the Commonwealth to a pretrial statement of its evidence and its theories of proof." The "essential elements" of the crime were correctly stated; the defendant's case was not prejudiced by the judge's conduct of the trial. "Long before trial commenced, there was an unequivocal statement of the offense charged."

from the beginning. The words *misguided attempt* and *under the guise of* do rather slander the prosecution's intentions. Since I do not know the prosecution's motivations, the question to be asked by students of this case is, What are the legal terms under which manslaughter could be committed in the vicinity of an abortion? That has certainly not been clearly answered in this case, or else it has been answered with a quite expanded area of liberty which may impinge on the manslaughter statute with fatal results. Except for Dr. Edelin's lack of mens rea of the crime charged, much of my foregoing comment on the reasoning behind the court's ruling could be summarized by saying that it was an unhelpful fuzzing of the old manslaughter statute by the court's use, in a matter distinct from abortion, of the *Wade-Bolton* definitions. This in turn seems likely to lead to a misguided reconstitution of the law of manslaughter.

We may also ask, How else than by bringing this or some other indictment was the Commonwealth of Massachusetts going to find out how the manslaughter statute, and case law, would be applied in the vicinity of an abortion procedure? How else could it be determined whether case law is flexible enough to take detachment of the placenta to be, under modern medical conditions, part of the meaning of being born independent of a mother's body (capability for independent breathing and circulation still to be evidenced)?

In order to bring these and associated questions into the light, the reader may ask, How could there be insufficient evidence of wanton or reckless disregard of another's life unless *first* there was insufficient evidence that there was a liveborn person? Only the three justices held there to be insufficient evidence on *both* these points which surely must be connected—live birth being the primary question. Dr. Edelin was not charged with recklessly performing an *abortion*. The majority opinion settles the question of manslaughter-recklessness without reaching the question of live birth. By indicating that it seems reasonably clear to me that Dr. Edelin did not have the guilty mind (mens rea) requisite to the crime with which he was charged, I am agreeing that these two issues can be separated to the degree the court separated them. Perhaps I want to believe that—imagining myself to be in Dr. Edelin's position. I do not address (as the court did not) the question of negligence or even gross negligence with which Dr. Edelin was *not* charged.

Still the logic of the matter works the other way as well: one must decide whether there was a person in the legal sense before inquiring whether an accused acted negligently, grossly neglegently, or recklessly in regard to that person's life. A judgment that there was insufficient evidence of negligence or recklessness is bound in some degree to be influenced by a court's notional understanding of what would have been required to establish the existence of a person.

This is my explanation of the bad reasoning behind the court's decision to acquit solely because of insufficient evidence of criminally reckless conduct toward another. That was reasonably clear in its own right to this prospective juror (as I imagine myself to be). But the court felt bound, because of the inherent logic of a manslaughter charge, to expatiate on the other point as well. Therefore it selected only the cargo-transport language of *outside* and *clear of* the woman's body, with no further refinements from the case law of manslaughter; it brought to bear *Wade*'s twenty-eight and twenty-four weeks and by implication its "meaningful life" standard; and it introduced *length* and *duration of life* without proper qualifications as a standard to be applied in manslaughter cases.

This is also my explanation of the greater cogency of the views of the three justices who would have acquitted because of insufficient evidence on *both* points. They were free to argue, without straining the law, for Edelin's innocence of reckless conduct toward another because they also were convinced that there was no legal person on October 3, 1973 (or at least that there was not enough evidence that there was such a person). These justices held the mens rea and the actus reus of the crime together. Neither had been proved. Therefore they did not feel bound to introduce as much potential disturbance into the law of manslaughter in order to reach the verdict of acquittal.

For example, we find in Kaplan's opinion for the court a reference to the legal significance of the disputed evidence for breathing only in the section representing the views of these three justices. In addition to the *location* of the fetus when it may have breathed, these justices identified the question that also needed to be faced—namely, "whether the breathing, such as it could have been, demonstrated postnatal 'life' as required for conviction under the manslaughter statute." When saying the jury needed a standard to go by, these justices apparently approved the defense's quoted standard—a medical definition [23]—as

23. "LIVEBORN INFANT. Liveborn infant is a fetus, irrespective of its gestational age, that after complete expulsion or extraction from the mother shows evidence

compatible with the life of a newborn required by the law of manslaughter. The three observed that a minimal demonstration of independent existence beyond "fleeting respiratory efforts or gasps" was less exacting proof than the standard usually applied in manslaughter cases involving newborns.

They thus articulated a test for "independent life" in addition to the *spacial* test of complete expulsion or extraction, outside and clear of the body of the mother. That decisively set aside the references to probability of meaningful life outside the womb along with the indeterminate reference to duration of life which the court introduced in considering not only the meaning of *viability* but also the meaning of *liveborn*. Here, alone, do I find crucial reference to the manslaughter law uncorrupted by *Wade-Bolton*. Given acceptable legal signs of life, the death of a newborn can be brought about negligently or wantonly in no time at all, so to speak, or in no great span of time. However, I ought to point out that, from a lawyer's point of view, these justices not only articulated their test for independent life, they went beyond that to weigh the evidence and decide the issue. That ordinarily is regarded as a usurpation of a jury's role.

On the matter of a prejudicial shift from the indictment to the crime defined (or ill defined) by the judge's instruction, the three justices used "inside-outside" language in assessing Dr. Edelin's prenatal and postnatal conduct. If the fetus died while still in the uterus or only partially removed, there was no manslaughter even if it breathed there and even if something "lethal" was done during that three- to five-minute interval before the fetus was "clear" of the body. (This would include the sweep of the physician's fingers to detach the placenta). Conversely, if the fetus died when entirely clear of the mother's body but did not breathe there, in the requisite sense, again there could have been no manslaughter. In either case, there was no live person whose death could be caused by reckless conduct. Whichever way the judge's instructions were interpreted, there could have

---

of life—that is, heartbeats and respiration. Heartbeats are to be distinguished from several transient cardiac contractions; respirations are to be distinguished from fleeting respiratory efforts or gasps . . ." (American College of Obstetricians and Gynecologists, Committee on Terminology, Obstetric-Gynecologic Terminology 452 [Hughe's ed., 1972]). One can only wish that the court or some of the justices had noticed the subsequent statement and plea of the American College (see chap. 1, n. 5, above).

been no action compatible with manslaughter. There was no actus reus of manslaughter, apart from examining Dr. Edelin's *bona fides* in believing there was not. I add, if he had proceeded somehow recklessly in performing that abortion, such action would have been cause for a malpractice suit, not manslaughter. Moreover, the prosecution waffled by moving from that three- to five-minute interval to trying to prove outside or partially outside breathing, and by composing a not unreasonable notion—what I, above, called a transitive interpretation—of the delivery process under these modern conditions.

So far so good. Still the reader pondering this case must, I think, ask the most important question: Cannot an indictment for manslaughter be one way the people of this nation try to find out, through the prosecutor's office, whether the courts will update the law of homicide and manslaughter to include detachment of the placenta (when it is the organ of a possibly viable infant) to mean "independence of" the mother's body equivalent to cutting the umblical cord in old-fashioned birth?

If not, then this needs to be done by legislation, either by articulation of the law with respect to causing the death of a fellow human being or by standard-of-care provisions in comprehensive legislation dealing with abortion. Although invited to do so by *Wade,* the states so far have made little headway, against that inflexible regime, toward protecting by law and from all possible harm the potentiality or the actuality of human life from possible viability to term. This being the case, we cannot agree with the conclusion of the court that the precedental importance of its decision is reduced because the *Edelin* case arose in an "interregnum"—"a kind of interval not likely to be repeated." For, as we have seen, *Wade-Bolton* was far more a regime or dispensation in its influence in this case than it was an interregnum.

Chief Justice Hennessey's Dissenting Opinion

The Chief Justice dissented from the court's conclusion that the defendant was entitled at his trial to a directed verdict of not guilty. Yet, despite the many errors Hennessey found in the court's opinion, he still would have reversed the verdict of guilty and ordered a new trial. Hennessey's target, again, was the trial judge's instructions. It is difficult to present the fault Hennessey found in the judge's instruction because of the chief justice's evident belief that the court was assuming an improper appellate role, both as to law and toward the facts to be decided in this tangled case, and because he alone among the justices seems to have kept clearly in mind the fact that the supreme judicial court should not retry the case. Still Hennessey believed that Dr. Edelin deserved better instructions than the trial judge gave.

The defendant's state of mind was a crucial consideration in this case. A physician needs protection from the "overhanging risk of incurring criminal liability at the hands of a second-guessing jury." [24] In the *Edelin* case, protection against unjustified second-guessing should have been accomplished, not by precluding the jury's consideration of disputed facts, but by appropriate jury instructions. The defendant was entitled to an instruction concerning the "reasonableness" standard: "that the defendant formed his judgment of nonviability either in bad faith, *or unreasonably,* based upon facts he knew *or reasonably* should have known" (italics added). The standard of reckless conduct in a manslaughter case is at once a subjective and an objective one. Hennessey found no instruction concerning the reasonableness of Dr. Edelin's subjective beliefs at the time; yet not only the bona fides of his beliefs but also the reasonableness of those beliefs were to be assessed by the jury—without instruction as to this more objective requirement.

Such an instruction, it seems to me, might have worked to Dr. Edelin's disadvantage in a new trial. Still one must admire the chief justice for adherence to the law as he viewed it, joining his brothers on the court in reversing the conviction while knowing they were going to enter a judgment of acquittal.

Hennessey is clearly pursuing his quarrel with "the Justice Kaplan opinion" (as he called the court's opinion) in stating the instructions he thought proper. For the sense of the court's opinion seemed to him to be that "the proclaimed medical judgment of the defendant overrides the opposing evidence and extinguished the issues of fact." Such a subjective test would have to show "actual malice" or proof that the defendant had "*actual* pre-abortion knowledge of viability." Such proof "equates with murder not with manslaughter." In a manslaughter case, "the medical judgment of the physician may not be proof against criminal conviction where it is shown that his judgment

24. Quoting Mr. Justice Stewart in *United States* v. *Vuitch,* 402 U.S. 62, 97 (1971).

was in bad faith *or unreasonable*." It was for the jury to say whether the defendant's medical judgments were within the bounds of "reasonableness": the defendant was entitled to have that issue decided under adequate jury instructions. Even in face of Chief Justice Hennessey's evident leanings (as I read his opinion) as to the probable outcome of a new trial, he was a "legalist" still willing to reverse the judgment of the trial court because of the lack of more stringent instructions.[25]

The rest of the Hennessey opinion is more interesting for moral reflection upon the intersections of medicine, law, and ethics. The court's opinion was in error, says Hennessey, both in the way it high-handedly dealt with the facts and in its statement of the applicable law.

"The Judge Kaplan opinion indulges in a weighing and discarding of evidence in a manner permitted only to the jury." The fact that crucial evidence was controverted (whether or not the fetus was viable or born alive) and that there were alternative explanations of acknowledged facts (the three- to five-minute delay) in now way warrants an appellate court to direct a verdict of acquittal. Such matters were for the jury to decide. As Hennessey said in a note, "The weight and believability of the evidence has possible relevance at the appellate level only as to the issue whether the defendant might be entitled to a new trial because the jury's verdict was against the weight of the evidence." Within the bounds of appellate judicial restraint, Hennessey rehearses some of the evidence. However, his argument was not that upon weighing the evidence a jury should declare Dr. Edelin guilty or not guilty, but simply that the supreme judicial court should not have preempted a new trial by entering a verdict of acquittal.

On the law applicable to this case, Hennessey believes the court to be equally in error. Here we take up again, and in a new way, some important themes already discussed in this chapter. There was for Hennessey substantial evidence of live birth—enough to meet "even

25. Imagining myself to be a prospective juror, I would certainly need an instruction concerning "reasonably knew" (if Hennessey is correct as to the law). Under such instructions, it would seem to me more difficult to reach the conclusion (expressed above) that Dr. Edelin was clearly not guilty of the mens rea of reckless manslaughter. Facing the difficulty of evaluating such an "objective" component in Dr. Edelin's "subjective" state of mind, perhaps the reader will join with me in becoming a conscientious objector to jury service. One way to do this is to join that sect of Mennonites who practice quite literally the New Testament injunction that brother should not go to law against brother.

the defendant's assertion that there must be proof that there was a chance for 'meaningful life' or survival for a 'minimum period,' within the meaning of *Wade-Bolton*." Again, the chief justice is only saying that such disputed evidence was there for the jury to decide, *not* that the jury should have weighed the evidence a particular way. He adds at this point, however, "I am not sure what those terms mean"; and in the next sentence he expresses, I believe, an undeniable implication of the law of manslaughter: "I do state that it is not for any doctor to guide his conduct by his own estimate as to the duration or quality of life likely to occur."

On the matter of wanton or reckless conduct, Hennessey "would agree that there was not sufficient evidence for the jury's consideration *if* [he] could accept the majority's premise that the judge in his instructions permitted the jury to consider only the postnatal conduct of the defendant." He reading of the instructions was that "the judge permitted consideration of both prenatal and postnatal conduct." To interject an analogy, the death or injury suffered by a baby in an automobile accident must occur after the birth of the subject for there to bè an actionable cause in the baby's behalf; but the pre-accident, prenatal behavior of an automobile driver involving another car driven by a pregnant woman would not be excluded from consideration in a trial. Or suppose a fictional case. A person with malice aforethought wishes to accomplish two things. He wants a baby to be born alive (so that it will inherit an estate), and he wishes the baby then to die (so the money will pass to him). He accomplishes this by giving the pregnant woman an injection that will cause premature birth and, by slower action, kill the bady. Let us also suppose that the accused is a physician who did this while performing an abortion. Would it not be outrageous to exclude his prenatal actions from consideration at the trial?

Hennessey argues that a valid instruction to include prenatal conduct (and he so reads the judge's words) falls within the meaning of *Wade-Bolton* and within the meaning of the common law. Thus Hennessey commends the judge's conduct of the trial (e.g., his allowing the prosecutor in his closing statement to use prenatal evidence as proof of the indictment for reckless conduct) and his instruction for not limiting the jury's consideration to postnatal conduct. The jury necessarily understood the charge to be based on "all relevant conduct" of the defendant.

"Given a live birth," he argues, "the common law of Massachusetts permits consideration of the defendant's prenatal conduct in support of a manslaughter indictment." There were no Massachusetts cases to cite; but "this is not surprising in view of the applicability, prior to *Wade-Bolton,* of the Commonwealth's anti-abortion statutes." In other words, instead of appealing to *Wade-Bolton* as an interregnum modifying the manslaughter law to be applied in this case, Hennessey appealed to the long-standing antiabortion statutory regime to explain why case law in Massachusetts contains no cases applying the common law meaning of manslaughter to infants in abortion-related instances. The centuries-old precedents of the common law were the reigning principles; that law would not have been applied ex post facto in this case, nor would it have been a violation of the defendant's right to due process.

That went to the point of the legitimacy of considering Dr. Edelin's prenatal conduct.

> Given birth followed by death, it would be extraordinary if the common law did not permit consideration of all relevant conduct of a defendant in a manslaughter case. Clearly the doctor's duty to the viable fetus arises at the time he knows or reasonably should know that he could be dealing with such a subject. In any case where he is fairly chargeable with such knowledge during the prenatal stage, it would be incongruous to exclude proof of his conduct during that period.

Within that strong statement of the applicable law of manslaughter, Chief Justice Hennessey expresses again his sole reason for reversing the judgment of the trial court: A charge of recklessness must show that the defendant "reasonably should know" that he was dealing with a viable fetus that could be born alive, and the instructions did not explain the reasonableness standard in terms of which the jury was to weigh the prenatal and postnatal evidence (pro and con).

In support of his argument against the court's belief that the *Wade-Bolton* regime modulated the manslaughter law at least to the extent of precluding consideration of prenatal conduct, Chief Justice Hennessey became the only justice in the *Edelin* case whose opinion cites, from *Planned Parenthood,* the words of the United States Supreme Court which strongly implied that Missouri's standard-of-care provision was unnecessary because "a physician's or other person's criminal failure to protect a live born infant surely will be subject to prosecution . . . under the state's criminal statutes."

Then in a single sentence Hennessey's partly dissenting opinion expresses the only conceivable way in which *Wade-Bolton* and the law of manslaughter can be understood together while neither invades or weakens the other:

> Just as the States may now provide criminal anti-abortion statutes which apply to the stage subsequent to viability, so may the laws of homicide apply in cases of a viable fetus, a live birth and subsequent death caused by prenatal and postnatal conduct.[26]

26. It is worth calling attention to certain *possible* conclusions of fact which Chief Justice Hennessey believed a jury *could* reach (if the instructions had explained "reasonable knowledge") because these are examples pertinent to the goal of drawing a clearer line between abortion as a lethal procedure and abortion as a severance procedure:

> The jury could . . . find from the evidence that the hysterotomy method is consistent with the production of a live child, but that the techniques used by the defendant made a relatively easy operation difficult. They could find that, prior to the sixteenth week of pregnancy, hysterotomy procedure involves separation of the placenta after initial incision into the uterus and before the fetus is removed from the mother's body. At or prior to the sixteenth week the fetus is very small, weighing about 100 grams, and it is possible, after separating the placenta, to remove the fetus and sac intact. A twenty-four-week fetus, however, would weigh 600 grams and intact removal would be impossible. The defendant knew that the gestational age of the fetus was far beyond sixteen weeks and that it was far heavier than 100 grams. The defendant knew, before the operation, of medical opinions relating to twenty-four weeks, and he himself thought it was twenty to twenty-two weeks. There was evidence of a weight of 700 grams, and he could be held to a (pre-operative) fair idea of the size from his prior examinations of the mother. It could be found that he unnecessarily used a technique which endangered the fetus's chance of survival. There was further evidence from which it could be inferred that anesthesia techniques were unnecessarily used which could be deleterious to the health of a viable fetus.
>
> From all this the jury could conclude that the defendant, knowing he was engaged in a late-term abortion and that a live birth was possible, acted with disregard for the consequences to the subject. Additionally it could be found that he proceeded with methods which unnecessarily endangered the subject. The defendant's total failure to have regard for the subject's well being was consistent with his testimony that he regarded the death of the fetus as "presupposed."

As trier of the facts, a jury *could* (or it might not) have found the foregoing to be the case—provided only that Dr. Edelin got what he deserved from the judge, namely, an instruction to the jury about the meaning of "reasonable" presumption of knowledge. Since the latter was lacking, Chief Justice Hennessey reversed the judgment

A Lawyer's Opinion of the Case

I asked a legal consultant to give me his opinion of the *Edelin* case. He is a lawyer in Massachusetts. His name, I shall say, is Oliver Wendell Sinequanon; I have not asked him his ethnic origins, nor do I imagine that matters much to him. As a lawyer, he is not interested as I am in retrospective analysis of the *Edelin* case. His interest is rather a practical and a prospective one; he wants to determine what the law will be judged to be in the case of present and future physician-clients who come to him for legal advice concerning their present and future liability. He needs to *predict* in their behalf, as I do not. At the same time, Sinequanon is an intelligent man, not a legal craftsman or tactician only. I judge that his view may be of as much interest to general readers as it was to me.

Sinequanon began abstractly, probably because he was speaking with me. Then he presented a scenario of what probably went on during the justices' deliberations, which led to the outcome in this case. It is a plausible story; but a story nonetheless. That scenario is still of great interest because it gathers up into story form many of the themes we have reviewed; the suppositive story enlivens those themes. Finally, my counselor Sinequanon got around to making some observations about a lawyer's practical position in offering sound predictive advice to physician-clients now practicing in Massachusetts.

The issue that ultimately disposed of the case, according to my lawyer friend, was the question of prenatal and postnatal conduct—in the legal context of the justices' views. Three justices (Kaplan, Braucher, and Wilkins) held that the manslaughter statute, especially after *Wade-Bolton,* may look only at the postnatal conduct of the aborting physician. In this case, these three justices agreed, the judge's instructions were so limited. They voted for reversal and acquittal because there was not enough evidence of postnatal reckless or wanton behavior to go to the jury. As they point out in a separate part of the opinion, they would also have reversed because of insufficient evidence of live birth and because of prejudicial variance

---

and would have ordered a new trial. His partly dissenting opinion suggests that developments in the case law of manslaughter *could* accomplish the result sought by standard-of-care provisions. These are the two options. Leaders of public opinion—least of all, the medical profession—should not oppose *both.*

between the accusation and the proof at trial. But prenatal-postnatal was the dispositive issue, and that led to the concurrence of other justices.

Reardon and Quirico held that the manslaughter statute, even after *Wade-Bolton,* allowed consideration of both prenatal and postnatal conduct. Yet "the law of the case" set by the judge's instructions permitted (they said) the jury to consider only Dr. Edelin's postnatal conduct. These two justices also held that there was sufficient evidence to go to a jury on live birth and there was no prejudicial variance between the accusation and the proof. Still the first point controlled the decision in this case: the judge's instruction limiting consideration to Dr. Edelin's postnatal conduct (*contra* the manslaughter statute).

Chief Justice Hennessey found concordance between conduct cognizable under the manslaughter statute and conduct cognizable under the judge's instruction: both embraced both prenatal and postnatal behavior; and he agreed with Reardon and Quirico on sufficient evidence to go to a jury on the question of live birth, and on no prejudicial variance in the accusation. Hennessey voted to reverse and remand for a new trial because the trial judge failed to instruct the jury as to the standard to be applied to the knowledge reasonably to be expected of Dr. Edelin during his prenatal and postnatal conduct.

All justices agreed that the evidence of Edelin's postnatal conduct was insufficient to establish wanton or reckless conduct. The view of Kaplan, Braucher, and Wilkins on the law of manslaughter, especially after *Wade-Bolton,* as well as their interpretation of the instructions, allowed them only to look at such postnatal conduct. Reardon and Quirico interpret the judge's instructions to be limited strictly to postnatal conduct, which although faulty (measured by their view of the law of manslaughter) established "the law of the case" and controlled this particular decision. Hennessey's reading of the instructions comports with his idea of the manslaughter law: both prenatal and postnatal conduct are to be examined. While unanimously reversing the conviction, it was thus by a five to one vote that the court determined to order acquittal. The court reached this result without dealing with the issues of live birth or prejudicial shift in the accusation.

Now for my lawyer-friend Sinequanon's scenario, his suppositive story of what went on in the ebb and flow of the justice's deliberations to obtain reversal and acquittal. I myself felt a little threatened by his presumption in claiming to go behind the robes of mystery with which (for the common good) we surround the legitimate magisterial authority of ultimate judicial decision-makers.

After the initial conference following the hearing of oral arguments, all six justices voted for reversal but split, three to three, on acquittal or new trial. The result was clearly incomplete and unacceptable, since it meant no disposition of the case. Presumably the court could have ordered a rehearing and even have appointed another judge to sit with them to break the tie. For any number of obvious reasons this was not the chosen course of action.

At a second conference Kaplan was unable to convince Hennessey, Reardon, and Quirico that the law of manslaughter in Massachusetts, even as impacted by *Wade-Bolton,* limits consideration to the postnatal conduct of an aborting physician. However, Kaplan did convince Reardon and Quirico that the only proper interpretation of the instructions is that the trial judge limited the jury to examination of Edelin's postnatal conduct. These instructions, in other words, were the controlling "law of the case" regardless of the manslaughter statute. Against my incipient protest, Sinequanon said: "Note the tone of Kaplan's footnote 20: 'We need not underscore the seriousness of a possible conclusion that the judge's charge was actually ambiguous on the point and could be understood either way by individual jurors.' "

An interesting argument, he went on. In the first place, *ambiguous* is a mislabeling. Hennessey reads the charge as all inclusive—that is, covering both prenatal and postnatal—not ambiguous. Secondly, even if ambiguous, the only danger evident in ambiguous instructions is the danger of a new trial of the case after the ambiguity has been eliminated. Of course, the ambiguity could not be eliminated because the court split three to three on this very point of law. And presumably this ambiguity is now a part of Massachusetts jurisprudence.[27]

27. I protested that Sinequanon was rather peremptorily settling the main issue in dispute among the justices, namely, the pre-*Edelin* law of manslaughter. He seemed too sure Hennessey was right about "reasonableness" and that (on the conduct issue alone, where the case rested) Hennessey, Reardon, and Quirico were right about a jury considering any actions or omissions relevant to the charge. Oliver Wendell

calmly drew down from his shelves a casebook used in law schools (not in Massachusetts only; he himself studied law in another state). Turning to the section "Legislative Grading of Unintended Killings," he showed me how, in order to explain the meaning of reckless manslaughter to law students everywhere in the United States the text uses precisely the two Massachusetts cases Hennessey chiefly relied on. The text says the judge instructed the jury correctly in *Commonwealth* v. *Welansky* 316 Mass. 383, 55 N.E. 2d 902 (1944). That judge's instructions are used in teaching the law; I too quote extensively so that the reader may join the class:

> Usually wanton or reckless conduct consists of an affirmative act . . . in disregard of probable harmful consequences to another. But whereas in the present case there is a duty of care, . . . wanton or reckless conduct may consist of intentional failure to take such care in disregard of the probable harmful consequences to them or of their right to care.
>
> To define wanton or reckless conduct so as to distinguish it clearly from negligence and gross negligence is not easy. Sometimes the word "wilful" is prefaced to the words "wanton" and "reckless" in expressing the concept. That only blurs it. Wilful means intentional. In the phrase "wilful, wanton or reckless conduct," if "wilful" modifies "conduct" it introduces something different from wanton or reckless conduct, even though the legal result is the same. Wilfully causing harm is a wrong, but a different wrong from wantonly or recklessly causing harm. If "wilful" modifies "wanton or reckless conduct" its use is accurate. What must be intended is the conduct, not the resulting harm. The words "wanton" and "reckless" are practically synonymous in this connection, although the word "wanton" may contain a suggestion of arrogance or insolence or heartlessness that is lacking in the word "reckless."

Then the trial judge in the 1944 *Welansky* case proceeded to quote from the 1844 *Pierce* case on which Hennessey also relied:

> The standard of wanton or reckless conduct is at once subjective and objective, as has been recognized ever since Commonwealth v. Pierce, 138 Mass. 165, 52 Am. Rep. 264. Knowing facts that would cause a reasonable man to know the danger is equivalent to knowing the danger. . . . The judge charged the jury correctly when he said, "To constitute wanton or reckless conduct, as distinguished from mere negligence, grave danger to others must have been apparent and the defendant must have chosen to run the risk rather than alter his conduct so as to avoid the act or omission which caused the harm." If the grave danger was in fact realized by the defendant, his subsequent voluntary act or omission which caused the harm amounts to wanton or reckless conduct, no matter whether the ordinary man would have realized the gravity of the danger or not. But even if a particular defendant is so stupid (or) so heedless . . . that in fact he did not realize the grave danger, he cannot escape the imputation of wanton or reckless conduct in his dangerous act or omission, if an ordinary normal man under the same circumstances would have realized the gravity of the danger. A man may be reckless within the meaning of the law although he himself thought he was careful. [Sanford H. Kadish and Monrad G. Paulsen, *Criminal Law and its Processes,* 2d ed. (Boston: Little, Brown and Co., 1969), pp. 313–14]

I understood my practical lawyer-friend to be asking whether the ambiguity now a part of Massachusetts jurisprudence could spread to the common law of other jurisdictions, even as those cases *contra* have been cardinal in legal instruction to date.

Thus by using the very ambiguity he abhors, Kaplan found a way out of the situation. With Reardon and Quirico agreeing on the interpretation of the instructions, the legal doctrine of the law of the case is applied and not only reversal but acquittal results. Reardon and Quirico could dispose of the case in this manner without, from *their* point of view, allowing *Wade-Bolton* to change the law of manslaughter in Massachusetts. By sticking by "the law of the case," they could acquit Edelin and avoid the chaos of a new trial. All the justices, of course, were well aware of the list of organizations filing briefs amici curiae in support of the defendant.

Sinequanon suggested that there may have been an aura surrounding this case which highlighted the wisdom, propriety, and maybe the necessity of making a final determination at the appellate level to forego further rending of the social fabric by a second trial. (That was the "danger" which Kaplan awakened in the minds of Braucher and Wilkins.) Perhaps this was all the more wise, proper, and necessary because of the South Boston school situation. . . . Here I stopped his sociological speculations.

To appreciate how thin the legal thread is by which Edelin's acquittal hangs, note the following, Sinequanon went on. The Supreme Judicial Court of Massachusetts was able to muster a majority in favor of acquittal by finding five justices who insisted on interpreting the instructions to apply manslaughter law to postnatal conduct only. Of the five, two acquitted only by deciding not to overrule a jury instruction which they felt incorrectly stated the law. They were not bound to accept the trial court's instruction; they chose to do so and justified their decision by invoking the doctrine of the law of the case. Had the trial court instructed the jury clearly that both prenatal and postnatal conduct could be considered, the objection of Justices Reardon and Quirico would have been met and presumably they would have voted to affirm. (Their concurrence indicates they had no interest in instructions concerning reasonableness, unlike the chief justice. Setting a standard for the reasonableness of Edelin's belief that the fetus was dead was Hennessey's mechanism for preventing undue second-guessing of professional medical decisions by a lay jury.)

If explicit jury instructions had been given that prenatal and postnatal conduct could be considered, the court presumably would have voted four to two for reversal because the objection of Reardon and

Quirico would have been answered. That would still leave open the issue of disposition of the case, assuming at least three for acquittal and one for a new trial. Under such circumstances acquittal may well result, but this is not clear and there may not be specific guidance on this narrow technical point. If the instructions had also satisfied Hennessey on the reasonableness-of-belief issue, the vote on reversal or affirmance would have been three to three, and the verdict below would have been upheld.

Running through my lawyer-friend's speculation was, of course, that the commonwealth still had the burden of proof even in face of erroneous instructions. These become the law of the case in terms of which to judge whether that burden was borne successfully. That—I understood him to say—was the reason Reardon and Quirico could be persuaded to give controlling effect to the instructions, which in their view were contrary to the manslaughter law. Likewise, Kaplan had to bifurcate the liveborn / conduct issues—if for no other reason than to gain the agreement of the other justices and so avoid the danger of the social disruption that might be occasioned by a new trial.

I understood Sinequanon already to have turned his thoughts to the present practical value of any lawyer's counsel to a physician-client. The legal issue now is, he said, How should a trial court with a similar case before it instruct a jury on the same or similar facts? How should a lawyer advise a client in such a situation? On the issue of the application of the manslaughter statute to the prenatal conduct of the aborting physician, it is dealer's choice: three justices say that as a matter of law only postnatal conduct may be considered; three say as a matter of law that all relevant conduct, including prenatal, is covered by the manslaughter statute. On this issue the judge in another trial may not know what the law is, but he does know that he can't be reversed.

That seemed a bit too cynical even for me. But the quandary of legal prediction seems very like the uncertainty physicians feel; and it is no consolation for anyone to point out that both lawyers and physicians have helped to create the predicament they are in. This leads me directly to the question posed in the final section of this chapter.

Is There a Legislative Solution?

Looking back over the important moral questions that arise at the intersection of medicine and law at "the first of life," perhaps the simplest solution would be that proposed by Sissela Bok. She suggested that abortion should be prohibited after viability, except to save the life and health of the mother.[28] That has support in the fact that physicians do not like to do late abortions; the earlier the better for all consciously concerned. Such a prohibition, well publicized, would encourage early decisions. Furthermore, *Wade* says expressly that the several states may even go so far as to prohobit abortion to promote their interest in the potentiality of life after viability has been reached.

Whether Bok's legislative solution is a good one (or will work) depends on the answer to two sets of questions—one addressed to the medical profession, the other addressed to our courts, including the Supreme Court, in view of the cases we have examined.

If endangered health were one exception allowing abortion after possible viability, would this be *stringently* interpreted—not loosely, even fraudulently, as in the days before *Wade-Bolton?* Would abortion be practiced as a "severance procedure" whenever it is possible to do so without very *serious* risk to the health of the mother? The medical ethics reaffirmed by the American College of Gynecologists and Obstetricians would support the most stringent medical effort to promote both patients' lives. Indeed, many physicians believe that, with proper management, there are no *medical* reasons, no "life and health of the mother" reasons, for abortion in any case; or, at least, that such situations are very rare. In juxtaposition with the *Wade-Bolton* "area of liberties," this would seem to mean that a physician's care can be extended alike to his two patients when the fetus is possibly viable. At the same time, the liberty of abortion for the first twelve weeks greatly lessens the pressure that once led to loose interpretations of the woman's "health." Only the most cynical should suppose in advance that medical ethics at the first of life could not recover some of its former vigor.

28. "The Unwanted Child: Caring for the Fetus Born Alive after an Abortion," *Hastings Center Report* 6, no. 5 (October 1976) : 10–15. See also chap. 1, no. 26 and text.

Whether Bok's proposal is choiceworthy depends, secondly, on whether such state statutes could be legally effective; and that would require first of all that an affirmative answer be given to the question, Will the statutory provisions bear constitutional scrutiny? We have noted the plain language of *Wade*. But the Court has subsequently imposed barriers which suggest that legislative attempts to "reach back" may be struck down, or at least that such laws will have to be drafted with great care. For if abortion should be a severance procedure whenever possible, if the medical profession means to care for both patients with the medical management now available to it, and if in our society we do not mean to diminish the law's protection of human life, the following are some of the elements of statutes prohibiting abortion after possible viability that must be deemed to have no constitutional flaw. Let the reader judge whether or not the courts would have to reverse their present trend.

Viability would have to be *defined* on the safe side—twenty weeks and 500 grams estimated weight. That was the National Commission's "operational definition" of a "possibly viable infant." Such a definition does not *locate* viability: physician discretion in *determining* viability was left free within those operational or cautionary measurements. Language like "unless the physician certifies that the fetus is not viable" could appropriately be used—still leaving physicians free to *locate* the viable and the nonviable. The language of *Planned Parenthood* upholding Missouri's definition of viability would not seem to be stretched too far by encompassing this requirement.

Such a statutory definition would have to be reexamined once a year, and the states' comprehensive abortion statutes revised accordingly. Alternatively and more practically, legislation could empower an appropriate administrative agency, such as the health department, to update on a periodic basis the definition set forth in the statute. That is the rapid pace of medical advancement in salvaging newborns (which itself may be questioned; but, wherever we are in the "state of the art," its benefits should not be arbitrarily extended to some and withheld from other *particular* lives). Or a contrary alternative might be chosen: the courts themselves could admit medical evidence on the question of viability—to go to the jury—and case law could develop accordingly. Courts could be freed or directed by statute to do so. Such legislative solutions should be our proximate goal.

However, we can go deeper still by recalling some of the basic moral assumptions of the present age that have been examined in the foregoing chapters. One such tenet is atomistic individualism, which erodes every bond of life with life—those bonds into which we enter (spousal) and those into which we are born (filial). This prevalent philosophy has now been brought down to the teen and preteen ages under the concept of "privacy" in *Planned Parenthood*. We shall again confront that radically individualistic concept when we come to the *Quinlan* case. Another such tenet—so silently operating as to be virtually unquestioned today—is Cartesian dualism. In lay language, this means placing a partition between the person: mind, or soul, and freedom on one side, and the body, biology, sexuality, and procreation on the other. The "religious" do this by talking enthusiastically about the *human* act or about interpersonal relations; others, by resting every ethical question upon subjective autonomy or on a reasonableness anchored in no reality. Such dualism is also the clue that explains the persuasiveness of quality-of-life judgments. A third tenet of our age I call the Baconian project—that is, the pervasive notion that, for every problem produced by technology used for the relief of the human condition, there will be an as-yet-distant technical solution. That, too, is among our certainties.

Put these fundamental assumptions (now strangely called "liberal") together, and we have *trends*—the (almost) inexorable trends toward a future nobody actually chooses or need choose. It is, therefore, pertinent for me to ask the reader to think with me along the line of these trends extended into one of our "possible futures." I applaud anyone who believes these extensions implausible. In the preceding chapters I myself have stayed close to the cases we have examined and have searched for ways in which the protections of human life enshrined in Western morals and law may be preserved. I have sought legislative and judicial solutions.

Under continuing attack from the tenets I have mentioned, however, this may be a forlorn hope. There must be a *human nature* (and *belief* in a human nature) that will rise up in revulsion against these dehumanizing trends; there must be in us an ineradicable *creation* (and *belief* in a doctrine of creation) or Providence or the Holy Spirit to bring about an earthquake (mildly called, above, a sea change) in contemporary moral opinion if these trends are reversible. With amniocentesis and genetic abortion, the human uterus is already a device for "people selection." It is a "half-way technology." More such technologies will follow. The intensive care nursery is another such technology now sometimes used for the same purpose. I have not noticed any great public upsurge against these practices, to be considered fully in chapters 5 and 6, below. Instead, exquisite defenses, tortured efforts to wrest free from Western morality and law, are most publicized. Perhaps I am a person of little faith; still it requires *some* faith or other to believe that modern societies will change course. Therefore, I judge it proper to ask the reader—perhaps only as a thought-experiment—to follow these trends into one possible future.

In the course of time it seems evident that—in the intersection of medicine, law, and ethics at the edge of the first of life—we are moving toward acceptance of extracorporeal gestation and abortion as a severance procedure at any stage of pregnancy. Women will at last be free from nature, if they wish to be. Our society need not (as I have shown in this chapter) weaken the law's ancient protection of each particular individual life. Nevertheless, with in vitro fertilization progressed as far as maintaining such life for two weeks, and with the salvaging of prematures pushed back to just after twenty weeks gestation, there remain only eighteen weeks of uterine support left to duplicate and replace. Then, I suggest, our protection of life by implementing the correct notion of abortion as a severance procedure may prove to be simply a way station on a longer journey into the night.

Indeed, the achievement of extracorporeal gestation, along with "severance" of one individual from another from womb to tomb (or rather from seed to dust), will not be so much a product of medical technology. It will rather be a fitting consequence of our atomistic, individualistic culture and its dualistic understanding of "freedom." Long before technological severance has become complete, it is far more likely that the law's ancient protection will have been withdrawn, and the morality on which it was based will have become so dim a memory that generations to come will have lost even the ability to ask themselves whether that humanistic ethics was not better for humankind. Our self-image, women's self-image, men's self-image will have changed radically. There will be no birth, no begetting; or need not be. And where birth and begetting rests that radically on radical *choice,* parenting will no longer be. Most of all, our children's self-image will have changed radically; they will become what they know they came from. They will be "products"—if not made-to-order, still chosen as ordered by finally autonomous wills.[29] No surprises, all "selections." And, I fear, boundless freedom will mean boundless submission—as Dostoevski discerned.

Farfetched, the reader may think. At the moment neonatologists in charge of intensive care nurseries seem to be halting further technical advance at twenty-four weeks. While there are good reasons for stopping here or earlier—reasons related both to the welfare of such infants and to not learning to fabricate our progeny—we need to ask why precisely that otherwise nonrational boundary is being mutually agreed to. It happens also to be the line at which, on anyone's reckoning, abortion must not be allowed if many viable fetuses are not to be destroyed. It is also the case that to leave that earlier span of gestation where it is will insure maximum advance in the identification and elimination of defective fetuses without running the risk of doing anything unlawful. So by this tacit agreement, extracorporeal gestation may not be in our futures.

One could wish that this was because of respect for nature over technology, or because of our ancient protections of human life from either destruction or imperious interference with its dying. Instead, I suggest, that on both sides of this line our half-way technologies will be left free to engage in people-selection by quality-of-life judgments without too much danger of arousing public memory of a moribund moral sensibility. We have yet to consider policies of neglect of defective newborns, in two chapters to come. Here it is sufficient to say that such policies as well as widespread acceptance of the practice of abortion are the ineluctable fate of every modern technological so-

29. See Paul Ramsey, "Shall We 'Reproduce'?" *Journal of the American Medical Association* 220, nos. 11 and 12 (June 5 and June 12, 1972): 1346–50, 1480–85. Also, the little poem I quoted in *Fabricated Man* (New Haven: Yale University Press, 1970), p. 60:

> I have a pet hen whose name is
> Probable. She lays eggs in concept,
> being a sophist-bird. But not in
> reality at all; those would be
> inferior eggs: for thought is superior
> to reality.
>
> —Frederick Winsor, *The Space Child's Mother-Goose.*

ciety—and, so far as the eyes can see, of humankind on this planet. Let no reader suppose that these projections of mine are a fruit of my well-known opposition to so-called liberal abortion practice. To the contrary. Far more fearful than more than one million legal abortions a year in the United States (those are *individual* souls, the religious might say; God will take care of them) is the fact that the human womb, with women's own consent, is being transformed into a machine for making better babies, interchangeable ones; and, as in a factory, those products that are flawed are discarded. But there will be future factories to replace our present primitive artifices. The human self-image is turning into the image of technological production.[30] This looming peril concerns the soul of the human species on this planet. God can take care of that too, the religious might say, but let's not make it so devilishly difficult for him to save humankind from self-destruction.

30. Some medical writers already refer to infants as "products of pregnancy"—when they have defective chromosomes (*Medical Opinion,* May 1976, p. 6). See Hans O. Tiefel, "The Language of Medical Science and Moral Concerns," *Hastings Center Report* (forthcoming) for, in general, the consequences of using *scientific* language in *humanistic* discourse.

PART TWO

The Last of Life

4

"Euthanasia" and Dying Well Enough

In order to think straight about the question of the morality of euthanasia, I want first of all to convince you that:

1. It is better if you do not know the Greek language or the root meaning of the word.
2. You do not need to learn that, while to kill someone directly (or with direct intention) is damnable, you are excusable if you kill someone only indirectly (or with indirect voluntariness).
3. You do not need to deploy such subtleties as saying you are accountable for another's death if you were the *active* agent of it, but not accountable if you were *passive* while the death occurred.
4. You do not need to prove to the waiting world of philosophers and theologians that there is a crucial moral distinction to be drawn between acts of *omission* and acts of *commission,* even though the consequence is the same.
5. You do not need to puzzle for very long over how to classify treatments according to the distinction between "ordinary" and "extraordinary" medical means of saving life—the first [supposedly being] morally mandatory and the second [supposedly] dispensable. both in past Christian medical ethics and in the view of most physicians.

These distinctions may be important to take up in other connections—I happen to believe some are—but neither separately nor together do they serve to solve or dissolve or even to clarify the question of euthanasia; they serve to confuse moral discourse. Yet it seems nearly impossible to dislodge such language.

The title of this chapter is taken from a recent study pamphlet issued by the General Synod (Church of England) Board of Social

Responsibility. "Man should be enabled to 'die well' " is the theme of that pamphlet. It goes on to say: "This is the literal meaning of the word 'euthanasia' and, if we were starting afresh, there would be a good case for using this word to express our common concern for the welfare of the dying. But this is no longer possible, since the word has now become established in popular usage with a more precise meaning." [1]

That "more precise"—and corrupted—meaning, I suggest, is that human beings should sometimes choose death as an end. The choice of one's own death or that of another as an end is now the meaning packed into the word *euthanasia*. Therefore, it occurs to us, when discussing the morality of the matter, to attach certain predicates that describe the manner in which death is brought about or the means to death as a chosen end. We speak of "active" or "passive" euthanasia, of "directly" or "indirectly" disposing a patient to death, of whether death came by acts of omission or by acts of commission, by action or by abstention.

I would get rid of all those terms. We are wrongly led to them by our popular and irreformable usage of the word *euthanasia* for "choosing death as an end."

Choosing Life and Life's Choices

The conviction that one should always choose life lies at the heart of the practice of medicine and nursing. In that sense, medical ethics must be pro-life. In this respect modern medicine was profoundly influenced by Judaism and Christianity.

The immorality of choosing death as an end is founded upon our religious faith that life is a *gift*. A gift is not given if it is not received as a gift, no more than a gift can be given out of anything other than kindness or generosity (to give out of flattery or duplicity or to curry favor is not a gift).[2] To choose death as an end is to throw the gift back in the face of the giver; it would be to defeat his gift-giving. That, I suppose, is the reason suicide and murder were called "mortal sins," deadly states of the soul as surely as despair over God or despair in face of the forgiveness of sin.

1. *On Dying Well: An Anglican Contribution to the Debate on Euthanasia* (Church Information Office, 1975), p. 2. Church House, Dean's Yard, SW1P 3NZ, London, England.

2. Charles Fried, *An Anatomy of Values* (Cambridge, Mass.: Harvard University Press, 1970), p. 15.

So also religious faith affirms that life is a *trust*. And not to accept life as a trust, to abandon our trusteeship, evidences a denial that God is trustworthy, or at least some doubt that he knew what he was doing when he called us by our own proper names and trusted us with life. We are stewards and not owners of our lives.

Or again, if as Christians we believe that death is the "last enemy" that shall be destroyed, then to choose death for its own sake would be a desertion to the enemy and a kind of distrust in the Lord of life, the Lord over the death of death.[3]

Many people today think it odd to believe that illness unto death or the gradual decay of our mortal frames is a sign that God is calling his servant home. That seems to make nature God. "Vitalism" is the usual charge. I suggest, to the contrary, that such a view is no more an oddity than to believe that the birth of a child is God's gift of life and a sign of hope. Both are, to the seeing eye, biological processes. Both are capable of being "rationalized"; and as faith recedes humankind seizes dominion: babies made to order, death by choice. To the eyes of faith, however, God gives and God takes away. And it is no novel conclusion of religious philosophy that God always works through "secondary causes." If that is true, then some current assaults on "vitalism" or "physicalism" are liable (if successful) to run God entirely out of the world.

What, then, does one choose in a medical-moral policy of allowing to die or refusing further treatment—if that is not dominion (or co-dominion) over human life instead of trusteeship or stewardship, if that is not based on a fundamental denial that life is a gift and a trust? What, then, does one choose in a medical-moral policy of "dying well enough" if one does not choose death as end or means? No one has answered this question better than Arthur Dyck of Harvard University: a person "does not choose death but how to live while dying." Physicians decide how a patient should live while dying, betubed or as comfortable as possible. Such choices about "how the last days of the dying patient are to be spent," Dyck goes on to say, are "no different in principle from the choices we make throughout our lives as to how much we will rest, how hard we will work, how little or how much

3. Paul Ramsey, "The Indignity of 'Death with Dignity,'" *Hastings Center Report* 2, no. 2 (May 1974), pp. 47–62. I believe it was Blackstone who said that suicide is wrong for two reasons. First, it is a crime against the king, because it deprives him of a subject. Second, it is a sin against God, because one rushes precipitously into the Lord's presence without being summoned.

medical intervention we will seek or tolerate, and the like"[4]—or, I would add, no different from choosing orange or apple juice for breakfast, to smoke or not to smoke, the shore or the mountains for a vacation.

These are life choices. They are indeterminate decisions in that it is difficult to say how we make them or to justify one option rather than another. But none is a choice between life and death, or who shall live and who shall die. Indeed that choice is now out of our hands. The dying patient is, of course, in a narrow passage—no longer thinking of going to the shore or to the mountains. His choices indeed are limited. Still, his choice of how to live while dying is a life choice; it need never be a choice of death as end or means. One compares a certain state or condition of dying with another, one treatment with another, or treatment with no treatment. All such decisions are consistent with accepting life as a gift and a trust. None seizes dominion over human life and death. We may be mistaken; indeed, we may be bad trustees and exercise our stewardship of God's gift of life wrongfully. Still, worthy or unworthy, we remain *trustees* making choices among the goods of life, and we do not lay claim to dominion, co-dominion, or co-regency over human life itself. As Dyck puts it, "choosing how to live while dying" stands in diametrical opposition to actions that "have the immediate intention of ending life (one's own or another's)." Only the latter "repudiates the meaningfulness and worth of one's own life." Only the latter "irrevocably severs any actual or potential contact with others and shuts them out of one's life." Only the latter usurps dominion, claims co-regency, or throws back the gift in the face of the giver. Only the latter chooses death as means or end. The former is a life-choice, one among the choices of a life still received.

The Meanings of Euthanasia

The word *euthanasia* has come to mean choosing death as one among life's choices. Since we cannot restore the word to its original meaning, I think we simply must speak of the immorality of euthanasia and of the morality of "dying well"—or, more soberly, of "dying well enough." That may be to beg the question, or at least to anticipate a

4. Arthur J. Dyck, "An Alternative to the Ethics of Euthanasia," in *To Live and to Die,* ed. Robert H. Williams (New York: Springer-Verlag, 1973), pp. 98–112.

conclusion. But there is little wrong with that among readers who are even now on the watch.

It is often said that "ceasing to oppose death," or "letting die," is *indirect euthanasia* while "intervening to start or hasten the dying process" would be *direct euthanasia*. It is important that we entirely reject this language, and not solely because of the subtle suggestion frequently introduced that an apologist for the morality of letting die is only a reluctant euthanasiast. The alternatives are simply between "dying well enough" (death itself never chosen either as end or as means) and choosing death as an end (and in that, he who chooses the end chooses the means also).

The language of "direct-indirect" was carefully honed in traditional moral analysis in order to sort right from wrong in dilemmas quite different from the one we are now considering. That language is properly used in the case of *indirect* therapeutic abortion (where a physician removes a cancerous uterus in order to save a woman's life knowing full well that he also kills the unborn child within) and in the case of collateral civil damage in acts of war aimed at legitimate military targets. In those cases, direct and indirect intentionality or direct and indirect effects have to do with the twofold (or manifold) effects flowing from a single action, or from a single act of the will, targeted upon some good while the agent foresees (and so "indirectly" wills or permits) some evil side effects.

The only instance in which such language and its moral meaning need be invoked in discussing the question of euthanasia is a minor one. It is also very obscure how factually to analyze what is being done in that instance. I refer to the use of pain-relieving drugs which are supposed also to be life shortening. That, indeed, is an instance in which from a single volition and action two effects are (ambiguously) foreseen to follow.

The moral analysis is clear enough. Any physician knows whether he is trying to relieve suffering or trying to bring on death. His aim is the former, even if he knows that he is also doing the latter. No one doubts that he should relieve extreme pain and suffering, even if a shorter life for the patient is an indirect result of the medical care he initiates.

Once in an interdisciplinary discussion, a scientist friend of mine, a proponent of euthanasia on utilitarian grounds who believes we should comparatively evaluate human lives in their declining trajectories—slowing some, hastening others—was poking fun at the "absurd" distinction between the direct and indirect results of pain-relieving drugs. I asked him what he would think if we had drugs to relieve suffering that certainly did *not* shorten lives or hasten death. He replied that he'd oppose funding the research to discover any such way to deal with the suffering of the dying. My rejoinder was: Then you *can* tell the difference between the direct or intended and the indirect or unintended of the twofold effects of medications! As between the two, he simply wanted physicians sometimes to bring on death, and incidentally, of course, relieve the suffering of the dying.

In the case of pain-relieving drugs, the moral grounds for approving their use even if death comes sooner is clear enough, and I believe convincing. As stated in the Anglican pamphlet:

> There is a clear distinction to be drawn between rendering someone unconscious at risk of killing him and killing him in order to render him unconscious. . . . There is a decisive difference between the situation of a medical practitioner whose patient dies as the result of an increased dosage of a pain-killing drug and who would use a safer drug had it been available, and that of a public executioner in states which employ this means of carrying out the death penalty who chooses drugs for their death-inducing properties. Two rivers may take their rise at a very little distance from one another on a mountainous plateau, but this slight difference may determine that the one flows north and the other south.[5]

What is in doubt is the factual situation. To suffer unrelieved pain is also debilitating and life shortening. "Giving the right drugs is not tantamount to killing the patient slowly. The relief of pain itself may well lengthen life: it will certainly enhance it."[6] "This is not 'protracted euthanasia' . . . as it has been called, but a way of enabling someone to live actively up to the moment of death."[7]

My point, however, is to urge that we jettison the expressions *direct* and *indirect* from discussions of euthanasia unless it is very clear that

5. *On Dying Well*, p. 9.
6. Ibid., p. 48.
7. Ibid., p. 47. The word *actively* may be questioned.

we are talking about this single issue: the use of pain-relieving drugs. Except for this sort of medical decision, the alternatives are (1) to choose death as an end and also the means thereto (to add *deliberately* or *directly* says no more than already stated by the word *choose*) or (2) to let die and to help the dying to die well enough (and that entails no choice of death, direct or indirect, as end or means).

The remaining verbal distinctions—the alleged difference between passive and active euthanasia, between acts of omission and acts of commission, between acting and refraining—can be taken together for coment. Again, those may be the right-making or wrong-making features in the analysis of some moral questions, but not of the treatment of terminal patients. Of course, euthanasia is an active choice of death as an end and of the means thereto. Death is brought about by commission, by an action. For Jews and Christians—and for other religious outlooks as well—euthanasia is wrong because it is wrong to choose death. But the alternative policy is not correctly characterized as "passive" euthanasia (a passive choice of death as an end or by negative means). Death's cause is not advanced by acts of omission or by abstention. Death's cause is advanced by the disease itself, and beyond some point it is useless to continue to fight it.

It is rather another cause that is advanced by choosing an alternative course of *action*. When a doctor says, "There's nothing more to be done," he means, in context, "There's nothing more to be done to cure or to save this particular life," not "nothing more to be done" except to switch to inaction, passivity, omission, refraining. "It is entirely misleading," the Anglican pamphlet correctly affirms, "to call decisions to cease curative treatment 'negative euthanasia'; they are part of good medicine, and always have been." [8] The cessation of curative treatment is followed immediately by an exceedingly active practice of medicine involving "commissions" of many sorts in caring for the dying. In words drawn from a Protestant hymn, from trying to "rescue the perishing" one turns to "care for the dying." Not even the turning from what was formerly the indicated treatment is an inaction, much less the care and treatment to which one then turns. Still that turn is not a turn toward death as a goal of human actions. No one chooses death as end or means. We choose rather to care for the still-living dying. That is "affirmative action" of the highest order. One

8. Ibid., p. 40.

refrains, of course, from what was formerly the needed curative treatment, but that is promptly replaced by the now needed caring treatment. The latter policy is as active as the former. Both serve life and neither chooses death as end or as means.

Cicely Saunders, M.D., is the leader of the hospice movement in Great Britain. The word *hospice,* used in place of hospital or "sunset village," is a medieval term meaning a way station for pilgrims. She once remarked:

> I am in the happy position of not being able to carry out drastic life-prolonging measures because we just do not have the facilities at St. Joseph's. Other people have made the decision, at a prior stage, that this is a patient for whom such procedures are not suitable or right or kind. This makes it very much easier for us than for the staff of a busy general ward. I think that it is extremely important that the decision be made by a person who has learned all he can about the family, about the patient himself, and about the whole situation. The further we go in having special means at our disposal, the more important it is that we stop and think what we are doing. . . . I have had much correspondence with the former chairman of the Euthanasia Society in Great Britain, and I took him round St. Joseph's after I had been working there some eighteen months. He came away saying, "I didn't know you could do it. If all patients died something like this, we could disband the Society." And he added, "I'd like to come and die in your Home." I do not believe in taking a deliberate step to end a patient's life—*but then, I do not get asked.* If you relieve a patient's pain and if you can make him feel like a wanted person, which he is, then you are not going to be asked about euthanasia. . . . I think that euthanasia is an admission of defeat, and a totally negative approach. One should be working to see that it is not needed.[9]

A reporter asked Dr. Saunders why even for emergencies they did not have an intensive care unit at St. Joseph's or St. Elizabeth's. She re-

9. Cicely Saunders, "The Moment of Truth: Care of the Dying Person," in *Confrontations of Death: A Book of Readings and a Suggested Method of Instruction,* ed. Francis G. Scott and Ruth M. Brewer, Oregon Center for Gerontology (Corvallis, Oregon: A Continuing Education Book, 1971), pp. 118–19.

plied, "Why, all we *have* here is intensive care!" That says better than I can why we should resist calling the practice of dying well enough by such names as "passive" or "negative" euthanasia, and why we should never let ourselves be put in the position of having to prove that refraining is somehow better than acting and that we are less accountable if evil comes about only through our omissions.

Replacing Past Principles in Care for the Dying

There was a final point listed at the beginning of this chapter, namely, you do not need to puzzle for very long over the categorical distinction between "ordinary" and "extraordinary" means of saving life. By that I mean that those terms as classes or categories of treatment are no longer useful and may in fact be helping to open the door to a policy of choosing death as an end. Yet before we can discard the classificatory or categorical meaning of *ordinary / extraordinary,* we shall need to search for adequate replacements. It is easier to criticize and discard the use of that language in treatment refusals than to propose substitutes.

Past moralists used the term *ordinary means for saving life* as an ethical category; it *meant* imperative. They used the term *extraordinary means* as one of moral permission; it *meant* electable or morally dispensable means. Like all other offense-terms, or terms of approval, these terms are formal and empty classifications, and their use is incurably circular, until filled with concrete or descriptive meaning. So, *forgery* means wrongfully writing someone else's name with intent to defraud, not simply writing someone else's name. *Lying* means wrongfully vocalizing an untruth, not singing "I die! I die!" if one is a Wagnerian opera singer. *Murder* means wrongful killing, not just any killing. We still have to ask, What sorts of cases count as these wrongs? A discussion of what constitutes ordinary or extraordinary medical means is like debating which cases of writing someone else's name constitute forgery, what killings are wrongful, or which words uttered inconsistent with the mind's apprehension are to count as lying. In all these instances, when we judge a specific situation or action to fall under one of these terms, we have to ask, What are the morally relevant features?

In the matter under our consideration, this question might be answered simply by classifying certain treatments as ordinary, others as extraordinary. This would mean that ordinary and therefore imperative medical treatments are to be determined by "standard medical practice." This is to say, the meaning of the ordinary / extraordinary standard would be entirely reduced to determining which operations or other treatments physicians agree are standard or customary at any stage of medical practice and which are heroic measures. I suggest that we must search for a more nuanced replacement or replacements for the traditional distinction.

When we ask the more searching question, there are five medical policies that are defendable tests or standards for when and how medical care should be extended or when it should be withheld or withdrawn. The options are:

1. The ordinary / extraordinary distinction.
2. A standard-medical-care policy.
3. A patient's right to refuse treatment.
4. A medical indications policy.
5. A quality-of-expected-life policy.

These medical policies are not disjunctive alternatives. Some overlap or may be combined with others. We have just seen that a standard-medical-care policy is one way to particularize the traditional ordinary / extraordinary distinction. A patient's right to refuse treatment —provided one has a patient competent to refuse treatment, which is the only meaning to be ascribed to refusal as a *human* act—may well include a reference to quality of expected life. And it is legitimate to ask whether competent refusal of treatment may morally go so far as to refuse "ordinary" or "standard" treatments, or only extraordinary ones. Finally, a medical indications policy needs to be distinguished from a quality-of-expected-life standard; and it is not unrelated to ordinary / extraordinary or to standard medical practice. Perhaps it could be said that a medical indications policy is a more subtle and more patient-oriented modulation of what was meant by ordinary / extraordinary and the customary medical practice standards. Perhaps a medical indications policy is the growing edge of those summaries.

In this chapter, and in the ethical intersection of medicine and legal cases to follow, I shall argue for a medical indications policy.

That obviously contrasts with a quality-of-expected-life standard, which was (some argue) an element in the meaning of the ordinary / extraordinary distinction and, I concede, may still be a test applied by a patient competent to refuse medical treatment. In the sequence of the history of Western medical ethics from ordinary / extraordinary to standard medical practice, I shall argue that the significant moral meaning of these similar and related standards can be reduced almost without significant remainder to a medical indications policy.

In *The Patient as Person* I focused chiefly, if not exclusively, on care for the dying when I discussed the meaning of mandatory treatments and electable treatment.[10] Historically, this was a mistake.[11] That is to say, the Roman Catholic moralists who worked out the distinction between ordinary and extraordinary means did precisely *not* have in mind those patients who have already entered the process of dying, those for whom treatment would now be entirely useless, those who are already "in the article of death." [12] Past moralists had in mind rather those patients whose lives could be meaningfully prolonged by radical or heroic measures. That is why they cited such reasons as excessive costs, too long a journey, reluctance to leave home, the repugnance of disfigurement as good reasons for refusing treatment, and they called such measures "extraordinary." I suppose also that these past thinkers never imagined it could be a medical duty to aimlessly prolong dying.

Today we are beginning to think it may be right to do unto others (i.e., refuse treatment for voiceless patients, whether dying or not) as conscious competent patients in former times could do for themselves (refuse extraordinary or heroic measures and some standard ones as well). Thus the original meaning of the ordinary / extraordinary distinction is applied to cases for which it was never intended. That leads straight to quality-of-expected-life judgments in the case of the desperately ill or "incurables" who are voiceless. We are beginning to think of them as dying.

I suggest that the older language be abandoned. For systematic

10. Paul Ramsey, *The Patient as Person* (New Haven: Yale University Press, 1970), pp. 113–64.

11. Charles Curran brought this obvious point to my attention in his *Politics, Medicine, and Christian Ethics: A Dialogue with Paul Ramsey* (Philadelphia: Fortress Press, 1973), p. 158.

12. St. Augustine, *The City of God,* bk. 13, chap. 6.

purposes, past medical ethics on these matters can be summed up as follows: (1) In the treatment of the dying, there is no need for family, physician, or the conscious dying patient to invoke the ordinary / extraordinary distinction. They only need to be sensitive and apt to determine when attempts to cure or save life are no longer indicated —that is, when in place of any longer bothering the dying with vain treatments, the indicated medical care calls upon us to surround them instead with comfort and a human presence while they die. (2) The conscious competent patient who is in the process of dying may, of course, choose that medical procedures continue to aid him in his struggle against death. (3) Also, a conscious competent patient who is not yet under the power of his own dying may refuse "extraordinary" treatments.

Why not say that the classification "ordinary / extraordinary" can simply be reduced to (1) a determination either of the treatment indicated or that there is no treatment indicated in the case of the dying, and (2) a patient's right to refuse treatment? The answer to that question is that there are medically indicated treatments (these used to be called "ordinary") that a competent conscious patient has no moral right to refuse, just as no one has a moral right deliberately to ruin his health. Treatment refusal is a relative right, contrary to what is believed today by those who would reduce medical ethics to patient autonomy and a "right to die." In this connection we need to recall that the reasons alleged to warrant refusal of extraordinary treatments were worked out in times that were medically primitive. Because of progress in medical practice, more and more extraordinary treatments have today become ordinary. These are surely medically indicated and desirable. Various national health services and government programs are aimed at removing from families the disastrous costs of major medical procedures. Prostheses can correct disfigurement or loss of function. In former times also it could be claimed that a patient refusing treatment (or refusing to travel) simply died more or less by himself. Today, I suspect that the cost of dying—the cost of palliative care—may often be great; and also great can be the psychological burden cast upon family, friends, and neighbors. A duty on the part of others to assist in "dying well enough" is entailed in every refusal decision; this needs to be taken into account as well as relief to the family or to its budget. A medical indications policy is applicable both to the nondying and to the dying, to the conscious and the unconscious. Instead of a conscious nondying patient's right to refuse treatment we need to emphasize his free and informed participation in medical decisions affecting him when there are alternative treatments.

Why some hesitation in recommending that we drop the traditional language entirely? Certainly not because of any doubt about the rightfulness of stopping further curative attempts in the case of the dying. Indeed, today we have commendably shifted debate about the meaning of those ancient terms to the case of the dying. And I do believe that a medical indications policy, properly understood, entirely covers the cases of the dying and the ill or incurable (without confusing them).

Still there was an important nuance in the older language that may be lost especially in our contemporary talk about a patient's right to refuse treatment. The terms *ordinary* and *extraordinary*—however cumbersome, opaque, and unilluminating—directed the attention of physicians, patients, family, clergymen, and moralists to *objective* consideration of the patient's condition and of the armamentarium of medicine's remedies. These considerations determined whether decisions to allow to die or to continue to try to save life were morally right or wrong decisions. This language asked all persons involved to consider whether treatment refusals would amount to "choosing death"; that was not among permissible life choices.

The translation of these terms to "a patient's right to refuse treatment" enthrones, to the contrary, an arbitrary freedom. It ascribes to subjective decisions the power to *make* medical interventions right or wrong. Choosing or refusing treatment is submitted to voluntaristic determination. In contrast to that, the distinction between ordinary and extraordinary means was a way of referring to refusals that are simply suicidal and those that may not be. The search for the specific meaning of imperative as opposed to electable means of saving life (objectively relative to a patient's *medical* condition or to his *human* circumstance) excluded a patient's right to choose death as end or means *simpliciter*. He chose to remain at home, not to travel far away; he chose against disfigurement. These were all *life* choices; none a choice of death as end or means.

Certainly no patient has a right arbitrarily to refuse treatment *with medical assistance*. Physicians, too, have consciences and integrity in their professional judgments. Therefore I add that the search for *objective* grounds for describing a treatment as ordinary or extraordinary (objective even when relative to the patient's condition) have also the virtue of not turning physicians into "animated tools" (to use Aristotle's definition of a slave) that simply assist a patient to attain anything he wishes. Instead, a patient's need and real claims upon our care have to be read from the human and medical reality of his case, not from his expressed wishes alone. His freedom and dignity do not encompass the right to do wrong, a right to assault the value of his own life with or without medical assistance. Treatments are not electable because elected, desirable because desired.

If there is a right to die (a right to choose death as an end), then that implies, "as is normal with rights, a correlative duty on the part of others to secure to the individual the exercise of his right." [13] Not yet have we assigned the right to die, the right to choose death as an end (if that is the meaning of "a patient's right to refuse treatment") the same moral status as the right to life. If the claim were verified that an individual has a right to arbitrary self-determination in the matter of life and death, and if then he chooses to live, there would be a duty upon others to protect his life; and, equally, if he chooses to die, there would be a duty upon others to assist his dying.[14] I, therefore,

13. *On Dying Well*, p. 7.

14. A quick and easy way to establish a public policy favoring euthanasia would seem to be to abolish the crime of "assisted suicide." The 1975 Assembly Bill 1207, introduced in the Wisconsin state legislature by Representative Barbee, reads like a joke but apparently was seriously intended. The bill provided that a person may request any person fourteen years of age or older to cause the death of the requestor; requests may be written or oral; no person under seven years of age may make a valid request; persons under eighteen years of age must notify their parents or guardian prior to making a valid request; the requestor, if married, shall notify his spouse; permission from parents, guardian, or spouse, however, shall not be a condition precedent to making a valid request; and any person who causes death pursuant to a valid request will not be civilly liable for his actions or guilty of murder, manslaughter, or homicide in any degree.

More significant to contemplate was the Incurable Patients Bill, introduced in the British Parliament by Baroness Wootton as a "private bill," which was opposed by the government, debated in the House of Lords on February 12, 1976, and defeated by a vote of eighty-five to twenty-three (*House of Lords Official Report* 368, no. 31 [London: Her Majesty's Stationery Office]). The central clause in Lady Wootton's bill reads: "No person shall be under a duty to interfere with any course of action taken by an incurable patient to relieve his suffering in a manner likely to cause his own

fear that the translation "a patient's right to refuse treatment" moves too far in the direction of subjective voluntarism and automated physicians. Having gone to that state of affairs in the matter of abortion, let us not do so as we approach medical euthanasia.

After this excursus, we now return to the main meaning and translation of *ordinary / extraordinary,* namely, a medical indications policy that readily allows for treatment indicated or no further curative treatment indicated in the case of the dying. We should now be prepared to see that this wording does not mislead. It rather directs attention to the objective condition of the patient, *not* to abstract classification of treatments or to the wishes of any of the parties concerned—not even to the previously expressed opinion (as reported) of Karen Ann Quinlan. Treatment indicated or no further treatment indicated is not determined by anyone's stipulation. Within whatever margin of error, this is an objective medical determination. That means that disagreement—for example, between physicians and the family of a comatose patient—may be *real* disagreement over an objective medical situation and about what should be done in a particular case.

At the same time, a comparison of treatments, or of treatment with no further curative treatments, is objectively relative to the patient's *present* condition—not to some notion of standard medical care in a physician's mind. A routinized understanding of "ordinary / extraordinary" is the security blanket of some physicians—who nevertheless have been known to call some ethicists "absolutists!"

---

death, and any intereference intentionally undertaken contrary to the known wishes of the patient shall be unlawful." That provision does not acknowledge a positive duty on the part of others correlated with the right to die. Lady Wootton's bill simply says that no person has a duty to *interfere* and makes it unlawful to interfere if the patient's wishes are known. No duty to assist suicide would by inference be cast upon the medical profession, only a duty not to intervene.

A reading of the debate in the House of Lords shows the difficulty of ever drafting legislation that institutionalizes as a *rule of practice* either the duty to kill, to assist, or not to interfere. Is it not also revealing that proponents of the right to die often want the correlative duty to be cast upon someone else—the medical and nursing professions—and want the deadly deed done in the caverns of hospitals, far from public view? I am told that even in Texas for a hundred years no one has even been arrested for the crime of assistance in suicide. Perhaps we should remove that from the criminal law *except* for physicians or nurses, and see how many from the general public step forward to do their "duty" in the service of this so-called right. That might be some sort of test—like the king who watched from his window to see who among his subjects would trigger the execution of a criminal.

So far in this chapter I have been concerned simply with the clarification of terms, to the end that the prohibition of euthanasia can be more fully understood. This is a firm principle or moral norm that should govern medical care. I myself have suggested that there may be exceptions to the rule against hastening or causing or choosing death.[15] A little flurry of debate once swirled around those exceptions. I do not now enter the lists to defend them. My point has rather been a far more important one—against the trend, clearly evident in contemporary discussions, to weaken the principle prohibiting choosing death. Loose language, I believe, is its source.

"Reasonableness" as a Standard for Substituted Judgments

Two standards, then, are still in contention to replace the classifications "ordinary" and "extraordinary" in helping to specify when to institute and when to withhold or discontinue medical treatment: medical indications and some version of a patient's right to refuse treatment. We now need to bring these translations or replacements together. Or rather, we need to ask whether these two more nuanced or particularized meanings should be confused. This is done whenever it is supposed that competent persons—parents, family, or physicians—may enlarge the medical indications for treatment of incompetent patients to include also quality-of-expected-life considerations that properly may be a part of patient-directed treatment refusals. Can substituted judgments be the same as the choice of patients capable themselves of participating in their own refusals on the basis of their own life plans?

Perhaps we should say that *medically indicated,* or not, is the expression to use when we are speaking of the voiceless dying or of the voiceless nondying, while reserving the word *reasonable* for use when we are speaking of patient participation in treatment decisions, or of patient refusals. On the other hand, *indicated* therapy and *reasonable* therapy seem to be interchangeable terms; verbally, either might be used in all cases. However, I shall argue that *medical indications* is the better and more circumspect term to use in clarifying the nature of medical-moral decision making.

15. *The Patient as Person,* pp. 157–64. See chap. 5, below, section entitled "Are There Exceptions?"

Here we need, first, to bring under scrutiny the so-called reasonable man standard in addition to the five alternative policies listed above.[16] I shall argue that general reasonableness tends to incorporate subjectivism and voluntarism into its meaning. As a consequence, a patient's normal right to refuse treatment turns into an arbitrary sovereignty that cannot be the basis of any ethics. I shall further argue in this section that general reasonableness, subject as it is to the vagaries and preferences of persons who presume to apply that standard, is an inadequate protection or guide in choosing treatment (or no treatment) for voiceless patients. Both convenant fidelity to the life and interests of another as well as the stringency of fiduciary obligations of familial or medical or legal guardianship require that a medical indications policy alone be applied when another, voiceless, human life is at stake.

Then I shall bring into view a theological proposal that the test for extending or withholding aid should be a patient's potentiality for significant personal life, for some relationship to God, and for interrelationship with other human beings, in the midst of the struggle for biologic survival which threatens to submerge these values. Like the general reasonableness standard, personal intersubjectivity is a test no one should presume to use in estimating (operationally, for medical practice) the worth of the life of another.

Finally, this chapter will conclude with an example of a medical indications policy. "Substituted judgments" and the "reasonable man" standard in the law can take proper hold only by first *discovering* some particularized interest in the ward or incompetent person who is in the charge of others.

Robert M. Veatch [17] proposes that we translate ordinary / extraordinary into reasonable / unreasonable—that is, treatments for which there is good reason to accept them and treatments for which there is not. He packs very little objective reference, however, into reasonableness or the reasonable man standard. That gives me occasion to say

16. From that list, "a patient's right to refuse treatment" flying under the banner of an extreme libertarian view of reasonableness, is the alternative discussed and rejected in this section.

17. "Guardian Refusal of Life-Saving Medical Procedures: The Standard of Reasonableness" (unpublished). Unfootnoted quotations in the text are from this article. See also Robert M. Veatch, *Death, Dying, and the Biological Revolution* (New Haven: Yale University Press, 1977). Page references will be made to this volume.

that I would have to unpack some physicians' judgment concerning indicated treatment. If they include nonmedical value judgments and social or economic indices or predictions in making decisions about "medically" indicated treatment, I would have to say that the proper standard is what they ought to have judged to be the medically indicated treatment. Still, in our common search for replacing terminology, it seems to me that the reasonableness standard would need more, not less, circumscription. Veatch, for example, holds that an adult competent patient has a *legal* right to refuse *any* treatments *whatsoever* proposed exclusively for his or her own good.

I question that sweeping interpretation of the law to date; however, this is not the main point here. Still it is worth commenting upon Veatch's remarkable feat of legal interpretation. In his book he states flatly that "no competent patients have ever been forced to undergo any medical treatments for their own good no matter how misguided their refusal may have appeared."[18] One might conclude from that announcement that the law has abandoned any interest whatsoever in protecting human beings from their own misguided medical decisions. A reader might not think that the courts would determine whether patients are competent or not by taking some notice of how misguided their treatment refusals are. However, this clearly is the case, as Veatch tells us. After again proclaiming that "there is a clear right of the competent patient to refuse treatment for any reason" (as if no objective reason exists that might affect the court's judgment concerning a patient's competence), Veatch almost grudgingly admits that "the right not to be declared incompetent while exercising that refusal is only beginning to emerge."[19] What sort of refusal right is that? It is certainly not as absolute as the reader might have supposed. A right to refuse treatment "for any reason" is not found in the law; it is found to be emerging. Here is a policy area where action is called for. From a consideration of specific cases Veatch concludes that "the circle of incompetency is shrinking rapidly."[20] That is to say, the withdrawal of the state's protection of human beings from misguided refusals is increasing rapidly; the right not to be declared incompetent, while refusing treatment for any reason, may be gathering strength and

18. *Death, Dying, and the Biological Revolution*, pp. 117–18.
19. Ibid., p. 146.
20. Ibid., p. 152.

precedent. Still Veatch's analysis is more a call for action than it is careful legal interpretation. This had to be the case because to date the law's meaning of *reasonable* and Veatch's meaning are quite different. So the moral meaning of reasonableness is the chief point to look for in his writings.

Veatch and I would agree that whether a competent adult patient's refusal is *ethically* right is not identical with whether it is *legal*. On the moral question, however, his reasonableness standard drives him in a circle—a circle of subjectivism that is neither the ordinary meaning nor the law's meaning of *reasonable*. To be ethical, patient refusal must be backed by "some attempt at justification." The patient is "morally obliged" not to refuse treatment "frivolously" or because he is "bored." The reason given ought to be "weighty"—but then Veatch gives his case away by adding "at least to the judgment of the one doing the refusing"; the competent adult ought to give what to *him* is a weighty reason. That adds up to saying that the universe of moral discourse to which he appeals—the reasonableness standard to which he appeals—can actually mean anything whatsoever.

"Useful / useless" does not help either, because "some treatments may be quite useless for achieving certain goals while useful for achieving others." Everything depends on what is a "reasonable objective," and that Veatch leaves to patient autonomy. Verbally he seems to be referring to objective right-making or wrong-making features of the patient's situation, but only verbally. A patient might use "uselessness" as a "good reason" for refusing treatment (and remember, he *should* put forward some attempt at justification) in two possible senses: "the uselessness of the treatment given the patient's objectives" and the "burdensomeness of the treatment according to the individual's sense of what counts as a burden." Both reveal the patient as a "reasonable man" to be *incurvatus in se*. Therefore in the case of the competent adult patient the reasonableness standard turns out to be entirely subjective and arbitrary—much more so than a physician's sometimes wobbly use of "indicated" treatment. The latter is, at the least, anchored in medical reality. At the moment, I do not see why as a patient I could not prefer to be whimsical, even frivolous, in refusing treatments if that was my mood, or why a boring life should not be too burdensome for me. I might also add that toward the end of a long life devoted to trying to give "weighty" reasons or at the least proposing some justification for human actions, I do not know why that should not be entirely too "burdensome" according to what counts as a burden to me when I come to be "in hospital" (as the British say).

In his book Veatch proposes that the words *ordinary, extraordinary,* and *euthanasia* be "banned from further use." I have agreed with that. But then Veatch proposes "two moves": the adoption of the patient's perspective and the use of the language of reasonableness. But in Veatch's case, the subjectivism of his first move controls the meaning of the second. For when Veatch asks, "What exactly does the reasonable person consider a reasonable or unreasonable refusal?," his reply finds a *useful* treatment (even if not necessarily a life-saving one) to be unreasonable if, among other things, it gives rise to any significant patient-centered objections based on physical or mental burden, familial, social, or economic concern, or religious belief.[21] That *language* is acceptable in the case of competent patients sharing or leading in decisions concerning their own cases. Still as a medical ethical policy it is without chart or compass, since on Veatch's view every individual patient has his own chart and compass, which is all medical practice need consult.

To avoid translating ordinary / extraordinary treatments into even more obscure and less helpful directives, I expressed some reluctance in moving altogether to "indicated / not indicated" unless the meaning of such a policy is carefully articulated. The action guides to be found in ordinary / extraordinary certainly cannot be translated into or replaced by reasonable / unreasonable as Veatch understands those terms. Veatch seems to me to allow, morally, patient refusals that are simply suicidal [22] and, moreover, to expect physician compliance, if not cooperation, in such decisions.[23] One wonders why Veatch both-

21. Ibid., pp. 110, 112.

22. In his book Veatch denies this. "It is a mistake," he writes, "to make the ethics of refusal of death-prolonging or even life-saving medical treatments stand or fall on the ethics of suicide" (*Death, Dying, and the Biological Revolution,* p. 115). I fail to see the logic of his denial when in addition to "death-prolonging" are added even "live-saving" medical treatments, and the refusal of either is subject to unlimited patient autonomy, provided only that the patient has self-justifying reasons. Veatch simply stipulates that patient refusal is not suicide; he avoids the problem by a definition.

23. As a defender of liberty, Veatch of course attempts to avoid this consequence. Physicians should be able, on grounds of conscience, to withdraw from the case.

ered to require a competent patient to offer justifying reasons in the first place, since he has no standard against which to measure whether these are good reasons or not. *Reasonableness* plainly means in this instance no more than the patient's autonomous subjectivity—a strange use of the term *reasonable.*

I still suggest that the language distinguishing between ordinary and extraordinary treatments be abandoned and that the following translations be substituted: (1) a conscious, competent, "incurable" patient would have a relative right to refuse treatment in the course of shared decision-making concerning his or her case; (2) a determination of and obligation to use the treatment indicated among the available alternatives would be required in the management of unconscious nondying patients; and (3) in the case of a dying patient, conscious or unconscious, a comparison and choice between further salvic treatments and no such treatments would be called for. Where a prognosis of fatal illness, severe uncorrectable defect, incurability, or nonrecovery has been made in the case of voiceless nondying patients, there will be some cases in which purely medical interventions will serve to improve patients' conditions of life, others in which nothing helps. In either case, there remains an undiminished obligation first of all to sustain life and, in the second instance, to use palliative treatments where possible. That states the rule of the ethical practice of medicine, favoring life when the patient has no capacity to refuse treatment or to share in physicians' or family decisions to omit or neglect treatment or otherwise initiate the incompetent, incurable patient's dying. That states a *rule of practice*—even if it may be rebuttable in rare exceptions. In ethics, an "exception" ought not to be assumed to weaken a rule of practice, nor should exceptions add up to a revision of the rule. Likewise, if exceptions are made by court rulings after hearing the *individual* case, the law's protection of life, regardless of

---

First, however, he attenuates possible conflicts of conscience by affirming that a physician's professional ethic is not to "preserve life" but "to do what is in the patient's interest." We have seen what that means for Veatch. As a consequence of his voluntarism, the substantive solution is that of two wills in conflict in which the physician's should give way: "To opt for their own interests rather than the patient's cannot possibly be morally acceptable." He does not feel the force of the judge's words about the "impossible choice" placed on hospitals and physicians by an unconscious patient, in need of an urgent operation, for whom a proxy refuses standby blood transfusion (*Death, Dying, and the Biological Revolution*, pp. 161–62, n. 93).

its condition or quality, should be preserved, undiminished by the substituted judgment of private individuals.

Veatch's "reasonableness" leads him in the opposite direction. His argument that parents or guardians have a moral and legal right to refuse *life-saving* treatment for children or incompetents will not bear scrutiny. That, legally, is not demonstrated by cases in which parents were permitted to refuse even *important* medical treatments short of life-saving ones. Nor is it demonstrated by permitted omissions that resulted in real harm. The law does, of course, try to accommodate its protection of children from harm with a public policy of allowing as much room as possible for parental liberty. We may grant that, in striking a compromise, parents have been allowed to follow courses of action or inaction which do harm or place children at risk in ways most of us would judge to be insensitive or negligent. Veatch correctly acknowledges that treatment refusals cannot be "transferred directly" to cases involving life or death.

The crux—the missing link—of his theoretical argument, however, is the notion that from a competent adult patient's legal and moral right to refuse treatment for *himself* one can derive an adult's right to refuse treatment for *another* for whom he or she has moral and legal responsibility. Veatch makes this move by assuming that "substituted judgment" in law and morals means putting a competent adult person's normal or reasonable judgment in place of an incompetent's. That is quite wrong. The search is rather for what the incompetent would wish and for his real interests. Even the law does not yet think autonomy over another life a reasonable thing.

In any case, on Veatch's understanding of reasonableness we can raise serious objection to his statement that "it would be bizarre if parents were able to make a treatment-refusing decision for themselves on the grounds that the treatment would be too great a burden on them while at the same time not be able to make a decision to reduce the burden for their child for whom they have even a stricter duty of benefit." In light of the meaning of "too burdensome"—the meaning of unreasonableness—which the adult should offer in justification of his own treatment refusals and which is relative only to his autonomous weighing of his interests, that capacity is no standard at all for assessing such an adult's moral or legal right to refuse treatment for another. Since a child cannot express or has no sense of what counts as a burden, and since a child cannot express or has as yet no patient objectives in terms of which to measure "usefulness," only the parent's sense of these things would count—and count as cryptoprotection. Even granting a competent patient's moral right to refuse treatment on grounds pleasing (i.e., reasonable) to him, there is nothing bizarre in saying that the life of another person in his charge should be surrounded with greater protection. In fact, it would be bizarre *not* to do so, legally and morally; otherwise the incompetent patient's interests are entirely dissolved and absorbed without distinction altogether into the parent's judgment or interests, whatever these may be. There's nothing surprising in this result: there can be only *one* autonomous will legislating what shall be reasonable.

However, Veatch goes on to ask "just how reasonable guardian refusals have to be before they are accepted by society and the courts acting for society." That was a question he thought not necessary to ask in the case of competent adult patient refusals. But guardian refusals must be "sufficiently reasonable." What that means has yet to be determined—for certainly guardians or parents in their own cases had to meet no standard for refusal except their own estimation of their (usefulness or burdensomeness). Is *that* the standard society should tolerate in life and death proxy decisions? No, Veatch replies. The standard applied to the competent is not exactly the same as the protection our law fosters for a voiceless one; society cannot permit "radically deviant" guardian judgments to be imposed on incompetents (e.g., Jehovah's Witnesses' refusals of blood transfusions for their children).

Yet Veatch insists that the "most reasonable" standard should not be required morally or by a court of law. His sole support for this view is that "we permit parents and other guardians to make many deviant choices for their wards" and children—in education and lifestyles. Veatch notes no difference between accepting deviant or less than reasonable standards in *that* range of liberties and permitting the same in *life or death* decisions in proxy refusals for children! He concludes that "some guardians should, in principle, be permitted to refuse some treatments for their wards because the treatment is judged to be a grave burden or useless, even though without the treatment the incompetent will die and with the treatment life would be preserved, even though a majority of the society might not share the judgment that the refusal was the most reasonable course."

At the outset the word *reasonable* seemed to suggest an objective standard, at least for persons not capable themselves of accepting or refusing lifesaving treatment. In the end, reasonableness means only social subjectivism and relativism. "Guardians must be permitted to refuse treatments [on behalf of incompetents] provided those treatment refusals do not deviate too radically from the social consensus of what is reasonable—provided, that is, they hold reasonable minority views." A reasonable minority view within a larger reasonableness which is simply consensus means that society determines only the outer limits of the protection of life. Within a rather wide span the protection of the life of incompetent persons is made entirely private. "Treatments for which there are good reasons to accept them and treatments for which there are not" is a distinction that really has no foundation—at least none ordinarily associated with the word *reason* or with medical practice.

Both the reasonable man standard and substituted judgments have, in American law, sought a basis for objective judgment. At first I was inclined to suppose that reasonable / unreasonable and *medically* indicated / unindicated treatments were only different terminology replacing ordinary / extraordinary. In other views of reasonableness, this is the case. Vincent J. Collins, M.D., for example, uses the term *reasonable* therapy in a sense entirely interchangeable, I believe, with my use of *medically indicated.* Collins weighs *reasonable* medically and would of course withhold unreasonable treatments.[24] But Robert Veatch would not. The latter's standard seems to be the sovereignty of the competent patient's refusal and the competent proxy's imposed refusal limited only by an existing range of social tolerance. To reach any other conclusion in regard to incompetent patients—i.e., any conclusion other than that someone must be able to refuse lifesaving treatment for them—would be to treat them as second class citizens. Someone must be able to exercise for them the claimed autonomy over choosing life or choosing death. If adults have such autonomy, incompetents are discriminated against unless the same autonomy is imputed to them and exercised for them. Fortunately, our law under the Fourteenth Amendment treats every human offspring, regardless of

24. Vincent J. Collins, M.D., "Care for Terminal Suffering—Therapeutic Rationalism versus Euthanasia" (unpublished paper). Compare the expression *therapeutic rationalism* in Collins's "Considerations in Prolonging Life—A Dying and Recovery Score," *Illinois Medical Journal,* June 1975.

its condition, as a citizen with rights to protection of life equal to that of any other person. I also suggest—but cannot here undertake to demonstrate—that the trajectory of the legal doctrine of substituted judgment, as this has developed case by case, is tending more and more to mean, morally, death by a thousand qualifications, or serious risk thereof.[25] Even that doctrine, however, does not encompass—what Veatch cautiously includes—proxy refusal of lifesaving treatment in rare circumstances on account of burden to persons other than the incompetent whose life is in question.

On this last point Veatch's unpublished article goes a step beyond the position taken in his book. There he discusses "the most difficult of all problems, the situation where a dying [?] child's life could be saved, but with a burden some would consider too great"—for instance, in the case of a mongoloid child or a baby severely impaired with *spina bifida*. Here Veatch rejects "the general argument of *burden to others* as a legitimate reason for refusing treatment for one who is incompetent. That leaves the criterion of *burden to the patient*."[26] His rejection of burden to others as a criterion for proxy death decisions, however, does not seem to me to make any material difference, for the following three reasons: (1) extreme extensibility enters into a proxy's estimation of "burden to the patient"; (2) a parent's understanding of the meaning of "too burdensome" is given sovereignty over medical judgment (physicians simply present the prognosis; the family makes the decision);[27] and (3) Veatch in an astonishing manner manages to reach the conclusion that a state of being dead does not depend on the consent of relative or guardian, but the state of being *pronounced* dead does depend upon that consent! "Being dead or alive may be quite independent of the wishes of relatives, but the treatment of persons as if they were dead or alive can logically still be a matter of choice of a relative. . . ."[28] It would seem, therefore, that if a family does not find enough latitude in "reasonable" estimates of burden to a voiceless, dying or nondying child, they can take the definitional route to determine the criteria by which the child should

25. See John A. Robertson, "Organ Donations by Incompetents and the Substituted Judgment Doctrine," *Columbia Law Review* 76 : 48–78.

26. Veatch, *Death, Dying, and the Biological Revolution*, pp. 133–34.

27. Ibid., pp. 142–23.

28. Ibid., pp. 73–74.

be pronounced dead.[29] Anyone persuaded by Veatch's reasoning cannot possibly need to resort to "burden to others" as a special category of reasons for treatment refusals bearing on the life of an incompetent patient.

Thus Veatch's reasonableness standard draws its meaning mainly from a patient's right to refuse treatment. That (both verbally and in medical reality) is one possible translation of ordinary / extraordinary—in the case of competent patients, who may indeed make quality-of-expected-life judgments by weighing all the costs and risks against the minimal benefits of treatment. When applied to children or wards, however, Veatch's reasonableness standard does not come close to a medical indications policy. This is made quite clear by his idiosyncratic comments in the present article on the New Jersey Supreme Court's decision in the *Quinlan* case, to be fully discussed in chapter 7. "The most reasonable course was not at issue," Veatch writes. "Rather Mr. Quinlan was permitted to exercise his judgment even if he happens to hold a minority view provided it is within the limits of reasonableness." That certainly is not established by speculation that the courts would intervene if the Quinlans decided to permit drug experimentation for a fee or to charge admission to view their daughter. To the contrary, as I shall show below, the court reached an opinion concerning Karen's reasonable wishes and imputed that to her privacy rights. For support it appealed to the agreement of the vast majority. It did not certify a deviant opinion, tolerable in our society. It did not elevate the family's or any other individual's privacy or autonomy. The anomaly of its decision is that it did then invoke the initiative of Joseph Quinlan and the concurrence of physicians and of a committee to give effect to Karen's individual rights. Veatch does not absolutely reject the idea of an *advisory* committee to review treatment refusal decisions. Its members should be, as closely as possible, peers of the patient; that, indeed, is the only way to begin to contain the subjectivity of Veatch's reasonableness standard. Treatment refusals should be based on individual values; proxy refusals, on *familial* values, no one else having a veto. "If anyone is going to override the right of privacy to make judgments about medical care . . . it must be a publicly legitimated agent of society such as the court." However, Veatch is quite mistaken when he says the court "found that parental

29. See below, note 34 of this chapter.

refusal of treatment is sufficiently reasonable that the state need not intervene." [30] To the contrary, the court did not even find that Joseph Quinlan held a reasonable minority opinion. It found instead what Karen's choice would be and that this would be the majority opinion in our society. Within that overall judgment, the court directed that a concurrence of decision makers could lawfully implement its ruling. Even the court's invocation of its own and everyone's reasonable substituted judgment, I shall argue, has too great latitude; and it invites an aftermath not readily cabined. The Quinlan decision could and should have rested upon a medical indications policy.

In our present exploration of principles, however, we next need to examine a theological proposal that would translate the medical and moral meaning of ordinary / extraordinary into a child patient's expected capacity or incapacity for minimal interpersonal relations. The following section—as well as the final section which concretely illustrates a medical indications policy—unavoidably anticipates and begins the discussion to be completed in chapters 5 and 6 on the treatment of defective newborns. I know no other way to articulate the ground rules with specificity and vividness than to discuss alternative treatment policies contextually. That means beginning the ethical analysis that will engage us—God save the marks missed—in the case studies that will be the topics of the remaining chapters in this volume.

Minimum Personal Relatedness: Entrance for Quality-of-Life Criteria?

In his article "To Save or Let Die: The Dilemma of Modern Medicine," [31] Richard A. McCormick speaks of "the ambiguity of the term 'hopelessly ill' ": sometimes that means irretrievably in the dying process; sometimes, a life that can be sustained only in a wretched, painful, and deformed state. He criticizes the AMA statement,[32] disavowing intentional killing, for limiting the cessation of extraordinary

30. See also Veatch's "Hospital Ethics Committees: Is There a Role?" *Hastings Center Report* 7, no. 3 (June 1977) : 22–25.

31. Richard A. McCormick, S.J., "To Save or Let Die: The Dilemma of Modern Medicine," *Journal of the American Medical Association* 229, no. 2 (July 8, 1974) : 172–76; reprinted in *America,* July 13, 1974, pp. 6–10. Subsequent discussion and rejoinders are found in *America,* Oct. 5, 1974, pp. 169–73, and in McCormick's "Notes on Moral Theology: April–September 1974," *Theological Studies* 36 (1975) : 121–23.

32. *Journal of the American Medical Association* 227 (1974) : 227.

means to cases in which "there is irrefutable evidence that biological death is imminent." In other words, McCormick is quite aware that he is not discussing "letting die." The problem, he writes, has shifted "from the means to reverse the dying process to the quality of life sustained and preserved." The title of his article is, then, unintentionally quite misleading. It also, I believe, misleads its author. For in setting forth his own moral grounds or substantive reasons justifying "no treatment" in the case of defective newborns, McCormick silently assumes that such a guideline will not leave many of these nondying patients worse off with help refused. He seems not to see that the next logical step in moral reasoning must be to hasten their deaths.

McCormick's argument is worth examining in its own right. Before doing so, however, let me note that since 1968 he and I must have passed one another in the dark. For I well remember that, as one of the panelists on the occasion of my Beecher lectures at Yale medical and divinity schools, McCormick argued (as I clearly do now under the rubric "medical indications policy") that treatments which would be extended to normal infants should be the standard for abnormal nondying patients as well. Both should also receive similar treatment if irreversibly dying.

McCormick recognizes, of course, that *meaningful life* is a slippery, even dangerous, term to employ in the practice of medicine or in public policy. Yet he believes we must face "the frightening task of making quality-of-life judgments." He wants to get at a defensible root meaning of that expression, one that is nonfunctional, nonutilitarian. The only option he sees is a "vitalism" that takes life to be an absolute value.

Interpreting a statement that Pope Pius XII made in an allocution to physicians,[33] McCormick proposes that human life is only a relative

33. McCormick's interpretation of the November 24, 1957, address of Pope Pius XII to the International Congress of Anesthesiologists on the prolongation of life (*Acta Apostolicae Sedis* 49, p. 1030) has not gone unchallenged. (See *The Pope Speaks* 4, no. 4 [Spring 1958] : 393–98, for the full text in English.) John F. Monagle, Office of Human Values in Medicine, St. Vincent Hospital and Medical Center, Toledo, Ohio, interprets the pontiff's remarks as simply a restatement of "the time-honored norm of ordinary-extraordinary means," in an article he deems to be a refutation of McCormick's replacement norm of "the quality of life as potential to human relationship" (*Marriage and Family Newsletter* 7, nos. 1, 2, 3 [January, February, March 1976] Collegeville, Minnesota). Anyone reading the entire address will see that, as Monagle points out, the pontiff's remarks are framed on all sides by

good, subordinate to spiritual values, and our duty to preserve it is a limited one. "The meaning, substance and consummation of life," he writes, "is found in human *relationships*. . . ." These sweeping statements are more closely defined—indeed severely limited—when there is a question of determining when our duty to preserve life ceases.

In the first place, says McCormick, the effort to support bodily life must not be disproportionate. "One who must support his life with disproportionate effort focuses the time, attention, energy and resources of himself and others not precisely on relationships but on maintaining the condition of relationships. . . . The very Judeo-Christian meaning of life is seriously jeopardized when undue and unending effort must go into its maintenance." That stipulation, McCormick recognizes, embraces external conditions, poverty and costs, separation from family, etc., which was the meaning of refusal of treatment on the part of a competent, conscious patient.

In the second place, McCormick distinguishes between conditions *external* to the individual which threaten or submerge "life's poten-

---

a restatement of the classical ordinary / extraordinary distinction (the words *burdensome / too burdensome,* Monagle says, derive their meaning from the former distinction, not vice versa), and by crucial reference to the sacrament of extreme unction, now called the sacrament of the sick. The phrases "too burdensome" and "render the attainment of the higher, more important good too difficult" take their meaning, Monagle writes, from the next sentence which reads, "Life, health, all temporal activities are in fact subordinate to spiritual ends." *In context,* he argues, all temporal goods and activities (these include McCormick's detectable capacity for personal interrelatedness) are subordinate to *les fins spirituelles,* which means eternal life. So goes the argument for the multi-valued norm of treatments classified as ordinary / extraordinary against what Monagle believes to be "the tyranny of a single-value theory: the potentiality for human relationship." I shall not undertake to adjudicate the McCormick-Monagle dispute over Pius XII's meaning. See however chap. 9, n. 18, below, and related text, for an explanation of the pontiff's meaning which was issued shortly after the 1957 address.

To take the matter out of the arena of textual controversy, the reader can gain an understanding of the issues at stake by reading two recent articles. The first is by John R. Connery, S.J., "The Quinlan Case," *Linacre Quarterly* 43, no. 1 (February 1976) : 25–28. Connery gives the standard ordinary / extraordinary interpretation of Pius XII's words; he does not milk them for further meaning. The second is by Lisa Sowle Cahill, "A 'Natural Law' Reconsideration of Euthanasia," *Linacre Quarterly* 44, no. 1 (February 1977) : 47–63. Cahill uses McCormick's interpretation in constructive ethical analysis of her own. These obviously are different paths, whatever the text meant. Perhaps I should add that at other points in her article Cahill cites words of Pius XII that seem to me to be more to the point; perhaps, unfortunately, the topic the Pope addressed on those occasions was not "the prolongation of life."

tiality for other values," and the patient's *internal* condition, "the very condition of the individual." The former "we can and must change" as a matter of social justice; the latter we sometimes cannot alter. Thus, he argues that "an individual's condition itself [may represent] the negation of any truly human—i.e., relational—potential." In summary,

> life is a value to be preserved only insofar as it contains some potentiality for human relationships.[34] When in human judgment this potentiality is totally absent or would be, because of the condition of the individual, totally subordinate to the mere effort for survival, that life can be said to have achieved its potential.

The guideline reads in the case of "grossly deformed and deprived infants": "If [because of the infant's condition, the potential for human relationships] is simply nonexistent or would be utterly submerged and undeveloped in the mere struggle to survive, that life has achieved its potential."

Several comments can be made at this point.

1. McCormick's position is altogether praiseworthy for the stringency of his understanding of meaningful life, for the small opening his position gives to decisions to neglect, for its attempted distinction between deprivation due to external conditions and "the condition of the individual patient," and for its requirement that "these decisions . . . be made in terms of the child's good, this alone"—in contrast to the marital, financial, and other considerations some physicians, we shall see, introduce or allow parents to introduce into medical-moral judgments.

2. It is noteworthy, however, that the argument of his article (whatever Pius XII may have meant) is based upon a (stringent) reading of ordinary / extraordinary as this was traditionally applied in the case of conscious nondying patients. The argument shifts these narrowly reinterpreted criteria to a class of nondying patients who are not capable

34. Robert Veatch takes a *definitional* route to reach the same result: "Death is most appropriately thought of as the irreversible loss of the embodied capacity for social interaction." Presumably when that point is reached a statutory definition of death would have the purpose of preventing "the basic indignity of treating a corpse as if it were alive" (*Death, Dying, and the Biological Revolution,* pp. 42 and 64).

of sharing in the decision that the duty to preserve life has ceased. The meaning of mandatory and dispensable treatments which I propose and shall use in the case studies to follow—and which is determined by a comparison of treatments indicated and not indicated—deliberately focuses instead on dying patients. This is not only the sole meaning to be given to "letting die"; it is also the only way to avoid the subtle move from comparison of beneficial and nonbeneficial treatments to a comparison of lives or stages or conditions of life said to be beneficial to their possessors.

3. When have Christians—or medical ethics in the Judeo-Christian tradition—heretofore reasoned that when a human being has achieved his potential, this can be taken as a sign that God is calling his servant home? that the duty to preserve life ceases? It is one thing for Charles Curran and others to argue that the onset of the dying process may be taken to signify that this is the case, and for them to conclude that no further moral distinction should be made from that point on between caring for the patient while he dies and accelerating the dying process.[35] It is quite another matter for McCormick to argue—as a general proposition, implicitly not limited to the dying nor to defective newborns alone—that our duty to preserve life ceases when to the seeing eye (one's own or another's) it appears that that life's earthly human potential has been achieved. As a guideline for medical practice, the former signification has at least some advantages.

4. It is hard to see how conditions external to the individual and "the very condition of the individual" can be kept as distinct as McCormick, admirably, tries to keep them. McCormick stipulates that the test must be that the internal potentiality for human relationships would, because of conditions of the individual, be either totally lacking or totally subordinated to the mere effort for survival. Can that distinction be well founded? One need not here object that potentiality for human relationships amid the struggle for survival is an accordion principle—inviting expansion—nor need one ask, Will the huddled masses be invited to emigrate to heaven because their lives can be said to have achieved their potential? McCormick has stipulated that "we can and must change" those conditions as a matter of social justice.

Still "the very condition of the individual"—his medical condition

35. See *The Patient as Person*, pp. 157–58.

—is often the effect of environmental deprivation and not only due to "inborn errors" or intrauterine hazards. Then is not the distinction somewhat abstract and, in pratice, often difficult to apply? We can and should call urgently for social conditions to be corrected. Doubtless the thrust of social action and institutional reform should be in that direction. But is not environmental deprivation often as severe as genetics in its devastating effects on human potential? Taking time into account, we know that not enough changes are going to be made soon enough to provide the relief needed by many socially deprived individuals. For *them* there are external conditions we cannot alter, not just the internal conditions of a meaningful life. If intensive care of defective newborns should, at a point, cease because of expected quality of life, how can we avoid also concluding that a pediatrician's "intensive care for the 1,200 gm. offspring of the 13-year-old unmarried girl from the ghetto" [36] ought also to cease? In the end we must repeat a question McCormick asked *before* he separated off "the very condition of the individual": "Can not these conditions, *whether caused by medical intervention* [or conditions] *or not,* equally absorb attention and energies to the point where the 'higher, more important good' is simply too difficult to attain?" (italics added). Defenses of the benign neglect of defective newborns are also arguments for the benign neglect of at least some of the environmentally deprived. If any of the recent arguments hold for triage in feeding the world's hungry, or if we simply fail to remove all causes of severe environmental deprivation, then there are likely to be individuals whose struggle against overwhelming obstacles seems so unendurably inhumane that they also would become prime candidates for medical neglect if they fall into the hands of a physician.

5. Finally, I ask, how can we fail to encompass within McCormick's guideline also some of the aged who are not dying? I ask, would not McCormick be forced to say also of some geriatric cases that "there comes a point where an individual's condition itself represents the negation of any truly human—i.e., relational—potentiality"? Again, the issue is not "letting die" but a culpable failure to help them live better until and, of course, also *while* they die. Therefore I suggest that McCormick's expressed position is capable of eroding the dis-

36. Robert E. Cooke, "Whose Suffering?" *Journal of Pediatrics* 80, no. 5 (May 1973) : 906–08.

tinction between voluntary and involuntary euthanasia, and between letting die and actively accelerating death, unless and until its application is limited to the dying—in which case his criteria would not be needed. In genuine cases of letting die, it is sufficient to refer to beneficial or nonbeneficial treatments. A medical indications policy is effective for both the dying and the nondying. In the case of the dying, to withhold or to withdraw attempted curative or salvic treatments may sometimes or often be indicated. But then it is not necessary to appraise a patient's capability of achieving human values to which life is subordinate—unless there are spiritual values to be experienced through suffering death in the context of comfort and human caring.

We now return to McCormick's analysis. Some there will be who, when agreeing and acting in accord with his principles, will still want to say that they are not using quality-of-life criteria, they are simply not using extraordinary means. That would be "fair enough" but nonetheless, he implies, a routinized appeal to that distinction. Such people should realize that "the term 'extraordinary' has been so relativized to the condition of the patient that *it is this condition that is decisive*" (italics added). Here again we come to the crux of the issue. Everything depends on whether the term *extraordinary* has been relativized to the *dying* condition of the patient or to a nondying patient's developmental human potential or to a geriatric patient's lost further potential. All are conditions of the patient. Here it is, unannounced, that McCormick takes the step from discussing whether treatments are in some measure beneficial to patients to discussing whether patients' lives are beneficial to them. Either can be deemed relativized to the patient's condition.

Then—to my puzzlement, not to say amazement—McCormick sets down the paragraph cited below. My puzzlement comes from the fact that he is still thinking about "allowing to die," having spent the first several pages of his article demonstrating that this is no longer the issue in many cases. My amazement is over the fact that he still speaks of the lives of defective newborns as valuable—presumably to us—although some of them should not be treated because of dim or no potential.

> It must be emphasized that allowing some infants to die does not imply that "some lives are valuable, others are not" or that

> "there is such a thing as a life not worth living." Every human being, regardless of age or condition, is of incalculable worth. The point is not, therefore, whether this or that individual has value. Of course he has, or rather *is* a value. The only point is whether this undoubted value has any potential at all, in continuing physical survival, for attaining a share, even if reduced, in the "higher, more important good." This is not a question about the inherent value of the individual. It is a question about whether this worldly existence will offer such a valued individual any hope of sharing those values for which physical life is the fundamental condition. Is not the only alternative an attitude that supports physical life as long as possible with every means?

The response to that last question is a medical indications policy. The answer obviously is that letting die is a justifiable, even commendable, alternative *for the dying,* but that this requires no comparison of patient-*persons* or of different stages or conditions of the same patient-person in order to determine his quality-of-life struggles or prospects. It requires simply a *comparison of treatments* to determine whether any are likely to be beneficial in any way other than prolonging dying (which is of no benefit to unaware patients, and for the conscious ones only in special circumstances, such as affording them an opportunity to make a will or to have their last reconciliation with God or a family member).

Below that surface question, however, lies a deeper philosophical and theological ethical question. How can a still-living human being have a "life worth living," "incalculable worth," "value"—not only *have* value, and "inherent value," but *be* a value—and exert no claim upon us or upon medical care? Of course, in his dying process such a valued patient-person (because of who he is, not his function or his prospective realizable potential) claims care and comfort and human company to the end: that is the meaning of "letting die." But what on earth is the meaning of a "value"—having "incalculable worth," inhering in a fellow human being who is not dying, who may even refuse to die—from which issues no claim upon the rest of us earth creatures, no duty to protect that life, no duty to provide helpful, possibly improving treatment before the time he enters into the throes of his dying process? Does that not say that some incurable nondying lives should be treated prematurely as if they are already in God's hands and no longer with us? that their "value" is to God and in God's sight alone even though they still live among us? Is that not to distinguish—as Jews and Christians do not—between love to God and love to some of our neighbors? Shades of the National Commission's rhetoric about "respect for the *dignity* of the dying subject," from which issued no claim on behalf of a fetus during an abortion procedure or on behalf of a still-living abortus about to be used in nontherapeutic experimentation!

McCormick seems to have been led into these quandaries by his strange use of value language distinguishing between the nondying and the dying in an earlier article. There he wrote that, when we say that there comes a point when medical means ought not to be used which in earlier circumstances we would have been obliged to use, "we are putting in some sense or other a different evaluation on that life than we would if it were nondying life." We "evaluate dying life differently (in the above sense of evaluation). . . ."[37] What is that

37. Richard A. McCormick, S.J., "The New Medicine and Morality," *Theology Digest* 21 (Winter 1973) : 317. The author's use of value language and a teleology of values was already leading toward maximizing the values of life as the sole test. Thus, the moral difference between so-called passive and active euthanasia rests upon the expectation, or belief, that the latter leads to disproportionate evil while the former does not. There can be proportionate reason for letting die, not for what used to be called intentional or direct killing. See below, chap. 5, sec. entitled "Are There Expections?" for analysis of McCormick's use of my exceptions to always caring for the dying in support of his quality-of-life criteria.

McCormick denies, of course, that his view makes human life a mere means to higher values. In "Notes on Moral Theology" (*Theological Studies* 38, no. 1 [March 1977] : 84), he affirms that "to say that life is a good to be preserved insofar as it contains some potentiality for human experience is not to make life a *bonum utile,* a kind of negotiable thing. . . . It is merely to talk about our duties—and especially the why of those duties—toward the preservation of a *bonum honestum,* the dying human person." If I understand that statement, McCormick here uses talk about our *duties* in a fashion equivalent to his use of our "putting in some sense or other different evaluations" on patients according to our determination of how they should be treated. Enough has been said about that in the text above.

A more serious question should be raised. Is McCormick simply confusing the dying and the nondying? Or does the foregoing statement *define* dying (or death) as the lack of capacity for human experience, in a fashion not unlike Veatch at n. 45, below? Does McCormick *equate* these conditions? In a footnote at this point McCormick quotes an interesting text of Thomas Aquinas's. He says the quotation is "in place"—which may mean supportive of McCormick's viewpoint. I hope, however, that I can count on Aquinas's diminished reputation among contemporary Catholics to prevent McCormick from drawing any medical policy proposals from this particular "some sense or other" which McCormick refers to in the "evaluations" to be distributed to the nondying and the dying? He tells us plainly. " 'Evaluation' here refers to the delineation of our duties to protect and support a good." Fair enough. But then the different evaluations which, in that sense, we place upon the nondying whom we put on a machine and the dying from whom we withhold such machines reduce to the distinction between beneficial and nonbeneficial *treatments,* treatment indicated and no further curative or salvic treatment indicated. To that meaning we should repair.

Warren T. Reich,[38] among others, criticizes McCormick's position. Reich, first of all, rejects McCormick's account of the value of life, in the Judeo-Christian tradition, as "the condition for other values." That, he says, is a bilevel view of man, making physical life an *instrumental* value for attaining *spiritual* goods. The charge is dualism—in contrast to our Western religious tradition in which "human life is valued holistically as the body-spirit life of the entire person," the "total (valued) life of man" from which the substratum of physical life is not to be set apart. Second, the infinite and intrinsic values of human life "are *not* essentially hinged to an individual's physical or mental abilities," his capacities for "spiritual goods," "not even his interrelatedness." Third, Reich asserts that "McCormick's basic normative method is a form of religious consequentialism or personalistic utilitarianism." Perhaps "ideal utilitarianism" or "multi-value consequentialism" would be better descriptions.

Reich's alternative approach is to translate extraordinary *means* to read extraordinary *circumstances.* Circumstances alter cases, not the internal conditions of the individual or his struggle to realize human potentialities or interrelationships. Circumstances in a given *situation* may diminish the obligation to treat. Newborn life should be "protected against homicide by omission as well as commission, without categorical discrimination as to the condition of the person." Yet un-

---

text. It reads in part: "Since happiness may not be attained except by living humanly or in accord with reason, when the use of reason is gone, human living is not possible. Consequently, in what concerns living humanly, the condition of madness must be equated with the condition of death" (*Commentary on the Nicomachean Ethics* [Chicago: Regnery, 1964], 1 : 85).

38. Reich, "Defective Newborn Children: An Inquiry into 'Quality of Life' Ethics" (Paper delivered at a conference on *spina bifida* babies, Skytop, Pennsylvania, May 4–7, 1976). See pp. 316–7, below, for an instance in which Reich's analysis may be applicable.

der given circumstances, treatment *itself* may impose unacceptable hardship; not that the patient's inner spiritual hardship spells the end of an obligation to treat. ". . . when the very means or effort to sustain life inseparably involves a truly grave excessive hardship, the obligation to continue may diminish to the point where one is no longer obliged to continue the efforts." Reich's position seems to me to be equivalent in most significant respects to my comparison of treatments, not patient-persons. That certainly is true of two of Reich's guidelines: Treatment may be stopped when excessively burdensome qualities are (1) directly *associated* with the means used (e.g., pain) or (2) *caused* by the life-sustaining treatment (e.g., maiming). Reich's third guideline—"when excessively burdensome qualities are perpetuated by life-sustaining treatment"—sounds remarkably like McCormick's position. Perhaps he means that care and comfort should be chosen for the dying life instead of a longer dying process; and the same choice should be made for the nondying instead of burdensome treatments that themselves diminish the patient's reception of care and comfort and a human presence.[39] Both are encompassed in a medical indications policy. Still I judge we must await further clarification of Reich's earlier distinction between "human qualities which account for the normative value of all human lives" and "other, more contingent qualities" that may indicate to an individual's obligation to sustain life, in contrast to McCormick's bilevel anthropology.

An Example of a Medical Indications Policy

To concisely particularize a medical indications policy when applied to voiceless patients I want now to summarize the practice of Dr. R. B. Zachary, pediatric surgeon at Children's Hospital, Sheffield,

39. This might be compared with the reason given in Jewish ethics for refusing a hazardous experimental treatment: such an operation, for example, may be refused because it might *shorten* one's life, and every moment of life is precious. A compilation of the sources and discussion of the issues raised on when life may be shortened by hazardous procedures is to be found in R. J. David Bleich, *Bioethics and the Jewish Tradition* (Course Syllabus, the Academy of Jewish Studies without Walls, sponsored by the American Jewish Committee and the University of Haifa, 1975). See also Bleich's "Theological Considerations in the Care of Defective Newborns" (Paper delivered at the conference on *spina bifida*, Skytop, Pennsylvania, 4–7, 1976).

England.[40] There are two groups of *spina bifida* babies on whom Dr. Zachary chooses not to operate. In this there is decisive proof that the relentless use of all medical means is *not* the only alternative to a routine use of the distinction ordinary / extraordinary or to admitting the entrance of a quality-of-expected-life policy into medical practice.

The first group consists of babies who Zachary is reasonably certain will die within a few days or a week. Withholding treatment in these cases is strictly limited to impending death; it is not related to whether the operation should be classed as "ordinary" or "extraordinary," much less to a prognosis of long-term dysfunction. None of the babies in this group should be operated on because to do so would have no bearing at all on whether it lived or died. No one can help them; there is no obligation to try to do the useless. This is Zachary's first test for whether treatment is indicated or not indicated.

The second group is a subset of all those severely afflicted babies who, even if left untreated as newborns, are not dying and indeed may live for many months or a year or more. Some of the babies whose impending death Zachary does not claim to know with reasonable certainty do actually die within the early period. But after 30 years as a pediatric surgeon he is unable to predict among the majority of spina bifida babies which ones are going to die. Many may live for months or a year or more, or in fact for many years. In general, babies who are treated live longer than babies who are not treated (just as adults with chronic bronchitis are likely to live longer if they have their coughs treated). The presumption favors treatment; impending death, the course of which cannot be significantly altered, is one reason in human judgment for setting that presumption aside. Eligibility for treatment, then, requires only a *lack* of reasonable certainty that the baby will die in a few days or a week. Still, some among the class remaining do die in the early period; that cannot be clearly forecast.

Yet within the class remaining Zachary identifies another group not to be treated. His indication for not operating in some of these cases is again a medical one: those where the wound on the back is not suitable for operation (e.g., a very wide wound or a gross kypho-

40. The contrasting policy of his colleague Dr. John Lorber is part of the matter discussed in the next chapter.

sis), and indeed if the operation were performed it is likely that healing would not occur, that there would be wound breakdown, and that infection could be far worse than if no operation were done at all. In these cases, the baby would be given simple dressing. While many heal spontaneously (one such baby grew up to be a part-time research secretary), a surgeon could not assist that process and he might make the baby's condition worse.

If, however, the nondying patient is suitable for operation, and if the primary physician or midwife observed some kicking movements of the legs after birth, Zachary advises urgent operation. The baby has some muscle power which otherwise might be lost; this activity is worth preserving. The purpose of the surgery is to reduce handicap to a minimum; and this, he believes, is medically good. Zachary does not say that an operation is medically good even if the baby remains abed or eventually dies at eighteen months; he does not *say* that because he does not *know* that that will be the case. The purpose of surgery is to preserve activity in the muscles; and it is equally true to say that where there is some activity in the muscles, the baby stands a chance of sitting up, probably standing, maybe walking—and that it has a reasonable chance of achieving adult life. The aim of operation is in either case to help the child remain active, however slightly, whether for a short or a longer life (whichever may be its future). It is the loss of function in unoperated cases that is important; where careful neonatal surgery may prevent this loss, that is sufficient indication it should be done even in cases where long life may not be the eventuality. In reference to complications associated with this central-nervous-system disorder, Dr. Zachary says simply, "Untreated hydrocephalus is a bad thing to have." [41]

41. The best article to date on the morality of neglecting defective newborns is David H. Smith's "On Letting Some Babies Die," *Hastings Center Studies* 2, no. 2 (May 1974) : 37–46. On one point, however, Professor Smith seems to be mistaken; or rather, he and Zachary hold opposed views about identifying the dying process of a newborn. "They have no visible personal past," Smith writes. "No opportunity to develop a normality of their own functioning. . . . Thus, in the absence of a benchmark in past life for saying *this particular person* has started to die, I do not see how one committed to care . . . could ever switch from cure to companionship" (p. 44). A Tay-Sachs baby, for example, has a visible personal past; it develops a normality of functioning prior to the visible onset of its dying which then can only be prolonged. But is that necessary? Cannot babies born dying be identified? Since this is largely a medical judgment—and in the absence of discussion among physicians focused pre-

"The fundamental purpose," Dr. Zachary writes, "is not to add years to their lives but to add life to their years." [42] That means, the purpose of surgery is to reduce disability and to improve a person's capabilities whatever years his life has to run, whether it is one or two or twenty-two years. The life added to those years is evidently often only a minimum improvement or a prevention of more severe impairment of biologic function. To be sure, minimal improvement may in fact *double* the activity of a patient, by adding a further 10 percent activity to the 10 percent that now exists. To lift one's head, and not become an object of pity, is better than not to. To sit up is better than not to be able to. To get out of a chair and walk to a toilet is better than not to be able to. The measure is not walking a mile or running to catch a bus. These are the good with which surgical and orthopaedic procedures properly deal. "There is a widespread misconception that surgery for this condition is designed to save the life of the newborn baby," he writes. "Nothing could be further from the truth. The purpose of urgent surgery is to preserve what muscle activity there is and the purpose of nonurgent surgery is to remove a swelling on the back." [43] That's the simple meaning of adding life to their years.

Thus, Arthur Dyck's dictum applies to the first category of spina bifida babies whom Zachary fails to treat: he chooses "how they shall live while dying"; he does not choose or even negligently bring about their deaths. The dictum, "Do no harm"—or, do not risk greater harm—applies to the second category not treated; the wound is

---

cisely on this point—I judge that we must side with Zachary on this first class of patients he chooses not to treat. See below, chap. 5, n. 35, for Smith's decisive moral reasons against the open-ended policies of neglect.

42. The above program of rational therapy is sketched and defended by Dr. Zachary in the following papers: "The Neonatal Surgeon" (The Forshall lecture delivered at the 23d Annual International Congress of Pediatric Surgeons, July 9, 1976), *British Medical Journal* 2 (Oct. 9, 1976) : 866–69; "A Rational Policy for Decision Making in Spina Bifida" (Paper delivered at the symposium at the Royal National Orthopaedic Hospital, London, February 26, 1975); "Paediatric Surgery and Legislation: Congenital Anomalies—A Rational Basis for Treatment" (Paper delivered at the European Congress of Catholic Doctors, May 24, 1976); "Aggressive Surgery" (Paper delivered at the London Medical Group Conference "To Treat or Not to Treat"); "Ethical and Social Aspects of Treatment of Spina Bifida," *Lancet* 2 (1968) : 274 ff.

43. Zachary, "The Challenge of Spina Bifida," Editorial, *Journal of the All India Institute of Medical Science,* New Delhi, April 1976.

judged to be inoperable. As for the class of spina bifida babies who are to be given treatment (an urgent operation to save muscle power; nonurgent operations to close wounds or to remove a protrusion that would excessively burden nursing or home care, shunts to prevent hydrocephalus, technics to deal with incontinence), how shall we aptly describe what Dr. Zachary recommends doing? He modestly describes the indicated treatment as adding life to their years, not years to their life. I once immodestly proposed (at the Skytop conference) that Dyck's expression could be stretched to embrace the treatment of spina bifida babies: that it should not be a part of the ethical practice of medicine ever to choose death, that in decisions to treat or not to treat a physician chooses how a voiceless patient shall live the last days of his life. Dr. Freedman said he'd accept that if the expression was changed to how the patient shall live the last *years* of his life. Evidently, then, Zachary's reservation of this description to *impending* death is correct. And as a consequence, we need his expression "add life to their years" (or months) to encompass judgments concerning treatment that is indicated for (in some sense) incurable but nondying patients.

Zachary believes that his practice is supported by Richard McCormick's views on to treat or let die. Let the reader judge whether this is the case. I myself do not find Zachary making reference to the child patient's present or future capacity to rise above the overwhelming struggle for existence so as to enter meaningfully into relationships with God and with fellow human beings. Instead, he treats personally the body of these patients; he does not treat the body as an instrument, nor bodily life as an instrumental value distinguishable from the persons who live those bodies. Zachary's medical maxim is simply, "Untreated hydrocephalus (or an unclosed wound, if treatable) is a bad thing to have." Perhaps McCormick's criteria and Zachary's are compatible. There may be no disagreement because each is describing a quite different sort or degree of childhood affliction. As I have pointed out, McCormick speaks of the child patient's struggle for survival being so overwhelming that there is no room left for minimal human relationships. Zachary does not find the patients he treats for spina bifida to be so overwhelmed. The fact remains, however, that Zachary's tests for no treatment are not the same as McCormick's. Zachary asks simply whether within human judgment the child's death is impending or whether the wound is inoperable. That is a clear example of what I have called a medical indications policy, which would define the province of medicine unless and until there is a patient capable of himself refusing treatment lest his established life projects be overwhelmed by continuing the struggle for survival.

Zachary insists rather that handicap and unhappiness are not dependent variables. There are degrees of handicap and degrees of happiness; but these do not in his experience vary directly with one another. So he rejoices in individual patients he has seen achieve a worthwhile measure of self-fulfillment in the face of great odds. But I do not find him attempting as a physician to distinguish between handicaps that are compatible with happiness or personal fulfillment and those that are not. Neither does Zachary, by using some expression more bleak than "happiness," allow his clinical judgment to become infected in the slightest degree by considerations of the quality of expected life. This is because decisions not to treat are strictly related to impending death or to inoperable conditions. He completely rejects the attitude that would withhold treatment for fear a patient will live longer, or that would view new complications of treatment as a possible opportunity for the child to die.[44] That would not be a clinical judgment. Yet we have seen that Zachary makes clinical judgments not to treat. One, at least, of his happy outcomes was the part-time research assistant he years before decided should *not* be operated on, but who healed anyway and then was offered beneficial

44. Zachary, "Aggressive Surgery" (Paper delivered at the London Medical Group Conference "To Treat or Not to Treat"). When a physician decides (from a comparison of treatment with no treatment) that an operation to close the wound is counter-indicated, it still is important that he not "choose death"; for the patient may heal spontaneously. Suppose, then, two physicians: oné when making the decision not to operate in the newborn period wished the patient could die, the other did not. Those attitudes will likely manifest themselves later on when that small patient is presented with complications calling again for medical decision. The first physician might wonder whether this later state of illness is the patient's last chance to die—since his view was that unfortunately the patient escaped the net on the first occasion, when he advised no treatment or wanted it to fail. He might diagnose renal failure and sedate the patient heavily to allow him to sleep away in peace. The second physician who did not choose death in the first instance, would likely check the blood more carefully; he might discover that urea was not high and find instead that the patient's urinary diversion was not working. Thus a physician's clinical judgment may be clouded by his ethical attitude toward a severely handicapped child, by his view that if there is any chance that the handicapped patient will die from an untreated illness advantage should be taken of it.

treatments. Whether life will be beneficial to its possessors is not a question Dr. Zachary asks. That was not his meaning when he wrote that in the most serious cases the purpose of treatment is not to add years to their lives but to add life to their one or two years. The enhancement of human bodily life, or prevention of its deterioration, is not, in clinical judgment, merely an instrumental value.

One thing more must be said. A medical indications policy will take *impending* death decisively into account in the treatment of voiceless patients. Yet terminal patients are frequently interchanged with dying patients, in ordinary speech; incurability with virtual death. McCormick, we saw, spoke of the ambiguity of the meaning of "hopeless cases." Veatch speaks of "chronic death," and even goes so far as to define *dying* as having "a specific progressive, normally irreversible ailment which will eventually end in death and which has become so debilitating that it has seriously disrupted normal life patterns." [45]

Indeed, I would argue that continued use of ordinary and extraordinary as classifications of treatments indifferently applied to all patients encourages the melding of *terminal* with *death impending* (since "ordinary" treatments are obligatory in either case). Then it is that a policy of quality of expected life gains entrance, applied thoughtlessly to the incurable whom, it is confusedly proposed, one should "let die."

At this point, the question will always be asked (in the tone of an objection): How can the "process of dying" be identified? How do you know that an infant or a comatose patient is dying? I do not. The reply must be that this is a *medical* judgment and that physicians can and do determine—in human, no doubt fallible judgment—the difference between dying and nondying terminal patients. In the case of those whose death is impending, further attempted salvic treatment can only prolong dying. In the case of nondying terminal patients, however, care calls for making treatment available to sustain them even when this only improves their condition or adds meager life to their days. Both the dying and the incurable if conscious and competent have, in addition, a right to refuse treatment or, better said, to participate in the choice of their treatment (including the choice of no further attempted cures).

It can also be pointed out that a reasonably certain prognosis of

45. Veatch, *Death, Dying, and the Biological Revolution*, p. 3 and n. 1.

incurability is also a medical judgment, like determining the dying process. Physicians should in both cases compare treatments, where there are alternatives; and they should choose the course that is medically indicated in either case: helping the incurable and refusing to prolong the dying of the dying, unless the patient himself is capable of refusing treatment in the first instance or of requesting heroic measures in the second.

Assuming no capacity for conscious choice on the part of a patient, the distinction between the incurable and the dying becomes crucial for the morality of substituting the judgments of the well for those of the ill. A medical indications policy is the only way to take a middle path between relentless treatment of the voiceless dying, which refuses to let them die even when disease or injury has won, and killing or hastening death or neglecting to sustain those who simply are voiceless incurables. The latter has to date been deemed to be manslaughter in some degree. Morally, it is never right to turn against the good of human life. In the case of one's own life, public policy could go so far as to place that in an area of liberties. But to allow private individuals to turn against the good of *another*'s life would be to promote injustice.

5

The Benign Neglect of Defective Infants

I cannot address this issue without first making certain retractions from my past ethical analysis. I beg forgiveness, therefore, for the necessity of beginning with a few self-referential remarks. In the Beecher Lectures I gave at Yale University's medical and divinity schools in spring 1969—published as *The Patient as Person*—I considered at some length the ethics of allowing terminal patients to die or, better expressed, the ethics of "(only) caring for the dying" instead of continuing to pester them with vain "cures." [1] At the same time I was writing my longest systematic treatment of the morality of abortion.[2] This concluded with a recapitulation of the moral arguments for sometimes allowing terminal patients, generally adult patients, to die free from further "curative" medical interventions. Then I wrote:

> These considerations need now to be applied to nascent life. . . . Before we rush to the justification of direct "fetal euthanasia" if the child is likely to suffer from grave physical or mental defect, surely the first question is the morality of a relentless and unqualified effort to save fetal life. The first question to be asked is whether the respect which can be claimed for nascent life may include also the claim to be allowed to die, and not be kept alive by the application of all the extraordinary means by which medical science can now do this.[3]

But then I cited a bad example: a severely malformed infant girl whom a New Jersey court ordered to be operated on over the objec-

1. Ramsey, *The Patient as Person* (New Haven: Yale University Press, 1970), chap. 3.

2. "Reference Points in Deciding About Abortion," in *The Morality of Abortion*, ed. John T. Noonan, Jr. (Cambridge, Mass.: Harvard University Press, 1970), pp. 60–100.

3. Ibid., pp. 97–98.

tion of her parents. I commented that "God in his mercy was beyond the jurisdiction of this human court. The child died before the operation could be performed." [4]

I do not regret having raised the question of "whether respect for the sanctity of life and therefore for nascent and for newborn life does not include sometimes keeping one's distance from its dying, protecting its dying no less than its life from arbitrary intrusion." [5] But I do regret that I addressed myself, in the final pages of a chapter on abortion—even in an interrogatory mood—to another grave moral question to which at the time I had given little thought.

Incidentally, that appeal not to rush to abortion to prevent defective children from a life of suffering has today been outdistanced, even as has my logical reasoning that many arguments favoring abortion would also justify infanticide. Since we should treat similar cases similarly, if *x* degree of defect would justify abortion, the same *x* degrees of defect would with equal cogency justify infanticide. So today we have a number of physicians who have come out of the closet to announce publicly their policy of benign neglect of defective newborns; [6] and some philosophers, acknowledging the obvious fact that birth makes little or no significant difference in the humanity or the moral status of young life, have put forward arguments in favor of infanticide as well as abortion.[7]

In any case, today there is an urgent need for a more penetrating analysis of what happens to our traditional ethics of conditionally allowing terminal patients to die when it is transferred to the case of defective newborn infants. Circumstances may alter one's judgment in the two sorts of cases.

4. Ibid., p. 98.

5. Loc. cit.

6. Anthony Shaw, "Dilemmas of 'Informed Consent' in Children," *New England Journal of Medical* 289, no. 17 (October 25, 1973) : 885–90: Raymond S. Duff and A. G. M. Campbell, "Moral and Ethical Dilemmas in the Special-Care Nursery," *New England Journal of Medicine* 289, no. 17 (October 25, 1973) : 890–94; John Lorber, "Results of Treatment of Myelomeningocele: An Analysis of 524 Unselected Cases With Special Reference to Possible Selection for Treatment," *Developmental Medicine Child Neurology* 13 (1971) : 279–303; "Criteria for Selection of Patients for Treatment," Abstract, Fourth International Conference on Birth Defects, Vienna, Austria, 1973.

7. Michael Tooley, "A Defense of Abortion and Infanticide," and S. I. Benn, "Abortion, Infanticide, and Respect for Persons," in *The Problem of Abortion*, ed. Joel Feinberg (Belmont, Calif.: Wadsworth Publishing Co., 1973), pp. 51–104.

Now, how shall an ethics of allowing to die, of only caring for the dying—now refined as a medical indications policy—be transposed to the case of defective newborn infants without any theoretical mistakes from which flow grave injustice and lack of care for human life in the practice of medicine?

The Dying and the Nondying

In the reported cases of the benign neglect of defective infants, it is quite obvious that not all are born *dying,* and certainly none are competent to refuse medical treatment.[8]

A Tay-Sachs baby is born destined to die. But presymptomatically it is not dying any more than the rest of us are. For about the first six months it is like any other baby; living and growing and presumably enjoying human existence as any other infant would. In religious perspective there is no reason for saying those six months are a life span of lesser worth to God than living seventy years before the onset of irreversible degeneration. A genuine humanism would say the same thing in other language. It is only a reductive naturalism or social utilitarianism that would regard those months of infant life as worthless because they led to nothing along a time line of earthly achievement. All our days and years are of equal worth whatever the consequence; death is no more a tragedy at one time than at another time. When the symptoms of irreversible degeneration show themselves and the child is in the throes of its very own dying, investigational therapies—including a search for a cure at high risk to an afflicted child—are quite in order. But from some point in the dying of Tay-Sachs

8. Dr. Raymond S. Duff described the following case:

> One time a decision was made to stop a respirator and let a baby die. The mother, only partially recovered from a caesarian section, wanted to hold her baby to "give him love and comfort so he won't die alone." Assisted by the father and the staff she was present when the respirator was stopped. The parents held and rocked their baby for 45 minutes when his heart stopped beating. She gave the baby to the nurse with the comment, "Please handle him tenderly." Then the parents signed the autopsy permit (at their request, this had been discussed earlier), and they left the unit.

That may well have been a child born dying, and not an instance of involuntary euthanasia by failure to use available beneficial or at least life-sustaining treatment. Beverly Kelsey, "Shall These Children Live? A Conversation with Dr. Raymond S. Duff," *Reflection* (Yale University Divinity School); reprinted in the *Hastings Center Report* 5, no. 2 (April 1975) : 5–8.

children they ought not to be stuck away in Jewish chronic disease hospitals and have their dying prolonged through tubes. The ethics of only caring for the dying holds without any modulation or modification in the case of a child no less than in that of an adult terminal patient who has entered upon the process of dying. No treatment is indicated when none exists that can do more than prolong dying.

Surely there is a distinction to be made between, on the one hand, children permitted to die whose deaths "resulted from pathological conditions in spite of the treatment given" (category 1), and, on the other hand, those permitted to die who simply had severe impairments, usually from congenital disorders (category 2).[9] The latter more than likely died *because* they were not treated. Of the former alone could it correctly be said, as physicians report nurses saying, "We lost him several weeks ago; isn't it time to quit?" or "For this child, don't you think it's time to turn off your curiosity so you can turn on your kindness?" or that the facilities in which they were treated are "hardly more than *dying* bins."

One lay Catholic moralist points out that many defective children often refuse to die, and from that fact he concludes that we should move to a policy of actively killing them.[10] Here was surely a slippery slope where the first mistake was to step on it. In medical care, we rightly compare treatments in order to decide what is indicated as responsible activity on the part of those who are still living toward those who are now dying. But we ought not to compare and contrast the persons—the patients who are dying—with one another in other respects. We have no moral right to choose that some live and others die, when the medical indications for treatment are the same.

That means that the standard for letting die must be the same for the normal child as for the defective child. If an operation to remove a bowel obstruction is indicated to save the life of a normal infant, it is also the indicated treatment of a mongoloid infant. The latter is

9. Raymond S. Duff and A. G. M. Campbell reported 299 deaths of defective infants at Yale-New Haven Hospital over a thirty-month period, 1970–72. Of these, 86 percent (256) belonged to category 1. Sixty-six percent of the deaths in this category were the result of respiratory problems or other complications associated with extreme prematurity. Category 2 comprised the remaining 14 percent (43) of the total deaths ("Moral and Ethical Dilemmas in the Special-Care Nursery," *New England Journal of Medicine* 289, no. 17 (October 25, 1973).

10. Daniel C. Maguire, *Death by Choice* (Garden City, N.Y.: Doubleday & Co., 1974), pp. 11–12.

certainly not dying because of Down's syndrome. Like any other child with an obstruction in its intestinal tract, it will starve to death unless an operation is performed to remove the obstruction to permit normal feeding.

Dr. John Lorber of Sheffield, England, is now famous for choosing to let some spina bifida or myelomeningocele babies die while others undergo a series of operations over many years. The latter lead impaired lives, but lives Lorber judges to be worth living. He claims he is able to make this determination on the first day of a baby's life by applying five measurements or tests. Now, I do not think that a series of ordinary treatments—closing the open spine, antibiotics, a contraption to deal with urinary incontinence, and a shunt to prevent hydrocephalus—today adds up to extraordinary medical care, except perhaps in the case of a conscious, competent patient who is able himself to refuse treatment. But the point is that Dr. Lorber does not claim that the infants he chooses to "let die" are now dying, or that to intervene medically only prolongs their dying. Indeed, those babies are heavily sedated. Is the reason for that to keep pain at bay? I doubt it.[11] There is rather some ground for suspicion that, since drowsy babies need to be fed less frequently, the spina bifida babies chosen not to be treated are sedated so that they will begin dying of hunger and slowly sleep away.[12] At least, that would be one way of

11. Dr. Anthony Shaw ("Dilemmas of 'Informed Consent' in Children," *New England Journal of Medicine* 289, no. 17) asks, in Case B: "To what extent should palliative treatment be given in a case in which definitive treatment is withheld?" That was surely a euphemistic use of the word *palliative,* since under that head Dr. Shaw criticizes the decision in the Johns Hopkins Hospital case to allow the "lingering death" of a Down's syndrome baby whose parents refused permission for an intestinal operation. The hospital failed to request a court to take jurisdiction and order such an ordinary operation. In Shaw's comment on Case D, the question becomes: "Where does one draw the line between palliation of the infant's suffering and actively shortening the infant's life?" That, indeed, becomes the question if one first commits the category mistake of identifying *both* with a physician's prevention of suffering, instead of calling the latter by its proper name: the choice and promotion of death, which is no part of a physician's vocation. Indeed, Dr. Shaw expressed sympathetic understanding for the view that selective neglect is a woman's second chance to secure an abortion! ("Doctor, Do We Have a Choice?" *The New York Times Magazine,* January 30, 1972.

12. The questions I raise about Lorber's practice are based on participation in the conference on *spina bifida* babies, May 4–7, 1975, at Skytop Lodge, Skytop, Pennsylvania, at which he was one of the speakers. In the literature, I can cite Dr. John M. Freedman, "To Treat or Not to Treat: Ethical Dilemmas of Treating the Infant with

avoiding the notorious case of allowing a defective infant to starve to death in fifteen days, as was done at Johns Hopkins Hospital a few years ago when a Down's baby was refused an operation to remove its intestinal obstruction. So my first point is clear: the fact that dying patients sometimes need no more attempts to be made to save them ought not to be carelessly applied to the case of defective newborns. Sometimes the neglected infants are not born dying. They are only born defective and in need of help. The question whether no treatment is the indicated treatment cannot legitimately be raised, unless there is special medical reason for saying that treatment might make them worse and in any case could not help. The comparison should be between treatments measured to the need. As God is no respecter of persons of high degree, neither should we be. The proper form of the question to be asked is: Should we not close a wound in a newborn expected to be normal? Should we not provide him with devices

---

a Myelomeningocele," *Clinical Neurosurgery* 20 : 134–46. Freedman is "ambivalently" a proponent of vigorous treatment. His article concentrates on the additional neurological impairment of the untreated who do not soon die. He asks, concerning such a child, "Is he to be sedated and fed inadequately so that he slowly dies of starvation, without making too much noise?" (p. 141). The optimistic treatment of spina bifida babies became technically possible in the late 1950s. Before that, Freedman raises the following skeptical questions concerning their reported deaths:

> Why should a child with myelomeningocele be stillborn? . . . Forest [a researcher Freedman is citing] found that the incidence of stillbirths dropped precipitously from a high of 40 percent of all births with this defect in 1958 to a low of zero in 1962. The drop in stillbirths occurred concomitantly with increasing optimism and enthusiasm for the treatment of infants with myelomeningocele. In marvelous English understatement, Forest states that "the percentage of stillbirths is by no means as fixed and unalterable as has generally been supposed." Was this the result of obstetrical euthanasia [formerly practiced]? An additional four to 10 percent of the infants die within the first 24 hours. Why? Whereas some of these infants have other congenital malformations or prematurity, a large number die of "hydrocephalus"; a most unusual age to die of hydrocephalus. . . . Deaths by omission or commission would appear to account for a significant proportion of the mortality in the immediate neonatal period. [Pp. 136–37]

Freedman's ironic comment concerning the "statistical deaths" of spina bifida babies simply demonstrates that infant euthanasia was a widespread practice before around 1950 when vigorous treatment of this condition became possible. Some pediatric surgeons and allied specialists seem now to be returning to that practice under the guise of refraining from instituting extraordinary treatment. Their omissions become overt commissions when heavy and unnecessary sedation is prescribed. Then these babies do not die of their affliction; they do not die natural deaths.

correcting his incontinence? Should not physical conditions likely to impair any child's mental capacity be stopped if possible; or if not, subdued?

In chapter 4 it was argued that the traditional medical morality expressed by the distinction between ordinary (or mandatory) and extraordinary (or only electable, dispensable) means reduces almost without significant remainder to (1) our duty always to care but only to care for the dying and (2) a conscious patient's right to refuse treatment; a medical indications policy contains the precision and the justifiable latitude to embrace both sorts of cases. We have seen that the first meaning does not apply to some current cases of medical neglect of defective infants. Many of the neglected infants are not born dying; neither are they born capable of refusing treatment. So the second meaning is equally impertinent.

One need not even argue this second point. Ethically, the generally announced policy of the benign neglect of defective infants should be called by its proper name: "involuntary euthanasia." I have elsewhere argued in the case of the dying that in the exceptional case when our care and comfort and presence can no longer reach them, there is no longer any morally significant distinction between omission and commission, between standing aside and directly dispatching them.[13] They are now in God's hands and no longer subject to our love and care. Now the reverse judgment must be made: when care is not even attempted in the case of defective nondying infants, there is no morally significant distinction between action and abstention. Morally, what in this case is not done is the same as doing. The benign neglect of defective infants—who are not dying, who cannot themselves refuse treatment, who are most in need of human help—is the same as directly dispatching them: involuntary euthanasia.

That, at least, is the opinion of Dr. R. B. Zachary, also of Sheffield, England, who believes in vigorous treatment of spina bifida babies. In a letter (October 31, 1975) to Dr. Elspeth Rhys-Williams of the International Pro-Life Information Centre in London, whom I had addressed, Dr. Zachary wrote:

> The question that puzzled me was that a considerable number of patients used to survive with ordinary care, and yet some

13. *The Patient as Person*, pp. 161–64.

authors were claiming "100 percent success" in selecting their cases, namely that all those cases which did not have surgery died, within three months in some cases or others said within six or eight months. Yet I myself was seeing at some other centres patients who were several months of age, or two or three months of age, who had not in fact died when that had been the intention.

It then became clear that the policy of management has something more to it than mere conservative treatment, and is expressed in a paper by Lorber that the children received no treatment for any complications and in fact no medical treatment other than "analgesics" as required. Now, in these newborn babies I have not known them to be suffering from such pain as to require analgesics, and if in fact the word is a mistake and it should be "hypnotics," I can only say that I have not known them unable to sleep. It appears that a policy has been adopted by some doctors of giving these babies chloral hydrate or phenobarbitone and in some cases go on to morphia (in the form of Nepenthe) in quite substantial doses and the babies are then fed on demand. Naturally, if the baby is very sleepy it will not demand any food and is likely to die either directly from starvation or from infection in a malnourished infant. Now, it is absolutely clear that there is no therapeutic indication for the administration of chloral hydrate or phenobarbitone or morphia and its administration would certainly not be considered in other cases which were to receive treatment. Moreover, we are constantly reminding our students that they ought to have a good and sound reason before prescribing drugs. It is not surprising therefore than many of the babies die within a very few weeks and hence there is the discrepancy between the results of conservative treatment in some places and others.

It is also clear that a comparison of the results of operative treatment and not operative treatment is completely invalid if active steps such as this are taken to accomplish the death of the child. The administration of these drugs is in fact undertaken by those who say they do not believe in euthanasia for these children. Sometimes the term "passive euthanasia" is used, but if that were so there would be no direct administration of drugs. It is indeed active euthanasia but slow euthanasia and I think if people are convinced that it is the right thing to do they should not shrink from calling it by its proper name.[14]

Our law on this is quite clear. I can only refer to the admirable article by John A. Robertson, assistant professor of law at the University of Minnesota, entitled "Involuntary Euthanasia of Defective Newborns: A Legal Analysis," [15] for a full account of the case law—

14. Printed with permission of Dr. Zachary. Dr. Zachary's practice, which I characterize as a medical indications policy, was discussed in chap. 4. Zachary decides whether curative (or improving) treatments are indicated or not. His practice is a *comparison of treatments,* to determine whether operations would effect improvement in these patients' neurological or other medical conditions. He does not compare patients to be brought about in the future (the "quality of life" to be delivered). He decides whether he can help or only care for these voiceless patients—not whether they can be given what some call a "life worth living."

15. *Stanford Law Review* 27, no. 2 (January 1973) : 213–69. See also Dennis J. Horan, "Euthanasia, Medical Treatment, and the Mongoloid Child: Death as a Treatment of Choice," *Baylor Law Review* 27, no. 1 (Winter 1975) : 76–85; and other articles in the same issue. Turning our attention somewhat more to the decision-making process, an article coauthored by a lawyer and a pediatrician offers the following advice:

> Physicians could consider informing parents that criminal liability might be attached to nontreatment cases, so that parents could be sufficiently informed of the risk to seek legal advice. In addition, such parents might be informed that even if they do not wish to keep the child, they are legally obligated, at least until parental rights are formally terminated, to provide it with medical care. If parents insist on risking prosecution, the physician might then inform them that he is [still] legally obligated to take steps toward saving the infant's life. . . . The parents cannot terminate the physician's legal duties by withholding consent or even by discharging him. The law does not permit a physician to avoid criminal liability by submitting to the wishes of the parents and doing nothing, if this will lead to injury or death of the infant.

The essence of due process, these authors also suggest, "entails turning over decision-making to someone more likely to be disinterested than the parents or their private physician" (John A. Robertson and Norman Fost, "Passive Euthanasia of Defective Newborn Infants: Legal Considerations," *Journal of Pediatrics* 88 (May 1976) : 883–89).

The title of Dr. Anthony Shaw's article, cited above, is significant: "Dilemmas of 'Informed Consent' in Children." "The answer to Mr. A's question," he writes at one point, "should have been, 'You *do* have a choice. You might want to consider not signing the operative consent at all.' " Informed dissent is thus placed on a par with informed consent to life-saving procedures in children. Philosophically, Shaw's point of view rests upon an understanding of human freedom exercised from an Archimedean neutral fulcrum, capable of shifting "arbitrarily" one way or the other. One chooses the choice. Dissent from life is as valid as consent to life for those in whose

the common law—on this matter. When a child has been born to parents, with an attending physician, in a hospital, all parties have entered into a role and a relationship with another human being who claims their care. Any refusal or failure on their parts may render them—parents, physicians, hospital administrators—guilty of offenses ranging all the way from child abuse to negligent or other degrees of manslaughter. The only reason this is not publicly apparent is because of the "benign neglect" of prosecuting attorneys, and because the medical neglect of newborn children was practiced until recently under institutional cover. One of the physicians who brought the practice out into the open knew the common law well enough to state at the conference mentioned above that he was going to press for an amendment to his state's child-abuse statute that would, in effect, remove physicians' neglect from the meaning of *child abuse,* thus relieving them of the obligation to *report* such cases. That alone, however, would not immunize them from some sort of criminal prosecution for acts of medical neglect between consenting adults (parents and physicians) when done in private.[16]

Constitutional law also enforces the protectability of the defective newborn. Right-to-life people perhaps should reread *Roe* v. *Wade*[17] with the question of the newborn infant in mind. There the Court, referring to the earlier case *United States* v. *Vuitch,*[18] said "we would

---

behalf we must make the choice, provided only that we are informed of a serious medical prognosis. To date both Western law and morality favor pro-life decisions—unless one refuses treatment for oneself, and that too reaches its moral limit at suicidal refusals of ordinary treatment.

16. Dr. Anthony Shaw, op. cit., indicated his own willingness to invoke the law in some cases to protect children in need of treatment from parents who would deny them care. Case E involved a Down's syndrome baby needing an intestinal operation, whose mother "thought that the retarded infant would be impossible for her to care for and would have a destructive effect on her already shaky marriage." In this case, a local child-welfare agency, invoking the state child-abuse statute, obtained a court order directing surgery to be performed.

Subsequent to his article, Dr. Shaw indicated his intention to seek an amendment of the child-abuse statute of the Commonwealth of Virginia. His amendment would not exclude appeal beyond the mother's decision in Case E. Thus it would not nullify the bearing of the criminal law upon medical neglect cases. I venture to say, however, that any amendment making it a private decision not to report abuse in cases of medical neglect will foster more child neglect than Dr. Shaw means to espouse.

17. 410 U.S. 113 (1973).

18. 409 U.S. 62 (1971).

not have indulged in statutory interpretation favorable to abortion in special circumstances if the necessary consequence was the termination of life entitled to Fourteenth Amendment protection." That, the Court said "inferentially" means that a person in the legal or constitutional sense is anyone born. The Court chided the law of Texas for inconsistency in protecting unborn life, and for making any exceptions ". . . [I]f the fetus is a person who is not to be deprived of life without due process of law, and if the mother's condition is the sole determinant, does not the Texas exception appear to be out of line with the Amendment's command?" What does that "inferentially" mean as to the protection constitutionally commanded for the defective newborn? Finally, the Court chided the law of Texas for not defining the woman as "a principal or accomplice."

One may not like that reasoning, but the question is, What does that imply concerning the criminal guilt of a physician and parents who enter into a private conspiracy to deprive an infant of its life, and who negligently do the deed? Are they not principals and accomplices in negligent homicide, or in conspiracy to deprive another human being (a "person" in the eyes of the law, if not psychologically) of his civil rights, his Fourteenth Amendment rights?

Moreover, on July 1, 1976, the Supreme Court [19]—striking down the effort of the state of Missouri, in its comprehensive abortion statute, to impose a "standard of care" upon physicians in case a live-born infant results from an abortion procedure—observed that the Missouri statute was redundant: any physician's failure to exercise that care was already covered by the criminal laws of Missouri and any other state. The Court in this instance must have known that the possibly viable infants "delivered" by an abortion procedure are likely to be defective, from induced prematurity if not from the procedure. Nevertheless, these infants have Fourteenth Amendment rights and their lives are protectable by the criminal law.

If the meaning of the distinction between ordinary and extraordinary means is to be found in only actively caring for the dying and in a patient's right to refuse treatment, it seems reasonable to conclude at this point that this distinction cannot be invoked in the case of very many defective newborn infants. "Benign" motives may be behind the practice of neglect, but the practice itself is morally the

19. *Planned Parenthood* v. *Danforth*. See chapter 1, above.

same as involuntary euthanasia. On this point we need to learn from the Jewish teaching concerning the creation of Adam:

> Therefore only a single human being was created in the world, to teach that if any person has caused a single soul of Israel to perish, Scripture regards him as if he had caused an entire world to perish; and if any human being saves a single soul of Israel, Scripture regards him as if he had saved an entire world.[20]

Dr. Raymond S. Duff discerned the reasons for a practice of pediatric medicine in accord with a medical indications policy: "Some patients without treatment live anyway, though in a greater state of misery. . . . Therefore, though death may be preferred to life with treatment, life with treatment is yet to be preferred over life without treatment."[21] That was a road not taken in the recently announced policy of the neglect of defective newborns. Dr. Duff's remarks were in the context of lamenting certain of our legal restrictions upon homicide: "some persons might prefer to avoid mostly useless treatment if death could be certain."

Dr. Duff would launch the practice of pediatric medicine upon a sea of uncertainty, upon economic and social indices for predicting the quality of a child patient's future and that of his family. That medical policy reaches to high heaven in its assumed future providence over the relief of the human estate, and it is bound to produce chaos in the practice of medical care here on earth. Instead, I have argued, the care extended to defective newborn children—and to other patients whose death is not impending and who cannot refuse treatment for themselves—should be cut to the measure of a medical indications policy (a comparison of treatments, or of treatment with no treatment). The underlying reason our law locates negligence in the matter of the life or death of small and uncomprehending patients in the class of homicides is that to neglect to save them (when we can, and when their birth within natural and elected covenants of life with life claims the protection of particular persons, parents, physicians, nurses, and hospital administrators) falls *morally* in the vicinity of homicide or involuntary euthanasia.

20. *Sanhedrin* 37a. "Neither shalt thou stand idly by the blood of thy neighbor" (Leviticus 19 : 16); for Jewish thought, this verse voids any appeal to neglect or to "passive" euthanasia as excuses.

21. "On Choosing Death," Testimony before the Senate Subcommittee on Health, Edward M. Kennedy, Chairman, June 11, 1974.

It is also crystal clear that one powerful force leading us toward involuntary euthanasia is the continued use of *ordinary* and *extraordinary* as classifications not limited to dying or to conscious patients and used as terminal justifications for sometimes withholding treatment from patients who are neither. Moreover, if passive euthanasia comes in the form of the unconsented withholding of treatments that are medically indicated, then active, involuntary euthanasia cannot be far behind. That is not because the slope affords no footholds, but again because to neglect to extend medically indicated treatment to uncomprehending patients is only in degree distinguishable from other homicides *in moral reasoning*. It happens to be a good moral argument (granting the premise, which I do not) to ask, If we may withhold medically indicated treatment (or only give treatments called for by quality-of-life expectations), why may we not directly kill instead? *Nonvoluntary euthanasia* and *substituted judgments* about fortunate death will be the terms that ease our passage to direct killing.

Justice and Equal Treatment

There is still another moral aspect of the practice of neglect. This is a question of justice. Some physicians who have reported that they let some babies die (perhaps hasten their dying) also report that they make such life or death decisions not only on the basis of the newborn's medical condition and prognosis, but on the basis of familial, social, and economic factors as well. If the marriage seems to be a strong one, an infant impaired to *x* degree may be treated, while an infant with the same impairment may not be treated if the marriage seems about to fall apart. Treatment may be given if the parents are wealthy; not, if they are poor.[22] Now, life may be unfair, as John

22. In a published interview, Dr. Raymond S. Duff seems to me to be ambiguous on these points, even contradictory. On the one hand he says, "My guess is that neither social nor economic considerations influence the decisions we are talking about to any significant degree. I never felt that a troubled marriage or the economics of the family has really had a major influence. Parents may fight with one another but they still adhere to what they both consider is fair to the child." Yet two or three paragraphs later he reported the case of a couple who had to decide "how many lives would be wrecked: one of dubious value plus four others, *or* the one of dubious value. There was no real choice the family felt" primarily because of space, money, time, and personal resources. That couple of modest means noted that the wealthy can "buy out" of the choice. Yet, again, a few paragraphs later, when asked whether there would be "a substantiative difference in the number of infants allowed to die"

Kennedy said; but to deliberately make medical care a function of inequities that exist at birth is evidently to add injustice to injury and fate.

Wiser and more righteous is the practice of Dr. Chester A. Swinyard of the New York University medical school's rehabilitation center. Upon the presentation to him of a defective newborn, he immediately tries to make clear to the mother the distinction between the question of ultimate custody of the child and questions concerning the care it needs. The mother must consent to operations, of course. But she is asked only to make judgments about the baby's care, while she is working through the problem of whether to accept the defective child as a substitute for her "lost child," i.e., the perfect baby she wanted. In the prism of the case, when the question is, Shall this open spine be closed? Shall a shunt be used to prevent further mental impairment? the mothers can usually answer correctly. In the case of spina bifida babies, Dr. Swinyard also reports very infrequent need of institutionalization or foster parents. That results from concentrating the mother's attention on what medical care requires, and not on lifelong burdens of custody.[23] One must entirely reject the contention

---

if society was equipped with uniformly excellent, well-staffed custodial institutions, Dr. Duff replied, "I doubt it," citing "several parents who felt it is not right for their child to exist primarily to provide employment for others." He also distinguished the decision to "let die" in Yale-New Haven Hospital from the treatment accorded defective children in Nazi Germany by saying that in the current cases "family and physicians took into account not only the child's right (to live or to die) but the needs of the family and society, and, to some extent, future generations," protesting that "if we cannot trust these persons to do justice here, can anyone be trusted?" (Beverly Kelsey, "Shall These Children Live?"; reprinted in the *Hastings Center Report* 5, no. 2).

The more technical and presumably well-considered article by Duff and Campbell is quite clear on these points ("Moral and Ethical Dilemmas in the Special-Care Nursery," *New England Journal of Medicine* 289, no. 17). There, the references to "the family economy," "siblings' rights to relief from the seemingly pointless, crushing burden," "the strains of the illness . . . believed to be threatening the marriage bonds and to be causing sibling behavioral disturbances," "fear that they and their other children would become socially enslaved, economically deprived, and permanently stigmatized, . . . [in] a state of 'chronic sorrow,' " stand without modulation, or without the claim that the family-physician decision was made simply for the sake of the defective child.

23. Swinyard's practice, as I understand it, is quite different from withholding prognosis of the child's condition. The parents of a child with meningomyelocele are not "simply told that the child needed an operation on the back as the first step in correcting several defects . . . while the activities of care proceeded at a brisk pace" (Duff and Campbell, "Moral and Ethical Dilemmas").

of Duff and Campbell that parents, facing the prospect of oppressive burdens of care, are capable of making the most morally sensible decisions about the needs and rights of defective newborns. There is a Jewish teaching to the effect that only disinterested parties may, by even so innocuous a method as prayer, take any action which may lead to premature termination of life. Husband, children, family and those charged with the care of the patient may not pray for death.[24]

One can understand—even appreciate—the motives of a physician who considers an unhappy marriage or family poverty when weighing the tragedy facing one child against that facing another; and rations his help accordingly. Nevertheless, that surely is a species of injustice. Physicians are not appointed to remove all life's tragedy, least of all by lessening medical care now and letting infants die who for social reasons seem fated to have less care in the future than others. That's one way to remove every evening the human debris that has accumulated since morning.

There is a story that is going around—in fact I'm going around telling it—about how the pope, the chief rabbi of Jerusalem, and the general secretary of the World Council of Churches arrived in heaven the same day. Since they had been spiritual leaders here below and ecclesiastical figures to take notice of, they had some difficulty adjusting. Such was the equality there that everyone had to take his place and turn in the cafeteria line. After some muttering protest they fell into the customs of the place, until one day a little man dressed in a white coat came in and rushed to the head of the line. "Who's that?" asked the pope resentfully. "Oh, that's God," came the reply. "He thinks he's a doctor!"

If physicians are going to play God under the pretense of providing relief for the human condition, let us hope they play God as God plays God. Our God is no respecter of persons of good quality. Nor does he curtail his care for us because our parents are poor or have unhappy marriages, or because we are most in need of help. Again, a true humanism also leads to an "equality of life" standard.

A policy of selectively not treating severely defective infants appeals ultimately, it is true, to whatever constitutes the greatness and glory of humankind to give us a standard by which to determine the bottom line of life to be deemed worth living. Thus Joseph Fletcher proposed fifteen "positive human criteria" and five "negative human

24. R. Chaim Palaggi, Chikekei Lev., I, Yoreh De'ah, no. 50.

criteria" as an ensemble quality-of-life index.[25] Then he reduced the number in an article entitled "Four Indicators of Humanhood—the Enquiry Matures." [26] There is no need for us to examine Fletcher's criteria—three of which seem to declare anyone who does not have a Western sense of time to be a non-person. Fletcher is simply a sign of our times. Many, more serious ethicists have joined in the search for "indicators of personhood." The fundamental question to be faced is whether the practice of medicine should be based on any such set of criteria (presuming they can be discovered and agreed upon).

To that question I want first to say that that's no way to play God as God plays God. That was not the bottom line of his providential care. When the prophet Jeremiah tells us, "Before I formed thee in the belly I knew thee; and before thou camest forth out of the womb I sanctified thee; and I ordained thee" (1 : 5), he does not mean to start us on a search for the "indicators of personhood" God was using or should have used before calling us by name. Neither did the psalmist when he cried, "Behold . . . the darkness and the light are both alike to thee. For thou hast possessed my reins: thou hast covered me in my mother's womb. I will praise thee; for I am fearfully and wonderfully made: marvelous are thy works; and that my soul knoweth right well" (139 : 12b, 13, 14). No more did God, at the outset of his Egyptian rescue operation, look around for "indicators of peoplehood," choosing only those best qualified for national existence. "The Lord did not set his love upon you, nor choose you, because you

25. "Medicine and the Nature of Man," in *The Teaching of Medical Ethics,* ed. Robert M. Veatch, Willard Gaylin, and Councilman Morgan; *Hastings Center Report* 2, no. 5 (November 1972) : 1–4. See also the correspondence in vol. 1, no. 1 (February 1973), p. 13.

26. *Hastings Center Report* 4, no. 6 (December 1974) : 4–7. These accordion concepts of "meaningful / meaningless," "humanhood," "relationships that can be considered human," and "man's ability to relate" (called, incorrectly, "minimal" criteria) are used throughout *Dying: Considerations Concerning the Passage from Life to Death,* an Interim Report by the Task Force on Human Life of the Anglican Church of Canada (Office of the General Secretary, 600 Jarvis Street, Toronto, Canada, June 1977; presented to the 1977 session of the Synod on August 11–18, 1977). Representing no official or authoritative views of the Anglican church of Canada, the report proceeds to address our duties toward defective newborns as if they are "human-looking shapes" or at most "sentient" creatures: ". . . the only way to treat such defective infants humanly is not to treat them as human" (p. 14). A widening controversy over the report was reported in *The New York Times,* July 28, 1977. The Synod sent the report back to committee.

were more in number than any people; for you were the fewest of all people. But because the Lord loved you, and because he would keep the oath he had sworn unto your fathers, hath the Lord brought you out with a mighty hand" (Deuteronomy 7 : 7, 8a).

Many of God's life and death decisions are inscrutable to us. People are born and die. Nations rise and fall. Doubtless God in his official governance does—or at least permits—lots of things (as the Irishman said) which he would never think of doing in a private capacity. Nor should we, who are not given dominion or co-regency over humankind. But there is no indication at all that God is a rationalist whose care is a function of indicators of our personhood, or of our achievement within those capacities. He makes his rain to fall upon the just and the unjust alike, and his sun to rise on the abnormal as well as the normal. Indeed, he has special care for the weak and the vulnerable among us earth people. He cares according to need, not capacity or merit.

These images and shadows of divine things are the foundation of Western medical care, together with that "Pythagorean manifesto," [27] the Hippocratic oath. As *John* Fletcher has written:

> If we choose to be shaped by Judeo-Christian visions of the "createdness" of life within which every creature bears the image of God, we ought to care for the defective newborn as if our relation with the creator depended on the outcome. If we choose to be shaped by visions of the inherent dignity of each member of the human family, no matter what his or her predicament, we ought to care for this defenseless person as if the basis of our own dignity depended on the outcome.[28] Care cannot fall short of universal equality.

Indicators of personhood may be of use in psychology, in educational theory, and in moral nurture, but to use such indices in the practice of medicine is a grave mistake. Even the search for such guidelines on which to base the care of defective newborn infants would launch neonatal medicine upon a trackless ocean of uncertainty, directly into arbitrary winds. Thus, one of the physicians at

27. *Roe* v. *Wade,* 410 U.S. 113.

28. John Fletcher, "Abortion, Euthanasia, and Care of Defective Newborns," *New England Journal of Medicine* 292 (January 9, 1975) : 75–78.

Yale-New Haven Hospital, explaining on television the newly announced policy of benign neglect of defective infants in that medical center, said that to have a life worth living a baby must be "lovable." [29] Millard S. Everett in his book *Ideals of Life* writes that "no child should be admitted into the society of the living" who suffers "any physical or mental defect that would prevent marriage or would make others tolerate his company only from a sense of mercy. . . ." [30] Mercy me, to that we must say no. Medical criteria for care should remain physiological, as should also the signs by which physicians declare that a patient has died. Decisions to treat or not to treat should be the same for the normal and the abnormal alike. Searching for an index of personhood to use (comparing patient-persons, not treatments or treatment with no treatment) is rather like founding medical care on theological judgments about when God infuses the soul into the human organism.

In face of the slipperiness of such criteria as "lovable" or capacity to live without the mercy of others, some doctors suggest that the defective themselves be consulted. They should be asked whether they themselves should have been assisted to live or allowed to die; or whether medical aid should be extended if they have a child afflicted as they are. That, it is suggested, would be a realistic way for us to tell the difference between a life worth living and one that is not. But who does not realize that answers to such questions would be a comparison of normal life with defective life—the same as a mother's initial reaction to such a tragedy—and not a comparison of life with no life? No one can weigh life against nothingness; and, of course, an abnormal person saved by modern medicine will say he wants no *affliction* such as his to be the fate of others. Faced with the question, he may very well say that he *wants no child* afflicted as he is. That will be his man-

29. CBS News, January 2, 1973. In their landmark article ("Moral and Ethical Dilemmas") Drs. Raymond S. Duff and A. G. M. Campbell used the expression "meaningful humanhood." Dr. Duff in a subsequently published interview explained that criteria to mean "the capacity to love and be loved, to be independent, and to understand and plan for the future" (Beverly Kelsey, "Shall These Children Live?"). Asked whether a mongoloid child may have "meaningful humanhood," Dr. Duff seemed to hedge, leaving the decision to parents who "pay the fiddler to call the tune," while the physician and hospital policy need only sometimes decide "whether the family's God is fair to the child."

30. Cited by Daniel C. Maguire, *Death by Choice,* p. 7. Here Maguire indicates no disagreement with such criteria.

ner of speaking. Still no one can look into the chasm between life and death and weigh the difference—not without first being alive, which makes quite a difference. Such speculations are rather like the "wrongful life" cases that have been brought to our courts [31]: suing one's parents for having been born illegitimate, or of parents with borderline intelligence, or in unhappy surroundings. The courts have held that the petitioner would not be there to sue if he had never been born. Likewise, no one has "standing" in the moral universe to tell whether he should ever have been or not. Life is not a good; it is an inexplicable gift. When we speak of *good* we speak of *life's* well-being. It is a duty of parents and physicians and the human community in general to sustain the life of a defective infant—who is not born dying and who cannot refuse treatment—and to insure that its life shall be as good and as free from disability as possible.

The proper treatment of defective newborns, especially proper care in the paradigmatic case of spina bifida babies, cannot be determined without a more radical rethinking than is usually proposed of the meaning of traditional medical ethical concepts. I have suggested that the distinction between ordinary and extraordinary measures in the case of patients who are not dying (and who cannot themselves refuse treatment) means discrimination between indicated and non-indicated treatments. It requires choice among beneficial treatments and a simple refusal to use medically nonbeneficial measures. The question to be asked concerning nondying patients incapable of consent is, What will help? What will ease?

Failure to take this route entails treating defective newborns who are not dying *as if* they were competent conscious patients refusing treatment. To continue discussion of these crucial cases under the alternative "to save or let die" forces an ethicist or a physician to move from consultation about beneficial and nonbeneficial treatments to consultation about conditions of life that are beneficial to the possessor thereof. This obscures the distinction between voluntary and involuntary euthanasia, or at least erodes the moral grounds for making that distinction. It also erodes the moral reasons for distinguishing

31. A convenient reference and discussion of these cases is in *The Problem of Abortion*, ed. Joel Feinberg (Belmont, Calif.: Wadsworth Publishing Co.), pp. 161–80. At one point Duff and Campbell expressly claim they are enabling infants "to escape 'wrongful life,' a fate rated as worse than death." We need to know, by whose ratings? The suicide rate among normal people is *higher* than among so-called defective people. That's one way to "consult" them.

between letting die and actively dispatching defective newborns, or hastening their deaths. Comparison of human lives and not comparison of treatments (including only palliative treatment) becomes the issue.

A New Class of Eligible Pediatric Research Subjects?

Let us return now to the paradigm case where choices are made to treat or not to treat defective infants. Before about 1950 physicians had no real choice when confronted by a baby suffering from spina bifida and myelomeningocele, with hydrocephalus in prospect. The operative results were no better than the nonoperative results. Then a decision to let die, or rather not to operate, could properly be made rather than pester the victim with vain trials. Today vigorous treatment makes a significant difference for the majority of babies with these afflictions, even when measured by the standard of their attainment of "meaningful personhood." Moreover, Dr. John M. Freedman of Johns Hopkins bases his support of vigorous treatment on the additional fact that the worst cases—those in which the patients are not much helped but refuse to die, a *minority* who do live long, perhaps in a hospital—have significantly fewer neurological and other deficits if treatment is not withheld.[32]

Now suppose that for the worst off of these infants we choose to return to the time before 1950 by using some nonphysiological standard—predicting functioning personhood in order to classify some not

32. John M. Freedman, "To Treat or Not to Treat: Ethical Dilemmas of Treating an Infant with Myelomeningocele," *Clinical Neurosurgery* 20 : 134–46. Dr. Chester A. Swinyard reports a study of 295 patients at Royal Children's Hospital, Melbourne, Australia. Ninety-four percent of the untreated patients died within two years; 4 percent lived from two to five years. The death of these infants is not impending. Swinyard's opinion is that many difficult problems would arise if the selection procedures now recommended for spina bifida patients were applied to other severe defects (Chester A. Swinyard, Shakuntala Chaube, and Fred J. Epstein, "The Dilemmas of Informed Consent", Paper presented at conference on spina bifida babies, Skytop, Pennsylvania).

Dr. Freedman's explanation of Lorber's "first day" policy is reported to be as follows: "Dr. Lorber has been caught in a trap that faces many of us who run big centers for those patients. He has been dealing with 1,200 or more children. It's far easier to provide optimal care for a small group of children"—such as at Johns Hopkins, where Freedman practices ("Let Blighted Babies Die, or Not," *World Medical News,* November 17, 1972, p. 28).

to be treated. I repeat that the vast majority of these infants are not born dying; so the option is not to save or let die. What then is it? You may be sure that positive acts and a positive policy of involuntary euthanasia stands in the wings.[33] Indeed, that is already with us, in the form of heavy sedation to hasten death.

But if we do not extend the medical care that can be conveyed to these infants, another and a "better" policy also stands in the wings, one that was used in the period before 1950. If the defective infants are not to be treated, they can be used in medical research, enabling their lack of actual potential to benefit others by experimentation—at minimum risk, of course, out of respect for their unearthly dignity. Will not the call soon go forth:

> Professor McCance and the members of his Medical Research Department want to be informed, if and when children are born in lying-in homes or women's wards in hospitals affected with Meningocele or similar abnormalities, which will make it unlikely or impossible that the children will survive longer than a short time.
>
> Professor McCance and his department wish to make some experiments on these children, which will give them no sort of pains, but they feel not entitled to make these experiments on normal, healthy children. When the birth of these children comes to be known, Professor McCance is to be informed at once by telephone. . . .

These were the words of an order issued by the deputy regional commissioner of the Northern Rhine Military Province in Germany, June 22, 1946.[34] In fact, I can think of no argument advanced in favor

33. Dr. John M. Freedman, cited above as a proponent of vigorous treatment, endorsed the termination of life of some defective newborns ("Is There a Right to Die—Quickly," *Journal of Pediatrics,* 80, no. 5 [May 1972] : 904–05). Replying in the same issue, Dr. Robert E. Cooke pointed out that "unwanted by both family and society" as a criteria for termination of life would also bring to an end a pediatrician's "intensive care for the 1,200 Gm. offspring of the 13-year-old unmarried girl from the ghetto," and he argued that "therapy without cure, if it contributes to *care,* is a necessary part of medicine in spite of the fact that the physician must sometimes suffer. Death of the unoperated patient is an unacceptable means of alleviating this suffering" ("Whose Suffering?," *Journal of Pediatrics* 80, no. 5 : 906–08).

34. Supplement 2 of the Document Books, *Trials of War Criminals Before the Nuernberg Military Tribunals Under Council Control Law, No. 10, Vol. I;* Docu-

of live fetal or abortus research in the United States in recent years that would not logically also justify medical experimentation with myelomeningocele infants who have been condemned under a policy of involuntary euthanasia, which can only benignly be called a policy of benign neglect. Most of the appeals or warrants favoring research on the still living abortus were, in fact, stated or implied by the deputy commissioner's order. Indeed, it can be argued that these defective infants would, if they could, serve the common good; and it will certainly be argued (1) that it would be a terrible "waste" not to advance pediatric research more rapidly by doing research with them and (2) that the opportunity to bring aid to other children should not be missed.

As modern societies move toward euthanasia, separation from such a social policy should be the attitude of the medical profession. Its integrity and professional ethics should not allow the practice of killing or, for that matter, experimentation on the unconsenting dying or the neglected. Instead, the proposal of Lord Brock on the subject of euthanasia is commendable.[35] He acknowledged that "the killing of the unwanted [the defective] could be legalized by an act of Parliament." Speaking for physicians, however, he wrote that there are "certain things which are part of the ethics of our profession which an Act of Parliament cannot justify or make acceptable." He goes so far as to say that "we may accept the need for euthanasia on social grounds but we cannot accept that doctors should implement it." Accepting the *need* for euthanasia on social grounds may not be the same as accepting the morality of euthanasia, or even being neutral toward the latter notion. Many an individual and some pacifist churches

---

ment Karl Brandt no. 93, pp. 250–51. Nuernberg, October 1946–April 1949. An attentive reader might suppose that the year *1946* is a typographical error, or a historical mistake on my part. Let such a reader face the facts and beware of ever again supposing that only the German *Volk,* under unique political circumstances, were capable of such crimes. Professor McCance was *British.* His request was made to German hospitals through British military government, which at the time was responsible for the supervision of all hospitals within the British zone of occupation. This document and the British precedent was introduced in *defense* of SS Lt. Gen. Karl Brandt by his counsel, Robert Servatius—better known to history as counsel for Adolf Eichmann in Jerusalem. I am indebted to Rev. Charles Carroll for this citation.

35. "Euthanasia," *Proceedings of the Royal Society of Medicine* 63 (July 1970) : 661–63.

have in some sense accepted the need for military preparations on social grounds. But far from holding the *morality* of warfare or participation in war to be an open question, they have maintained a special moral norm on that issue; and our world would be worse without them.

Suppose the medical profession in Germany had said, "We may accept the military need for throwing prisoners into icy waters to see how quickly they freeze to death, for the socially useful purpose of finding out when a ship on an important mission should or should not turn back in case a sailor falls overboard, but we cannot accept that doctors should implement that research." That might not have been a very courageous witness to a more universal ethics, but it would have been something not to be scorned. Similarly, it would have been entirely commendable if the German medical profession had said with one voice: "As ordinary citizens we can accept that the killing of unwanted retardates could be legalized by an act of the Third Reich, but as doctors we know there are certain things that are part of the ethics of our profession which an edict by the Führer cannot justify or make acceptable." Then the medical profession and the confessional church might have stood side by side against outrageous crimes against humanity, as both should in the future stand against essentially the same thing (done with less political passion) in the course of our advancing medical technology under the aegis of "social needs."

As the Nuremberg medical trials recede into the past, our great medical centers move more and more in the direction of incorporating socioeconomic considerations and cost analysis into the rationing of medical care. Are we not approaching a time when statements such as the foregoing ones, and such as Lord Brock's, may need to be addressed to the director of the budget? The need for medicine to take such a position may not show that we are at a high point in the moral history of mankind. Yet, an appeal can still be made that everyone recognize (and require) special moral obligations of a physician —even if in the descent from civilization to barbarism we are at the point of doing some rather immoral things through the agency of social technicians.

It was a wise physician who said, ironically, concerning the coming practice of infant euthanasia, that he would approve "if the parents administered the syringe of KCI prepared by the judge, and all the lawyers, priests, economists, psychologists, and journalists within a 50 mile radius were witnesses and no physicians, nurses or medical or nursing students were allowed to be present." [36]

ARE THERE EXCEPTIONS?

One could perhaps construct some exceptions to the principle of giving equally vigorous treatment to defective newborns as to normals. Before doing so I must refer the reader to what is my own understanding of the relation of an "exception" to the moral principle or rule to which it is attached [37]—since I find that a number of ethicists sometimes refer to a couple of my exceptions on the matter of letting die and directly killing and then proceed to turn the exception into a general moral principle or rule justifying (at least) "passive" involuntary euthanasia. Also, physicians should understand that among ethical analysts exceptions or counter-examples are sometimes not so much practical proposals as clarifying "thought experiments."

My first thought is a proposed *redescription* of one sort of defective newborn, not logically an "exception"; moreover, it is a hypothetical and moot point, worth mentioning anyway. It is not at all necessary to take an anencephalic baby (born without a brain in its brain chamber) as the demonstration case of a defective newborn that certainly ought not to be treated, and then build up from there other cases of gross defects that should not be treated. In "To Save or Let Die," McCormick gives anencephalous as an example of a case where no treatment is justified; a child afflicted with mongolism, on the other hand, is for him a case claiming treatment. He does not give examples

36. Albert R. Jonsen and Michael J. Garland, eds., *Ethics of Newborn Intensive Care* (Berkeley, Calif.: Institute of Governmental Studies, University of California, 1976, pp. 174–75, n. 12, and p. 190). (This volume contains the proceedings of the conference to be discussed in the next chapter.) The Church of England study pamphlet made a similar suggestion: if a euthanasia bill was again introduced into Parliament and "should it display any prospect of being passed into law, it might be wise to insist on the inclusion of a clause excluding from its scope any practitioner in therapeutic practice and confining the right to administer euthanasia to a limited number of persons who are at the same time excluded from therapeutic practice" (*On Dying Well: An Anglican Contribution to the Debate on Euthanasia.* Church Information Office, 1975. Church House, Dean's Yard, SWIP 3NZ, London, England, p. 60).

37. Paul Ramsey, "The Case of the Curious Exception," in *Norm and Context in Christian Ethics,* ed. Gene Outka and Paul Ramsey (New York: Charles Scribner's Sons, 1968), pp. 67–135.

that would serve to close the gap between these two cases in showing the practical meaning of his ethical analysis.

But, for one thing, an anencephalic baby is born dying, and here the morality of letting die clearly applies as it does to a Tay-Sachs baby when it is seized by irreversible degeneration. For another thing, even if it were possible to treat anencephalic babies, this should not be done—but not because they would be the demonstration case in support of a policy of not treating nondying defective newborns. Instead we could and should, consistent with our present understanding of brain life and death, take the definitional route in resolving that hypothetical case. Such an infant is "human," of course, in a generic sense; also it was a unique individual of our species. However, it has not been born *alive*. If we use here at the beginning of life the same physiological signs of the difference between life and death which we use at the end of life, an anencephalic baby does not have the unitary function of major organ systems within which the brain has primacy. That is why they soon "die," as we say. Such infants demonstrate their status by dying, in all senses, rather quickly. So an anencephalic baby, it could be argued, no more enters the human community to claim our care and protection than a patient remains in the human community when his brain death (and consequent heart death and lung death) is only disguised behind a heart-lung machine.

There should be no hesitation in withholding treatments that would prolong the existence such babies have, just as I would not hesitate to stop the sustenance of vital functions in a terminal patient who is no longer alive interrelatedly in brain and heart and lungs. But withholding treatment is not the point, since on our supposition they are not born dying. By acceptable indices of life they are not "alive." Within this gruesome thought experiment, one should be willing to "kill" such brainless products of human generation if (contrary to fact) they persisted in "living" in that condition. One should be willing to bury a reflexively reacting corpse (though other reasons override such an action), but not a terminal patient whose heart is still beating naturally, showing signs therefore that the brain is not wholly dead. I put the word *kill* in quotation marks, as well as the words *alive* and *living*. Actually, if these infants were never born alive it is morally impossible to commit homicide upon them (actively or negligently), just as it is impossible to do so to the corpse of the newly dead, some of whose vital signs may be maintained by machines. In short, I suggest (under these fictional circumstances) that we deal with the issue of anencephalic births by the definitional route: they are not alive human beings. The respect due them would be more like the respect to be given to the corpse of a deceased, and it is an expression of the tenderness due the unfortunate mother who gave birth to a dead baby. For these reasons our present practice should be continued: let these babies "die" all the way.

My second suggestion would be a true exception or qualification attached to our moral duty to treat all defective infants who are not born dying and who, of course, cannot for themselves refuse treatment. If care cannot be conveyed, it need not be extended. A mongoloid can receive care. So can a Tay-Sachs baby while it is dying. For the latter we may choose how it will live while dying. In the case of the former, we can add life to its years. But we face an entirely different issue if there is a sort of birth defect for which there is no therapy and if the suffering infant is in insurmountable pain. In such a suppositive case, care cannot be conveyed. Indeed, in regard to adult patients I have elsewhere argued that those circumstances abolish the moral distinction between only caring for the dying (allowing to die) and directly dispatching them.[38]

So now I must ask, is there a birth defect comparable to insurmountable pain or to such deep and prolonged unconsciousness that places terminal patients beyond the reach of the caring human community? From my limited knowledge of it, I am inclined to say that the Lesch-Nyhan syndrome seems a good candidate for this comparison, and that such a suffering infant *may* be an exception to the foregoing ethical analysis. Not, of course, to the moral rule that if possible we should always treat nondying defective newborns: there is no therapy for Lesch-Nyhan genetic illness. It is rather an exception to the rule that, when attempted remedy fails or there is no available remedy, when instead we should move to affirmative caring and comforting action, there is never any reason for stopping caring actions. From cure to care: but then does care never cease? Such a limit, if there is one, would have to be found in the nature of care itself, not in anything extrinsic. Care itself reaches or posits that limit. The fact that there is no remedy for Lesch-Nyhan disease, for example, would not

38. *The Patient as Person*, pp. 157–64.

be a reason for ceasing care. But it did seem to me, in the abstract, that giving palliative comfort could not be effectively conveyed to these babies. That seemed a barrier one runs up against by caring until one *can* care no longer.

Lesch-Nyhan disease is a genetic defect, identified and described in a series of cases in 1964, which is passed on only to male children. Its victims are unable to walk or sit up unassisted; they suffer uncontrollable spasms and mental retardation. Initially, I should say, care can and should always be conveyed to such victims, though as yet there is no cure. When, however, the babies' teeth appear they will gnaw through their lips, gnaw their hands and shoulders; they often bite off a finger and mutilate any part of their bodies they can reach. There they lie, bloody and irremediable. Is this not a close approximation to the supposable case of insurmountable pain which in the terminal adult patient places him beyond human caring action and abolishes the moral significance of the distinction between always continuing to care and direct dispatch?[39] When care cannot be conveyed, it need not be extended.

A pediatrician who read these pages expressed dismay over the idea of ever introducing into the special-care nursery the practice of promoting dying; and he told me something about the human care that can be extended to Lesch-Nyhan babies despite the fact that there is now no curative treatment. If he is correct, then my thought experiment need be pursued no further. At any rate, my remarks on this case are exploratory—an extended question. All the more so since Dr. William L. Nyhan of the University of California announced[40] some promising if small degree of success in developing a drug that relieves the illness of which he was co-discoverer (with Dr. Michael

39. Of course, a Lesch-Nyhan baby is not dying. But see *The Patient as Person*, p. 160, n. 59, for an "exception" that may be compared with that syndrome in the respect that it consists simply of descriptions of fact like the symptoms of Lesch-Nyhan's disease given above. An "exception" need not be expressed by a general term like *insurmountable pain*. The case of epidermolysis bulloso (lethalis) might serve as a better example of an exception to the rule that care should never cease until it must. A baby born with that genetic affliction cannot be effectively comforted. Any touching—routine in normal care—causes blisters to erupt on the skin. These blisters are often quite large, and infection results. Taken back to the hospital, the blisters can be subdued and the baby sent home, again to be cared for and comforted —into pain.

40. *The Chicago Tribune*, August 23, 1975.

Lesch). The development of treatments make it questionable, indeed, whether as a *rule of practice* swift or slow involuntary euthanasia ought ever to be introduced into the special-care nursery. This is not because physician-researchers would then slacken their pursuit of remedies for this and other illnesses of newborns. The good reason for doing no such thing would be that for whole teams of the caring profession (physicians, nurses, interns, medical students) to begin to induce death as a practice would be one more step in the erosion of the moral distinctions between voluntary and involuntary euthanasia and between allowing to die and direct killing. Moral theologians have already done enough for the advancement of that cause.

I can no longer postpone responding to the uses of and the objections to my venture into exception-making in the case of caring for the dying—in the case of the no longer competent person and, now here, in the case of the helpless, never competent human being. I suggested in the case of terminal patients that there may be sorts of cases when the patient (because of intractable pain or deep coma) is *totally inaccessible* to human care of any sort. Such a condition could render continuing to care no longer a duty (because useless); and, since always caring for the dying was the issue, I suggested that the *moral* reason for continuing to distinguish between allowing to die and *direct killing* looses its force when the patient becomes totally inaccessible. If care even in the form of minimal human presence with a patient can no longer be communicated, then it was also a matter of indifference to them whether care continues until and while they die or whether their deaths are accelerated. Perhaps these were daring proposals; in any case, they have been misused.

First of all, it was always apparent, at least to those familiar with ethical analysis, that as I said at the beginning of this section an exception logically need not alter or weaken the principle or rule to which it is attached. *Total inaccessibility* simply indicates a point beyond which care discovers it cannot go. Just as one never sees darkness, but instead finds that one no longer sees, so is this true of the darkness into which the dying go beyond care's reach. Far from weakening the rule to always care for the dying, care has to be ever alert, the eyes must be vigilant, to see when care can no longer accompany the dying in their passage.

Secondly, I hope it is clear from the Lesch-Nyhan example that warrants for a rule of practice may be different from warrants for an individual action. Robert M. Veatch calls this the "red light rule": Always stop at a red light. "A far better rule might be," he points out, " 'Stop and wait for every red light unless the road is clear' "; or, to give another example, "unless you are speeding a child to a hospital." The word *unless* states the exception. The red light rule without any exceptions, however, is a better general rule of practice, even if that means people waste time at lonely intersections. Civil disobedience—the courage to go against the rule when morally warranted—may be better than to allow for exceptions in a rule of general practice.[41] An example of the value of holding a rule of practice to be without exception may be the case of intractable pain. It would certainly be bad medicine to institute the practice of dispatching patients when they are in insurmountable pain, since we know that even surmountable pain is not managed skillfully in most hospitals. Instead we should improve terminal care. The exception, "unless the patient is in insurmountable pain," might too readily become an excuse for bad medical management of pain. Above I said something similar with regard to Lesch-Nyhans infants—while at the same time believing it to be right in an individual instance to act contrary to a generally justifiable practice.

41. *Death, Dying, and the Biological Revolution,* p. 97. Veatch has in mind a rule of practice against direct killing, which I argued was admissible morally in the inaccessibility cases I ventured to describe as possibilities. Veatch is entirely correct in his caution about a rule of practice. Again, anyone familiar with my writings on the methods of ethics should recall the difference between asking, What rule of practice best expresses convenant fidelity? (general rule agapism) and asking, What singular action best expresses covenant fidelity? (act agapism). (*Deeds and Rules in Christian Ethics* [New York: Charles Scribner's Sons, 1967]; and "The Case of the Curious Exception," in *Norm and Context in Christian Ethics.*) I know no further general rule into which to gather these two sorts of moral warrants or by which to decide that one or the other should, morally, always be overridden. Perhaps I was not as cautious in proposing those exceptions in *The Patient as Person* as I am now in the Lesch-Nyhan example. Perhaps I counted too much on the logical point that specific *sorts* of exceptions do not weaken the rule to which they are attached. In any case, it seems in order to refer anyone interested in these points to my long-standing recognition that there may be warrants for rules of practice that conflict with what covenant fidelity may require in individual actions. With Veatch's backing, perhaps I should say that conscientious objection may be the course to follow even in face of justifiable rules of practice. I ask the reader to note (p. 275, below) what I say I would be willing to join the Quinlans in doing for Karen Quinlan—even in face of the analysis to follow concerning the rule of practice in law and the aftermath of the Quinlan case.

The Church of England study pamphlet, which we examined in chapter 4, made the same point about a rule of practice in a medical ethics: ". . . a professional ethics cannot be built on altogether exceptional cases, even if in some such exceptional cases a man who contravened it might rightly be held not to be morally culpable." This is even more obviously true of the law.

> It is perfectly consistent to argue that morally speaking euthanasia is permissible in some extreme cases, but that it would be wrong to alter the law to allow it in such cases, because this might inescapably, in practice, let in cases in which euthanasia should not be allowed by law. The law is a blunt instrument for dealing with moral complexities. . . .[42]

This is to say, a legal and professional rule of practice can be justified by asking what prohibitions will be generally productive of maximum care of the dying. Even a conscientious objector is braced to his best, morally, by rules of practice that are generally expressive of the most care.

Thirdly, I want it understood that my understanding of care was and is what might be called (to borrow philosophical terminology) a "role and relations" ethics. It was and is a question of *agent* morality. The sole question raised was whether there ever comes a time when the care of a human agent (parent, physician) no longer reaches the subject cared for, when the eyes of faith and love no longer see, and it would be fanaticism to think so. If such a time does come, care for the dying would become as aimless as earlier further medical attempts to save or cure that life became purposeless. A gift is not a gift unless received; care is not what we suppose unless received, even if minimally. If not at all, there is no obligation to continue to do the useless. Since mine was and is an ethics of agent agape and, in medical ethics, a strong sense of agent care, I never suggested that one should base moral judgments in any degree upon an evaluation of the patient-

42. *On Living Well*, p. 12. Daniel C. Maguire objects to this line of reasoning about professional and legal ethics ("Death and the Moral Domain," *St. Luke's Journal of Theology* 20, no. 3 [June 1977]: 197–216). His article, however, gives evidence of the correctness of it, by substituting *suffering* for insurmountable pain as sufficient ground for incorporating euthanasia into law. Suffering is already an accordian category, even though Maguire still writes as if he is talking about very rare, exceptional cases.

subject as such. There was not the slightest suggestion that one should decide *first* whether the patient-subjects are so overwhelmed by their struggle for existence that they have lost effective capacity for meaningful relationship. No quality-of-life judgments were given entrance; only uselessness of agent care was suggested. These outlooks may seem very similar, but the accent is quite different.

For these reasons, I consider that, of the objections to my proposed conditions for ceasing care, the most telling ones were those published earliest. The early criticisms also did not obscure the fact that by the exceptions in the case of deep coma or intractable pain I proposed to draw a line beyond which the prohibition against direct killing would have lost moral significance. Following a decision to stop attempts any longer to cure or to save the life of the dying, the entire *moral* reason for prohibiting direct killing or accelerating dying, I argued, was our obligation always to care for the dying. It was not a routinized rule distinguishing between omission and commission or between direct and indirect action as regnant moral principles. If, then, care that never ceases is such by always abiding and ceaselessly caring,[43] and if such care finds that this most important work of love on earth has come to its end, then the patient's impenetrable inaccessibility to care, I argued, means that the distinction between direct killing and allowing to die has now become a matter of indifference. The conditions for ceasing to extend care while the dying die, and the line beyond which directly dispatching them or hastening their deaths becomes indifferent or permissible, involve the sorts of cases (if there are any) in which patients are entirely inaccessible to any human communication from our side. But I added that no ethicist or any person other than a physician would possibly be able to determine when a comatose patient was *utterly unreachable* by any agent's care.

One reply was that no one—physician or philosopher—can determine that such is the case. Thus Daniel C. Maguire called in question my claim that those exceptions in the case of patients irretrievably in-

43. Cf. Søren Kierkegaard's profound thought that "love hopes all things" only because love always hopes, is always hopeful. *The Works of Love*. Princeton, N.J.: Princeton University Press, 1946, pp. 199–213. Applied to the above two crucial medical decisions, care means always hoping to cure and to save life until that becomes, in the case of the dying, useless; and care means always abiding with the dying patient until that becomes useless.

accessible to human care were "carefully circumscribed." They are not, he wrote, since "medical men and bioethicists are not at all sure just when the dying patient enters into 'impenetrable solitude.' The judgment of inaccessibility will usually be highly subjective." [44] Richard A. McCormick, S.J., made the same point. Physicians "are in no better position than anyone else to tell us whether the patient is experiencing anything or is beyond care." To my question, Must it always be assumed that a comatose patient is never beyond sensing any presence with him? McCormick answers, "No, it need not be assumed." But whether he is beyond or still within range of caring would be an assumption; and physicians are no more competent than anyone else in giving a satisfactory answer.[45]

There was, however, among these early responses a far, far more telling objection, one that perhaps is decisive for anyone who does not mean to abandon the inviolability of human life that has been definitive for Western law, morals, and medical ethics to date. Against my suggestion that our duties of caring are limited by the limits of care's communications, Richard McCormick asked whether the limits are not instead to be found in "the self-consciousness of the patient." Let the reader not run off in the wrong direction upon first hearing that objection. For McCormick wrote: [46]

> Helmut Thielicke, arguing that it is self-consciousness that is the characteristic sign of human existence, suggested that conscious-

44. "Correspondence," *Commonweal,* October 6, 1972, pp. 3–4. I have had ample reason to be "sorry" (as Maguire suggests in his letter) that I reached for those possible exceptions—and did not yield to the plea from my young friend and mentor, Leon Kass, that they be eliminated from the manuscript of that first book of mine on medical ethics.

45. Richard A. McCormick, S.J., "Notes on Moral Theology: April–September, 1972," *Theological Studies* 34, no. 1 (March 1973) : 68. Granting this objection to have great weight—perhaps, telling effect—against my prolongation of medical and familial care into those thought experiments, I still am not quite convinced that a physician cannot in human (fallible) judgment find sufficient reason to make the stringent determination I suggested. This particularly may be believed true if we rightly allow into his diagnosis a continuous period of time during which a physician has treated a comatose patient. As a member of the family I would want to seek his expert advice on whether another blood transfusion, or high caloric feeding, or respirating with more oxygen than room air, or any help at all is doing any good beyond prolonging the dying of a loved one. Similarly, I would also seek his help in knowing whether visits to the hospital and sitting by the bedside are now giving *me* the comfort, no longer the patient. Good medical-moral judgments do not need to be beyond possible error. I know few crucial moral decisions that may not be mistaken.

46. "Notes on Moral Theology," *Theological Studies* 34, no. 1 (March 1973) : 68.

> ness of self can find expression in dimensions beyond our hermeneutical grasp. "It is conceivable that a person who is dying may stand in a passageway where human communication has long since been left behind, but which none the less contains a self-consciousness different from any other of which we know."[47] If this were the case, would genuine caring demand that we *not* put an end to this self-consciousness? [Italics added]

That truly would be a good reason for an absolute prohibition against ever deliberately dispatching patients, although it is an argument from the unknown and the unknowable. Should an abiding care extend that far? or for this reason? I am the more persuaded that this is true because Hans Jonas—a person to me of exemplary moral wisdom—holds a similar view about respect for the inviolability of an embodied human life.

In his landmark article "Philosophical Reflections on Experimenting with Human Subjects,"[48] Hans Jonas wrote that, given a clearly negative condition of the brain,

> the physician is allowed to allow the patient to die his own death by *any* definition, which of itself will lead through the gamut of all possible definitions. . . .
>
> It is one thing to cease delaying death, another when to start doing violence to the body; one thing when to desist from protracting the process of dying, another when to regard that process as complete and thereby the body as a cadaver free for inflicting on it what would be torture and death to any living body. For the second purpose we need to know the exact borderline between life and death—we leave it to nature to cross it wherever it is, or to traverse the whole spectrum if there is not just one line. [For the first purpose] all we need to know is that the coma is irreversible. For the second purpose we must know the borderline with absolute certainty; and to use any definition short of the

47. Helmut Thielicke, "The Doctor as Judge of Who Shall Live and Who Shall Die," in *Who Shall Live?*, ed. Kenneth Vaux (Philadelphia: Fortress Press, 1970) pp. 147–94.

48. Hans Jonas, *Philosophical Essays* (Englewood Cliffs, N.J.: Prentice-Hall, Inc., 1974), pp. 105–31. The context was the ultimate violation that Jonas discerned to be permitted by "updating" the definition of death for the purpose of "salvaging organs" or otherwise invading the dying. (Originally published in *Daedalus*, Spring 1969; it also appears in a new, revised version, with a comment by Arthur J. Dyck, in *Experimentation with Human Subjects*, ed. Paul A. Freund [New York: Braziller, 1970].

maximal for perpetrating on a possibly penultimate state what only the ultimate state can permit is to arrogate a knowledge which, I think, we cannot possibly have. *Since we do not know the exact borderline between life and death,* nothing less than the maximal definition of death will do . . . before final violence is allowed to be done.

[Turn off any sustaining artifice on an irreversibly comatose patient]; but let him die all the way. Do not, instead, arrest the process and start using him as a mine while, with your own help and cunning, he is still kept this side of what may in truth be the final line. Who is to say that a shock, a final trauma, is not administered to a sensitivity diffusely situated elsewhere than in the brain as still vulnerable to suffering, a sensitivity that we ourselves have been keeping alive. [But the question of a possible suffering is] not the real point of my argument; this, I reiterate, turns on the indeterminacy of the boundaries between *life and death*. . . .[49]

Thus in his article first published in 1968, Hans Jonas argued for the inviolability of human life because of the unknown and the unknowable borderline (if there is a line and not a continuum) between life and death. His position is strikingly similar to McCormick's objections in 1973 to my appeal to a patient's impenetrable inaccessibility as grounds for suspending care and allowing instead direct action which we cannot know is not an ultimate violation of a still living patient. In a subsequent article Jonas successfully answered the charge of "vagueness." His argument was "a precise argument . . . *about* vagueness, viz., the vagueness of a condition. Giving intrinsic vagueness its due is not being vague." [50] Under such circumstance one

49. Ibid., pp. 129–31 (Jonas's italics).

50. "Against the Stream," *Philosophical Essays,* p. 134. Continuing the discussion of the issues he had raised, Jonas cleared up one possible misunderstanding. His language about "dying his own death by any definition," the "gamut of all possible definitions," "traversing the whole spectrum," and "letting him die all the way" could include even cellular death. It left Jonas's real position open to easy dismissal. If, he wrote in response (p. 135), by "whole organism" someone means "every and all parts of the organism," then Jonas did not mean "death of the whole organism," through the gamut of every possible definition, etc. He meant rather "death of the organism as a whole." Jonas's wholistic notion of an embodied human life does entail recognition that the effect of the functioning of respiration and circulation, though performed by subsystems (with the brain in some sense the presiding organ system), extends through the total system. By letting die all the way he meant through the

refrains from any direct action that would be violative of a fellowman who may be this side of the inexact and doubtfully known borderline between life and death. To accept Jonas's view would mean, for example, that instead of taking the definitional route I proposed above in regard to an anencephalic baby, it should be allowed to die all the way (as actually happens). The McCormick argument (citing Thielicke) was to raise a similar, serious question whether I had given intrinsic vagueness its due when I suggested even verbally stringent circumstances in which to bring about human death.

That is certainly the way to go if—in order not to deceive the public—those exceptions of mine should be withdrawn.[51] Moreover, these are the serious moral objections to allowing any exceptions to an ethics of respecting and protecting life, to always caring for patients so long as care can abide with them. The decisive objection is not the possibility than an exception may illogically be believed to weaken the principle to which it is attached, or even the more serious one

---

death of these interrelated whole-body organ systems. His object was directed against decreeing death before the death of the "organism as a whole" in the sense now explained: before a comatose patient is "in the domain of things," no longer an organized life.

More important than this correction was Jonas's philosophical position, his philosophical anthropology against the stream of modern thought. At work in the trends he opposes Jonas discerned "a curious revenant of the old soul-body dualism." To which he responded:

> It is no less an exaggeration of the cerebral aspect as it was of the conscious soul, to deny the extracerebral body its essential share in the identity of the person. The body is as uniquely the body of this brain and no other, as the brain is uniquely the brain of this body and no other. . . . My identity is the identity of the whole organism, even if the higher functions of personhood are seated in the brain. How else could a man love a woman and not merely her brains? How else could we lose ourselves in the aspect of a face? Be touched by the delicacy of a frame? It's this person's, and no one else's. Therefore, the body of the comatose, so long as . . . it still breathes, pulses and functions otherwise, must still be considered a residual continuance of the subject that loved and was loved, and as such is still entitled to some of the sacrosanctity accorded to such a subject by the laws of God and man. [P. 139]

(At the three ellipses, I omit "even with the help of art," i.e., mechanical means; I disagree with that, and moreover Jonas's anthropology does not require it.) Here truly spoke a Biblical man—against ancient and modern dualisms, against (shall we say) "quality of cerebral life" judgments as the decisive grounds for respecting and protecting embodied human life from deliberate harm or destruction.

51. But see nn. 39 and 45 above.

(mentioned above) of whether any exception should be written into a rule of medical practice or into professional medical ethics allowing the taking of human life or positively hastening death. Whatever may be said of those proposals, they were certainly proposals of a "medical indications policy" for ceasing any longer to try to communicate care. The serious objection to searching for such exceptions is that—even within the stringent limits of indications of a patient's impenetrable solitude silencing any need on our parts to feel an obligation to continue to extend care—one still might do the deadly deed to someone still in a penultimate stage, to someone who while beyond showing response to us may still be within reach of violation at our hands, and so not altogether in God's keeping.

But then the objectors shifted, and the objection changed (I must judge) into a misunderstanding of those thought experiments about possible exceptions.[52] Criticism changed into appeals to them in support of outlooks in medical ethics I never thought of espousing. For example, dropped from view was the fact that I was exploring whether or not there are stringently circumscribed sorts of cases in which the prohibition of *direct killing* is suspended. My defense of direct killing was, at least, a daring proposal. Following those early and weighty objections, however, I suddenly seemed to be cast in the role of an ally in search of conditions under which it would be right to *let die,*

52. I cite, in passing, Daniel Maguire "The Freedom to Die," *Commonweal,* August 11, 1972 (wiith the "Correspondence," *Commonweal,* October 6, 1972); Lisa Sowle Cahill, "Paul Ramsey: 'Covenant Fidelity in Medical Ethics,'" *Journal of Religion,* October 1975, pp. 470–76; and her "A 'Natural Law' Reconsideration of Euthanasia," *Linacre Quarterly* 44, no. 1 (February 1977) : 47–63. Cahill has the better argument: that those exceptions are not so much qualifications as they are extensions or fulfillments of the originating principle in medical care. "Ramsey would better argue that the present requirement of our covenant fidelity is to hasten the death of one already in the dying process" ("Covenant Fidelity," p. 475). By pinning direct action to the acceleration of *dying,* she at least avoids the mistake of employing those exceptions to help solve the case of patients who are simply incurable or grossly defective. So there need be no switch to minimum quality of life standards. An actual case to which her reasoning leads would have to be that of a dying patient in unbearable, insurmountable pain, so that to end the suffering one must hasten the end of the sufferer. This, Cahill argues, is not an "exception" but simply an *extension* of always caring. By either line of reasoning, I agree, it would be right to hasten death, if there is such a case and if one has satisfied oneself concerning the effect such a moral *rule of practice* would have upon the management of pain generally; or, in the alternative, if one would justify conscientious objector action, in particular cases, against a right rule of practice.

which was never in doubt. Then, that search took on the meaning of letting patients die who are in fact not dying. The search became a search for conditions under which it would be right to neglect voiceless patients because of the utter seriousness of the defect or condition from which they suffer. To that in advance I must say that I'd rather be charged with morally justifying first degree murder in the limited circumstances I described (or charged with justifying conscientious objection in single actions that go against the prohibition of medical killing as a rule of medical practice) than to add a feather's weight on the balance in favor of quality-of-life judgments—unless these are a part of a competent patient's balancing determination of goods and harms in his own case.

To invoke these proposals of mine in support of the growing policy of benign neglect of defective newborns would show nothing so much as the erosion of the distinction between voluntary and involuntary euthanasia, and between letting die and neglect, which is morally equivalent to intentionally getting rid of sufferers to prevent their suffering or deformity. This comes about, I have suggested, because the categorical meanings of ordinary and extraordinary still hover over the moral debate among theologians and physicians alike; those meanings have not been radically reexamined or replaced by decisions made on the basis of medical indications.

Thus, in a restatement of his standard of minimal capacity for human relatedness, Richard McCormick now approves of those exceptions of mine that, with a greater weight of moral reason, he once criticized.[53] I am grateful for his praise, yet more than a little dis-

53. "A Proposal for 'Quality of Life' Criteria for Sustaining Life," *Hospital Progress,* September 1975, pp. 76–79. Despite the more latitudinarian title of this article, I judge that it expresses more limiting verdicts than those brought into consideration in chap. 4, above. Here McCormick requires that in order for a human life not to be sustained, not to be treated, it must be "*totally without any* potential for human experience or relating" (italics added)—not simply that the odds against such potential are or seem overwhelming, or that the burdensomeness of the affliction is so great that in the constant struggle a possibly remaining capacity to experience human interrelatedness cannot be fulfilled. If I am not mistaken in noting the greater stringency of the words *totally without any potential,* do they not subtly reflect the fact that my proposals (brought here into alliance) were about circumstances under which continuing to extend care might be replaced by more than the removal of efforts to sustain human life? by positive acts of direct killing? In any case, in this article favoring quality-of-life criteria, McCormick insists that we must "distinguish between two sets of conditions: those that allow us to do things well, easily, com-

tressed over that for which I am now praised. In my "excellent book, *The Patient as Person,"* I "insightfully" point out that "our basic duty in dealing with those who are desperately ill and dying is not to dispatch them; it is to company with them in a human way. Ramsey's description of this duty is the most beautiful and Christian available." Then McCormick brings up "intractable pain" which isolates and "absorbs the patient," "disallowing companying"; and "irretrievable [where I said impenetrable] unconsciousness," "preventing companying." These instances "reflect" McCormick's position—i.e., including "capacity for minimal experience." He summarizes: "If treatment, whether medical or surgical, will only preserve a life of prolonged, excruciating, and, therefore, isolating pain, or a life totally without any potential for human experience or relating, then that treatment could be an example of *nocere,* to do harm."

My accent upon agent morality (parents' and physicians' role and relations toward the patient) has now been shifted to the condition of the patient-subject, and my focus on our estimation of life's worth and that patient's life's worth has been shifted to the patient's capacity for minimal experience in the midst of his struggle and suffering. These shifts are not insignificant. Instead of asking when agent morality reaches its limits or exceeds its capacity to convey care and a human presence to the dying, we now must ask *primarily* whether the patient-subject has "any potential for human experience or relating." The two questions are connected, of course, but I did not begin by founding the decision to care on any inherent capacity of the patient-subject to reciprocate relatedness; rather, I based it only upon the comatose patient's receptivity to care or his minimal awareness that there are persons still present with him. I said nothing about determining the life's ability to "achieve its potential." For McCormick that means determining the conditions of life requisite for "minimal achievement of other values." There seems to me no need to ask about potentiality for other values; we need only ask what fidelity to another human life, perhaps lacking any further potential and lacking reciprocity, requires of an agent. Persons are not reducible to their

---

fortably, and efficiently, and those that allow us to do them at all" (pp. 77–78). The latter criterion is the minimal quality of life used as the standard for ceasing to treat. My sense is that this is more stringent than some potential for human relatedness or higher values; perhaps I am mistaken.

potential. Patients are to be loved and cared for no matter who they are and no matter what their potential for higher values is, and certainly not on account of their responsiveness. Who they are, in Christian ethical perspective, is our neighbors. They do not become nearer neighbors because of any capacity they own, nor lesser neighbors because they lack some ability to prevail in their struggle for human fulfillment. I merely supposed—and still suppose—that Christian love and its derivative, a strong sense of medical care, could reach their own limits of usefulness, in their inability to convey the care or attention intended.

I urge McCormick to return to his earlier substantive and weighty objection, founded upon a profound respect for human life even in face of its unknown and unknowable accessibility. I also urge that one question he raised earlier be brought up and directed against his own present position which ever so slightly admits quality-of-life criteria. When inaccessibility to care cannot be determined beyond a reasonable doubt, he wrote in 1973, "when we have no concrete cases on which to build our exception-making clauses, or at least no evidence for them," he wrote, "the exception tends to gather in instances that have no place there at all. That this can erode our adherence to the original principle seems clear." [54] It does seem that the evidence for absence of any potential is at least as problematic as evidence for utter inaccessibility to care or to a human presence. The logic of exception-making clauses is not to erode or weaken the principle to which they are attached. Even if it were, the "logic" of quality-of-life criteria is "softer," to say the least. However minimal, such criteria tend to gather in instances that have no place at all in McCormick's own present position. Perhaps my friend and colleague in religious ethics and I should both retract, go back to the drawing boards, and ask whether the ordinary / extraordinary distinction which hovers over all discussions of treatable and untreatable sorts of cases, protectable and unprotectable lives, has been questioned with sufficient radicality.

54. "Notes on Moral Theology: April–September, 1972," *Theological Studies* 34, no. 1 (March 1973) : 68–69.

6

An Ingathering of Other Reasons for Neonatal Infanticide

Since we are moral beings it is necessary, of course, to convince ourselves that our benevolence is beneficent, that mercy-neglecting or mercy-killing is at the same time mercy-doing.

In May 1974, at Sonoma, California, a conference was held on ethical issues in neonatal intensive care, sponsored by the health policy program and the department of pediatrics of the School of Medicine, University of California, San Francisco. There were twenty participants in the Sonoma conference, an interdisciplinary group: pediatricians, psychologists, medical social workers, professors of community medicine, medical economists, legal experts, journalists, and bioethicists—one of whom had a background in theological ethics, at least one other in philosophy. The proceedings of this conference have now been published.[1] In addition to the papers presented by various specialists, the participants polled themselves on four questions. I shall begin with the questions the participants asked themselves, even though it is impossible to tell from the report which were the decisive considerations, from a list of alternatives given, that led each of the twenty to vote as he or she did.

How We Vote

The first question was: *Would it ever be right not to resuscitate an infant at birth?* The Sonoma conference answered unanimously in

1. Albert R. Jonsen and Michael J. Garland, eds., *Ethics of Newborn Intensive Care* (Berkeley, Calif.: Institute of Governmental Studies, University of California, 1976). The conference was originally reported fully in an article by A. R. Jonsen, S.J., Ph.D.; R. H. Phibbs, M.D.; W. H. Tooley, M.D.; and M. J. Garland, Ph.D., "Critical Issues in Newborn Intensive Care: A Conference Report and Policy Proposal," *Pediatrics* 55, no 6 (June 1975) : 756–68. When the papers presented at the conference were issued in the volume mentioned above, *Pediatric News* ran a summary (February 1977) of the questions and answers the twenty participants gave at

the affirmative. Unquestionably, that was the right answer, both medically and morally. I myself know no one, from whatever ethical perspective, who would not say yes to that, given a moment's thought. This I suppose has always been the right answer to that question; the practice of medicine has not come upon a new moral landscape simply because of the "success" of neonatal intensive care, over the last fifteen years, in salvaging younger and younger prematures. Provocation for further thought, and foreboding, arises only when we look at the list of some twenty-eight reasons or indications which the participants gave themselves to choose from in arriving at that conclusion.

Presumably a particular participant could have answered yes to the first question because "the infant is dead, as evidenced by tissue decay"—i.e., no resuscitation is prescribed.[2] Anyone can sleep peacefully tonight if that was the reason for the conference's unanimous affirmative answer; likewise with a number of other medical indications the conference gave itself. Other conditions, however, may have been the reason or reasons particular participants joined the unanimous agreement not to resuscitate. I select a few examples at the other end of the spectrum.

One possible reason is stated as follows: "if baby is dying (or is 'dead') and there is no hope of correcting the present lethal condition or foreseeable related complications so that, if resuscitated, the baby would probably die in infancy." That is listed under the heading of "General Physical Status"; it nevertheless is quite ambiguous. With the words *or foreseeable related complications* this condition moves toward the "General 'Human' Status," to be particularized next. For if the baby is dying (or is "dead"?) and there is no hope of correcting its present lethal (dying) condition, what is the meaning of going on to speak about "foreseeable related complications" which are so severe that "the baby would probably die in infancy"? These are divisible specifications that should have been separated.

Under "General 'Human' Status," we have three possible reasons

---

Sonoma, which we shall take up first below. *Ob-Gyn News* and *Family Practice* ran reports on February 15, 1976. See also, comments in *Pediatric News,* March 1977.

2. What does it mean to resuscitate an infant who is "dead as evidenced by tissue decay"? On a strict construction of the word *only,* the following condition seems to be an equally good reason not to resuscitate: "if baby is in pain which resuscitation will only prolong"; or, "if the infant is anencephalic."

for not resuscitating the neonate: (1) "if the quality of life is and will be intolerable as judged by most reasonable persons (the infant's life will predictably involve greater suffering than happiness and it will probably be without self-awareness or socializing capacity)";[3] (2) "if the infant has no chance (or small chance) of normal life"; and (3) "if the infant is clearly below human standards for meaningful life." Again—because we must perceive our benevolence to be beneficent—we move this time by steps having increasing length: from "intolerable" to "predictably greater suffering than happiness"; from absence of "self-awareness" to "socializing capacity" and on to "normal" life; from normal life to "human standards for meaningful life."

Under "Family Situation," the following are listed as possible good reasons for failure to resuscitate if the baby is severely defective: (1) if the death of the infant would minimize the suffering of the parents; (2) if the death of the infant would avoid unbearable financial costs to the family; (3) if the death of the infant would avoid emotional burdens to its siblings; and (4) if the parents already have a defective child.

These were some of the twenty-eight particularized reasons given the participants to be used in answering the first question, or which they gave to justify their responses. Some, one, or all of them in indefinite combinations and with differing weights could be backing for an affirmative answer to the question. A fair comment on the poll is that here surely is one way—on issues other than medical ethics as well—by which we as a people are bound to corrupt ourselves: first, secure a consensus that leaves the reasons behind or even a consensus that may have been itself a fiction arrived at for divergent or contrary reasons; then, publicize the consensus to sway others because the persons composing it are obvious experts and authorities. Moreover, this was interdisciplinary ethical policy making; can anything be better?

I have spent some time on the range of reasons offered under the first question, because many from this list were also offered as grounds for answering the three remaining questions. The reader should keep in mind the broad spectrum of reasons—and especially the quality-of-life statements proposed as possible reasons—as we turn now to the

3. How can a human being be probably without self-awareness or socializing capacity and at the same time predictably experience greater suffering than happiness?

remaining questions. I shall indicate only some of the different conditions introduced in each case into the framework of possible justifying reasons.

The second question was: *Would it ever be right to withdraw life support from a clearly diagnosed, poor prognosis infant?* The answer was unanimously in the affirmative. Here the reasons offered range from "if the infant is slowly dying; continued therapy only delays death" to "if the infant is defective and *unwanted* by its parents and unneeded by society." The latter was a new entry; as also were "if the parents are judged unable to nurture a severely handicapped infant" and "if the death of the infant would serve to overcome the demoralizing effect on the nursery staff of prolonged treatment of a hopeless case." If I do not entirely misunderstand the procedure used in arriving at a consensus, the latter considerations *could* have been the most weighty reason or even the *sole* reason one or another participant had for withdrawing life support.

I have no further comment, except to say that my comment on the first question applies *in toto* to the present question as well.

The third question was: *Would it ever be right to intervene directly to kill a self-sustaining infant?* The twenty participants answered: seventeen, yes; two no; one, uncertain. In this case we are given some information of why the participants voted as they did. Among the seventeen in favor of neonatal infanticide, "many, especially physicians," we are told, said they meant that "they would not condemn another" who did the benevolent deadly deed, while they themselves would *not* do so. "Others" indicated their yes was "intellectual, but they were emotionally uncomfortable with the action."

Of the two who said no, only one gave the explanation "only passive euthanasia is permissible." The other, by saying no, registered the fact that such action would be "subjectively impossible for the respondent." The one voting "uncertain" was in that state of mind because "although the act intends mercy, society seems wisely unwilling to approve of this kind of power in the hands of physicians." It seems to the present student of medical ethical questions that one need not be at all uncertain on this point. The respondent was probably wisely less uncertain than he said.

Again the quality-of-life formula quoted in full under the first question is repeated here as a possible sufficient reason for going on from negligent to direct infanticide. Around that, the reasons range from the most strict ("irretrievably dying a lingering death"; "dying painfully, or is in extreme pain or its life would be pain-ridden") to the opposite end of the spectrum ("if the infant is defective and unwanted by parents and unneeded by society"; "if the parents wish the death of the infant").[4]

The fourth and final question was: *Would it ever be right to displace poor prognosis infant A in order to provide intensive care to better prognosis infant B?* The respondents answered: eighteen, yes; two, no. The negative answers were weak, indeed: one said simply that a policy favoring such action would be too easily abused; the other said the whole question was not a matter of morality, not a matter of right and wrong, but purely a question of "practicality."[5]

4. Here my favorite anonymous physician at the conference entered the proviso: "If the parents administered the syringe of KCl prepared by the judge, and all the lawyers, priests, economists, psychologists, and journalists within a 50 mile radius were witnesses and no physicians, nurses or medical or nursing students were allowed to be present."

5. It seems likely that this respondent was Dr. Jane Hunt, psychologist at the University of California at Berkeley, whose personal communication is reported in A. R. Jonsen et al., "Critical Issues in Newborn Intensive Care" (*Pediatrics* 55, no. 6, p. 763), as follows: "I maintain that [neonatal triage] turns out *not* to be a proper ethical question because there is *no* ethical solution. One rule is as good as another, unlike the military triage. You can never articulate a policy which separates 'common good' from 'special interest' because the latter can be put forward as cogent argument for the former."

In *Ethics of Newborn Intensive Care* the following "additional comment" was added to the reasons for answers to the last question: "This situation is not a *moral* problem but a tragic, necessary situation to be approached practically (like the lifeboat situation with too many wanting to get in). The *moral* problem would appear on the larger social scale if an affluent society permitted such needless, tragic scarcity to be chronic." That may be Dr. Hunt's revision, for the 1976 volume, of her personal communication quoted above from the 1975 *Pediatrics* article.

Ethicist Albert Jonsen introduced the notion of triage as a general analogy enabling the conference to incorporate expansive patient quality and social conditions into neonatology. It must be asked why he did not introduce the participants also to our *law* in the lifeboat case (casting lots to insure *equality* of opportunity to be saved and precisely to avoid loose appeals to personal capacities or to corresponding elements in the common good which, as Dr. Hunt said, is apprehended in terms of many goods / special interests); and also why he did not introduce them to some of the ethical reasoning about the conditions under which triage is ethically justifiable, on which there is a literature. On both points see Paul Ramsey, *The Patient as Person,* pp. 252–66. Triage has been justified heretofore only when *one* social value is at stake—survival, for example. If medical practice moves to neonatal triage based on judgments of social worthiness (or on judgments of social tolerance: wanted by

Again the range of reasons offered was exceedingly wide. On the conservative side, one may start with "if infant A is *dying*, and infant B is truly viable (intact or nearly so)." Concerning that, we may ask in the first place, why infant A, considered alone, should have its *dying* prolonged in an intensive care unit? A medical indications policy ought to have no problem here. Babies are not born to accomplish their dying up against intensive care that has no purpose other than extending their time of dying. The existence of these life-sustaining technologies seems to have misshapen the minds of pediatricians to suppose in this instance that there is a problem of triage between infant A and infant B.

At the other extreme, the most expansive *statements* of quality-of-expected-life standards were, interestingly enough, suppressed. These criteria are still there in such qualifications as "grossly abnormal life," or little or no chance of "meaningful existence" on the part of infant A. Instead of making references to self-consciousness, socialization, wantedness, impact on siblings, or society's greater need for infant B, the respondents used emphatic language ("there is *demonstrable certitude* that displacement is *necessary* to provide care for infant B and that there is a *vast difference in prognosis* for the two infants"); they used quantifications in very low percentages ("at best 5% chance for meaningful existence") and resorted fulsomely to physical and other measurements. Resort was also made to tighter procedures. Thus do we quantify and resort to questions of "Who decides?" when it becomes clear that quality-of-expected-life, which nevertheless we do not hesitate to use as a standard, *entails* in principle the view that a particular human life is replaceable by another.

A final additional comment, entered by one respondent favoring replacement of infant A by infant B, stated that "displacement is *permissible* in this situation [when the lives of babies are the question], but would not be so for adults who must be given security that they will not be bumped from life support machines to accommodate 'better prognosis' latecomers." When I first read that I thought it was simply a strange reversal of our ordinary feeling and moral judgment that infants who are fragile and most in need of help have, if any-

---

parents, needed by society), it would in some ways be better to say, with Dr. Hunt, that such a policy would be simply a question of practicality, not a matter of morality or of right / wrong.

thing, a greater claim on human care and protection. On second reading, it seems clear that the very notion that a particular life has value and is noninterchangeable with any other has been entirely dropped; also dropped was any nuancing of care for the most vulnerable. This respondent offered no reason why aged and ill patients should not be bumped except their *apprehension* that they might be. If we had an effective "lie serum" which would entirely remove any such apprehension in the aged ill, remove this particular perception of what was going on, we could move at once to adopt in every hospital, nursing home, and home for the aged the medical ethical policies proposed here for the neonatal intensive care unit. Perhaps research on such a serum should be funded by NIH; then we would be free to do the greatest good for all which now we are free to do only in neonatal practice because infants are not apprehensive about their disposal.

"A Moral Policy for Neonatal Care"

Next it will be helpful to examine the section bearing the above title in the article which in 1975 first reported the Sonoma conference.[6] The authors state that this article was written subsequent to the conference, that it was sent to the participants for review, that the response was generally favorable, that there were several significant dissenters whose comments are duly noted,[7] but that the joint authors believe the participants would accept that statement of "a moral policy for neonatal care" as "an accurate reflection of the mood and tone of the Conference."

The critical point to be noted, and a telling objection, is the circularity between the ethical principles assumed and the resultant policy. In contrast to the image of a serpent with its tail in its mouth, it is quite impossible to say which is the head and which is the tail.

6. A. R. Jonsen et al., "Critical Issues in Newborn Intensive Care," *Pediatrics* 55, no. 6. Perhaps I can insert here the information that the article, which we are about to consider in other connections, apparently endorses the basis for choice among lives which we had before us at the end of the last section. The authors affirm that "for the adult the time intervening between verdict and death may be of great personal value. For the infant, the intervening time has no discernible personal value." As a reason for saying that "the morality of active euthanasia is far from settled" in the case of infants, that is a paltry reason. For "personal value" in the foregoing statement must simply mean a high degree of apprehension—which is a remarkable reductionism of that value.

7. See, for example, n. 5 above.

Whether ethical considerations weigh upon medical practice and policy or whether medical practice or policy is eating away the tail of medical ethics cannot be decided. The attempt is to obscure and bury that question under the ambiguous expression "moral policy."

At first it seems that *moral policy* means what I called a consensus at the surface of action-decisions, arrived at from many moral points of view or from diverse, even contradictory, ethical perspectives, and based on any number of considerations with which participants in a moral policy may deem to support it. Thus, the authors say that "when many individuals with diverse moral convictions face a series of decisions about similar cases, there should be a way to accommodate the diversity of private beliefs within some degree of broad agreement about how such cases should be managed." The broad agreement at the conference about how to manage four cases, based upon a multitude of divergent *private* moral convictions, seems to be a good example. "We call this effort making a moral policy."

But then in the very next sentence the authors go on to affirm that "this policy should describe not only substantive moral principles with which the majority can agree, but also the social arrangements that will facilitate discussion and action on the basis of those principles." This seems to imply that agreement concerning substantive moral principles should be achieved first, and then the practices to facilitate them in neonatal medicine can be determined accordingly. Thus, we are told, "a moral policy mingles statements of principle with statements of procedure." That, interpreted, can only mean that a moral policy sets out to obscure the lexical ordering between ethical principles and practice-procedures.

The "mingling" seems to be deliberate obfuscation when we look at the ethical propositions that are supposed to be the substantive moral principles with which the majority agreed. For it is clear that these ethical principles—if they are such—already contain everything that was said, or needed to be said, in the answers given to the questions about policy or procedure which the participants asked themselves. It is quite impossible to tell which produced the substantive moral principles—the participants' *agreement* on those principles, or predetermined policy decisions for neonatal medicine. In other words, conceivably a diversity of private beliefs was buried under initial broad agreement about how cases should be managed.

As a first step away from each participant's diverse private belief, consider the following selection from the ethical propositions—the substantive moral principles—on which, it is asserted, there was agreement. These propositions constitute the "moral policy." In each case the question to be asked is whether the alleged moral principle does not already contain the consensus on those four questions and everything significant for neonatal policy or its actual practice in the management of cases—with only minor details yet to be settled. Behind that question there is a more ultimate one: Did the movement at the level of practice and management determine the substantive moral principles needed to justify itself? What then is the meaning of a moral policy except to justify decisions actually being taken? The serpent, tail in mouth, goes round and round.

One of the ethical propositions reads, "Physicians have a duty to take medical measures conducive to the well-being of the baby *in proportion to* their fiduciary relationships to the parents" (italics added).[8]

Another reads: "Life preserving intervention should be understood as *doing harm* to an infant who cannot survive infancy, or who will live in intractable pain, or cannot participate even minimally in human experience" (italics added). Where did that ethical proposition come from, unless from a practice of neonatal medicine already agreed to? Even if there is no way to answer that question, we clearly have here an entirely circular dependence of moral policy and medical practice upon one another (a chicken and egg problem) with no rational ground beneath either, no necessity explained for either to come first, no sufficient moral reason to support either.

Another "ethical" proposition, astonishingly, presumes to determine the role of law and the interest of the state in the protection of life. This one reads, "If a court is called upon *to resolve disagreement* between parents and physicians about medical care, prognosis about quality of life for the infant should weigh heavily in the decision as to whether or not to order life-saving intervention." Leave aside those quality-of-life instructions to the court. The obvious question is, Whence came the notion that it is an ethical proposition that courts only intervene in cases of disagreement to protect life from negligent

8. The baby we are talking about is a legal person with full Fourteenth Amendment rights who is not to be deprived of his or her right to life. In proportion to *what* does the Sonoma conference propose a doctor's duty be diminished?

parents and physicians, or from the same parties who may decide to destroy the life in question? Procedurally, of course, courts do intervene only when a case is brought before them. This usually happens when there is disagreement between family and physicians. However, a case can just as well be brought before the courts by a prosecutor—if he can find out what is going on *by agreement* between these parties. In any case it is clear that these authors, as a matter of medical policy, want decisions concerning infants to be privatized between family and physicians; and *therefore* they came up with this instruction to the court if it should be called upon to intervene. And this wished-for rule of medical practice and wished-for role of courts they called an "ethical proposition." [9]

I shall cite only two more of the components of the moral policy. One reads: "If an infant is judged beyond medical intervention, and it is judged that its continued brief life will be marked by pain and discomfort, it is permissible to hasten death by means consonant with the moral value of the infant and the duty of the physician." The last fourteen words, qualifying the *means* to be used to hasten death or to kill, are palliative expressions; they, of course, exclude throwing the baby out the window as incompatible with the moral value of the infant, and so forth. The last ethical principle I select reads: "In cases of limited availability of neonatal intensive care, it is ethical to terminate therapy for an infant with poor prognosis in order to provide care for an infant with better prognosis."

Again, these two substantive ethical principles simply state the practical management conclusions the conference reached, with only further technical determinations to be made. The only wonder is why anyone felt impelled to invoke ethical principles or a moral policy. I myself do not think that today morality exerts all that much influence on policy, or that ethicists are equal among the authority figures in any interdisciplinary discussion of the issues we face or in determining the way policies and practices are going. Still I can tell the dif-

9. In the commentary on the proposed moral policy, this article absurdly supposes that the only state interest is in 'the fair and efficient distribution of benefits throughout . . . society as well as the promotion of health and well-being of its citizens. If promotion of the child's well-being unavoidably jeopardizes other equally worthy endeavors, a reconciliation of the competing interests must be sought." That is *wishful* legal reasoning; but still the wish may be father of those legal consequences eventually.

ference between ethical reasoning and medical policy, as these authors do not. Instead they need to believe that their benevolence is beneficent, and they manage to sustain that belief by concocting something called a "moral policy," which is only a reflection of the trends of medical practice. Can intellectuals no longer tell the difference between good reasons and palpable rationalizations?

In commentary upon this allegedly independent operative moral policy, the authors, I regret to have to point out, cited Richard McCormick's article "To Save or Let Die." [10] This was in support of the ethical proposition that an infant in order to be saved must "have some inherent capability to respond effectively and cognitively to human attention and to develop toward initiation of communication with others." Clearly McCormick's position was misused and abused in this summary of this conference's determinations; yet his language was invoked, and his standard of minimal personal interrelatedness was *used*—and then abused by vast extension. Clearly, in decisions to resuscitate at the first of life or decisions to discontinue treatment once begun, McCormick would allow no reference to whether others who should bear that burden of care are up to it or not. Clearly he would not allow considerations to be brought in about the patient's predictable future based on correctable social circumstances that deprive a patient of familial or institutional medical care. Clearly McCormick would not endorse the practice of directly killing infants in neonatal intensive care units. Clearly McCormick does not weigh in the balance "impact on siblings," or "wanted by parents," or "needed by society." His standard is limited exclusively to conditions inherent in the defective child. I am confident also that he would not endorse replacing infant A by infant B because the latter has a *better* prognosis for developing its human potentiality and relating with God and with fellowman. What we should do for an individual patient depends only on that particular patient. Abuse of an ethicist's position, I well know, is no argument against it. Still I think it is fair to ask McCormick to recognize the enormity of the task of containing his standard, which already is racing through medical ethical deliberations today. I ask this, first of all, because quality of life *to the patient* was the first concern at this conference. I ask this also because his original posi-

10. See above, chap. 4, sec. entitled "Minimum Personal Relatedness: Entrance for Quality of Life Criteria?"

tion allowed neglect based on a particular patient's overwhelming difficulty in achieving human relatedness; and because the next quite logical step is, for the same reason, to bring on death and not only to let die. This next step is in some sense an entailment of his position, at least in the case of infants without minimum capacity for interrelatedness who refuse to die soon enough from simply the withdrawal of treatment. The latter inferences were not an abuse—like the wide ranging quality-of-life judgments and benefits to others, which the Sonoma conference proceeded to draw out from McCormick's position in the course of its deliberations.

The commentary on the proposed moral policy for neonatal intensive care next sets out to use the medico-moral principle "do no harm" as the most appropriate principle to guide decisions regarding neonatal survival. That proves to be no guide at all because the traditional pro-life meaning of "do no harm" is entirely removed from that formulated rule of practice.

The following strange use was made of a well-honed position in both theological and philosophical ethics. Positive commandments, such as "bring aid" or "be fruitful and multiply," do not apply *urbi et orbi* to everyone; negative commandments, such as "do not kill," are more stringent, they apply *urbi et orbi* to everyone. Thus "do no harm" is a negative and therefore more stringent requirement, while "bring aid," which may be of higher value than the harm prohibited, is nevertheless not a universal requirement. Thus, one can say that to do no harm is a universal prescription in medical ethics; to bring aid is medicine's constant task. To get around that, the authors of this article reporting and interpreting the Sonoma conference accomplish a verbal flip.

Since "do no harm" is a universal negative requirement admitting of no exceptions, the authors could not let themselves even make reference to the fact that medical killing or neglect that brings death has heretofore been regarded as the ultimate harm falling under that principle, in a proper explication of it. Correlated with that, "preserve life," a positive commandment, has rightly been regarded in good medical practice as a medical imperative having limits or exceptions. (For example, perhaps, a physician does not have the resources to preserve the lives of both of two babies; that gives him no leave to bring harm to one.) Two things must be accomplished: the stringency of "do no harm" and its supremacy over "bring aid" must be assaulted; in case of conflict, "bring aid" must be elevated almost, if not quite, to a position of lexical priority.

This is accomplished by directing at least a programatic skepticism against the notion of harm. We need to determine, these authors say, what *harm* means; *harming* must be defined, as if we hitherto knew not its base meaning for the protection of human life. Thus "do no harm" is transformed into the same sort of injunction as "bring aid" (whether to the patient or to others)—admitting of degrees, variation, exceptions to neglect, exceptions to killing, displacement of one life by another if any of these things brings greater aid, etc. Thus by emptying "do no harm" of all known content, relativizing its meaning, and rendering it a formal principle only, that cardinal principle of medical ethics is changed into the equivalent of "bring aid." [11] The consequence of this intellectual sleight of hand is that, in order to bring aid to siblings, to family, to society, to the patient himself, harm may be done to an infant negligently or by direct action.

The foregoing brain-twisting reasoning set the stage for arguing that intensive care therapy positively "does harm" if (seeking to bring aid) it sustains neonatal lives of babies who are unable to survive infancy, who in the life sustained suffer severe pain, or who in the life sustained are unable "to participate, at least minimally, in human ex-

11. This discussion of harm is in some way related to the cardinal point Albert Jonsen convinced the National Commission for the Protection of Human Subjects to assume in their background deliberations on fetal research—viz., that one can harm a human fetus in research if and only if it is going to have duration of life; that it makes no sense to speak of harming a fetus by research during or following abortion; toward the soon-dying abortus one can only have an attitude of respect. See the revised and enlarged edition of my book *The Ethics of Fetal Research*. Something of the same dissolution of the meaning of medical harm seems to be brought forward now in the special care nursery—e.g., you cannot really harm a neonate who is going to die in infancy; neglecting it to death may be to bring aid; not to do so would be harm. If a reader is with me so far, I suggest the following intellectual exercise. Read Paul F. Camenisch's article "Abortion for the Sake of the Fetus," *Hastings Center Report* 6, no. 2 (April 1976) : 38–41. His is a fine analysis of the meaning and the ambiguity of any such statement. Then let the reader forget about the question of abortion and simply transpose the concept to the newborn: What can possibly be the meaning of negligent homicide for the sake of the newborn? The twistings and turnings of the reasoning reported above about the meaning of *harm* results, I suggest, from the essential incoherence of the notion of bringing about death for the sake of the newborn. By contrast, to bring about such a death for the sake of others is not incoherent; it is only morally and legally wrong.

perience." To bring that on anyone is to do harm; at the latter point McCormick was cited. The participants in this conference, however, were not minimalists.

Thus all that medical or legal harm ever meant was jettisoned. To continue the lives of some infants comes to mean to do them harm. From this a new concept can be developed (although not by the members of this conference), namely, the injury of continued existence.[12] Then one is not doing any harm or injury by discontinuing an infant in existence, and one can conscientiously proceed to bring aid to others thereby. That is to say, neonatology is then based selectively on an overall policy of bringing aid—harms done defined away.

This overturning of negative duties and positive duties constitutes a great divide. Looking back from *this* side of the divide, all previous medical violations of the principle of "do no harm," all fallings short of a physician's covenant with his patient, all other departures from the *equality* of particular lives regardless of their state or condition, every past weakening of humanistic ethics, and all past practical atheisms that lost hold of the awesome claims of a human life and tried to rise above good and evil—all look puny by comparison.

The main point, however, that I want to make here about this analytical interpretation of the Sonoma "findings" was stated at the outset. The interrelation between ethical principles and policy-practice (or neonatal management policy) is entirely circular. Ethical grounds and policy conclusions stand upon one another. Ethics and policy collapse into one another. I do not say that together they collapse. I only point out that, if this is a fair account of the deliberations at Sonoma, no one seriously *tried* to discover ethical grounding sufficient to sustain the policy proposals. For, as we have seen, the ethical propositions are merely anticipatory statements of the policy conclusions.

In the same year the first report of the Sonoma conference was published, the principle author of the present article published another joint article in which he again addressed the fundamental question of

12. H. Tristram Englehardt, Jr., "Euthanasia and Children: The Injury of Continued Existence," *Journal of Pediatrics* 83 (1973) : 170 ff. It has also been proposed that, instead of an enforced policy of eugenics, a better device in a democratic society would be to make it legally possible for a child born defective to sue its parents for "wrongful life"—that is, for perpetrating on him the injury of continued existence. See also Englehardt, "Ethical Issues in Aiding the Death of Young Children," in *Beneficent Euthanasia,* ed. Marvin Kohl (Buffalo, N.Y.: Prometheus Books, 1975).

ethics and policy formation. This is worth mentioning in conclusion for the slight but significantly different role accorded to ethical reasoning in relation to policy options. In "Public Ethics and Policy Making," [13] Albert Jonsen argued that the task of "public ethics [= "moral policy"?] is the articulation of relevant moral principles and the elucidation of options." He does not here claim that the "articulation of relevant moral principles" will be determinative of the choice of options, or even that it should be. Instead, the contribution of ethics to public policy is to "show how a policy would look and what its probable outcome might be if one moral principle is ranked above another," to identify trade-offs in a world of compromise in which the actualization of one moral principle will likely negate another. Thus public ethics is "the art of discerning the morally preferable among the practical possibilities."

I read that to say that, while there can be a ranking among possible public *policies* (reflecting how moral principles are ranked, some of which must be compromised by any option taken), there can be no rank ordering of moral principles themselves. Any ranking would help *determine* policy choices by a reasonable judgment about which principles are preeminent, which should be compromised. According to Jonsen, however, an ethicist (or reason itself) can only point out the free throws that are possible, and delineate the consequences of each. For example, he could point out that if "do no harm" has lexical priority over "bring aid," a certain kind of neonatal management policy will result (setting limits upon actions to bring aid), while another policy will result if we choose to make bringing aid preeminent. The art of doing that sort of public ethics (moral policy formation) does not seem to require an ethicist. More importantly, it does not require *everyone* or *anyone* to think ethically about the rank ordering principles of conduct do have.[14] Jonsen calls his views *infraethics,* a term I accept with an immoderate amount of glee.

13. Albert R. Jonsen and Lewis H. Butler, "Public Ethics and Policy Making," *Hastings Center Report* 5, no. 4 (August 1975) : 19–31.

14. Such an account of moral policy was the fatal flaw in Daniel Callahan's *Abortion: Law, Choice and Morality* (New York: Macmillan Co., 1970), which listed several bearers of "the sanctity of life" (individual lives, family lineages, the human species, etc.) in the context of total skepticism concerning the ability of moral reasoning to discover any rank order among them—indeed, with spirited moral resistance to the undertaking. See Paul Ramsey, "Abortion: A Review Article," *The Thomist* 37, no. 1 (January 1973) : 174–226, for a spirited—and I think conclusive—refutation of any such moral policy.

The point to be made here, however, is simply this: Even that sort of public ethics makes us aware of the fact that some rank ordering of principles of medical practice needs to be consciously sought and chosen after deliberation *in that mode*. Here the relation between moral policy, with its assemblage of ethical propositions, and neonatal care policy is simply that of mutual replication. Each sees the other in its own mirror.

In the volume of papers delivered at the Sonoma conference, the chapter by Albert R. Jonsen and Michael J. Garland [15] presents essentially the same circular view of ethical propositions and medical policy blended into a moral policy. One of the ethical propositions that I have not yet mentioned reads: "The responsibility of parents, the duty of physicians, and the interests of the state are conditioned by the medico-moral principle, 'Do no harm without expecting compensating benefit for the patient'." [16]

In support of that patient-centered concern, the authors say further, "He is independently valuable," adding that "this conception of the *independent and equal value* of human beings is basic in modern Western civilization. We assume its validity for our discussion and judge that the burden of proof lies on those who would deny it" (italics added).

The burden of proof seems easily borne. First comes selectivity based on assessing the patient by his or her ability "to respond affectively and cognitively to human attention or to engage in communication with others." This, the authors say, is "a conservative criterion"; it steers "a middle course between an undiscriminating policy of saving and sustaining all life and inconsiderately consigning to destruction the most vulnerable." Of course, if one first casts up extremes (of which the first was never a part of good medical practice), that ethical proposition falls easily somewhere in the middle. When the first extreme is paired with the second ("inconsiderately consigning to destruction the most vulnerable"), selective intensive care is necessarily

15. "A Moral Policy for Life / Death Decisions in the Intensive Care Nursery," in *Ethics of Newborn Intensive Care*, pp. 142–55. Unfootnoted quotations to follow are from this chapter.

16. This is followed immediately by the proposition: "Life-preserving intervention should be understood as doing harm to an infant who cannot survive infancy, or who will live in intractable pain, or who cannot participate even minimally in human experience." We have adequately exposed the legerdemain by which alone one can move from the first to the second proposition.

the consequence. For what the words just quoted mean is that intensive care must forge ahead in the perinatal region; not to do so would be to "consign to destruction." Thus again the principle and the policy are the same: to push ahead relentlessly saving more and more fragile lives one must, along the way, save from the harm of continued existence a number of other "independent" and "equal" lives.

Secondly, these authors state the ethical proposition that "in the final care of infants from whom life-sustaining support or curative efforts are withheld, analgesics should be used whenever indicated for avoiding pain, even though their use might hasten death." [17] That, too, has always been a part of good medical practice. Their discussion of this principle, however, "brings us into the euthanasia debate." Jonsen and Garland take a stand against active or direct killing. Their reasons are largely pragmatic: ". . . active euthanasia legitimizes a practice that is theoretically difficult to contain. . . . It seems foolhardy and dangerous to urge a policy of active euthanasia for dying neonates." (Of course, if they are dying there is no need for hastening death, only for not prolonging dying.) Jonsen and Garland may, therefore, have cast the two negative votes against question three.

Finally, in light of what was said about the independent and equal value of each infant life, the authors allow that "a new element is introduced" when a "comparison is introduced between two individuals" —i.e., poor prognosis infant A and better prognosis infant B. Here we have the self-reflecting mirrors of a principle stated and the neonatal policy proposed, while the conception of the independent and equal value of human beings, basic in our civilization, gives way as if it had the burden of proof. Triage showed the way. But in disaster medicine, the division among the injured is imposed for one reason only; the "common good" has now one focus only: the sheer survival of the community. Selection of the slightly injured for treatment first is demanded because they can help bury the dead before contagion breaks out and all may die together. Or else triage may be used by a company of men who are joint venturers in a single mission deemed

17. This *replaces* the principle stated in "Critical Issues in Newborn Intensive Care": "If an infant is judged beyond medical intervention, and if it is judged that its continued brief life will be marked by pain and discomfort, it is permssible to *hasten death* by means consonant with the moral value of the infant and the duty of the physician" (italics added).

to be of overriding importance. In neither case is one patient selected for no or delayed treatment by a *direct comparison* with another patient having a better prognosis. No one is allowed to die or be killed for the sake of saving a particular other person *per se*. Instead the division stems directly from the singularly focused and overriding social goal. One can hardly say, as in the foregoing instances, that poor prognosis infant A has an interest in the survival of better prognosis infant B. Triage among victims in disaster medicine is more dissimilar than similar to substituting one patient for another in the intensive care unit.[18] The latter must be based upon a frontal rejection of the independent and equal value of each infant life. This has to be our conclusion—unless neonatology proposes to advance inexorably onward into the perinatal area until the whole system threatens to break down and become a disaster area.

Suppose a fire broke out in the intensive care unit, and a nurse could save only three babies. If in the panic she retained her wits she would gather up the three infants who *least* needed intensive care and take them to safety. Such a case highlights a crucial aspect of triage medicine which, I must say, ethicist Jonsen failed to stress. In disaster triage medicine one treats first those *least* in need of it. In case of nuclear disaster, for example, which destroys the medical centers of a metropolitan area, leaving only the dog and cat hospitals on the outskirts, the remaining medical resources are first called upon to bind up a broken finger so that a patient can use a shovel to help bury the dead or fix a leg so yet another patient can hobble along carrying a stretcher or assisting the remaining medical team as together they move on to try to save, next, the more seriously injured. Set aside for last treatment or no treatment are *all* patients who would require intensive care.

To introduce the notion of triage *into* intensive care policy—distinguishing the worst from the next better prognosis—is an error *ab initio*. Triage starts with those least in need, in a crisis disposition of sparse medical resources. To bring the notion of triage, where justifiable, to bear at all upon neonatal intensive care would impell us to conclude that, in allocating a society's normal but still limited medical resources, intensive and costly care is the *last* thing we should undertake.

18. See also n. 5 above.

Roe v. *Wade* Generously Extended to Life after Birth

In the volume of the papers delivered at the Sonoma conference, the chapter by F. Raymond Marks, attorney for the Childhood and Government Project, University of California, Berkeley, needs next to be noticed.[19] One main assumption of this chapter is that, legally and morally, *Roe* v. *Wade* was a quality-of-life decision handed down by the United States Supreme Court; and without much, if any, further ethical or legal argument that decision can be extended to the intensive care nursery.

Right off, we are told that social viability is distinct from biologic viability and, more important, the claim is that *all* views of children—normal children no less than defective ones—are quality-of-life views. "The child is both a biologic creature and a social invention." Since we always have invented our children—by education, training, role models—the legal permission granted by *Wade* to decide *whether* a child shall be granted biologic viability means that "the opportunities for ego projection are evident and the effects nearly total." Since children in their life after birth can be killed many times over, their social viability destroyed, the pediatric clinician should relax: "he is not the majordomo of the only moments of truth in the lives of children." Does that mean, I ask, that his destruction of biologic viability is justified because those other moments may come? The joint authors of this chapter express "considerable trepidation" about some of the implications of their observations; nevertheless they forge ahead.

Reference to "wrongful life" legal cases is a minor paragraph; the authors come down on *Roe* v. *Wade*. That Supreme Court decision, it is asserted, "changed the right to life ethic. Birth, per se, and life, per se, were no longer the only values sanctioned. *Roe* recognized that there are competing values. A child's right to life had to be balanced against the mother's right to life, impact on the family of an unwanted child, and even the impact upon the child if it were born an unwanted child." From that quite incorrect interpretation of *Wade,* an extrap-

19. F. Raymond Marks, with the assistance of research associate Lisa Selkowitz, "The Defective Newborn: An Analytic Framework for a Policy Dialogue," in *Ethics of Newborn Intensive Care,* pp. 97–125. Unfootnoted quotations that follow in the text are from this chapter.

olation is promptly made of "important implications for the neonatology dilemma." "No matter what else it said about it, *Roe* is a quality of life decision." From that quite false assumption (as I shall show), quality-of-life decisions are promptly made the way to deal with lives after birth.

Professor Marks does acknowledge that "such ease in the use of the non-life fiction is presently unavailable in the case of defective neonates"—none such as the Court used in finding no protectable "person" before viability. Nevertheless, the argument presses on. The Court *did* use "the fiction of fetal nonpersonhood" in reaching its decision. At this point comes the leap to life after birth. The Court's decision in *Wade* and present hospital practice in the neonatal intensive care unit are parallel. Both "incorporate elements of a fiction": the fiction of nonpersonhood. In both cases, the fiction is useful: "we do not announce to the world" what we are doing; this is supposed to save the helping professions from some inexplicable self-corruption. The fiction of nonpersonhood in *Wade,* as well as the fiction of nonpersonhood in the special care nursery, "allows the actors to hide from themselves the fact that they have changed and departed from the rule while announcing their strict adherence to the absolute rule of the sanctity of life in all cases." Either fiction is a "manifesto."

There is more than parallelism, however. Before *Roe* v. *Wade* we were able to believe that we were saving some life or lives at the expense of statistical or anonymous lives only. That is to say, before *Wade*—under liberalized laws allowing "likelihood that the fetus will be born seriously defective mentally or physically" as an indication for abortion—statistical probability of defective births covered what was done. After *Wade,* according to Marks, (I would have said because of intrauterine monitoring) we know the particular defective life we are taking for the sake of others. Before *Wade* we were "unwilling to have this equation haunt us where we knew the identity of the lives to be taken or saved." Having established that in abortion we are now beyond figuring probabilities and are taking definite lives, Professor Marks then asks, "How different is the decision in the nursery from that of the pregnant woman?" Not much or not at all, he implies. Indeed, he seems to believe that making selection of children in the intensive care unit may be preferable to "inventing" our children through selective abortion. "The defective child is more 'unwanted' than the unplanned child." "Can we say that because the child was born alive," Marks asks rhetorically, "the balancing of lives permitted in *Roe* v. *Wade*—mother for child—is out of the question? Does not a failure to consider the trade-off condemn the parents as surely as the earlier refusal to consider abortion condemned the mother?" At this point, the author comes close to suggesting that natural parents should be able to turn over to the state within five months children manifesting defects that were not at first observed, just as (he says) adoptive parents may do in some jurisdictions. Thus natural human parenting with obligations arising therefrom would be replaced by artifice, and moreover by an artifice of adoption that does not, in an essential respect, "imitate natural parenthood perfectly" (Aquinas).

In addition to the foregoing, there are other decisional alternatives that Marks is willing to contemplate. One, which he doubts will be taken because it would involve "a major shift in our self-image," is as follows. In order to continue by neonatal intensive care to gain "additional normal babies," we could calculate that "killing defective babies" was an appropriate price to pay for the gain. That would mean "redefining human life to exclude the defective child"; with particularity and consensus we would define "the type of infant who, upon birth, would fit into the category of 'subhuman' non-personhood (infants with spina bifida, i.e., divided spine; or extensive brain damage)." That option is "not altogether futuristic [indeed, it is not], although it is dangerous [indeed, it is]." At this point I ask the reader to say whether Marks's momentarily rejected option is in any significant respects different from the fiction of nonpersonhood which he says was the way *Wade* went about allowing the actors to hide from themselves the fact that they have departed from the announced rule of the sanctity of life in all cases.

Indeed, it is evident that Marks never rejects the policy of nonpersonhood for certain classes of neonates. He opposes, for example, the proposal that slowly, case by case, a sort of common law will develop allowing for infant euthanasia—without our having ever to face the clear choice of a nonpersonhood policy. One reason he offers for rejecting the possibility that we simply glide into infant euthanasia is, in fact, a reason Marks believes we should *not* take that route. The "considerable effort" that has been expended attempting to distinguish between a "passive posture" and an "active posture" has been a waste.

"These distinctions are meaningless" and moreover drawing them "has a damaging effect because it hides the real issue." So he really believes that "a fiction will develop," the fiction of nonpersonhood (which, we should recall, has the virtue of hiding the real issue). An arrangement by which we could consciously adopt that option would be "briefly withholding birth certificates and names from high risk infants and those in certain categories." Thus, we return to the option of having "an open, but saving, fiction of non-personhood"—before called "unlikely" and "dangerous."

Finally, and with whatever verbal reluctance, the author announces that "we will urge serious consideration of the non-personhood policy." "This model is, in many ways, like present abortion practice." That claim may be correct and, again, it is supported by reference to *Roe* v. *Wade*. But Marks's quality-of-life interpretation of *Wade,* I shall argue, is entirely mistaken. In any case, the author's view seems to be (expressed, as too much else is, in the form of a question): "Is it possible to view euthanasia in some instances as a late abortion decision in much the same way that abortion has been viewed as a late birth control decision?" Indeed, it is possible. And talking about such a policy in a normless context is one way to promote its sooner actualization.

The state's interest in these matters is simply "an interest in preservation of our collective symbols." [20] This means the "useful fiction" which the author toyed with at first and then finally urged. Moreover, *Wade* was a Supreme Court decision that preserved our collective symbols as a rights-bearing people, while moving to comparative quality-of-life standards. In support of these propositions, the author brings in altogether too current, merely persuasive references to war and capital punishment (without any serious consideration of the *moral* arguments that, rightly or wrongly, have been used by serious thinkers to justify those state actions) in order to support his thesis—namely, that the state has only a symbolic interest in maintaining a

20. More than such an interest of the law in the protection of life peeks through in Marks's rejection of what he calls the state's "pre-audit of decision making." That means the invocation of the state's parens patriae power. In its place he would instate "a system of post-audit." That means "a system that broadly defined the class of infants who could be disposed of by their parents, a system that did not require certainty, that could then be coupled with criminal sanctions for actions taken against children who fall outside the category."

rule against murder. Where life is spent as part of known cost, life has become "currency"; all of us, however, have an interest in the state's interest in fictions or symbols that deny that this is our operating principle.

Thus "a fixed star, life-saving at all costs, has dropped out of the medical constellation." [21] This means identifying babies capable of developing into "normal human beings" and, until this is determined, having the useful fictional personhood which, the author admits, he has "repeatedly shunted aside." The "social time" for "letting a baby go" is in the first few hours; a better time, he says, would be later. To wait requires fictional nonpersonhood to preserve rather than eliminate options. To proceed in this direction, parents currently do not make very good decision makers; "they [still] feel the pressures of the prevailing life-saving ethics"; they do not yet regard children as currency and some of them are likely to resist making the trade-offs—i.e., substituting one life for another. The insistent question is: "Are parents in a different position from the mother in *Roe* v. *Wade?*" There is still "a mystique surrounding birth. It is a legitimate mystique, but a mystique nonetheless"—like, I suppose, the state's management of symbols. But now "with *Roe* v. *Wade* behind us," perhaps we are ready "to demystify our reality. Society not only invented its children, it has invented the rest of its reality, too." [22]

Now, a fetologist or a pediatrician well versed in the nature of fetal development (and busily engaged with his or her own speciality) *might,* understandably, have supported those conclusions by reference to *Wade*. But it is quite incomprehensible that a *lawyer* can believe the Court's abortion opinion admits of any such extension.

The law that was dispositive in *Wade* [23] was the Court's judgment

21. Two comments are in order here. First, an objection to "life-saving at all cost." I know no medical ethics that ever subscribed to that. Secondly, at this point, Marks speaks of the "quantum jump in technology that alters the definition of life-saving, and of life itself." If we are slaves to technology, this may be an apt *description*. If we are human beings, however, we can talk back to technology.

22. Barbara J. Culliton's report (*Science,* April 11, 1975, pp. 133–34) referred to the Sonoma conference as the "Valley of the Moon Conference." The setting may have been beautiful. I am inclined to believe it was very beautiful, since we academics know how to spend the money of wealthy sponsors, in this case the Robert Wood Johnson Foundation and the Henry J. Kaiser Family Foundation. Still the symbolism of Culliton's designation should not be lost: a valley on a dead satellite of our mother earth.

23. 410 U.S. 113 (1973).

that "the unborn have never been recognized in the law as persons in the whole sense." That statement of our law is well founded, although I myself believe it would have been more correct to say that *in the whole of our law* the unborn have never been recognized as persons in the whole sense. Here the Court refers both to the fact that in tort law recovery for prenatal injury assumes a right to life in the unborn, and to the fact that the devolution of property by way of inheritance assumes an interest of the unborn. The "perfection" of these rights and interests is "contingent upon live birth."[24] Therefore when Blackmun in the Court's opinion affirmed that "we need not resolve the difficult question of when life begins," that statement referred exclusively to the prenatal period. It in no way weakened—it rather enforced—the law's view that at live birth there is a legally protected person having interests and rights equal to any other. This was affirmed again by the Court in *Planned Parenthood,* as we saw; statutory "standards of care" governing physician conduct seemed redundant because at birth (premature or not) the manslaughter law begins to have full force.

Retracing the *Wade* opinion from the line of live birth (which was dispositive as to the law), we come to what the Court said about the period between viability and birth. If a state undertakes to enforce its legitimate interest in potential human life, "it may go so far as to proscribe abortion during that period except when it is necessary to preserve the life and health of the mother." Notably, the Court did not

24. In the case of a father who dies not knowing that a child has been conceived, one can argue that entitlement to inherit must have passed from one person to another legal person at a certain time, before the father's death and after the unsuspected conception, even though collecting the cash depends on live birth. For example, the hypothetical child mentioned here might after birth succeed in collecting the whole estate, unlike a child conceived by the mother subsequent to the death of the father by means of his frozen semen. In the first case, the child was "in the land of the living" while the father was also; whereas this was not so in the case of the second child. A statute governing postmortem artificial insemination from husband could attempt to fix that. Still, remembering how deeply imbedded natural parenthood is in our law—a will has to be very carefully drawn in order not inadvertantly to exclude adopted children—such an AIH statute could be challenged. The challenge could succeed with or without a showing, for example, that the mother wanted to disown the first child entirely and, being legally prevented from doing that, meant to cut his inheritance in half. Entitlement to an inheritance requires, I believe, two persons existing at the time of the devolution of the property. For this reason I suggested above that "in the whole of our law the unborn have never been recognized as persons in the whole sense" would have been a better formulation on which to base *Wade.* Not so strong a legal foundation, but a foundation nonetheless.

add another possible exception. It did *not* say that the state may go so far as to proscribe abortion "except when it is probable or when it may be certainly determined that the unborn will be born seriously defective." Marks would need that statement in the opinion to have any (but still insufficient) basis for making the foregoing extrapolations to the intensive care nursery.

From the beginning of the second trimester the state may intervene between a woman and her physician only by statutory requirements governing abortion reasonably related to protecting her life and health; and the state may not intervene between them during the first trimester in any way. The appeal in law was to the woman's right of privacy until viability. That places her and her physician's decisions in "an area of liberties," as I have argued. If *they* make quality-of-life decisions, or decisions based on "unwanted by the mother or unneeded by society," or substitute a defective fetus for another expected to be normal ("better prognosis"), this in no way means that the law subscribes to those decisions or gives backing to them; it permits them to be made in the area of liberty from state intervention. Most importantly, the reason the law recognizes this area of liberty is because the law as such does not know anything fetal physiologists or medicine in general or theologians or philosophers may speculate about "when life begins" prenatally. Still our law as defined by the Supreme Court does know when life begins in the sense of a person fully endowed with a right to life. Dispositive in the *Wade* opinion was the fact that "*the unborn* have never been recognized in the law as persons in the whole sense" (italics added). That entails that after live birth there is a person in the whole sense of the law's protection. Forbidding the misconstruction of *Wade* is also the fact that the Court recognized that the state may, if it chooses, insure its interest in the potentiality of life by going so far as to proscribe abortion after viability—upon which the Court placed only one limitation, which was to protect the life and health of the mother. Extending *Wade* to the proposed neonatal care policy is rather to be compared with leaping over the Grand Canyon on the way to the Sonoma conference. Both attempts must fail.[25]

25. I said above that it would be understandable but still a mistake if a fetologist or a pediatrician construed *Wade* as a quality-of-life decision which can be generously extended to neonatal intensive care policy. Such a specialist presumably knows

A slender argument could be made that the liberalized abortion law enacted by the state of New York in 1970 (now superceded by *Wade-Bolton*) was a quality-of-life statute. This was certainly the view of one chief consultant to the sponsors drafting the bill; he chose twenty-four weeks estimated gestational age as the cutoff point because, in order to detect birth defects, time must be allowed to culture fetal cells obtained by amniocentesis (such was the state of the art at the time); this in turn might require abortion that late in pregnancy to prevent a defective birth.[26] Moreover, most of the liberalized abortion laws passed by the states immediately before *Wade-Bolton* contained

---

fetal physiology well enough to recognize that there is a second patient long before birth. He or she will know the grounds for the 1859 statement of the American Medical Association deploring abortion; if the medical specialist disagrees with that conclusion, his or her disagreement *must* introduce a quality-of-life judgment. Said the AMA at its twelfth annual meeting (quoted by Blackmun, with no sense of the contradiction, in the midst of trying to show that early American abortion statutes were introduced and *stayed on the books* through the nineteenth century, after the discovery of the ovum, simply to protect the woman from abortion, which then was a dangerous procedure):

> The first of these causes ["of this general demoralization"] is a widespread popular ignorance of the true character of the crime—a belief, even among mothers themselves, that the fœtus is not alive till after the period of quickening.
>
> The second of the agents alluded to is the fact that the profession themselves are frequently supposed careless of fœtal life.
>
> The third reason of the frightful extent of this crime is found in the grave defects of our laws, both common and statute, as regards the independent and actual existence of the child before birth, as a living being. These errors, which are sufficient in most instances to prevent conviction, are based, and only based, upon mistaken and exploded medical dogmas.

To disagree with that, a fetologist necessarily resorts to some alternative determination of life; a neonatologist could then extend that to medical practice in the case of newborns. Appeals to *Wade,* however, have no probative value.

26. Susan Edmiston reported that Cyril C. Means, Jr., professor at New York Law School, recommended that twenty-four weeks would be a good cutoff point because of legislative precedent and because many birth defects cannot be detected until twenty weeks' gestation or later ("A Report on the Abortion Capital of the Country," The *New York Times Magazine,* April 11, 1971, p. 44). Professor Means made, therefore, a quality-of-life recommendation. Whether the pre-*Wade* liberalized abortion laws could be extended in principle or in law to the intensive care nursery depends very much upon whether the state legislature was aware of the fact that it stepped into the area of possible viability / perinatality when it followed Means's advice. Edmiston also reported that twenty-eight fetuses were aborted / born alive in the first nine months of the operation of the New York law; one lived to be adopted. Very likely the legislators believed they were drawing a proper line on viability.

provision for abortion on grounds of indication of fetal defect. Even though the legislatures of those states (New York included) deliberately adopted these provisions, they did so in the belief (in my judgment, even then mistaken) that twenty-four weeks was the line to be drawn on *viability*. "Liberalized" neonatology policy can therefore find no launching pad either in the pre-*Wade* liberal abortion statutes or in *Wade* itself. Viability (outside the womb or not, if a state so chooses) and live birth remain according to law the point of entrance into full personhood.

A Categorically Selective Policy for the Intensive Care Unit

At the entrance to the topic of this chapter we are told that "life saving intervention in an infant's existence inevitably raises certain questions about the desirability of saving *certain* lives. . . ."[27] Then follow the questions about "certain" neonates as distinguished from others and conflicted with others, which we have considered; and following this, as we saw, is the philosophy behind the answers. For some reason that initial sentence struck me as very odd indeed. Questions are not raised inevitably. People raise the right, the correct, the fruitful, the fit, or the appropriate questions; or the opposite sorts of questions. But people don't know how to do that "inevitably." If people begin with the wrong questions or with questions inevitably predetermined, the answers they give may prove equally predetermined. An illusory sense that we are freely and morally setting policy might remain a cherished relic of our peoplehood; nevertheless, our policy decisions would be fixed within the parameters set by the questions the intensive care unit puts to us.

I once asked a neonatologist whether, by continuing to save newborns who are increasingly younger gestationally (that is, whether by doing everything we technically *can* do—without considering whether we *should* or not), we were not producting a greater number of defective newborn lives. His answer was negative. His reason was that as we learn to save gestationally younger and younger lives (where consequent defect increases) we are at the same time learning more and more about how to decrease defect and bestow normality upon neonates that once would have been damaged. So on balance, he

27. A. R. Jonsen et al., "Critical Issues in Newborn Intensive Care," p. 756.

believed, pushing further the life-saving consequences coming from neonatal intensive care was a good thing. That response seemed to me then—and seems to me now—to be an inadequate one. Must we use earlier and earlier neonates as experimental subjects to improve the chances of normalcy for other infants whose lives we learned to save some years ago? Should not a categorical line—however arbitrary—be drawn in this relentless technological attempt to duplicate perfectly the human uterus? Could or could not medical science continue to improve the human prospects of newborns who are now saved in a span of gestational age nearer the natural birth line without, as a means, pushing the line of possible salvability further back? What is the necessity compelling us to reach back further into gestational age in order to improve the prospects of infants we some years ago learned to save? These were my questions.

I learn from the Sonoma conference volume that my questions may have been incorrectly phrased, and my respondent's answer correspondingly not to the point. That, at least, is my reading of the chapter by Jane V. Hunt, research phychologist at the Institute of Human Development, University of California, Berkeley.[28]

> Increased rates of survival are not inevitably accompanied by an increased incidence of handicapped children. In fact, the reverse seems to be true.
>
> The number of infants with normal or superior development at one year of age has increased over time, and the incidents of infants of poor development has declined. Survival rate has continued to improve over the years, but with increasing rather than decreasing incidents of normal outcome.
>
> If, as it now appears, neonatal intensive care has resulted in a shift toward normality (fewer deaths and fewer retarded), then it is quite possible that this trend will also be reflected in the smaller numbers of children with minor handicaps.

Concerning the respiratory distress known as hyaline membrane disease, in particular, "new methods of assisting ventilation have increased the survival rate and improved the outcome for infants with this problem."

28. Jane V. Hunt, "Mental Development of the Survivors of Neonatal Intensive Care," in *Ethics of Newborn Intensive Care,* pp. 39–53. Unfootnoted quotations that follow in the text are from this chapter.

For the remainder of the chapter Dr. Hunt adopts a "developmental model" in contrast to a strictly "neurological model." There are transient defects at birth. This developmental lag means that one cannot yet predict the permanence or the importance of the lag, while if the child is normal at one year it can then definitely be said that he or she will not be frankly retarded from the effects of neonatal events. The range of unpredictability based on transient abnormalities extends to at least four years from neonatal illness. To diagnose an infant as a "hopeless case" is a label that often generates a self-fulfilling prophecy. Indeed, "high-risk infants fare better if they go home to a supporting environment."

These observations, of course, go far beyond the range of decisions the Sonoma conference believed should be brought within the practice or immediate concern of neonatology. None proposed to join the Baconian project for the conquest of nature and suffering and for the relief of man's estate by a prognosis looking so far into the future. Dr. Hunt's observations are, nevertheless, worth recording here because—along with her assertion that normality has improved along with survivability—the fundamental question arising from them is, What is the new question inevitably raised by intensive care—what is the inevitable question—demanding to be unavoidably answered by a policy of comparing neonates with one another and by a selective quality-of-life policy?

Here, I judge, we see the wisdom of Dr. Clement A. Smith's observation, "Neonatology has always had its ethical problems" [29]—even before that word and the intensive care nursery were invented. If Dr. Hunt is correct, there is nothing new under the sun disclosed to us by intensive newborn care: no questions inevitably raised, no inevitable questions requiring a new ethics of medical practice. People may, of course, raise those questions; and to them give novel answers. But they ought not to bludgeon the public with the notion that the questions somehow raised themselves, nor should they speak as if a policy of neonatal quality-of-life selectivity is being forced upon them and upon society.[30] That may well happen, and if so it will be because

29. Clement A. Smith, "Neonatal Medicine and Quality of Life: A Historical Perspective," in *Ethics of Newborn Intensive Care,* p. 31. Dr. Smith is a professor of pediatrics emeritus, Boston Hospital for Women and Harvard Medical School.

30. An observant reader of this volume on the conference will spot altogether too many *imperative* statements, which require *moral* reasons to support them, expressed

of modern technology. I should rather say, the causal influence may be technology, but that will not be a *reason*.

But what of the *costs* of salvaging all these neonates, it may be asked. Is that not an impelling reason for neonatology to go to a selective policy based on criteria other than a medical indications policy? Here I interpose that an impelling reason is not the same as a good moral reason. But let us take up the question asked. As I read the cost / benefits chapter in the Sonoma conference volume, its main thrust bears upon whether, in the allocation of general medical resources, the present and expected future expenditure on salvaging neonates (costs in personnel resources as well as financial ones) should be expended upon them or might better be expended elsewhere on humankind's medical needs. Moreover, as a second interpretation of mine, the author does not believe that cost / benefit analysis settles any ethical question; prior ethical determinations must be made before costing the options can be deemed to have any morally imperative meaning.

Marcia J. Kramer, assistant professor of economics at the Health Sciences Center, State University of New York, Stony Brook,[31] "views the ethics of the treatment decision from an economic perspective." Yet, as I said, her very informative chapter affords no significant ground for selection within the neonatal intensive care unit. It bears instead on the whole enterprise within a society's allocation of its medical resources. Thus, when "qualifying" the claim that life should be sustained at any cost, Dr. Kramer sets that question within the context of "the *real* costs of employing scarce resources," measurable in terms of other lives not saved. Her prime illustration is drawn from the "developing nations" where the (imaginable) diversion of resources to intensive neonatal care could "reduce per capita income to a level incompatible with life." She, of course, rejects a morality that "would sooner reduce everyone to a subsistence standard rather than deny care to a single, ailing newborn, for whom the odds are not so favorable."

---

in terms of some compelling necessity ("must") which require only *descriptive* statements to support it.

31. Marcia J. Kramer, "Ethical Issues in Neonatal Intensive Care: An Economic Perspective," in *Ethics of Newborn Intensive Care,* ed. Albert H. Jonsen and Michael J. Garland, pp. 75–93. Unfootnoted quotations that follow in the text are from this chapter.

That extreme example is valid to a lesser extent for affluent societies as well. Therefore, Dr. Kramer addresses principally the question of allocation of medical resources in general, not differential cost and quality-of-life benefits within neonatal care. "Because the activities foregone by providing NIC may be of greater moral worth than the care itself, it is morally imperative that cost criteria be established for this as for any other service." Her question is whether to provide intensive neonatal care or not; not how to cut costs within it. Kramer's chapter parallels the supposable case that instead of convening a commission to study whether the United States should fund research to develop a battery-powered or a nuclear-powered totally implantable artificial heart, a commission was convened to determine whether we should develop *any* sort of artificial heart. Therefore, I fail to see how her analysis lends any support at all to the emotionally persuasive instances given in articles and speeches, totaling up the tens of thousands of dollars it costs to save an *individual* baby who may be subnormal.[32]

Moreover, cost / benefit analysis is, for Kramer, footless unless informed by prior moral principle; "unless morality happens to be imbedded in the preference structure, there is no assurance that . . . allocation rule[s] will generate ethical solutions to the treatment dilemma." Indeed she affirms that the cost / benefit method is "wholly inadequate . . . because it operates without reference to prior principles. . . . Implicit in the method is the assumption that the worth of a baby, like the worth of any other consumer good, is identically equal to the benefit that baby is capable of providing *to others,* and that the fact of its existence in and of itself entitles the infant to no claim on life." Dr. Kramer does offer the opinion that "for a society composed of morally upright individuals, cost-benefit analysis would produce a moral solution." That seems satisfactory as a way of stating the thesis that cost analysis is an empty or formal method only. But suppose that a society of morally upright individuals held the view that an infant's existence in and of itself entitles it to a claim on life—or, as Jonsen / Garland announced, that every human being has

32. Albert Jonsen, the principal author, continues to purvey such persuasive appeals (e.g., *Medical Tribune,* February 16, 1977). Kramer's chapter concludes with costing sorts of cases; but this in no way deflects the thrusts of the ethical or social policy pointed out above, nor does it turn her data into *reasons* for intra-intensive case selectivity by cost / normality judgments.

equal and independent value—how would such a society go about using cost / benefit analysis?

This crucial question cannot be directly addressed without first disposing of the currency now given to the supposed triviality or nonsensicality of distinguishing between, on the one hand, the primary purpose and direct effect of a medical or social policy decision and, on the other, the foreseen effects allowed or accepted (rightly or wrongly) by that policy. The primary purpose of highways, I suppose, is to get places, not to kill people. It may be that we accept more "statistical deaths" than we ought to accept. Surely it is arguable that lower speed limits should be set and that money spent on circuitous routes to get into the main traffic stream at lower costs in lives is a proper use of public funds. Still, wherever we draw the line on the costs of preventing statistical deaths in the enterprise of getting places, this in no way argues that we regard or should regard directly killing people as morally justifiable in order to get places—or to mine coal, or to carry out any other human enterprise.

To forget what is the primary purpose and immediate effect of a human activity is always a mistake. Direct intentional killings and calculable deaths allowed are thereby reduced to one quantifiable moral or public policy question. Of course in any primary human enterprise—whether it is highway safety or safety measures in coal mines or the allocation of medical resources—those neglected to be saved are not regarded as "priceless." We do not save lives at the cost of having no other common purposes; in that sense, we do not save lives at infinite cost. "Proportionate reason" certainly governs the deaths to be accepted in any human enterprise; and that sort of moral reason ought, indeed, to shape or possibly negate some goods we primarily intend, or the manner by which we accomplish our goals. To dismiss as trivial the cardinal distinction between direct killing and foreseeable deaths allowed turns all human lives into expendable currency. It also subverts the moral basis of Western law and morals in the untouchable value of a human life. That turns our constitutional principles into useful fictions.

The astonishing fact is that there are persons in the legal profession today who adopt that viewpoint. Having set aside the significance of the notion of permitted deaths, they are bound then to say that our prejudice against directly taking human life is only a fiction, a symbol by which we protect ourselves from limitless corruption. So we should preserve the "fiction" that a human life is noninterchangeable with any other, that a human life is in that fictional, symbolic sense "priceless"—meanwhile pricing it in legal and public policy. Maybe for a year or so we should try to save workers in coal mine disasters at exorbitant and unjustifiable public expense. Then for a following span of years we could turn to saving at great cost persons who failed to pay attention to storm warnings at sea. Such a policy of alternation in life saving would sustain in all of us the desirable fiction that we do value an individual human life above all else on earth.

Such a view *must* first reject the notion that there is a fundamental moral distinction to be made between directly taking human life and the certainly foreseen human lives that statistically will be lost in any human enterprise whose primary purpose and immediate effect is the achievement of some worthwhile goal. For myself I must say that (cynic though I am about the ethos of present society), if this *elitist* program was made plain to the people of the United States, there would be aroused a public protest of enormous proportions against the training of our future lawyers and justices to regard the claims of an individual human life—to regard the constitutional foundations of our republic—as something to be priced. Indeed, the point of this cost / effectiveness view of human life and policy making is precisely that it be never made clear. Only philosopher-kings know the truth; the people believe a noble lie; they must and should. As a Christian ethicist, I must also say that those of my colleagues who would reduce the distinction between direct killing and allowed deaths to a provisional distinction only, and who argue that the overriding point is the proportionate greater good, are unknowingly doing the same thing—pricing human lives.

The point here is to ask why professionals involved in neonatal intensive care are *impelled* to reject the basic distinction between direct killing and allowing the dying to die, and why those who still entertain the distinction do so only for pragmatic reasons (e.g., taking life would be a practice too dangerous to entrust to physicians).

Benevolence is the answer; beneficence assumed. We must "continue to gain additional normal babies" (Marks). More strongly expressed, we must not "consign to destruction" additional normal babies (Jonsen / Garland). Thus consigning to destruction is reduced to the same neonatal policy as failure to bring aid to additional normal babies.

Those expressions manifest a praiseworthy medical-moral passion to save life. But then the strain and burdens become too great—burdens not only financial but familial as well, burdens not only familial but also professional—in continuing to extend care to defective newborns. These are by no means novel dilemmas. What snaps, however, is the "equal and independent" value of each and every young life. That happens to be the principle on which the medical-moral passion to save life was founded and which created the intensive neonatal care unit in the first place.

The people-question to raise from within the intensive care unit (or concerning intensive care in contrast to other uses of medicine in the service of life), and the people-answer to be given to that question is simply this: What are the implications for intensive care policy of the equal and independent value of human lives? This question is not even a dilemma unless the situation addressed turns the question into another one: Who should be saved when not all can be? That again is no novel dilemma. It is the question of the allocation of scarce medical resources.

The intensive care unit does not *tell* us that the principle governing allocation *must* be selection according to expected-quality-of-life criteria or by comparison of patient-persons. But this does not mean that there is no principle of selectivity to be found—one that is in accord with the equal and independent value of human lives.

There are ways to assure equal opportunity to gain access to lifesaving treatment when, tragically, not all can be saved. For example, a lottery system or "first come, first served" in kidney dialysis; some such scheme would be better than resorting to the use of "social worthiness" criteria.[33] Perhaps neonatology faces this same choice. Developments in medical technology over the past fifteen years do not make or dictate the option people choose.

One extreme option would be a national medical policy decision, or a professional policy decision by pediatricians, which would declare in effect that additional normal babies would be gained, fewer would be consigned to destruction, if the limited human and material resources of pediatrics were redirected into community medicine, ade-

33. Paul Ramsey, *The Patient as Person*, pp. 239–75.

quate nourishment, and attention to poverty mothers, etc. Shutting down the intensive care unit altogether—which I do not propose—would have at least this virtue: no preemie would have cause to complain that he or she was treated unfairly, unjustly, unequally. None would be let go because he or she was unwanted by parents or unneeded by society. No preemie would be compared with another at risk of flunking someone's expected-social-worthiness test.

This extreme option illustrates the fact that, under conditions that necessarily limit our capacity to save young lives, a policy of selectivity should be by broad *categories* if such a policy is going to acknowledge the equal and independent value of human lives. Put positively: selection by broad categories of those not to be saved builds upon that cornerstone of Western morality and medical ethics. The need to neglect some may be regrettable, tragic; but it would not be unjust or unequal if done by definable *sorts* of cases to be set aside—sorts of cases "not to be saved." No one consigns anyone in particular to destruction; affirmative medical care is directed elsewhere, aid is brought to other categories of young life in need of help. One need not especially emphasize the very great costs attached to modern medical service, or the infinitude of medical needs. Basically, we need only say that people must manage to be and act morally under the conditions of finitude. That is nothing novel; it is the human condition.

Moreover, another "fatal" flaw in the notion of triage used at the Sonoma conference was ignorance of the fact that triage is by broad categories; it does not sort out individuals to let die or be saved. An individual would have his finger fixed first (if then he can handle a shovel) or his leg (if then he can carry a stretcher)—no significant reckoning would be made about whether he is a mongoloid or is otherwise unwanted or unneeded by society. If anyone at the conference based his answer to those four questions on *all* or a considerable accumulated number of those specifications of reasons, that amounted to a rather complete description of the *particular* patient (as close as reason can come to grasping the unique individual patient-person as a whole). Medical triage does not do this. Doubtless some severely impaired individuals were passed over by triage during the disastrous storms that struck the coast off the Gulf of Mexico some years ago. But they were not neglected *because* they were incapable of meaningful human relationships in general; and nobody seized the opportunity to make other judgments of social worthiness (to minimize the suffering of their parents, to avoid emotional burden to their siblings) or asked whether parents had another defective child or not.

It would be regrettable, tragic, if under a national health service—or more informally under our present diverse ways of determining the quantity and the "quantity of the quality" of medical service offered—the decision was made that a given, quite costly (in human as well as financial terms) heart operation was not done for *anyone*. Such an overall policy would still not be wicked (my strong term for unjust or unequal comparison of particular patient-persons). Indeed, I understand that if costs sets the limit (finitude) and indeed the choice of less evil (e.g., less prolonged) ways to die, it can be demonstrated that we ought not to continue to try to "conquer" cancer or heart failure. Those who now die of those causes do not have the choice of dying of something called "natural death." Instead all will die of *something*—for example, stroke, which leaves many paralyzed for many years. If we live long enough we are all going to die of something incurable, not "naturally"—whatever that may mean. So I see no moral objection to an overall medical policy decision which stipulates that certain *sorts* or *categories* of live-saving or life-prolonging technology will not be offered to *anyone*. Then no particular patient has just cause to complain that he was treated unfairly, unequally. The norm should be (under the conditions of finitude) that no particular patient be singled out for reasons other than the *category* of illness that sadly our possible policy decides not to treat.

It seems obvious that any selective policy within the present life-saving capability of neonatal medical technology can readily be set by categories of perinatal patients. No necessity forces us to go to expected-quality-of-life determinations case by case. There is no moral problem if the neonate has been determined, in human judgment, to be dying. Doubtless such an infant should have been given intensive care in the first place. But when in human judgment intensive care is only purposelessly prolonging its dying, the infant should be taken out of the unit and allowed to die. That, I think, is a settled canon of medical ethics.

Beyond that, the next step would be to determine sorts or categories of neonates who, regretably, are not to be saved by the modern upper limits of treatment capable of saving them. That issue should be settled in accord with the equal and independent value of the particular lives in question. What I have called a "medical indications policy" is one way to do that. But then one who is a physician does not add in the weight of the criteria: "If the quality of life is and will be intolerable as judged by most reasonable persons (the infant's life will predictably involve greater suffering than happiness and it will probably be without self-awareness or socializing capacity)."[34]

A medical indications policy could go so far as to stipulate abrbitrary lines to be drawn—for example, that no neonate below a designated weight and gestational age should be saved. Whatever operational line is drawn, physician discretion could still be free within limits to the one side or the other to decide to try to save or not to try to save the infant life. Still that would be a categorical, and therefore equal and just, determination concerning a class of patients, not particular individual ones, to be given access to life-saving treatment. It would be rather like the extreme of stopping intensive neonatal care altogether for the perhaps justifiable reason that such a radical reallocation could have more lives—in terms of both numbers and quality; or like a decision to offer a costly heart operation to infants and young people, but to no one over fifty-five years of age.

These suggestions follow from the formal maxim to treat similar cases similarly when informed by a substantive notion of justice or equality. Selection for treatment (or allocation of medical care) must be by categories and not by drawing distinctions between individual patients if these fundamental norms are not to be violated. As Gene Outka has written:

> Illness is the proper ground for the *receipt* of medical care. However, the *distribution* of medical care in less-than-optimal circumstances requires us to face collisions. I would argue that in such circumstances the formula of similar treatment for similar cases may be construed so as to guide actual choices in a way most compatible with the goal of equal access. The formula's allowance of no positive treatment whatever may justify exclusion of entire classes of cases from a priority list.

34. *Ethics of Newborn Intensive Care*, p. 182.

> Yet it forbids doing so for irrelevant or arbitrary reasons [reasons that deny the equal and independent value of particular patients]. . . . All persons with a certain rare, non-communicable disease would not receive priority, let us say, where the costs were inordinate, the prospects of rehabilitation remote, and for the sake of equalizing benefits to many more. . . . The relevant feature remains the illness, discomfort, etc., itself. The goal of equal access then retains its prima facie authoritativeness. It is imperfectly realized rather than disregarded.[35]

35. Gene Outka, "Social Justice and Equal Access to Health Care," in *Love and Society: Essays in the Ethics of Paul Ramsey,* ed. David H. Smith and James T. Johnson (Missoula, Montana: The Scholar's Press, 1974), pp. 200–01; first published in *The Journal of Religious Ethics* 2, no. 1 (Spring 1973) : 11–32. As Arthur J. Dyck has written, a "quality-of-life" standard is directly opposed to an "equality-of-life" standard ("The Value of Life: Two Contending Policies," *Harvard Magazine,* January 1976, pp. 30–36).

The special worth of David H. Smith's article "On Letting Some Babies Die" (*Hastings Center Studies* 2, no. 2, pp. 37–46), is that (a) he does not rely on any important moral distinction between killing and neglecting to death, in the case of uncomprehending patients; and (b) he sets the ethical question of the neglect of defective newborns in the context of the general ethical question of negligently or actively bringing about death. The question he presses is: What are the good reasons sometimes excusing or justifying accountability for the death of a particular life?

There are, of course, justifications for killing (by action or by abstention) someone for whom one is accountable (one's neighbor). To justify causing death to come upon another, the killing must always be *protective.* For protection to be a good reason, and not a rationalization, there must be another *particular* person whose life is physically threatened. The "obligation to protect can override the prohibition on killing, if the person against whom action [I add, or abstention] is taken is threatening the life of someone to whom one is obliged" (a fellow man or someone with whom one has a special moral relation). To excuse bringing on death by reference to general or statistical lives, which are not *immediately* threatened and for which other provision could be made, is morally inadmissible. Such reasoning "would prove far too much, for it would justify the killing of anyone [or neglecting them to death], of any age, who is in some way a social liability." From this Smith concludes that it is impossible to show that the defective newborn constitutes a direct and otherwise irremediable threat to specific other lives. "The deserted, defective newborn is precisely the child who may never be killed [or harmfully or fatally neglected] for the sake of others. . . . [A] baby with no advocate, and threatening no particular person, cannot possibly be construed to be a legitimate victim of *protective* killing [or protective neglect]."

Smith knows there is a distinction to be drawn between "maximal" treatment and "optimal" treatment. But the announced policies of selective, particularized, discretionary neglect cannot "claim to be judgments made about optimal treatment of the particular babies at hand." He also acknowledges that it may be the case that "resources used to care for him could be [better] used in other ways" to bring aid to

That surely is a selective policy based on medical indications *and on the equal and independent value of patient-persons.* If push came to shove, a policy of treating every *fourth* neonate presented would be more just—and a less violent departure from the foundations of Western law, morals, and medicine—than the Sonoma assemblage of multiple specific criteria which add up to a policy of selecting between one particular patient and another, and moreover on grounds other than illness and need.

If "entire classes of cases" have to be excluded from intensive care, these cases nevertheless remain within the human community claiming palliative care and comfort. Their dying should, of course, never be prolonged; but if not dying these patients do not deserve abandonment simply because intensive care cannot be offered them.

Professor Jerome Lejeune (who identified the chromosomal basis of Down's syndrome) once proposed the "Statutes of a New Facility for Research and Applied Eugenics." [36] This reads as follows:

Article I

> Considering the disputed issue of mankind's betterment, noting the burden imposed upon society by genetic and chromosomal diseases, and recognizing the limitation of the available solutions, a special Institution for Research and Applied Eugenics is created: "THE NATIONAL INSTITUTE OF DEATH."

Article II

> Under the scientific scrutiny of a board of specially appointed advisors, the NATIONAL INSTITUTE OF DEATH will:

---

others. Still "it does not follow from this that he is personally threatening anyone." Therefore he should not be made the particular target of selective neglect. Failure to bring aid to *sorts* of medical cases in order to bring aid to other sorts of cases would not, I infer, constitute a clear departure from principles of ethics that govern *protective* omissions or commissions that foreseeably bring on fatalities. *Categorical* distinctions would not prove too much; they would not imply that one could rightfully bring death to a particular person—to anyone of whatever age or condition—who is arguably a social liability or who may even be preventing us from bringing lifesaving treatment to others. *Categorical* distinctions retain the authoritativeness of equal access to lifesaving treatment, even if imperfectly realized. In priority or allocation decision, this must be the mode—if we mean to adhere to the "equal and independent" value of every human life.

36. Jerome Lejeune, "On the Nature of Men," William Allan Memorial Aware Lecture, American Society of Human Genetics, San Francisco, October 2–4, 1969; printed in *American Journal of Human Genetics* 22 (1970) : 121–28.

A. Decree on undesirable genes or chromosomes.
B. Deliver unhappy parents from unwanted pregnancies.
C. Discard embryos not fitting standard requirements.
D. Dispose of newborns not reaching minimal specifications of normalcy.
E. And generally, destroy, delete, or decry any human condition voted against by the above-mentioned board of advisors of the NATIONAL INSTITUTE OF DEATH.

Article III

To prevent any possible error, concern, or prejudice, the advisors shall be chosen from among knowledgeable persons not belonging to any philosophy, society, or race.

Lejeune's biting irony deserves wider circulation; for this reason I quote it here. Also, his final punch line enforces how correct Dr. Jane Hunt was when she objected that the (strange) notion of triage used at the Sonoma conceference afforded no ethical solution because "special interests" would provide the divisions of the "common good" to be made, and so of the comparisons made among particular neonates. Indeed the *negative* function of standards of justice and equality is precisely to *suppress* such special-interest and quality-of-life judgments.

7

In the Matter of *Quinlan*

The case of Karen Ann Quinlan nicely, and tragically, illustrates most of the themes elucidate in chapter 4. Moreover, the final decision in this case by the New Jersey Supreme Court shows the folly of failure to give legal effect to a medical indications policy. The two court decisions will be analyzed in this chapter. The issues raised cannot be probed to the bottom, nor can an alternative be outlined, unless the reader keeps clearly in mind and never forgets that at the time these opinions were handed down both the lower court and the supreme court found as a matter of fact that Karen Quinlan was dying. Without the respirator her death was impending—in a matter of minutes. When the legal decisions were rendered there was no reason to suppose—at least, none to which the courts gave any probative weight—that Karen was simply incurable or terminal. Her dying, then, was deemed irreversible; there was no need to speak broadly in terms of "irrecoverability."

Even the disagreement between the physicians and the Quinlan family might perhaps have been clarified by translating ordinary and extraordinary into indicated treatment and treatment no longer indicated—in the case of the dying. In any case, medical and human judgments in this regard need to be flexibly wise, not routinized, if the matter is not to wind up in the courts—where it does not belong except in rare instances of deliberate intent and actions that kill or positively hasten dying, or inaction in treating (where indicated) the merely incurable. The two outcomes that the courts in New Jersey reached, once a legal mandate was sought in the *Quinlan* case, are both regrettable. If the lower court's opinion had not been overruled, we would now have detailed court-ordered practice of medicine with the dying. On the other hand, the decision of the Supreme Court of New Jersey has opened a large hole in the law, which could encourage a broader comparison of the expected sapient quality of life

of patients (not limited to the dying) in place
treatments, leading to a decision to withdraw pr
only prolong dying.

I believe that basically these outcomes stem f
clearly that no treatment is beneficial to a con
when it can alter the dying process in no way an
long it. To allow Karen's release, however, the
reasons that are extensible to other sorts of nondying patients who are unconscious. That erodes the moral prohibition and the legal protections against involuntary euthanasia, as I shall show, the only stipulation being advice from an "ethics committee." Hard cases make bad law, and bad ethics too. Incentive in this direction has come from the contrived, confused, and imprecise use by physicians and ethicists alike of categorical "ordinary / extraordinary" language with no differentiation made between the conscious or unconscious dying and the nondying who for some reason are incapable of refusing treatment.

Basic Circumstance

Karen Quinlan was certainly not dead, but she was clearly dying; at least, that was the finding of fact in both courts. Earlier there was some suggestion that she be declared legally dead. That medically would have been a mistake. The thought behind taking the definitional route seemed to be that the sole reason for cutting off respirators is because the patient is already a corpse on which the face of life is maintained by machines alone. That assumption in ethical reasoning is a mistake. In any case, to declare that a person has died means that treatment is no longer possible; it then can only be attempted. That's different from saying that further treatment (of the still-living dying) is counterindicated.

Another valid reason for cutting off respirators is because to continue will not affect the still-living dying patient's condition in any significant respect except to prolong the dying. Then trial curative treatments are no longer indicated, whether they be "standard" or "heroic" measures.

Karen's father, Joseph T. Quinlan, spoke nobly to the court about his and the family's desire to have "Karen returned to her natural state so that we could place her body and soul in the tender loving of the Lord."[1] He wanted her "taken from the machine and ubes connected to her." Mr. Quinlan, however, expressed amaze-ent when asked whether he wanted the IV removed, replying, "Oh no, that is her nourishment." So in the formation of the Quinlans' conscience there was a sharp distinction to be made between the IV and the respirator. One was ordinary (imperative) treatment, the other extraordinary (dispensable) treatment.

I suggest that in a proper understanding of these terms (objectively relative to the patient's dying conditions),[2] the IV was equally aimless. In this case, it, too, was only prolonging Karen's dying. Surely it was not hunger that Karen felt. To be on the safe side, perhaps we should say that she might experience dehydration. Then *that* was the purpose of a glucose drip: to give the comfort of a cup of cool water to a patient who has entered upon her own particular dying. If a glucose drip prolonged this patient's dying, it should not have been given for that purpose, or as a means in a continuing useless effort to save her life. More than five years ago, I learned that there are certain sugars that it might be possible to use in cases such as this to give water for hydration without metabolizing calories and prolonging the dying process.[3]

The physicians in this case had a different formation of their professional conscience. (They, too, were practicing Catholics.) To be sure, there is disagreement in the testimony as to whether they momentarily agreed to the Quinlans' request and then changed their minds. And before the case came to trial, suggestions were made that the physicians' primary motive was fear of malpractice suits or of

1. *The New York Times,* October 22, 1975.

2. No reference needed to be made to her "sapient" condition, except as the reason physicians and family had to make the decision for her, Karen being unable herself to refuse further treatment.

3. Paul Ramsey, *The Patient as Person* (New Haven, Conn.: Yale University Press, 1970), pp. 128–29. The same point can be made by asking, What was the purpose of using high caloric feeding? Although that should be classed as nourishment, and thus be called "ordinary" in the classificatory meaning of that term, such forced feeding more effectively prolonged the dying process. Anyone who believed that to be the case must also say there was no medical indication to use such a drip. So, also, physicians frequently move from special oxygen mix to delivering only room air by respirator, in order to find out what they have been doing with the patient by respirator and whether continuing to do so has any medically indicated purpose.

criminal prosecution.[4] I do not believe that this was true. The doctors (a neurologist, Dr. Robert Morse, and a pulmonary internist, Dr. Arshad Javed) are neither sadists nor automatons. They, too, are people of conscience and said in open court that they would refuse to turn off the respirator even if ordered to do so.[5] Their formation of professional conscience was shared by other physicians who testified—Dr. Sidney Diamond, neurologist at Mount Sinai Hospital in New York, for example—and by Theodore Einhorn, the lawyer for Saint Clare's Hospital.[6]

That professional judgment is worth examining in considering this human, all-too-human, conflict of consciences. It is remarkably similar to the Quinlans', however sharp the contrast materially and in the practical outcome. The truth is that neither the Quinlans nor the physicians had made the translation into indicated treatment and treatment no longer indicated. As a consequence, they had opposed views of the classificatory meaning of ordinary / extraordinary.

It was simply the case that for the physicians the respirator had become a "standard medical practice" equated with the IV as a life-saving instrument. If there had been reliable information, when Karen was brought to the hospital, as to how she became comatose, how long she was in a state of respiratory distress, and what degree of anoxia her brain had suffered, Karen might not have been placed on a respirator in the first place. Not knowing why or how long Karen had been comatose, the doctors rightly began artificial respiration. Subsequent information and retrospective diagnosis reached the conclusion that she had ceased breathing for at least two fifteen-minute periods! Under those circumstances, I ask, would not the IV for feeding have also been counterindicated and not started? But having rightly begun curative treatment, the physicians then found they could not in conscience stop. To do so would have been for them a quality-of-life judgment, which the physicians (and their lawyers) rightly declared they are not competent to make. Similarly, for Mr. Quinlan to ask to have the IV withdrawn would have been to declare Karen's life to be not worth nourishing.

4. *The New York Times,* September 28, 1975. This view was repeated by Dr. Michael Halberstam in an Op-Ed page article in the *Times* on November 2, 1975.

5. *The New York Times,* October 21, 1975.

6. *The New York Times,* October 21, 22, 24, 1975.

I suggest that both were wrong. Treatments that were potentially lifesaving (or reasonably believed to be so) when first begun became means for aimlessly prolonging dying. Is it not a routinized conscience that keeps physicians from determining when this point has come?

In the physicians' professional conscience some treatments remained as extraordinary (dispensable) as Mr. Quinlan believed the respirator to be. Theodore Einhorn declared the situation would be different if Karen were "riddled with cancer [dying?] and in pain." Physicians would not order another resuscitator if her breathing failed, or implant a pacemaker in the event of a heart problem. "To do so," Einhorn said, "would be the height of misuse of technology." Then "physicians will say don't treat this patient any more. . . ." [7] Dr. Sidney Diamond—while saying that he knew of no physicians who would take Karen off the machine since it was performing a lifesaving function—went on to say that physicians would not order transfusions for Miss Quinlan if she "suddenly lost her defenses to infection and hemorrhaged," and he added, "surgery would, of course, be out of the question." [8] "Karen Ann" is the name these physicians gave to this patient's dying ensouled body plus the respirator.

We who are laymen in these matters can only express surprise, even incredulity, upon hearing that one alone among all these procedures—the respirator—is believed to be lifesaving and not an aimless prolongation of dying or a misuse of medical technology, and when told that stopping *that* would alone entail comparisons of patient-persons in quality-of-life judgments. Does not a justifiable use of any of these procedures entail similar comparisons of treatments, or of continuing curative treatment with discontinuing treatment?

The Trial Court's Opinion

In his opinion,[9] Judge Robert Muir, Jr., was limited to determining Karen's temporal interests. "The single most important temporal quality Karen Ann Quinlan has is life," he said; "there is no constitutional right to die that can be asserted by a parent for his incompetent adult child." [10] Unfortunately, the precedent in New Jersey

7. *The New York Times,* October 22, 1975.
8. *The New York Times,* October 24, 1975.
9. 137 N.J. Super. 227 (November 10, 1975).
10. Robert M. Veatch breaks that sentence into two parts, as it were, in objecting to Judge Muir's "tragically faulty analysis." "Mr. Quinlan did not ask for his daugh-

had been set by the *Heston* case.[11] By that decision, only four years before *Quinlan,* an adult unconscious Jehovah's Witness was ordered to be given a blood transfusion—despite the interest she had in liberty of religion. That also was certainly one of her "temporal" interests, superior to life itself and guaranteed by the First Amendment. Perhaps the available evidence of her religious faith was better than in Karen's case.

The tragedy was that the Quinlans did not simply ask the court to be appointed their daughter's guardian. That would have given them freedom of decision among medical consultants and among treatments. Such a case might have been won in the lower court in New Jersey. Among the rumors that have swirled around this case, one portrays the Quinlan's lawyer as a young man in a hurry to make a name for himself, and who gave the family bad advice. That, I have determined, was not true. A more probable opinion—and humanly quite understandable—is that Joseph Quinlan emotionally needed the moral support of the law in the awesome decision he was making. We shall see that the New Jersey Supreme Court also did not have the courage of the decision it had reached, and it, too, went in search of support from other decision makers.

Under the circumstances before him, Judge Muir felt he could not designate Joseph Quinlan as guardian of Karen's person. He

---

ter the right to die," Veatch writes; "he asked for the right to refuse medical treatment" (*Death, Dying, and the Biological Revolution,* [New Haven: Yale University Press, 1976], p. 138). Judge Muir did not deny a constitutional right to die *simpliciter;* he did not say that a competent conscience patient may not refuse medical treatment. He found rather that there is no such right "that can be asserted by a parent for his incompent adult child." The latter is a restrictive clause. Faced with Joseph Quinlin's particularized request to be made guardian of Karen's person, Judge Muil was forced to invoke the law's role as parens patriae. Veatch's idiosyncratic interpretation of the opinions in this case are a result of his own extreme patient libertarian and surrogate libertarian views. For example, neither Judge Muir nor the supreme court found the reports of Karen's previously expressed opinions to have sufficient probative weight on which to base a court-ordered substitute judgment to remove the respirator. Concerning that, Veatch affirms it to be "an affront to her memory that someone else's estimate of what she would want in her present condition is taken as more reliable than her own, *albeit casual* expression made in the vigor of youth" (ibid., p. 153; italics added). His position would reduce the state's parens patriae power, and its efforts to discover on what to base substitute judgments, to almost nothing.

11. *John F. Kennedy Memorial Hospital* v. *Delores Heston and Jane Heston,* 279 A.2d 670 (N.J. Sup. Ct. 1971).

found, correctly I believe, that there is no constitutional right to die that can be asserted by one person for another voiceless person. In addition to protections in the United States Constitution, the New Jersey State Constitution of 1947 provides for "certain natural and unalienable rights, among which are those of enjoying and defending life. . . ." [12] But surely it was a mistake for Judge Muir to designate the guardian *ad litem* (Karen's court-appointed guardian during the litigation) to continue in that capacity after the trial was over. Another guardian should have been appointed, one not tainted by these adversary proceedings.

Unless the law's protection of human life is to be breached, it is quite necessary to keep the case of the dying clearly distinguished from all other cases of withholding treatment, and also to insist that in withdrawing treatments from the dying no one intends their death (mens rea), but rather the intent is that they live unbetubed while dying and that they die by no human agency. Such elementary moral distinctions were too subtle for either court in this case. Yet we shall see that the supreme court *accepted* that reasoning; it was the more at fault for not basing its ruling on it.

After Judge Muir's decision, it seemed we were going to have medical decisions directly supervised by the court. Provision for Karen's "total care" (including the use of high calorie food and antibiotics to control infection—considered extraordinary means, above) "was worked out in Judge Muir's courtroom yesterday after the ruling was handed down." Moreover, the guardian announced that he would "not take one step either forward or backward" without conferring *with Judge Muir,* the physicians, and the Quinlans.[13] Judge Muir's statement that these are medical decisions was the only glimmer of hope that any procedure would ever be found wanting in medical purpose.

In response to a subsequent petition from the Quinlans, Judge Muir agreed to replace the guardian ad litem who was placed in an adversary position against the Quinlans during the course of the trial. But whom did he appoint? Another lawyer. We may well ask, why a lawyer or even a physician? Would not any respected member of the community, belonging to neither of these professions, do as well or

12. Art. 1, para. 2.
13. *The New York Times,* November 15, 1975.

better? It is true, the permanent guardian, Thomas R. Curtin, promptly announced that he would act in this capacity as a layman, not as a lawyer, and that he would consult with the Quinlans elsewhere than in his law offices. At the same time, however, he announced that the lawyer *he* would consult in his assumed lay capacity would be the original guardian ad litem—to whom the Quinlans had objected.[14] Beneath this network of errors there are basic social issues involving the over-professionalization of our notion of responsible role-playing today.

This might have been the final outcome: no breach in the fabric of protections of life in American law, and at the same time no protection of the dying from relentless medical interventions. The dilemma of ethics and modern medicine is that the New Jersey Supreme Court reached another decision only by weakening that fabric.

Since physicians are not automatons, I did not wish the court to order these physicians to stop the respirator. But Mr. Quinlan should not have expressed his own unwillingness to do so. At the conclusion of my first lecture at Columbia, I expressed my willingness to join the Quinlans' priest, the Reverend Thomas Trapasso, in accompanying them to Karen's room in Saint Clare's to pray while Joseph and Julia Quinlan disconnected both the respirator and the IV and held Karen in their arms while she died—adding that at least I would be willing to do so if that did not put me at risk of arrest on the charge of conspiracy and thus bring to an abrupt end the 1975 Bampton Lectures.

The New Jersey Supreme Court's Decision

The Supreme Court of New Jersey handed down its decision in the *Quinlan* case on March 31, 1976, Chief Justice Richard J. Hughes speaking for the court.[15] Lawyers for the Quinlans had relied on

14. *The New York Times,* December 12, 1975. Objection to the *exclusive* designation of lawyers or physicians as guardians ad litem was one of the points stressed in a discussion at Columbia University, November 13, 1975, on the topic of death as an ethical problem for the profession, attended by several hundred faculty and students. On that occasion Dr. Samuel Klagsbrun, Rev. Donald Shriver (President of Union Theological Seminary), and Professor Frank Grad addressed comments to my Bampton Lecture, dealing in part with this case.

15. *In re Quinlan,* 70 N.J. 10 (1976).

claimed constitutional rights of (1) free exercise of religion, (2) protection against cruel and unusual punishment, and (3) privacy. Before getting to these central issues, we should note several findings of fact and of law accepted by the court. Karen was not dead; her death was "impending." There was no course of treatment that would "lead to the improvement of Karen's condition," and without advanced medical procedures "the patient would expire." Karen's reported conversations with regard to others terminally ill lacked "significant probative weight" for the court to rest its opinion in any degree upon Karen's wishes in the matter. She had not and could not refuse treatment. Her condition was described as "decortication," a derangement of the cortex of the brain. Within Karen's comatose state there were "sleep-wake" cycles, but that in no way meant sometimes awake or responsive. Instead, her own doctors described her as in a "chronic persistent vegetative state," no longer having any "cognitive function" or hope of recovering such function. Apparently the court accepted the anthropology of Dr. Fred Plum who explained that the human brain works in essentially two ways, the vegetative and the sapient.

One can pause at this point and ask whether any living human being ought to be described as a "vegetable" or reduced to metabolism in newspaper editorials.[16] We can appreciate the need for gallows humor among medical personnel who daily deal with grim realities. For such language to escape from the hospital setting, however, and become common parlance racing through the human mind—or be given judicial notice—may be as dangerous as a bacteria escaped from recombinant DNA research racing through the human intestines of a population.

Having judged that Karen's reported conversations about terminal illness lacked probative weight either to establish her refusal of treatment or as grounds for a legal opinion, the court quoted at length from a statement of Bishop Lawrence B. Casey, in an amicus curiae brief submitted by the New Jersey Catholic Conference. It said, however, that expert testimony as to the nature of Mr. Quinlan's religious and ethical beliefs was considered by the court "only in respect to its impact upon the conscience, motivation, and purpose of the intending guardian." What the court called the Catholic view of "religious neutrality"—i.e., the belief that interruption of treatment, even when it

16. *The New York Times,* June 3, 1976.

causes the arrest of circulation, would be no more than the indirect cause of the cessation of life under the circumstances of this case—was a matter of "religious dogma or concepts" that could be admitted into evidence only as this view bore on understanding and measuring the character and motivations of Joseph Quinlan as prospective guardian. That seems an elaborate way to judge sincerity and trustworthiness. Those "religious" considerations were weighed by the court only to reach its negative answer to the question "Was the [trial] court correct in withholding letters of guardianship from the plaintiff and appointing in his stead a stranger?"

A Decision Not Rendered

The remarkable thing about Chief Justice Richard Hughes's opinion for the court, however, is that *urbi et orbi* it accepts those "religious concepts" about interrupting treatment and declares that reasoning to be an essential aspect of good medical practice. Before following the way the court went, it is necessary to take notice of this road not taken. For it is necessary to demonstrate that the court had quite another basis for a ruling granting Joseph Quinlan undivided guardianship and giving Karen relief from the medical regime on which she had been placed. It could have avoided the trial court's detailed court-ordered practice of medicine without resorting to the astonishing lawmaking that was its actual outcome. The case before the court was, by its findings, a *dying* patient. To assign Joseph Quinlan undivided guardianship would set no legal precedents beyond the case of patients whose death is certified to be impending and imminent. That would have signaled the fact that the New Jersey courts stood ready to remove the "brooding presence" of malpractice liability which the court declared "we cannot believe . . . has not had strong influence on the standards"—if not of Karen's two physicians then on the profession's "standard medical care" and its categorical use of the ordinary / extraordinary distinction. That would have freed Joseph Quinlan for full guardianship, and freed physicians to use a medical indications policy, limited as this case was to the dying. There was no need for the procedures the court elaborated and the strange standards it laid down that are already proving to be broadly extensible from the dying to the terminal and to the simply incurable. All this can be demonstrated by reasons of substance which the court said, and said at length, were sensible, and which it did not even intimate would lead to guardian decisions or medical practices that are unlawful.

The court's first venture into sensible terrain was a cautious and tentative one. It said that "the thread of logic in [the doctors'] distinctions [between a respirator and giving Karen large quantities of blood or resuscitation or a major surgical procedure—which they agreed would be a gross misuse of medical procedures] may be elusive to the non-medical lay mind, in relation to the supposed imperative to sustain life at all costs." Such elusive disagreements, the court said, "relate to medical decisions." Indeed, the court ought not to have mandated one or another *specific* classifications of ordinary and extraordinary treatments.

Still it is strange that a distinction familiarly used in medical practice (however elusive to lay minds and a source of *real* disagreement among physicians) should be thought to be a matter of "religious dogma and concepts" which cannot be allowed to enter a civil litigation simply because the Roman Catholic church traditionally has held this view. A past claim of that church to teach the "whole moral law"—principles and action-guides falling within the limits of human moral reason alone as well as a distinctive Christian morality—seems now to be turned on its head: any part of rational moral law becomes "religious dogma and concepts" simply because the church also teaches it. As we shall see, at numerous other points in its decision, the court indicated that it discerned the *reasonableness* of these concepts, indeed accepted them.

The court could have acknowledged some distinction between ordinary and extraordinary means (which in the case of the voiceless dying can mean no more than a medical indications policy). It could have recognized some distinction between directly intended action and acceptable associated effects. It could have found these to be secular concepts, and the search for what the distinctions mean in medical practice to be an ongoing secular enterprise. It need not have sacralized those concepts and that enterprise. The United States Supreme Court could not do without the distinction between direct and indirect action—even if that is a piece of scholasticism—when deciding cases involving mutually impinging and possibly conflicting interests. For example, there are now three tests governing in our highest court's decisions concerning the constitutionality of laws or practice of local, state, and national governments in the area of potential church-state conflicts. On questions ranging from public funds or buses going to parochial schools to choral music in public schools, the Supreme Court asks: (1) Does the activity have a *secular purpose?* (2) Is its *primary effect* a secular one? (3) Does the activity involve day-by-day "entanglement" between government and the churches? The first two tests are precisely the distinction between killing and letting die to which Bishop Casey testified, altering the questions to read: Does the activity have the intention to kill? Is that its primary effect? Why sacralize a quite necessary aspect of complex decision making and rule its substance entirely out of court when a complex medical issue is presented?

So I suggest that, to avoid Judge Muir's court-ordered medical practice, the New Jersey Supreme Court could have done more than take notice of the fact that medical decisions often involve a determination of what constitutes ordinary and extraordinary means, over which physicians sometimes elusively disagree. It might also have seen the sense in saying that whether everything mandated by law is being done to protect life very much depends on the chief purpose (i.e., the intention) and the primary effect of medical actions. Under circumstances strictly limited to the case of a dying patient, it could have ruled that the *purpose* in withdrawing nonbeneficial treatments from Karen Quinlan does not necessarily constitute the mens rea of a crime (the guilty mind choosing death, which the law seeks to suppress); and, likewise, its *primary effect* is not necessarily the action of wrongdoing hands. The court could have adopted that understanding of lawful medical decisions, even while the court stood its distance from disagreement among physicians—and in this instance between physicians and family—on matters too elusive for courts to determine; and while removing the bifurcation of Joseph Quinlan's guardianship and also weakening the threat of malpractice suits. That Joseph Quinlan believed Karen should be allowed to die ought not to have been held against him *because* he was a Catholic. That sacralizes a necessary secular set of concepts. In any case, many important aspects of our law and of medical ethics were influenced by Christianity. The court sacralized a secular concept that was religious in origin, and so removed it from substantive consideration today. That is an odd result. To have legally legitimated decisions in accord with these concepts in the specific circumstances of this case, it seems to me, would have adequately protected other lives from actions whose chief intention and primary effect may be to kill or to accelerate the death of an unconscious patient simply because the patient is not sapient or has a life not worth living.[17]

Chief Justice Hughes in his opinion noted not only the (removable) "brooding presence" of the threat of malpractice suits sustaining inflexible standards. He noted also a "widening ambiguity" in those standards themselves in the background of the disagreement presented to the court for litigation. In that connection the court made some clarifying remarks that, I suggest, might have been the substance of its decision. Instead, these remarks stand as observations made on the way to another outcome. "We glean from the record," the court said, "that physicians distinguish between curing the ill and comforting and easing the dying; that they refuse to treat the curable as if they were dying or ought to die, and that they have sometimes refused to treat

17. Professor George J. Annas, director of the Center for Law and the Health Sciences at Boston University School of Law, affirms that the court applied "the principle of double-effect, *sub silencio* to homicide" in the *Quinlan* decision. I have argued that "double effect" is not an apt characterization of letting the dying die; that expression is applicable only to such treatments as pain relieving drugs or generally to the twin effects of a given action. It has no meaning when used to characterize the treatments that are choiceworthy because they are medically indicated for different patients or different classes of patients. Sub silencio, however, the court did accept the distinction between activities whose chief purpose (intention) and direct effect is to kill and activities whose chief purpose and direct effect is to replace further curative treatments where possible with palliative and comforting ones. That, I suggest, might have been a sufficiently narrow basis for the court's ruling, distinguishing in the case of the dying between letting die and homicide. Later on in his article Professor Annas drops "double effect" and correctly says that the court committed itself (not so *sub silencio*) to the principle that "the refusal of 'artificial life support or radical surgery' is to be distinguished from 'self-infliction of deadly harm.'" Annas believes that, as part of the court's expansive package, that distinction is as questionable as the whole of which it was a part. I suggest that, standing alone, that distinction requires simply a comparison of conditions of life useful to their possessors while dying. I do agree, however, with Professor Annas that rather than search for this or for some other "narrow grounds (applicable to this particular case) on which to base its conclusion, the court chose instead to employ expansive and ill-defined language to deliver one of the most wide-ranging—and potentially dangerous—opinions in medical jurisprudence" ("In re Quinlan: Legal Comfort for Doctors," *Hastings Center Report* 6, no. 3 [June 1976] : 29–31). The language of "double effect" and a *categorical* distinction between ordinary and extraordinary means *applied to all sorts of cases* by bishops, priests, theologians, and physicians alike are clearly leading to involuntary euthanasia, and of patients other than the dying.

the hopeless and dying as if they were curable." The physicians who had testified that no doctor would withdraw the respirator from Karen Quinlan nevertheless indicated that many of them "refuse to inflict [by other means] undesired prolongation of the process of dying on a patient in irreversible condition when it is clear that such 'therapy' offers neither human nor humane benefit." The court went on to say: "We think these attitudes represent a balanced implementation of a profoundly realistic perspective on the meaning of life and death and that they respect the whole Judeo-Christian tradition of regard for human life. No less would they seem consistent with the moral matrix of medicine, 'to heal,' very much in the sense of the endless mission of the law, 'to do justice.' " Finally, in regard to the "somewhat hazy" record before it in the present case in regard to distinguishing between ordinary and extraordinary measures, the court remarked that "one would think that the use of the same respirator or like support could be considered 'ordinary' in the context of the possibly curable patient but 'extraordinary' in the context of the forced sustaining by cardio-respiratory processes of an irreversibly doomed patient."

While one could quibble over a word here and there, the quotations in the previous paragraph, taken together, are an excellent statement of the medical ethics expressed to the court by the New Jersey Catholic Conference in its amicus curiae brief. Having in its wisdom unsuspectingly expressed a secular version of that determination of good medical practice with the dying, why did not the court finally take that moral matrix of medicine to be "very much in the sense of the endless mission of the law, 'to do justice' "? Was anything else required to satisfy any interest *contra* on the part of the law, or to assure the state's interest in the preservation of life? Why did the court believe it necessary to take a different route to, I believe, a significantly different outcome?

Besides, when before has a state supreme court gone to such lengths to hear testimony concerning a church's teachings in order to assess only the sincerity and trustworthiness of one of its communicants and not also the objective manner in which he proposed to act as guardian? Confronted by Joseph Quinlan who held those "religious" concepts, Judge Muir, in line with the law's protection of life regardless of its state or condition, had to place the medical care of Karen Quinlan under the court's direction. Confronted by that same Joseph Quinlan the New Jersey Supreme Court bifurcated *him* (separating sincerity and sincerely held beliefs-to-be-acted-on). It was therefore forced to elaborate decision-making procedures and to express standards governing conduct (not Joseph Quinlan's), both of which are apt to convey into private hands superabundant discretion in matters of life and death.

The constitutional claims can be taken up in turn.

The court gave short shrift to the constitutional claim of free exercise of religion. "The right to religious beliefs is absolute," it said, "but conduct in pursuance thereof is not wholly immune from governmental restraint." It further observed that "ranged against the State's interest in the preservation of life, the impingement of religious belief, much less religious 'neutrality' as here, does not reflect a constitutional question. . . ." We have just seen that the court itself stated in every significant detail that moral matrix (miscalled "neutrality") of medicine, and deemed it a reasonable secular view.

Because of the state's interest in the preservation of life, Judge Muir had been impelled to say that conduct announced in advance to be in pursuance of these religious concepts presented a constitutional question. Yet it was precisely a muddled version of "religious 'neutrality' " (discontinuance of treatment, as precisely defined above) the New Jersey Supreme Court placed in the private realm and gave over to Joseph Quinlan to carry out. In doing so it set precedents for placing in the private realm, in regard to uncomprehending patients, life and death decisions that are not likely to be so neatly packaged or defensible. The state's interest in the protection of life was weakened by an appeal to the right to privacy and to the quality of recoverable function. A decision based instead on the court's own careful formulation of a secularized version of what it strangely and mistakenly called "religious neutrality" would have avoided Judge Muir's outcome—and its own outcome as well.

Short shrift was also made of the constitutional claim of cruel and unusual punishment. That claim, the court said in effect, was a category-mistake: in the case of the unfortunate Karen Quinlan, "neither the State, nor the law, but the accident of fate and nature, has inflicted upon her conditions which, though in essence cruel and unusual, yet do not amount to 'punishment' in any constitutional sense." Neither—I interpose—would returning Karen to her natural state, though in essence cruel and most unusual, involve the infliction by any human agency (neither by the state, nor by the law, nor by the physicians, nor by the guardian) of conditions not there already. A careful construction, in legal opinion, of that moral notion of care for the dying would have buttressed the state's interest in the protection of life more than is likely to be the consequence of the opening the New Jersey Supreme Court actually made between affording no relief and court-directed care of the dying.

The Law the Court Made

To afford relief, the New Jersey Supreme Court walked into the thicket of a right to privacy which the United States Supreme Court has found "emanating" from various provisions in the Bill of Rights and other amendments to the Constitution, and which in recent years, we saw in part 1, has been an open sesame to large-scale, "substantive due process," court-made legislation. This right, moreover, is expressly protected in the 1947 New Jersey Constitution.[18] From Karen's right of privacy, the court said, flows "the right of the physician to administer medical treatment according to his best judgment" and the right of a guardian of Karen's person to act on her behalf.

The potential conflict between these "rights" and the state's interest in "the preservation and sanctity of human life" gave the court the "most concern." That concern and potential conflict was resolved by exceedingly broad constructions based upon Karen's presumed exercise of her right of privacy and by finding her noncognitive condition to be the focal point, not her "impending death."

The court first pronounced that Karen could legally decide to refuse

18. Art. 1, para. 1. In basing its decision on the right of privacy, the New Jersey Supreme Court, of course, did so with the meaning that constitutional right has had since *Roe* v. *Wade* (410 U.S. 113). "Presumably this right is broad enough," Chief Justice Hughes wrote, "to encompass a patient's decision to decline medical treatment under certain circumstances, in much the same way as it is broad enough to encompass a woman's decision to terminate pregnancy under certain conditions." Thus as might have been predicted—as *was* predicted—when the United States Supreme Court took from the people and their legislators the power to determine the meaning of protectable human life and gave that over to private hands, it became reasonable to suppose that other comparable decisions would follow from so powerful a right as that sort of privacy. Let no one henceforth use the "future line-drawing argument" against the "wedge argument," and in particular not when the principles and reasons in support of one move clearly contain the seeds of future moves.

treatment, if she could consciously do so. This at once shifted the issue in principle or in emphasis from the care of the dying (and from surrogate decision makers in such cases) to refusal of treatment in general (and to surrogate decision makers in a much more encompassing range of cases). "We have no doubt, in these unhappy circumstances," the court said, "that if Karen were herself miraculously lucid for an interval . . . and perceptive of her irreversible condition, she could effectively decide upon discontinuance of the life-support apparatus, even if it meant the prospect of natural death." So far, so good, when that last provision is attached. But then the court had to distinguish its decision from the *Heston* case. It intimated that the court as recently as 1971 had been in error in considering that case "as if the patient's own religious decision [she was a Jehovah's Witness] to resist transfusion were at stake," and not "most importantly a patient apparently salvable to long life and vibrant health—a situation not at all like the present case." To which one reply is that to have construed that an unconscious adult Jehovah's Witness would in an interval of lucidity refuse a blood transfusion certainly stretches legal inference no further than to presume refusal "even if it meant the prospect of natural death" in the case of another unconscious adult dying patient. Secondly, a construction that she lawfully could do that would have been based on a First Amendment right, not simply on a right of privacy found only in the penumbra of several amendments.

The nuance in law significant now and for the future is what the court felt forced to say in order to distinguish *Quinlan* from *Heston*. It did not limit its contruction of Karen's refusal of treatment (which could be lawful and for which surrogate refusal could lawfully be substituted) to the withdrawal of procedures "even if it meant the prospect of natural death." Instead and "most importantly" was a patient's apparent salvability in *Heston* to "long life and vibrant health." That in principle or in emphasis shifts the ground for lawful surrogate refusals from dying unconscious patients—the court's finding of fact in the *Quinlan* case—to include (at the least) incurable unconscious patients as well.

Here is the point of entrance for substituted quality-of-life refusals of medical treatment in medical judgment or mutually between physician and family. The court then went on to expand *this* marked difference between *Quinlan* and *Heston* by speaking of vegetable and sapient life.

> No external compelling interest of the State could compel Karen to endure the unendurable, only to vegetate a few measurable months with no realistic possibility of returning to any semblance of cognitive or sapient life. We perceive no thread of logic distinguishing between such a choice on Karen's part and a similar choice which, under the evidence in this case, could be made by a competent patient terminally ill, riddled by cancer and suffering great pain; such a patient would not be resuscitated or put on a respirator, . . . and *a fortiori* would not be *kept against his will* on a respirator.

I noted, above, some breaks in that thread of logic, and at least one knot where the court might have paused and not reached this outcome. There is, for example, a moral difference between returning a patient to her natural state of impending death (not prolonging her dying) and returning a nondying patient to her natural state if that simply means noncognitivity or incurability (or some other measure of the "less than human") given as reasons for not using indicated medical procedures to sustain a patient's life. In addition, we may ask whether the court could not have relieved physicians from some of the pressure to keep a respirator going beyond the point where it would not initially have been started, by subjecting this inconsistency to examination. We can ask whether (allowing for medical discretion) some additional dicta about the dim difference between continuing a respirator and planned refusal of resuscitation or massive blood transfusions or major surgery for such a patient as Karen might not have been more helpful than dicta about vegetation and "cognitive or sapient life." Instead, the court based its ruling on nonsapience, and so concluded that "the interests of the patient, as seen by her surrogate, the guardian, must be evaluated by the court as predominant, even in face of an opinion *contra* by the present attending physicians."

What, then, of the *state's* interest in the preservation of life which played so strong a role in the lower court's decision? In answering this question, the New Jersey Supreme Court was still engaged in distinguishing *Quinlan* from *Heston* [19] and other similar cases. It used two tests in distinguishing between *Quinlan* and the medical pro-

19. *John F. Kennedy Hospital* v. *Heston,* 58 N.J. 576 (1971). By introducing the test of degree of bodily invasiveness to distinguish a respirator from a blood transfusion, the court was striking out on its own with slender or no legal precedent and was obscuring the gulf between this and previous cases. George J. Annas ("In re Quinlan") points out that in almost all the blood transfusion cases *invasive surgery* was involved as well. This highlights the fact that the test of *recoverability* in determining the state's interest in sustaining life was the crux of the *Quinlan* decision, not the degree of invasiveness needed to effect cure. The latter was largely a distraction, and one that served to make the crucial test seem to be one that can be cabined more easily. "Degree of invasiveness" also stirs memories of the categorical meaning of "extraordinary" treatments, in both medical and religious traditions, and takes the attention of the "faithful" away from the fact that by coupling "extraordinary means" with incurability and not just with impending death, a long step has in principle been taken toward substituted judgments leading to involuntary euthanasia. The doctrine of substituted judgment, in American law, has to date been governed by an incompetent's previous actions and intentions (when these are known) or by well-founded construction of what these might be. Substituted judgment in the *Heston* case would therefore have given legal effect to the patient's faith as a Jehovah's Witness. Instead, *Quinlan* links substituted judgment with that patient's prospects for long and vibrant life and, by contrast, with Karen's lack of such prospects. For an analysis of substituted judgment in case law before *Quinlan,* see John A. Robertson, "Organ Donation by Incompetents and the Substituted Judgment Doctrine," *Columbia Law Review* 76, no. 1 (January 1976) : 48–78. Robertson argues that when *correctly* applied the doctrine of substituted judgment is quite consistent with respect for persons and need not expand into judgments based actually on other people's interests put in place of the incompetent's. Nor is substituted judgment in law to date consistent with proxy death-choices.

Nevertheless a careful reading of Robertson's article shows the direction in which the legal doctrine of substituted judgment is moving in the present day. In cases involving the once competent, the never competent, and the not yet competent, the judgment of parent, guardian, and parens patriae are *floating free* from a searching effort, within human judgment, to discover or find an interest to be protected from them. The author is discussing organ donation, it is true, not substituted life and death decisions. Still his "objective" standard is to ask what the incompetent, if competent, would consent to. That seems to me a more subjective standard than to ask whether an incompetent potential kidney donor had or has an actual countervailing interest in placing himself at risk to save his brother's life. Thus, the legal doctrine of substituted judgment approximates Veatch's "reasonableness" test. Such an "immaculate conception," I said above, must come to mean death by a thousand qualifications. Nevertheless, I judge that Robertson's notion of substituted judgment cannot as such be extended to the *Saikewicz* case, to be discussed in the next chapter. In the absence of any actual interest to be discovered in an incompetent, the standard should be, he writes, that "it is in the incompetent's best interest to be treated as nearly as possible as the person he would be if his incompetence had never occurred." This means in treatment decisions to use as a norm the treatment offered to normal patients.

cedures required in those other cases. In the latter cases, first, "the procedure required (usually a transfusion) constituted a minimal bodily invasion." Second, "the chances of recovery and return to functioning life were very good." That means, the court ruled, that "the State's interest *contra* weakens and the individual's right of privacy grows as the degree of bodily invasion increases and the prognosis dims. Ultimately, there comes a point at which the individual's right overcomes the State interest."

That compact statement needs to be unpacked if the reader is to be able to think with or against the court's opinion and trace out its consequences for our society. First, the state's interest in the protection and preservation of life grows less and less as bodily invasion increases. As stated, that calculus commits our legal system to objective classes of ordinary and extraordinary procedures and to measuring these by the degree of bodily invasion. It commits our legal system to protect human life by less invasive procedures, by ordinary procedures so defined. Standard medical practice—invasive in some cases, less so in others—is a better standard than the court's, even if both legitimate routinized decisions.

The state's interest, secondly, grows less and less as "the prognosis dims," as the prospects of resuming cognitive life decrease. Later on in its opinion, the court asserted that *"the focal point* of decision should be the prognosis as to the reasonable possibility of return to cognitive and sapient life" (italics added). These, indeed, are sweeping generalities to which the court was drawn (away from strictly the circumstances of Karen's case) in endeavoring to break with the precedent of the *Heston* case.

Everybody's Substituted Judgment

One point remained to be determined, namely whether anyone else could decide for Karen. "If a putative decision by Karen to permit this non-cognitive, vegetative existence to terminate by natural forces is regarded as a valuable incident of her right of privacy," the court reasoned, "then it should not be discarded solely on the basis that her condition prevents her conscious exercise of the choice." Therefore the court appealed to the doctrine of substituted judgment.

It also appealed to the concurrence of a social consensus ascribing to Karen a decision to refuse treatment. "If [the] conclusion [of guardian and family] is in the affirmative this decision should be accepted by a society the overwhelming majority of whose members would, we think, in similar circumstances, exercise such a choice in the same way for themselves or for those closest to them." Therefore Karen's right of privacy was to be asserted by Joseph Quinlan who was given undivided guardianship.

In making this determination, it should be noticed that the court arrived at a doctrine of everybody's substituted judgment. Having reached its own judgment concerning what Karen would decide if she was lucid for a moment, the court needed further support for reasons psychologists may be able to explain. In undertaking "a nondelegable judicial responsibility" to reexamine "underlying human values and rights"—instead of leaving the matter in the hands of physicians—the court said its determinations had to be responsive "not only to the concepts of medicine but also to the common moral judgments of the community at large." That seemed a needed assistance as the court ventured to "answer with its most informed conception of justice in the previously unexplored circumstances presented to it," and also when it declared that "law, equity, and justice must not themselves quail and be helpless in face of modern technological marvels presenting questions hitherto unthought of."

The court rightly avoided court-ordered practice of medicine. But it failed to give the medical profession adequate direction as to "the State's interest *contra*" in life and death decisions. Rightly acknowledging that "there must be a way to free physicians in the pursuit of their healing vocation," the New Jersey Supreme Court's solution was procedural. It extensively absented the law from these questions. On *what* to decide, it pointed to less and less state interest in the preservation of life as the invasiveness of procedures grows and as the prospects of recovery of cognitive function lessens. On *who* shall decide, it gave Joseph Quinlan undivided guardianship, with the entailed right to consult additional physicians concerning Karen's treatment. That was, in itself, a correct move. Yet associated with physicians and guardian, there should be others who decide: the court called for the establishment of ethics committees. Its ruling embraced all these details, both the focal criteria we have discussed and the procedures.

> Upon the concurrence of the guardian and family of Karen, should the responsible attending physicians conclude that there is

> no reasonable possibility of Karen's ever emerging from her present comatose condition to a cognitive, sapient state and that the life-support apparatus now being administered to Karen should be discontinued, they shall consult with the hospital "Ethics Committee" or like body of the institution in which Karen is hospitalized. If that consultative body agrees that there is no reasonable possibility of Karen ever emerging from her present comatose condition to a cognitive, sapient state, the present life-support system may be withdrawn and said action shall be without any civil or criminal liability therefor on the part of any participant.

Professor George Annas [20] says the court "felt not completely comfortable" permitting a guardian alone to make this judgment for Karen; therefore it added physician concurrence and the concurrence of an ethics committee in a prognosis of irrecoverability—and, I add, the substituted judgment of everyone. Without necessarily agreeing with Annas about the court's discomfort, we must take very seriously his remarks about the layer of decision making to be supplied by a committee. On the one hand, the ethics committee could be called upon to make a determination that, as the Court ruled, "there is no reasonable possibility of Karen's ever emerging. . . ." If that is its business, Annas remarks, "an ethics committee will be of absolutely no help; that is purely a medical prognosis"; and surely the Court did not mean for the committee to practice medicine without a license.[21]

20. "In re Quinlan."

21. Robert M. Veatch makes this same criticism of the so-called ethics committee. (*Death, Dying, and the Biological Revolution,* p. 175.) It "should really be called a neurology committee and be made up only of neurological experts," since its task is to confirm the medical prognosis. The New Jersey Hospital Association in cooperation with state officials has now issued guidelines directing hospitals to set up advisory committees consisting of six or seven doctors, including a surgeon, an anesthesiologist and a neurologist or neurosurgeon. While the committees may include a member or members from the general public, the notion of committees consisting mainly of laymen has now been abandoned. They are to be called "prognosis committees" instead of "ethics committees" (*The New York Times,* January 27 and 30, 1977. See also Veatch, "Hospital Ethics Committees: Is There a Role?" *Hastings Center Report* 7, no. 3 [June 1977] : 22–25.) Annas's critique of the *Quinlan* opinion, however, is quite different from Veatch's. For Veatch, a medical prognosis is simply to be given to the family or guardian who alone should make the decision to treat or not to treat, with light supervision by the courts. A team or committee of physicians under whatever name is needed only to determine technical medical matters; a decision to withhold treatment is the family's business, and the ethics of it is as well.

If, on the other hand, that is not what is expected of an ethics committee, then it must decide about other matters. Read that way, Annas finds the court's statement "equally disturbing." It would be left to such a committee, by the competence here given it, to "be consulted on the definitions of 'reasonable possibility' of recovery and the meaning of 'cognitive, sapient life.' " So "one could read this as being the first time any United States court has sanctioned the use of a 'quality of life' criterion for making such decisions. Read together with the rest of the opinion this could be taken as a signal to let ethics committees reevaluate the care and treatment of defective newborns, the retarded, and the mentally ill." Moreover, such a committee was specifically relieved of any civil or criminal responsibility if that became its agenda.

Following its ruling the court strongly implied that similar proceedings for judicial declaratory relief would not necessarily be required for the implementation of comparable decisions in the field of medical practice in the future. So having designated a group of decision makers and having left behind the "impending death" which was the first finding of fact in this case, the court stepped aside.

Moreover, a note in the decision reads: "The declaratory relief we here award is not intended to imply that the principles enunciated in this case might not be applicable in divers other types of terminal medical situations such as those described by Drs. Korein and Diamond, supra, *not necessarily* involving the hopeless loss of cognitive or sapient life" (italics added). Dr. Sidney Diamond testifying for the state, would have continued the respirator on Karen, but said no physician would respond to a massive hemorrhage in her case, or perform a major operation: he seemed to link those refusals with Karen's loss of "human qualities"—which, in the note just cited, the court says is not a necessary condition. Dr. Julius Korein, testifying for the plaintiff, favored stopping the respirator and invoked the concept of "judicious neglect" and the use of what the court called "the foreboding initials DNR (do not resuscitate)" in the case of metastatic cancer involving the lungs, the liver, the brain—even though there is perhaps not yet a "hopeless loss of cognitive or sapient life." At the first mention of these cases, the court observed that the thread of logic in such distinctions was elusive, but it noted that such distinctions are related to medical decisions—with which the court was unwilling to rest the matter in cases of (as these surely were "impending death." Having rested its ruling more on the hopeless loss of cognitive or sapient life and mandated procedures for shared decision making, the court then suggested that the principles enunciated may embrace divers other cases of "judicious neglect" as well, "not necessarily involving the hopeless loss of cognitive or sapient life." It is hard to say what an ethics committee is going to do when it convenes, even if it interprets its task narrowly, beyond trying to determine the standards the court meant them to use and figuring how to use its calculus of invasiveness. It requires not much of a "slippery slope" argument to predict that, if ethics committees accumulate extra-legal legitimacy, the kinds of cases they encompass in making life and death decisions will expand.

Now, there are "peer review" committees in medical centers where medical *research* is carried on. The committees sometimes review the ethical aspects of human experimentation, and some have added representatives of professions other than medicine to their membership. In the wake of *Quinlan* we may expect a new and untried institution to spring up, one that reviews the ethical aspect of medical *treatment* in hard cases. That may or may not be welcomed by the lonely physician. But there seems to me to be grave question whether a committee structure will have the advantage the court thought. "The most appealing factor" of that mandated concurrence, it said, will be "the diffusion of professional responsibility for decision." I fear it will be exactly that: the diffusion of professional *responsibility*.[22] One may question whether ethical review with the addition of "social workers, attorneys, and theologians" to physicians on the committee will raise the level of decision much above that of an ethical physician free to consult with his colleagues and with others. I have for too long a time frequented theologians, ministers, and ethicists not to tremble at absenting the law from these questions as far as the court did in order to make room for those people.

There were one or two concluding remarks on the question of criminal liability that, for completeness' sake, should be mentioned. If the procedures are followed, the court ruled, "there would be no criminal homicide in the circumstances of this case. We believe, first,

22. On this point, see also George Annas, "In re Quinlan." He adds a portentous consideration: diffusion of responsibility makes decisions *easier*.

that the ensuing death would not be homicide but rather expiration from existing natural causes. . . . There is a real and in this case determinative distinction between the unlawful taking of the life of another and the ending of artificial life-support systems as a matter of self-determination," or determination by a proper surrogate. Long before in this decision, I have suggested, the court could have ruled *that* way, it could have made that distinction "determinative" instead of absenting the law and designating persons in their professional or other private capacities to decide questions other than when to withdraw life-sustaining procedures. But such a position requires impending death to be the focal point. "Secondly," the court went on, "even if it were to be regarded as homicide, it would not be unlawful." In context, one should ponder that long and hard—even granting that the positive law can do what it wants to do in making and unmaking "crimes." Does the court mean that the "principles" enunciated in this case will not be homicide—or if homicide, not unlawful—if these principles are "applicable in divers other types of terminal medical situations . . . not necessarily involving the hopeless loss of cognitive or sapient life"? If so, then, "ethics committee" means "death committee"; and the *Quinlan* decision has by its very words privatized what once was called homicide.

A Critique of the Opinion [23]

In its capital punishment decisions on July 2, 1976, the Supreme Court invalidated the mandatory death penalty.[24] One of the constitutional defects found in North Carolina's mandatory statute was its treatment of "all persons convicted of a designated offense not as uniquely human beings, but as members of a faceless, undifferentiated mass to be subject to the blind infliction of the penalty of death" (Justice Stewart). Does not *Quinlan*—we may ask—give over to the substituted judgments of private persons a power which *Woodson* denies to the state—namely, the power to treat all persons "convicted" of coma and irrecoverable sapience, and perhaps "divers other types

23. For an opposite view, see Robert M. Veatch, *Death, Dying, and Biological Revolution*. Veatch's opinion is that *Quinlan*'s "recognition of the right"—I would say the responsibility—"of the guardian to exercise the right of privacy on behalf of the incompetent patient is an exciting departure and . . . a key insight for future resolution of similar cases of incompetent patients" (p. 140).

24. *Woodson* v. *North Carolina*, 428 U.S. 280 (1976).

of terminal medical situations," not as individual human beings, "but as members of a faceless, undifferentiated mass"?

Moreover, having ruled that there was sufficient probative evidence that Karen would not want to live under the circumstances and that the assumption that she would want to die was well-founded because the "overwhelming majority" of us would want to do so, why should the guardian or family or physicians be empowered to "overrule" or "veto" a patient's right to die? Given Karen's imputed will, why should the concurrence of any particular persons be sought? The court had reached its decision and could have ordered the respirator stopped. As we have seen, the constitutional right of privacy is the individual patient's right, not the family's, not anyone else's. If a patient has such a constitutional right, members of the family ought not to be able to defeat the exercise of that right. Having acknowledged such an individual right of privacy, and having decided how it would be exercised, the courts should consistently stand ready to insure that right's exercise. There may be families whose wishes are contrary to those of Joseph Quinlan—who cannot bear the added guilt that would come from a decision to discontinue any means that might delay the death of the one they love. Suppose a case in which a parent or guardian wanted to continue the respirator, while the physicians petitioned to be allowed to stop it? By *Quinlan*'s reasoning (though not by the procedures it set up) a court should insure that an incompetent patient's right of privacy not be frustrated. The parent's or a guardian's will in this matter should be set aside; the court should act, in behalf of the patient's privacy and in behalf of his or her court-imputed decision. As we saw in analysis of *Planned Parenthood* v. *Danforth,* the Supreme Court held that the state cannot "delegate" to spouse or to parents a blanket veto power over a woman's private decision to obtain an abortion, and the courts stand ready in the case of incompetent women to insure their privacy in this matter. Having acknowledged something like a "right to die" in the content of Karen Quinlan's privacy, how could the court—in our supposed case—allow anyone to stand in the way of the exercise of that right? That would be to delegate to particular persons a power to take away a constitutional right. Judge Muir had ruled that "there is no constitutional right to die that can be asserted by a parent for his incompetent adult child." In place of that, the logic of the New Jersey Supreme Court's opinion is to say: There is a constitutional right to die that cannot be opposed by a parent for his incompetent adult child. That is a strange meaning to assign the state's power of parens patriae; but such is the logic of the *Quinlan* decision.

The *Quinlan* case has gone a long way toward obliterating the distinction between voluntary and involuntary euthanasia and weakening legal protection of life from involuntary euthanasia. The court *imputed* to Karen a will to die; it did not discover it. Then the court permitted others also to impute a will to die to an uncomprehending patient and to act in behalf of that patient's privacy so construed. It does not matter *who* is the designated agent; *others* now have an extraordinary extralegal power to bring death. And as we have seen the court did invoke the concurrence of everyone in our society in the conditions of human existence judged not to be worth preserving. It does not matter that the conditions of life needed to impute a will to die to an uncomprehending patient are now assessed by somewhat narrow criteria: impending death and irrecoverability of cognitive and sapient life. Indeed the court first vacilated between these two tests and then put its weight on the second. Less narrow appraisals of conditions under which no one would or should want to live will begin to be used. The *Quinlan* opinion goes so far as to suggest that this may be legally permissible.[25]

25. Professor Yale Kamisar of the University of Michigan Law School has suggested (in an unpublished address to an interdisciplinary seminar held in connection with the National Right to Life Convention in Boston, June 25, 1976) that as a thought-experiment we reread a crucial passage in the court's opinion, leaving blanks where the court mentioned this case's special circumstances and adding ourselves, *in mente,* the conditions or qualities of life in prospect:

> We have no doubt, in these unhappy circumstances that if [this senile old man, mongoloid child, etc.] were [himself] miraculously lucid for an interval and perceptive of [his] irreversible condition, [he] could effectively decide upon [death]. . . . The only practical way to prevent destruction of [this creature's] right is to permit the guardian and family to render their best judgment . . . as to whether [this creature] would exercise it in these circumstances. If their conclusion is in the affirmative this decision should be accepted by a society the overwhelming majority of whose members would, we think, in similar circumstances, exercise such a choice in the same way. For this reason we determine that [this creature's] right of privacy may be asserted in [his] behalf, in this respect, by [his] guardian and family.

I lodge the same objection to Kamisar's use of the expression *this creature* as I did above to the court's use of variants of the word *vegetable.* In *both* cases, however, that helps rhetorically to sustain an emphasis on quality-of-life decisions.

Consider, for example, the extraordinary formula by which the court "solved" its most difficult problem: how to weaken the state's interest. Apply its calculus to the case of a mongoloid baby needing an operation to remove a bowel obstruction or to deal with a heart condition; or to a spina bifada baby who is the offspring of a 13-year-old unmarried girl in the ghetto. The individual's right to privacy grows as the degree of bodily invasion increases and the prognosis dims. Along with that, the state's interest contra surrogate death decisions weakens as privacy grows and prognosis dims. Ultimately there comes a point at which the individual's rights overcome state interest.[26]

Moreover, a leading British philosopher has worried a great deal about and has on his own principles been unable to solve the hypothetical case of a Nazi who makes the substituted judgment that Jews should be incinerated and who himself is so thoroughly a Nazi that

---

Kamisar fears—quite rightly, I believe—that the New Jersey Supreme Court "may have provided the euthanasiasts with something that has eluded them for decades—the bridge between voluntary and involuntary euthanasia, between the 'right to die' and the 'right to kill.'" There are, he pointed out, "many thousands of others—severely mentally deficient and congenitally deformed children, adults suffering from senile dementia, severe mental retardation, massive brain-damage—whose symptoms may be as unequivocally described as irreversible as Miss Quinlan's."

26. The most striking feature of Kamisar's article "Euthanasia Legislation: Some Non-Religious Objections" (in *Euthanasia and the Right to Death,* ed. A. B. Downing [London: Peter Owen, 1969], pp. 85–133) is his *proof* that the founders, leaders, and spokesmen for the euthanasia societies in Great Britain and America proposed voluntary euthanasia only because the public was not yet ready to accept involuntary euthanasia. Only the latter, it is admitted, would do much good or help those most needing relief of the human condition. Against those who proclaim that they wish to drive home a wedge in the law's presumption and our moral presumption of a life-favoring will in anyone who cannot speak for himself, it is quite proper to us a wedge argument in return. Those who announce they don't want to stop at the line of voluntary euthanasia cannot consistently reply that it is possible to stop at that line. Those who defend a conscious patient's right to refuse treatment or to refuse dispensable "extraordinary" treatments cannot without further argument conclude that substituted judgment may legitimately withhold treatment or a class of treatments from *incurables* no less than from the *dying* who cannot speak for themselves. The traditional teaching about ordinary and extraordinary in Christian medical ethics must be recomprehended in terms of a medical indications policy, and substituted judgment must be reserved for the dying who cannot speak for themselves, if it is not in *morality* to provide euthanasiasts with the same thing Kamisar fears in the legal order: a bridge over to involuntary euthanasia. Indeed, this is already palpably evident in the writings of moral theologians and in the statements of some bishops and ministers concerning substituted judgments to neglect incurable defective newborns who are not dying.

he himself is willing to say that if he or his wife were a Jew he or she should also be incinerated. Suppose we say, "If a putative decision by X to permit this Jewish existence to terminate is regarded as a valuable incident of X's right to privacy, then it should not be discarded solely on the basis that something prevents his exercise of the choice. The only practical way to protect that right is to permit physicians and a hallowed ethics committee to render their best judgment. This decision should be accepted by a society the overwhelming majority of whose members would, we think, in similar circumstances exercise such a choice in the same way for themselves and for those closest to them."

I make no apology for this most remote possibility drawn from the Nazi era, or for two or three far more proximate analogies in this volume. My experience in public discussions confirms Yale Kamisar's suggestion that it is "not so much that the euthanasiasts are troubled by the Nazi experience as it is that they are troubled that the public is troubled by the Nazi experience." And as a Christian ethicist I have some good reasons that Kamisar does not have (he has enough) for believing that "it is necessary to distrust the malignity of the human heart." [27]

We are, of course, a long way away from anything the New Jersey Supreme Court said; and it is also true that court decisions are always prima facie related to the circumstances of the case alone. Still, in criticism of the *Quinlan* opinion, I have not used an external or causal slippery slope argument; ample concepts or principles have been adduced from the opinion that are quite capable of greasing the slope, or driving the wedge deeper. No one should discount the power of legal precedents to replicate themselves and even to generate kindred species. No one should be convinced by a *theoretical* counterargument that it is always possible to *stop* the extension of legal language and principles.[28] People who do so reason, who say that a line can be drawn somewhere just ahead of us down hill, often themselves ten or fifteen years ago voiced the same counterargument—about a line then just ahead which is now behind us and no longer persuasive as a legal or moral norm.

27. Yale Kamisar, "Euthanasia Legislation," pp. 114 and 119, n. 12.

28. Yale Kamisar, unpublished paper (n. 25, above). Moreover, courts would simply make *rulings* in particular cases, without disclosing their reasons and arguments for them, if judges and justices did not believe their reasoning also to be important and to have expected effect on future cases.

Nevertheless, Yale Kamisar is not correct in aiming his criticism of the *Quinlan* decision solely at the doctrine of imputed and substituted judgment. He does this because he sees no sensible distinction to be made between so-called passive and active euthanasia, between letting die and killing. Therefore, for him, the court eroded any distinction between voluntary and involuntary euthanasia, and it legitimated involuntary euthanasia by allowing consent to be imputed to unwilling patients and by allowing other persons to execute what they judge the patient would decide if he or she could. For Kamisar, a substituted judgment to let die is legally and morally the same as a substituted judgment to kill or a substituted judgment to neglect the medically incurable.

In decisions to "let die well enough" one does not need to go through the rigmarole of imputing and then substituting judgment for the patients. One simply needs a medical indications policy to determine what should be done for the *dying*. One needs only a wise determination of when the point comes at which salvic treatments will no longer be beneficial, when further treatment will do nothing except prolong their dying. It is not the doctrine of imputed and substituted judgment, standing alone, that abolishes the distinction between voluntary and involuntary euthanasia or makes the opening in our law for the entrance of involuntary euthanasia, as Kamisar fears. This happens when that doctrine is used (or when ordinary / extraordinary is used to distinguish classes of treatments) indifferently for the nondying who are voiceless and the dying who are voiceless. Both the categorical meaning of ordinary / extraordinary and the doctrine of substituted judgment, especially as this was interpreted by *Quinlan*, are opening the door to involuntary euthanasia.[29]

29. In the text above I consistently speak of "voluntary" and "involuntary" euthanasia. The latter, however, is likely to be euphemistically dubbed "nonvoluntary." That is the term used by Ruth Russell in *Freedom to Die* (New York: Human Sciences Press, 1975; Dell Publishing Co., 1976), p. 216. Professor Russell thinks that the term *nonvoluntary* euthanasia was appropriate in the case of the "seriously deformed" thalidomide babies (pp. 165–69, 223–27). These babies were not (at least many of them were not, including the famous Belgium baby) mentally deformed, only physically deformed. The Massachusetts man in the case to be examined in the next chapter, was "cognitive" and "sapient," although he only had the mind of a three year old; but the thalidomide babies were "mentally normal." Yet Russell favors "euthanatizing" them—and elsewhere complains about opponents who use the "wedge" or "slippery slope" argument (p. 213)!

The court did this in the totality of its decision and in the aggregation of the several ingredients of its ruling and reasoning. It did this in part by substituting the judgment of others for that of a patient incapable of refusing treatment. It did this also in part by failing to rest its ruling on its own clear discernment that there is a significant distinction to be made on medical grounds between choosing death for patients and deciding to return them to their natural, dying condition. It did this by speaking almost in the same breath of impending death and irrecoverable cognitive or sapient function. It did this by its calculus of increasing invasiveness, increasing patients' putative rights, and decreasing state interest in the preservation of life. It did this by its mention of "divers other types of terminal medical situations." It did this by then mandating procedures by which private parties and hospital committees should make life or death decisions, which if the procedure works will gain extralegal legitimacy—a sort of "administrative law" alongside the courts, beyond which (it was pointedly suggested) there may seldom be need for appeal. For these reasons I must judge that a careful examination of the final juridical outcome of the *Quinlan* case gives support to Kamisar's foreboding.

On June 9, 1976, Karen Ann Quinlan was moved from Saint Clare's Hospital in Denville, N.J., to the Morris View Nursing Home in Morris Plains—the first comatose patient admitted to that nursing home. There she would receive the same level of care as anyone else. While refusing to discuss the particulars of medication and ancillary care, the director did say: "I don't think it appropriate to use some super-fancy procedures to return her to a state that was unacceptable to begin with." He called that "acceptable practice." It was revealed that Karen now had been "weaned" from the respirator. Saint Clare's had told the Quinlans they would put her back on a respirator if she needed it again. An ethics committee was formed at the nursing home, whose members consisted of the chairman of the Morris County Welfare Board, a physician on the staff of Morris View, an associate minister of the Chatham United Methodist Church, the minister of the First Memorial Presbyterian Church in Dover, and the supervisor of social work at Morris View. This committee ruled unanimously on June 10 that Karen was in irreversible coma with no reasonable possibility of recovering a "cognitive, sapient state." They also agreed unanimously that normal levels of nutrition and antibiotics should be administered. "All we ever asked for," said Mrs. Qlinlan, "was the removal of the respirator even if she breathed for three weeks, a few months, or five years." [30]

In a quiet hour one can speculate what Karen Ann Quinlan will think, from the verandas of heaven, about the consequences on earth of the outcome of her case.

30. *The New York Times,* June 11, 1976.

8

The Strange Case of Joseph Saikewicz

On July 13, 1976, a UPI press release [1] reported a ruling handed down by the Supreme Judicial Court of Massachusetts. By a split vote the court ruled that "life-prolonging" treatments could be withheld from a severely retarded leukemia patient who was incapable of making such a decision. The patient was a sixty-six-year-old man, institutionalized and said to have the mental age of a three-year-old. He was suffering from acute myeloblastic leukemia, a cancer of the blood-producing cells. That disease, it was testified, is always fatal; treatment causes painful side effects, nausea and vomiting, bladder irritation, etc.; drug therapy can arrest the cancer and prolong life, however, for two to thirteen months in 40 to 50 percent of the cases. (The news report said *only* 40 to 50 percent!) The patient, obviously, was not competent to refuse treatment. If the patient had been a normal three-year-old there is no doubt that the substituted judgment of family, physician, or court's guardian would have favored sustaining his life, and he would have been treated.

An advantage of this ruling, as such, was that the *court* decided the rights of a particular patient. It did not place a severely impaired person's right to life into an "area of liberties," as the 1973 abortion decisions did with regard to the fetus for the first trimester and which, we have seen, some wish to extend to newborns. It did not cast upon private individuals the power to be both triers of the facts and of the law governing a voiceless patient's right to treatment.[2] That, however, was no advantage to the patient, Joseph Saikewicz—unless escape from the Belchertown State School was an advantage. The director

1. *The New York Times,* July 14, 1976.

2. The newspaper reports did suggest, however, that the *opinion* of the supreme judicial court, when issued, would (like *Quinlan*) specify procedures to be followed in the future so that similar cases need not be brought before a court of law. However, Joseph Saikewicz died before the court could write the opinion, and so those procedures were prevented from issuing.

of that institution and its lawyers argued that he should be treated because "the vast majority of competent individuals would choose treatment." The court-appointed attorney for the patient at first thought he should "at least get the treatments anyone else would get," but he later changed his mind. The trial judge said in an interview: "I think I'd want to die. If I couldn't be cured, I wouldn't want to live." [3] That suggests an abandonment of the state's parens patriae power and a radical misuse of the doctrine of substituted judgment. It suggests that Joseph Saikewicz's interests were ascribed to him, not discovered by the light that the law's protection of life may throw on a dilemma of medical indications for or against treatment. Here is one way to empty our mental institutions by attrition.

No more than three and a half months passed before the first effects of the *Quinlan* case on our law were felt—in the present case.[4] Failing to sustain and prolong the life of the retarded or of incurables and letting the dying die are different sorts of actions. The failure of the court in *Quinlan* to give legal effect to the moral quality of these different activities can only be deeply regretted. For surely a three-year-old is "cognitive" and "sapient." Was it only the incongruity of that degree of cognitivity and sapience in a sixty-six-year-old man that counted against his right to life? If so, this case was, morally, a case of court-supervised involuntary euthanasia. If so, the Massachusetts court was swayed by the New Jersey court's shift from "dying" or "impending" death (*its* finding of fact at the time) to "irrecoverability" and to "cognitive" sapient life as the basis of its opinion. Prognosis of recovery in Saikewicz's case was shifted to take into account his irreparable retardation (not length or chance of recovery from his illness alone—for which normal patients are treated). At the same time, the unlikelihood that Karen Quinlan would recover cognitive sapient life was replaced by the unlikelihood that Saikewicz would ever have an IQ of more than 25. Since "cognitive" admits of degrees, the use of such a standard already forecasts in principle its own expansion in human judgments. In turn, the resulting quality-of-life criterion reached back to render prognosis of reasonable prospect

3. B. D. Colen, "After a Lifetime of Neglect, Man Becomes Cause Celebre," Los Angeles Times–Washington Post News Service, *The Evening Gazette*, Wooster, Massachusetts, August 3, 1976, Op-Ed page.

4. *Jones* v. *Saikewicz*, no. 711 (Sup. Jud. Ct. Mass. 1976); Civil Action no. 76-173, on direct appellate review from the Hampshire County Probate Court.

of cure or recovery no longer simply a medical decision. Finally, Saikewicz's right of privacy appears to have been exercised for him directly contrary to *Quinlan*'s appeal to everybody's judgment in medically similar cases.

That, I suppose, could be called the worst reading of the outcome in the instant case. Conceivably, the ruling could have been a balancing judgment falling within a medical indications policy. That is, it is possible that the patient's expected quality of life did not adulterate the decision; that his retardation was only an undeniable component in figuring how and whether effective treatment could be delivered. Saikewicz had lived in state institutions since 1923. His inability to cooperate might cause some problems, although restrictions could have been placed to restrain him.

I call this a "strange" case because Joseph died before the court wrote an opinion on which its ruling that he not be treated was based. So we may never know the court's reasoning in this matter. On the record are two briefs, pro and con. These briefs are worth examining, because of recurring references to the precedent of *Quinlan* on both sides of the *Saikewicz* case. A third brief, amicus curiae, was submitted by the Massachusetts Association for Retarded Citizens.

Basic Circumstance

If untreated Saikewicz would probably live a month or so, but could die tomorrow or live six months. A man of his age had less chance of remission than a younger man under forty. Even so, there was a 30 to 50 percent chance of a remission that would extend his life from two to thirteen months. Judge Jekanowski of the probate court *found* that "it is to a very high degree medically likely that he will die sooner without treatment than with it." Most patients situated similarly to Mr. Saikewicz choose to undergo chemotherapy. The guardian ad litem noted that "a person that could make an informed consent would consent" to chemotherapy. The patient's two attending physicians recommended not giving the therapy. One of the physicians, however, Dr. Elisha Ross, testified that she would withhold treatment only because his condition seemed stable (the leukemia was "smouldering"), and that she might change her mind if he got worse. The other physician, Dr. William Davis, believed that chances of success would worsen daily, so the therapy should be begun at once if at all; he thought it should not begin now *or* later.

In recommending against treatment, Dr. Davis used very strange words indeed, which the reader should note and ponder (they are repeated several times in the briefs we shall examine). He did not want to treat Saikewicz because "the quality of his life has been good and he would be likely to die a painless death." That's right, you read that correctly. A physician appealed to this institutionalized, severely retarded patient's *good* quality of life, as against the pain of treatment, in what may have been a landmark *negative* quality-of-life court ruling! Was that a euphemism needed to cover a retreat from the generally pro-life orientation of professional medical ethics to date? The authorities at the Belchertown State School wanted to treat, and they brought the case to court. The guardian ad litem, Patrick Melnick, recommended to the probate court that chemotherapy not be attempted in Saikewicz's case, despite his own assertion that normal patients would elect to be treated.

Judge Jekanowski of the probate court, like the guardian ad litem, was at first inclined to give treatment; after oral argument, he, too, changed his mind. In his formal findings of fact, Jekanowski listed the considerations on both sides. Factors weighing against administering chemotherapy were the patient's age, his inability to cooperate with the treatment, probable adverse side effects of treatment, low chance of producing remission, the certainty that the treatment would cause immediate suffering, and *the quality of life possible for him even if the treatment brought about remission.* Factors favoring administering chemotherapy were the chance that his life would be lengthened thereby and the fact that most people in his situation when given a chance to do so elect to take the gamble of treatment. Judge Jekanowski's decision not to order chemotherapy was appealed directly to the supreme judicial court.

Francis X. Bellotti, Attorney General of Massachusetts, entered the case on the side of administering treatment (on the side of the Belchertown School authorities, the plaintiff-appellants). That brief we take up first. In a most unusual move, the attorney general's office also entered the case on the other side: its civil rights and liberties division entered a brief arguing in behalf of the defendant-appellee (Saikewicz, no less) that he not be treated. Those arguments we shall also examine. Following a resume of the amicus curiae brief submitted by the Massachusetts Association for Retarded Citizens, I shall propose a hypothetical opinion that the court might have written in support of its ruling that Saikewicz not be treated. The court's reasoning, I will suggest, could have been based on a medical indications policy if, but only if, it was unpersuaded by the appeals to *Quinlan* placed before it by the brief against treatment.

Arguments Favoring Treatment

The probate court had equity jurisdiction, but once the court determined that the therapy would more likely than not extend the life of Joseph Saikewicz—the brief favoring treatment argues—it then was without authority to withhold treatment. Chemotherapy is an acceptable form of potentially life-extending therapy even for patients sixty-six years old. The state's paramount interest was in seeing that every reasonable attempt would be made to preserve his life. Thus, the court had a duty to require treatment for an incompetent patient, once these determinations had been made. To rule otherwise would "place the state's sanction behind the devaluation of the life of a mentally retarded person." Here, at the outset, the attorney general's brief refers to *Quinlan,* which he said invoked the ward's right of privacy exercised in her behalf "only because a majority of people in a like situation would probably end all treatment." In the instant case, the probate judge had reached exactly the opposite conclusion. He allowed competent persons to impose their own private standards of life on an incompetent, and the judge imposed his own personal opinion about "the quality of life that the retarded patient must live" and ruled that it was "not worth continuing when combined with pain when under chemotherapy."

The brief contends that once the court made these two findings of fact—(1) that the patient is more likely to live longer with than without the treatment, and (2) that a majority of competent patients under similar circumstances choose to accept the treatment—the court's and the state's duty was clear.

In regard to the disagreement between the two physicians, both of whom recommended no treatment, Dr. Davis's testimony that "the risks involved will increase and the chances of successfully bringing about remission will decrease as time goes by" seemed reasonable. But then Dr. Davis's reason for withholding therapy, as we noted above, was that "the quality of Mr. Saikewicz's life has been good, and he would be likely to die a painless death without therapy." The attorney general argued in reply to that statement: "Dr. Davis does not base his reasons for recommending against treatment on medical grounds, but rather he relies upon ethical judgments on the quality of life and death. . . . There can be no substitution of Dr. Davis' judgment for that of the court." Indeed, both physicians implied that were Mr. Saikewicz competent they would offer him the choice of accepting chemotherapy. I add here: this means that *both* physicians testified that Saikewicz's quality of life had *not been good,* and that his incompetence was the primary reason for not offering him treatment. Here we have a crucial contradiction: a retarded person by virtue of his incompetence needs a fiduciary agent (physician, guardian, court) to act in his behalf. If then he is also in need of life-prolonging therapy, his very dependence on a fiduciary agent could become a self-generating argument against his obtaining the needed treatment.

The guardian of litem had reported his belief that it was in the best interests of the defendant to die because "he would be in pain and fear the last moments of his life if he were treated. He would be unable to understand this pain and fear." The court below weighed the immediate suffering caused by the treatment against "the quality of life possible for him even if the treatment does bring about remission." The brief favoring treatment summarized that judgment as "the 'quality of life' that Mr. Saikewicz would lead *undergoing* chemotherapy" (italics added). That is somewhat puzzling language. Where the judge found that "most people" in his situation would choose chemotherapy, the guardian said "100 percent."

The attorney general argued that "it is not for any court to decide that the 'quality of life' of a mentally retarded individual living in pain is so poor that the person is better off dead than alive. There is no way for us to know if this mentally retarded person 'fears' or 'understands' the pain; and there is no way for us to measure his desire to live or his appreciation of being alive." He might well have added that normal children three years old and younger who are treated may also fear and fail to understand the pain we are causing them. In a footnote, the brief also drew attention to the fact that

> failure to provide Mr. Saikewicz with chemotherapy may be in violation of his constitutional right to treatment. Similarly, to deny Mr. Saikewicz treatment, which a majority of competent

patients choose, on the grounds of the quality of life that Mr. Saikewicz would lead under chemotherapy (the quality of life being judged to be so poor on the basis of his retardation) may violate Mr. Saikewicz's right to equal protection under the law.

This case was clearly distinguishable from *Quinlan* in two ways. The first has already been mentioned: *Quinlan* allowed the guardian to invoke "the ward's right of privacy only because a majority of people in a like situation . . . would probably choose to end all treatment." Another key distinction between *Saikewicz* and *Quinlan,* according to this brief, was that the latter ruling was based on a forecast of no likelihood of the ward's recovery from "biological vegetative existence" to cognitivity or sapience. Here the defendant's incompetence was a result of his retardation and not his illness; and if his life were extended through chemotherapy "he would continue to live the cognitive life he has always led." To buttress that argument, the attorney general pointed out that "society has determined that defendant's life was of enough value to maintain him for the past 53 years in state institutions." Viewed from this perspective, what was done with Joseph Saikewicz gives the appearance that the state seized upon adventitious circumstances in order to place, at long last, a quite different evaluation upon Saikewicz's life.

Finally, on the substance of the ruling that this brief asked the court to render, it cautioned that its precedental reasoning would race through the law: "It is important that this Court not establish a principle that it cannot accept in its most extreme fact situation." [5]

5. Here the brief cites Justice Jackson's dissent in *Korematsu* v. *United States,* 323 U.S. 214, 246 (1944), the case that upheld placing Japanese Americans in detention camps: "All who observe the work of courts are familiar with what Judge Cardoza described as the 'tendency of a principle to expand itself to the limit of its logic.'" The landmark search and seizure case, *Boyd* v. *United States,* 116 U.S. 616, 635 (1886): "It may be that it is the obnoxious thing in its mildest and least repulsive form; but illegitimate and unconstitutional practices get their first footing in that way, namely, by silent approaches and slight deviations. . . . It is the duty of courts to be watchful for the constitutional rights of the citizens, and against any stealthy encroachments thereon. *Their motto should be obsta principiis . . .*" (brief's italics). And the flag salute case, *Board of Education* v. *Barnette,* 319 U.S. 624, 641 (1943): "Those who begin coercive elimination of dissent soon find themselves exterminating dissenters. . . . *The First Amendment was designed to avoid these ends by avoiding these beginnings*" (brief's italics). It is quite clear that at the point of medical, legal, and ethical intersections at the edges of life discussed in this volume, the so-called

There was, however, yet a third reference to *Quinlan*. This concerned the *procedures* the attorney general asked the court to provide to cover possible future cases. The recommended guidelines are opposite in intent to those the New Jersey Supreme Court decreed, even though parallel. The family should not be allowed to make the decision, not even in concert with physicians. Even the attending physician may not be totally objective. As the guardian ad litem noted in this case, it is difficult to be sure that the attending physicians do not have "the desire to put their resources elsewhere." Thus there must be a guardian—someone who is "concerned with no one's but the ward's interests"—participating in every decision of whether to treat a terminally ill incompetent patient. Such a guardian ad litem must be appointed in all cases, not just in the case of an institutionalized patient where the head of the state school (the plaintiff, in this case), who has taken care of the patient during his life, has properly a part in the decision-making process. Finally, to have a second opinion on a decision of such consequence, an ethics committee or its equivalent should "review any decision not to provide available treatment to a terminally ill patient and incompetent patient."

The standard of review in the *Quinlan* case, however, was "obviously inapplicable"; the question whether Joseph Saikewicz had "a reasonable possibility of ever emerging from [his] present comatose condition" was impertinent. Likewise with future cases like his. The standard of review should be the one argued in the brief—that is, whether physicians' decisions generally are that a patient is likely to live longer with available treatment than without it. (The brief omits to repeat at this point its other substantive argument as a component of its standard of review, where *Quinlan* has its application, if any—namely, whether the available treatment would be chosen and would be offered to normal patients.) In order to state "the only exception" to be allowed by this standard or by the review process, the brief again quotes from *Quinlan:* where the treatment amounts to no more than "an undesired prolongation of the process of dying on a patient in *irreversible* condition when it is clear that such 'therapy' offers

---

wedge argument is an excellent one. This is true because legal principles and precedents are systemically designed to apply to other cases as well. This is the way the law "works," and, I think, also the way moral reasoning "works" from case to similar case.

neither human nor humane benefit." The brief's underlining of the word *irreversible* shifts attention toward "the process of dying" (*Quinlan*'s finding of fact) and away from that sentence's mention of "humane benefit." *Quinlan,* as we have seen, vacillated between impending death and restoration of cognitive, sapient life (humane benefit?), and finally came down on the latter.

Thus the attorney general recommended that the supreme judicial court promulgate standards and procedures covering cases similar to the one before the court. The brief chose "wording," for the recommended procedures, that followed "as closely as possible those promulgated by the New Jersey Supreme Court"—but with opposite standards and consequences. I quote from the wording:

> Should the responsible attending physicians conclude that an incompetent patient is likely to live longer with available treatment than without it, or that the potentially life extending treatment amounts to more than a prolongation of an irreversible dying condition, they should consult with the hospital 'Ethics Committee.' . . . If that consultative body agrees that the patient is not more likely to live longer with available treatment than without it or that the potentially life extending treatment amounts to no more than prolongation of an irreversible dying condition, the treatment may be withheld and said action shall be without any civil or criminal liability therefor on the part of any participant. . . .

Under these procedures and with that standard the courts would not be called upon to make a decision every time an incompetent, terminally ill patient was in possible need of treatment.

Again I draw attention, in the wording of standards and procedures to be promulgated, to the omission of any reference to whether all or a majority of competent patients would choose the life-sustaining therapy in question, which was a major component of the substantive argument in the body of the brief. The omission is not without significance, because such a test only enlivens the imagination when one is pondering what *should,* morally or legally, be done. Consensus settles no moral or legal questions. A better test is to ask whether the treatment is *given* to nondying normal patients who are incompetent to decide for themselves; and to ask whether physicians are not inclined to argue a bit with a normal competent patient who wants to exercise his right to refuse the therapy offered. That should be the standard of care extended to voiceless patients.

I am obliged to say at this point that the omission of abundant other cases and precedents cited in the "Brief Favoring Treatment" may seem to elevate *Quinlan* into the role of the sole basis of the argument. Still I judge that any reader of the attorney general's brief from which I selected would judge that *Quinlan* was given extraordinary prominence. As for the "Brief Against Treatment," on the face of it there would have been no argument at all—or at least very little—without *Quinlan*. To that brief we turn next.

Arguments Against Treatment

The Civil Rights and Liberties Division of the Department of the Attorney General of Massachusetts moved for leave to participate amicus curiae in the *Saikewicz* case, which was granted. It was "unusual for the Department of the Attorney General to appear on both sides of a legal matter" and contrary to general departmental policy to do so. Exception was made, however, because "the need to develop standardized procedures for approval of medical treatment for incompetent individuals is an important civil rights issue which must be faced." This brief upholds the probate court's order as "a reasonable and proper balancing of the individual's privacy rights and the Commonwealth's responsibility."

The probate court is a court of equity. As such it is "empowered to stretch forth its own [hand or action] in whatever direction its aid and protection may be needed." By virtue of its equity jurisdiction, the lower court could "pass upon purely personal rights." That seems clear enough. I mention it only because here is this brief's first citation of *Quinlan:* In the exercise of such power, a court of equity has "the enormous power to make whatever orders it may deem necessary for the benefit of those not capable of looking after themselves." However enormous, that so far is only a formal power, empty as yet of content pertinent to this case.

The power to pass on purely personal rights, and to issue whatever orders a court of equity deems necessary in the interests of incompetent persons, acquires material content by the next reference to *Quinlan,* which claims that case evidences that the interests of an incompetent may best be served under certain circumstances by withholding treatment. So far, so good. To take one more step: if the probate court did not have the power sometimes to *disapprove* proposed treatment plans from whatever source (family, physicians, custodians, even guardians), it would become "merely a *conduit* for providing a consent [recommended by someone else] which the incompetent could not himself provide." Again, so far so good.

Indeed, since the latter point was inapposite to the present case (and obviously true), I do not know why the brief bothered to mention it except for the fact that here is yet another reference to *Quinlan*. The force of these remarks about the plenipotentiary powers of a court of equity was actually to argue that the supreme judicial court had to bear the burden of proof in order to override the court below. The issue was "whether the Probate Court, with such facts as were available to it, made a judgment which was not plainly wrong."

In the present case, the decision of the probate court was "necessarily an ad hoc judgment based upon all the facts available to it." It could determine that the commencement or continuation of treatment would be of no benefit to the incompetent patient "where the record established the lack of utility or net disutility of the treatment, based on solid medical evidence." Here was another reference to *Quinlan,* in a rapid sequence of such references interrupted by little other text. The sweeping standard of "net disutility" must refer in *Quinlan* (the reference itself is unspecified) to that case's extraordinary calculus about the state's interests in the right to life decreasing and the patient's right of privacy increasing as the degree of medical bodily invasion increases and prognosis of recovery of sapient life dims.

The brief against treatment, understandably, stressed the dim prospects for a patient like Joseph Saikewicz more than the brief favoring treatment. It also accented, more than did the opposing brief, that the patient's "lack of cooperation" was "regarded as very significant by the treating physicians." It then endorsed the probate court's weighing of the toxic effects of the treatment, the patient's inability to cooperate, and the lack of probability of remission, "together with Mr. Saikewicz's age and the possible quality of life, against the finding that most persons capable of consent would choose the treatment and the fact that [he] was likely to live longer with treatment." The treatment would "create an unbearable situation for Mr. Saikewicz with few benefits"; his longer life would be "months filled with pain, nausea, twice daily blood transfusions, and the likelihood of hemorrhage and infection." Such "additional life would be an horrendous experience for Mr. Saikewicz."

Then follow—again in rapid succession and without significant other argument or citation of other cases—two references to *Quinlan*. The first is in support of providing "comfort and company rather than utilizing extraordinary measures." In *Quinlan* this had in mind the *dying:* "Physicians distinguish between curing the ill and comforting and easing the dying; . . . they refuse to treat the curable as if they were dying or ought to die, and . . . they have sometimes refused to treat the hopeless and dying as if they were curable. . . . We think these attitudes represent a balanced implementation of a profoundly realistic perspective on the meaning of life and death and they represent the whole Judeo-Christian tradition of regard for human life."

The next reference to *Quinlan* was in support of "balancing" judgments in regard to incompetents: "As nearly as may be determined considering the guarded area of remote uncertainties characteristic of most medical science predictions, she can never be restored to cognitive or sapient life. Even with regard to the vegetative level and improvement therein (if such it may be called) the prognosis is extremely poor and the extent unkown if it should in fact occur." The present brief concluded from that, "the importance of the [*Quinlan*] decision is its weighing of the interests of the incompetent to some life with the harsh realities of her existence in a chronic vegetative state. The Court's decision was *a reasonable balancing of the interests*" (italics added).

Neither point, of course, was pertinent to the case of Joseph Saikewicz. Then there was equally impertinent reference, with cases cited, to "the Constitutional principle which permits competent adults to decline medical treatment" based on "the Constitutional right of privacy and the common law concept that individuals control their own bodies."

The final citation of *Quinlan* as precedent in the brief against treatment was located in the context of offering an interpretation of exceptions to the rule that the state as parens patriae will order treatment of incompetent patients to save their lives, over the objection of parents. This final appeal to *Quinlan* was to that opinion's distinction between its own reasoning and that of *Heston*. In *Heston* the New Jersey Supreme Court ordered treatment because the voiceless patient was "apparently salvable to long life and vibrant health," and the "medical procedure required (usually a transfusion) constituted a minimal bodily invasion." In *Quinlan* the principle—cited in full at this point by the brief against treatment, and with approval—was that "the State's interest weakens and the individual's right to privacy grows as the degree of bodily invasion increases and the prognosis dims. Ultimately there comes a point at which the individual's rights overcome the State interest." We have seen, however, that *Quinlan* wrestled that formula out of a mistaken reading of the blood transfusion cases, as if they involve only the slight invasiveness of a transfusion and not the major surgery often associated with the latter procedure, which Jehovah's Witnesses have, in their opinion, good religious reasons to reject. So do ethical-legal mistakes replicate themselves.

The brief concludes with a rather astonishing argument to the effect that since "there is no way to determine how Mr. Saikewicz would vote if he could," the probate court could rightly order that he not be treated without reference to ordinary legal efforts to discover how he would or might vote. This concluding argument explains the brief's stress on the plenipoteniary power of a court of equity, and on the burden of proof the supreme judical court must bear if it reversed its decision. It also explains the omission—at two points the omission is so palpable as to appear deliberate—of any reference to the guardian's and the probate court's finding that, in the vast majority of cases, normal patients suffering from the same disease choose chemotherapy when it is offered them. That would have been a way to discover at least some grounds for determining, in human judgment, how Mr. Saikewicz might vote. By these omissions the brief makes manifest the fact that, in substituting the court's judgment for the patient's, it wanted the balancing of pains and benefits to proceed with reference only to his likelihood of *significant* remission. That would be easier to settle, in this case, as a supposable balancing "objective" judgment, if Saikewicz's wishes in the matter were declared to be wholly beyond accessibility to any court. That is to say, the court should uphold the decision below because normal people's judgments afford no basis for knowing how a retarded person may value his own continued life.

Citing evidence of older patients who sometimes refuse chemotherapy, the conclusion to be drawn is simply that *nothing* tells us how Mr. Saikewicz would make a judgment. Freed from any norm drawn from how the vast majority of patients decide, the "best interest" of the patient can mean only some substituted judgment concerning his least detrimental alternative. Thus the appeal to the principle of substituted judgment—that "the guardian is regarded as acting upon the same motives and considerations as would have moved the incompetent"—seems to be a nominalistic or arbitrary stipulation that has already placed what the incompetent would do into the realm of the unknowable. To determine his will or interests, in any case, there is no limiting reference to the norm of other patients' choices under the same conditions of illness. Thus the right to treatment and Joseph Saikewicz's right of privacy were brought into stark conflict. The conflict, I should say, was between the known and the unknowable, with proxies and courts to resolve the conflict rather arbitrarily, having *Quinlan* in the background, and—the brief argued—with little or no weight given to the *normal* will to live when faced with similar medical threats. Nowhere, of course, is there any reference to the law's long-standing protection of life against any consensus.

Brief of the Massachusetts Association for Retarded Citizens

In its amicus curiae brief, the association for retarded citizens did not "take a position on the correctness of the [probate court's] specific decision in this obviously difficult case." The association, however, argued strongly for a "life-biased" ruling. It urged that "the *Quinlan* case is inapplicable because it involved a ward in a vegetable state for whom there was no possibility of any cognitive life." No simple "right to life" approach or a "right to privacy approach" could help to resolve this case. In particular, the association objected to the weight the probate judge gave to what he called "the quality of life possible for [Saikewicz] even if the treatment does bring about remission." The association stated its firm belief "that the 'quality of life' argument is an improper foundation on which to support a denial of treatment." Otherwise expressed, "the fact of mental retardation, as such, is not, and should not be relevant to any medical decision."

Emphasis should be placed, however, on the words *as such;* perhaps we can say that the association's viewpoint was that mental retardation should not be directly or solely determinative of a medical decision to treat or not to treat. For it disagreed with the contention of the brief favoring treatment that the court *could not do otherwise* than to order treatment once it found that chemotherapy would be chosen by most normal patients or given to normal patients too young to choose for themselves. For Saikewicz to "receive the same medical evaluation as a normal adult," the association said, did not exclude consideration of *medical* differences between his case and that of a normal patient. One such factor mentioned was the "pain which the ward, inherently, can never comprehend." Another was his possible resistance or noncooperation with treatment (though the brief warns that treatment should not be denied "because of the difficulties doctors encounter in furnishing treatment to such a person"). These are possible medical indications against treatment. Thus, the argument seems to be that there may be narrow medical grounds for withholding treatment that are related to a patient's mental retardation, even if mental retardation *as such* or quality of life judgments are never good or sufficient reasons for distinguishing retardates from normal patients afflicted with the same illness. While not favoring one side or the other of the ruling the court handed down, the association presented the case I have sketched—warning throughout that physicians, the guardian ad litem, and the courts "must be alert to determine whether that decision is medically sound, or merely medically convenient. . . . The greater evil is the risk that the mentally retarded, among others, will be denied equal treatment because of real or imagined difficulties in administering to them. . . ."

THE UNWRITTEN OPINION

The Supreme Judicial Court of Massachusetts handed down the ruling that the "Brief Against Treatment" asked for. Whether the court agreed with that brief's reasoning we shall never know, since no opinion was issued. On the tentative hypothesis that the court did agree with the argument of that brief, it reached two important conclusions in the Saikewicz case. First, the court depended on *Quinlan,* added further flaws to that opinion, and interpreted it in ways probably not intended by the New Jersey court as the meaning properly to be drawn from its standard of prognosis of unlikely recovery of cognitive sapient life. Secondly, the Massachusetts court applied in this case the normless substituted judgment it reached when it ordered a bone marrow transplant from a 13-year-old incompetent, of whom the guardian ad litem reported that

> after explaining the procedure and discussing the transplantation with him, the boy could not answer simple questions referring to what he had been told. In a written report to the Court, the guardian stated that he could not give permission for the boy to donate bone marrow because the boy could not demonstrate understanding of the procedure well enough to give a truly informed consent. On the other hand the guardian refused to deny this boy the "right" to help his dying brother simply because others did not have easy access to his cognitive processes.[6]

Likewise, in the present case—not involving help to any other particular person in a matter of life or death—it is possible that the supreme judicial court made its decision simply in face of the inaccessibility of Saikewiczs cognitive processes. That was the brief's final argument: there was no way to tell what the patient would do. If so, then the patient's incompetence (his reason for needing protection) became the reason for not protecting his life. In any case, no grounds were discovered for how he would vote by reasoning from how the vast majority of patients choose who are fatally ill with the same sort of leukemia.

Still it is possible that the court's ruling was not based in most substantive respects upon the brief's arguments against treatment. With a little imagination and perhaps stretching speculation a bit, it is possible to construct an opinion that would bring the court's reasoning far closer to a medical indications policy judgment. Perhaps its reasoning was not an extension of *Quinlan*'s "irrecoverability of cognitive sapient life" to encompass the irrecoverability of more than three-year-old cognitivity. Perhaps the expected low quality of future life was not brought into the question or seized as an excuse for nontreatment. Perhaps the invasiveness of the treatment was not measured against the patient's childlike inability to understand what was being done with him or his childlike inability to cooperate. Perhaps Saikewicz's

6. Melvin D. Levine, M.D., et al., "The Medical Ethics of Bone Marrow Transplantation in Childhood," *Journal of Pediatrics* 86 (January 1975): 145–50.

incompetence was not made the chief point on which the decision turned. Perhaps the court's unwritten opinion would have been closer to the viewpoint of the association for retarded citiens.

At least, Saikewicz's severe retardation need not have been isolated or elevated in isolation into the decisive consideration. Lack of cooperation from anyone *is,* after all, part of medical treatment to be taken into account. Instead of a quality-of-life judgment simpliciter, could this have been a quality-of-life-during-treatment judgment? Go back to Dr. William Davis's initially strange word when he expressed his view that Joseph Saikewicz should not be treated. "The quality of his life has been good," he said, "and he would be likely to die a painless death." That could well be a sympathetic physician's judgment that, incompetent as the patient was, he nevertheless had a relatively good life compared to the inexplicable pain now hopelessly to be imposed upon him. He was probably not as docile as a three-year-old child; there were probably some quite specific counterindications to treatment. Recall also that the brief favoring treatment spoke puzzlingly of "the 'quality of life' that Mr. Saikewicz would lead *undergoing* chemotherapy" (italics added): that was the quality of life open to this terminal patient, although a different sort of expected quality of life was often referred to in the briefs. So it could have been this particular patient's condition of life *during* treatment—the life to be taken from his months or a year undergoing treatment as opposed to the life to be added to those same months or years—that was placed in the balance.

It could, therefore, be suggested that the patient's fulfillment of his life's potential or his inherent capacity for life's value of interrelatedness, overwhelmed by his retardation, was not brought directly into the issue of his protectability; or, at least, that this played only remotely a part through more proximate indications that were relevant. One might try to resolve the case of Joseph Saikewicz in terms of what Warren Reich called "extraordinary circumstances" (his translation of extraordinary means). No categorical discrimination may have been made as to the condition of the patient-person. Then it was not the patient's inner spiritual hardship, or his lack of capacity, that spelled the end of the obligation to treat. Instead, under these given circumstances, perhaps it was because *treatment itself* imposed unacceptable hardship. As Reich wrote, "When the very means or effort to sustain life inseparably involves a truly grave excessive hardship, the obligation to continue may diminish to the point where one is no longer obliged to continue the efforts."[7] Saikewicz certainly was dying, without treatment—as the eventuality proved. Moreover, I said earlier[8] that, while not altogether persuaded by Reich's formulation, his position seems to me to be equivalent in significant respects to a comparison of treatments, or of treatment with no treatment—not a comparison of patient-persons.

Which unwritten opinion did the Supreme Judicial Court of Massachusetts intend to issue? What was the reasoning behind its ruling? Perhaps the law and our courts are not capable of decisions based on the subtleties of moral reasons I have just introduced. If not, then the ethical rule of practice should be the treatment of incompetents always in the way normal patients would be treated. Best of all, the ethical rule of practice should be whether the treatment is *offered* to normal adult patients, *given* to normal patients who because of age cannot themselves refuse treatment, *protected* in such patients by courts against any private decision to withhold them. If the court did not mean to issue the sort of opinion I have speculatively constructed for the strange case of Joseph Saikewicz, then the likelihood that we may never have the actual opinion—to say nothing of those promised procedural mandates for decision making—is a blessing in absentia.[9]

7. Warren T. Reich, "Defective Newborn Children: An Inquiry into 'Quality of Life' Ethics" (Paper delivered at conference on spina bifida babies, Skytop, Pennsylvania, May 4–7, 1976).

8. See p. 180–81 above.

9. See p. 335 below for the final decision in the Saikewicz case.

9

The California Natural Death Act

On October 1, 1976, California became the first state in the nation to grant terminally ill persons the right to authorize, by prior directive (sometimes called a "living will") the withdrawal of life-sustaining procedures when death is believed imminent.[1] On that date, Governor Edmund G. Brown, Jr., signed into law the Natural Death Act [2] passed by the California legislature on August 30, 1976.[3]

As of March 1, 1977, at least forty-nine death-with-dignity bills were pending in thirty-six state legislatures. Twenty-eight of these bills in twenty-three states are identical with, similar to, or quite clearly based on the California Natural Death Act. Texas Senate Bill 148 is one such example; it differs in no important respect from the California provisions to be discussed below. Arkansas, Idaho, New Mexico, and Texas have, in addition to California, already enacted legislation. Arkansas permits the execution of a document on behalf of a minor or incompetent adult by parent, spouse, child, or guardian; this might be called the right-to-die once removed. Legislation pending in seven states, while providing for some form of a living will, does not follow California in mandating a specific wording. The language proposed by the Euthanasia Education Council appears only in Vermont H.R.37. The Utah bill H.R.11 uses the directive proposed by Dr. Milton D. Heifetz.[4] Missouri H.R.104 is an example of a proposed statute that provides for the execution of "a document directing that no maintenance medical treatment be utilized," etc., without requiring a specific wording of the directive. The Missouri bill also differs from the majority of these bills by defining the failure of a physician to cease

1. *The New York Times,* October 2, 1976.

2. California Health and Safety Code, div. 7, pt. 1, chap. 3.9, Natural Death Act, secs. 7185–7195.

3. *The New York Times,* August 31, 1976.

4. Milton D. Heifetz, M.D., with Charles Mangel, *The Right to Die.* New York: G. P. Putnam's Sons, 1975, pp. 40–42.

maintenance medical treatment as a misdemeanor punishable upon conviction as provided by law. The vast majority of the bills provide no enforcement procedure. Instead they follow California in exempting from any criminal or civil liability the failure to effect a directive. Such failure—coupled with failure to transfer the patient to another physician—constitutes unprofessional conduct.

Opposition to this rash of proposed legislation arises from public apprehension that these bills, if enacted, will be a giant step toward euthanasia or "mercy killing" in medical practice and public policy. Opposition also comes from many physicians and health care professionals who believe that they can be trusted to act in the best interest of their patients, and who rightly resent any suggestion that cessation of treatment at an appropriate time is not already a part of good medical practice. I shall suggest in this chapter that there was more to be said for both these viewpoints before the *Quinlan* norms were adopted into our law, and before it was publicly announced that some physicians mean to withhold treatment from uncomprehending patients who are not dying. There may be need for legislation that links cessation of treatment with impending death, and such legislation may be one roadblock in the way of the medical adoption of policies of negligent euthanasia of the nondying.

The debate over the bill in California was typical of the debate going on in all the states. To speak first of the generally religious opinion in that state: the bill was supported by a battery of Protestant and Episcopal churches and associations of churches; it was strenuously opposed by the California Pro-Life Council; while the California Catholic Conference modified its position "from OPPOSITION to WATCH" shortly before the bill was passed.[5]

The bill was supported by the California Medical Association,[6] the California Nurses Association, the California Conference of Local Health Officers, the American Civil Liberties Union, and various senior citizens associations. However, Dr. Jerome Lackner, head of the state

5. Letter from the Most Reverend John S. Cummins, executive director of the California Catholic Conference, to the sponsor of the bill, Assemblyman Barry Keene, August 12, 1976.

6. The CMA declared: "Patients have a right to make some decisions about their own lives and have a right to die with dignity. . . . Although many physicians currently take enough initiative to make these decisions, others do not out of fear of legal ramifications."

health department, opposed the bill. His grounds were that by defining the very rigorous conditions under which a physician may withdraw treatment without fear of liability, the Natural Death Act may have implied that physicians are liable for ending treatment in patients who have not executed a proper directive. The bill would, in Dr. Lackner's opinion, discourage physicians from exercising proper discretion in discontinuing treatment procedures, which has always been a part of good medical practice. The sponsor of the bill, Assemblyman Barry Keene, pointed out that the bill specifies that the rights it confers are in no way meant to "supercede or impair" any other existing rights of physicians or patients. The California Medical Association announced that amendments to the law will be urged to spell out a broader exemption from liability for physicians.[7]

Portentous issues are at stake. It is, therefore, exceedingly important that we analyze the provisions of this law (which went into effect January 1, 1977) and suggest some appraisals of it. For when we speak of the California law as the first Natural Death Act to become law in the United States, there is some slight suggestion of more to come [8]—not to mention the amendments that already are being proposed.

Peripheral Protective Provisions

Before we get to the heart of the matter, there are some features of the California Natural Death Act worthy of note, even if they are peripheral protections. The first two are significant *omissions,* what the law did *not* do.

Perhaps most important of all were eleven words *omitted* from the preamble (7186) before final passage. Among the legislature's "findings" justifying the statute, the words "and an unreasonable emotional and financial hardship on the patient's family" were stricken out. Those are considerations for a patient who is conscious and competent *at the time* of treatment refusal to think about. Not yet as a society do we mean by law—not even following a prior directive—to allow physicians to let go one particular life in order to save others from grave distress. There are no words in the document to be executed in California directing (or allowing) a physician to weigh such

7. Herbert G. Lawson, "California's 'Natural Death Act,'" *The Wall Street Journal,* December 28, 1976.

8. Like the humor in introducing someone as "my first wife."

considerations when he comes to the time of actual decision about primary care of an incompetent or unconscious patient. Inscribed in the California law by this omission was something of the Jewish wisdom noted above: that no one who has any interest in the outcome should hasten the death of another, not even by praying for that person's death. In short, while relief of families from unreasonable emotional or financial burdens may be *an* effect of the act, and may properly be among the motives of persons who execute the directive, the chief purpose and direct effect of the statute has in view the proper primary care of patients whose death is *imminent*. That *necessary* condition must also be in itself a *sufficient* condition for decisions to withdraw or withhold treatments. Burdens on other people are not to be given weight by physicians, nor should they be given weight by the state in discharging its interest in protecting life.

It ought to be pointed out, however, that the words in question were still in the statute during most of the time the bill was publicly debated in California. I have no way to measure whether the widespread apprehension aroused by the bill [9] focused on that bit of social utilitarianism; nor can we tell to what extent the omitted provision aroused support for it from the first. A column by Herman Hoth in *The Sacramento Bee* [10] and a San Francisco station KCBS editorial [11] mentioned unreasonable financial and emotional burdens and hardships upon the patient's family among the reasons for supporting the bill. Perhaps other media also counted that as among the strengths of the bill. I can only comment that on balance the evidence can be read either way. showing how close one state in the nation came to institutionalizing letting go one particular life for the sake of others and yet at the same time evidencing that the entire public policy processes of this one state drew back from that measure of involuntary euthanasia.

There was another "omission"—one which was never in earlier versions of the statute but which has been proposed as a codicil to

9. Senate majority leader David Roberti opposed the bill because, he said, it would permit "physicians and social planners to commit euthanasia," and because he did not believe that aged and terminal patients were competent to make the decision or that they could be adequately protected from subtle coercions. A Stockton citizens' group passed out handbills on the capitol steps calling the bill "the legal murder act." Herbert G. Lawson, "California's 'Natural Death Act.' "

10. May 2, 1976.

11. July 7, 1976.

be added to some living wills by those who wish to do so. That is, the suggestion that anyone who cannot tolerate life if he suffers blindness or deafness, or whatever, should be able to direct his physician not to resuscitate him if that would save him from a continued life with those defects.[12] Here we do not need to take up the question of the morality of suicide. It is sufficient to observe that no one has a right to ask another's assistance, to ask medical assistance, in committing suicide under those or other self-selected conditions. That would mean turning physicians into technicians serving patients' wishes, however arbitrary or nonmedical may be their wishes to live no longer. It would be, to say the least, a cowardly way to commit suicide. Only one living will can have legal force in California, and that is the law's directive—no codicils added.

Next we should take up the protections with which the California statute specifically surrounds signatories of its directive. The directive must be "signed by the declarant in the presence of two witnesses not related to the declarant by blood or marriage and who would not be entitled to any portion of the estate of the declarant upon his decease" (7188). The "and" in that sentence is a conjunction; I suppose everyone realizes that declarants should be protected from persons entitled to inherit their estates. Not everyone, however, would grant that a declarant may need also to be protected from *anyone* related to him or her by blood or marriage, whether there is an inheritance or not. Here, surely, the California statute unknowingly incorporates the wisdom of Judaism that no one who has *any* interest in the matter (including family) can even pray for sooner death for another. An interest in unbearing the burdens of our roles and relations can distort care for persons needing help no less than hope of inheritance.

Two physicians must certify "terminal conditional"—which (as we shall see) is defined as impending death. Other protections are af-

12. This suggestion is tucked away in a "living" will developed by the Law and Ethics Working Group of the Faculty Seminar of the Center for the Analysis of Health and Medical Practices of the Harvard School of Public Health. Such a "will" should "leave an open paragraph where individuals might insert specific instructions regarding particular conditions under which they would not wish to be maintained in life." Examples given include "conditions such as paralysis or blindness, and degrees of suffering, . . . circumstances under which one does not wish to enter a hospital or nursing home" (Sissela Bok, "Personal Directions for Care at the End of Life," *The New England Journal of Medicine* 295, no. 7 (August 12, 1976) : 367–69).

forded by the act. About them all I must observe at the outset (as a theologian in the heritage of the Reformation) that no carefully drawn statute can rest upon the assumption that there is an "island" of purity in any human being immune from sinful self-interest (unfortunately called "total depravity" by my theological and intellectual forebears).

Not only must *two* physicians certify that death is imminent. When the original directive, or living will, is made, the attending physician is (among others) excluded. The two witnesses to a directive "shall not be the attending physician, an employee of the attending physician, or a health facility in which the declarant is a patient." All such persons are presumed possibly to have an interest in sooner death, whether they do or not. Neither blood nor marriage nor the role of a personal physician is presumed to have saved anyone assuredly from too great an interest in sooner death. At least, anyone in these roles and relations must be *seen* to have no easy way to give effect to his or her interest in the sooner death of another, if in rare cases they have such an interest.

Special care is taken to protect patients who, when signing the directive may be institutionalized in nursing facilities. One of the two witnesses, in such an instance, must be "a patient advocate or ombudsman" designated by the State Department of Aging. The intent of that provision is clearly stated: such patients "may be so insulated from a voluntary decision-making role, by virtue of the custodial nature of their care, as to require special assurance that they are capable of willfully and voluntarily executing a directive" (7188.5).

No one around the dying is assumed to be a pure rationalist. Neither are the dying themselves. Whatever may have been the prudence of the decision of a declarant when he signed the directive, those prior wishes are not to be inexorably carried out as if they remain so, or on the presumption that one's *real* will continues to be the one expressed in the declaration. Provision is made for written revocation; that is, rationally deliberate revocation. But provision is also made for revocation by defacing, obliterating, burning, or tearing the declaration. I like that: a human being is permitted to die irrationally if he wishes, or to continue to live less rationally than before. There are guarantees that his prior directive was made calmly and without duress. Revocation, however, may be made by a declarant "without regard to his mental state or competency" (7189). That's good, if we mean to respect human persons in their dying and not their worthy decisions only. Any person who falsifies or forges the directive of another or willfully conceals or withholds personal knowledge of a revocation shall be guilty of unlawful homicide (7194). Before final passage words were inserted into the directive saying, "If I have been diagnosed as pregnant and that diagnosis is known to my physician, this directive shall have no force or effect during the course of my pregnancy" (7188. para. 3). Finally, it is expressly stated that nothing in the statute "shall be construed to condone, authorize, or approve mercy killing, or to permit any affirmative or deliberate act or omission to end life other than to permit the natural processes of dying . . ."(7195).

Notice that not only any deliberate act but also any deliberate *omission* to end life is forbidden, other than acts *or* omissions specifically related to (a) the process of dying and to (b) prior competent declarations on the part of the patient. Otherwise, either action or omission may be some degree of homicide. And rightly so, when decision is made without authorization for another.

The Directive

The words of the directive, in its central paragraph, read:

> If at any time I should have an incurable injury, disease, or illness certified to be a terminal condition by two physicians, and where the application of life-sustaining procedures would serve only to artificially prolong the moment of my death, and where my physician determines that my death is imminent whether or not life-sustaining procedures are utilized, I direct that such procedures be withheld or withdrawn, and that I be permitted to die naturally (7188).

That is the only living will given legal effect in California.

Any reader of the present volume, and any careful reader of the directive, will see at once that it contains several quite ambiguous expressions. Among these are "incurable," "terminal condition," "life-sustaining procedures," "artificially prolong the moment of death"; how these relate to "my death is imminent"; and the bearing of "whether or not life-sustaining procedures are utilized," whatever was the prognosis meant by those earlier expressions.

Nevertheless, I believe that the California Natural Death Act contains language that is wrought with sufficient care. The directive must be read in the light of the definitions the act also contains. The ambiguous words in the preamble and in the directive are made rather clear, if not perfectly clear, in the definition of *life-sustaining procedure,* in the definition of *terminal condition*—even, finally, in the wording of the directive itself. An assessment of the California statute, I suggest, must address first of all the necessary and sufficient conditions that it instates for withholding or withdrawing treatments, not the peripheral protections we brought up first. Here is the real cutting edge of the medical, legal, and ethical intersections. For a proper understanding we need to go to the definitions.

Among the definitions (7187c), *life-sustaining procedure* means "any medical procedure or intervention which utilizes mechanical or other artificial means to sustain, restore, or supplant a vital function, which . . . would serve only to prolong the moment of death. . . ." So far, that remains rather loose language. What does it mean to say "serves only to prolong the moment of death"? In some senses of those words, a pacemaker is a mechanical means which sustains or supplants a vital function and whose constant and sole function is to "prolong the moment of death." The definition, therefore, does not conclude at that point; it goes on to say: "and where, in the judgment of the attending physician, death is imminent whether or not such procedures are utilized." Thus, *impending death* is the fundamental test. Moreover, the words "whether or not such procedures are utilized" imply that the terminal patient must be certified to be dying even in the presence of an artificial life-support whose withdrawal has been brought into question, or even in face of an available life-support whose initiation or first use has been brought into view. This last stipulation should be questioned.

Terminal condition (7187f) is defined precisely in order to distinguish it from *incurable,* just as *life-sustaining procedure* had to be more precisely defined than *prolong the moment of death. Terminal condition* means "an incurable condition . . . which, regardless of the application of life-sustaining procedures, would, with reasonable medical judgment, produce death, and where the application of life-sustaining procedures serve only to postpone the moment of death." Notice again the stringent requirement: "regardless of the application of life-sustaining procedures." The words "*whether or not* such procedures are utilized" qualified the *imminence* of death in the definition of *life-sustaining procedure*. Here the words *regardless of the application* qualify a condition—an incurable condition—to make it properly describable as "terminal."

The words *postpone the moment of death* are less obscure than the words *prolong the moment of death* (in the previous definition and in the directive). Perhaps the legislative drafters were trying to say something about the process of dying when they wrote "prolong the moment." However that may be, it is fair to say that the definition of *terminal condition* is, by itself, inadequate. The drafters wanted to distinguish *terminal condition* from *incurable*. It is doubtful that they succeeded in doing so. Most human conditions "caused by injury disease or illness" are incurable or terminal, if that means likely within reasonable medical judgment to produce death *without* the application of life-sustaining procedures. This is to say, many, most, or all medical treatments serve only to postpone the moment of death. If the test is reasonable medical certainty that a condition will produce death *regardless* of (i.e., even with) the application of life-sustaining procedures, that describes an "incurable condition" no less than a "terminal" one. One could be terminal for a very long time, by this definition—unless it happened that the patient dies sooner from another "incurable" condition. Few there are who are ever going to die of what the statute calls "natural death"; that expression has little meaning except in contrast to medicated death. Therefore, I suggest that a favorable reading of the definition of *terminal condition* and the only consistent reading of the act in its entirety must be one that stresses the phrase "death is imminent whether or not life-sustaining procedures are utilized" in both the directive and the definition of *life-sustaining procedure*. A terminal condition should be understood in terms of the impending death of the incurable.

If, however, the words *whether or not* and *regardless* are removed from the statute (as *arguably* they should be removed from the status of an additional restriction upon letting the dying die), then the interpretation I have just given of the California law tends to lose *some* of its force. The imminence of death, death impending, could too readily take its meaning from "incurable condition" or "terminal" illness," instead of the other way round. Still I think that the reading I have given is a correct one.

The signal feature of the California law is that the distinction between morally mandatory and morally dispensible means is anchored in a physician's reasonable certainty of the objective fact that death is imminent. If anyone would have it otherwise—if instead he cries classes or ordinary and extraordinary procedures—he opens the door to involuntary euthanasia. It does not matter that in legal terms the highest degree of such offense would be called "negligent" or "grossly negligent" homicide, or that in moral analysis the wrong is said to supervene by "omission."

Given that anchorage in physicians' certification that death is impending, however, the qualification "whether or not life-sustaining procedures are utilized" may say too much.[13] Would that require a patient to be able to accomplish his dying "up against" the life supports already initiated and up against any that are available? Would the referent of a physician's respect and protection be the ill and dying patient *plus* those machines? Is it not sufficient to say that the physician must determine that a procedure already begun or any that might be begun can affect the imminence of death only by prolonging the dying process? Perhaps that was what was meant by "prolong the moment of death." [14]

An Evaluation

There are persuasive arguments against these natural death acts. A neat summary of the objections is that "the existing ambiguity [is] better than the anticipated hardening of medical hearts." [15] Ambiguity, however, is not a correct word for the positive position defended. Liv-

13. These words are significant for Karen Lebacgz's objection to the passage of the statute as a whole (in agreement with the opposition lodged by the head of the state health department, Dr. Jerome Lackner). See her "Against the California Natural Death Act," *Hastings Center Report* 7, no. 2 (April 1977) : 14.

14. Professor Thomas Oden—a theological ethicist at Drew University, whose location in Madison, New Jersey, placed him into deep involvement in organized interdisciplinary discussion of the Quinlan case—is the only ethicist I know who begins his analysis on the presumption that life-sustaining procedures *in use* should be continued. Perhaps I should say instead that the moral and decisional questions in the focus of his analysis are whether or not to institute further efforts to sustain life, what are the grounds for not doing so, etc. In those decisions, Oden finds that quality-of-life criteria will today be ranked high by decision makers drawn from several professions and positions in life—whether or not those criteria *ought* to be made determinative. See his *Should Treatment Be Terminated?* New York: Harper and Row, 1976.

15. Michael Garland, "Politics, Legislation, and Natural Death," *Hastings Center Report* 6, no. 5 (October 1976) : 6.

ing wills, it is said, enshrine into law the false notion that, without them, physicians are masters, not servants, of their patients. The onus is on the individual to write a will if he wishes to avoid excessive resuscitation. Patient rights are conferred rather than recognized; if this notion takes hold, then the law could also confer the right to be killed. Physicians are made servants of the statute, thereby losing their ability to be the advocates of their patients. Freedom of medical practice is impaired, and families are excluded, on the false assumption that physicians generally resuscitate their patients to death, thereby imposing medicated indignities upon them. These statutory remedies are misguided efforts to protect physicians from lawyers, not patients from physicians. The latter protection is not needed because physicians generally make nuanced decisions to withhold or stop useless treatments.

A hardening of medical hearts should realistically be anticipated both in the presence and in the absence of a living will. A patient who has made a living will may be underresuscitated for fear of professional misconduct or—according to some statutes—for committing a misdemeanor punishable by law. A patient who has made no such directive is likely to be overresuscitated insofar as his not making one when he could is taken to be a signal of his wishes in the matter. The care of the dying will be depersonalized and taken out of the human judgments of physicians and families. There are less drastic legislative remedies that would recognize "allowing to die" in the practice of medicine and that might accord some status to informal documents submitted by patients to their physicians. Natural death acts are not only not needed; they are also predictably counterproductive.[16]

16. In the above summary of the arguments, I follow Richard A. McCormick, S.J., and André E. Hellegers, M.D., "Legislation and the Living Will," *America,* March 12, 1977, pp. 210–13). Two comments are in order: (1) The authors assume that *Quinlan* left general medical practice where it was before the case occurred. In chap. 7 I pointed out that the Supreme Court of New Jersey had good reason in its own findings for stopping there, but it did not do so and instead introduced its own novel juridical norms and procedures into the practice of medicine with incurables. (2) The article notes only the "terminal illness" language of the California act, while assuming throughout that "the dying process" is the focus of attention and that current medical practice (without the proposed acts and even in face of negligent manslaughter) is not tending to apply the traditional ethics of ordinary / extraordinary to nonconsenting incurables who may not be dying. The heart of that medical ethics in what should be its contemporary meaning is beautifully stated. The terms *ordinary* and *extraordinary* in their "full moral sense" are "utterly personal." There are "values more important than life in the living of life." There are also "values more important

Two intervening considerations, however, are persuasively in favor of statutes that by limitation to impending or imminent death are narrowly drawn to encompass only allowing the *dying* to die. One consideration is the fact that the final decision in the *Quinlan* case did not rest upon the court's *finding* that Karen was dying or its own endorsement of the practice of letting die (chapter 7 above). The second consideration is the trend to expand medical practice to allow the neglect of the nondying (chapters 5 and 6 above). In the face of these legal and medical actualities, a primary purpose and the immediate result of the California law seem to me, on balance, to be morally defensible. The statute gives legal effect to a specific formulation of a living will; it does not legalize arbitrary treatment-refusals. Moreover, I have also reluctantly come to the conclusion that carefully drawn legislation—as the California statute almost succeeds in being—may be the last, best chance we have to stem the tide that on its crest is bearing present-day society—every banner unfurled in the wind—toward the general practice of involuntary euthanasia. In other words, on the face of it the California law has merit; also, no better place is likely to be found at which to build a holding wall to protect the foundations of the Venice of Western law and morals from the daily watery bombardment that now threatens to take that city into the sea. So it seems to me that opponents of voluntary and of involuntary euthanasia have an additional good reason to support legislation like the California Natural Death Act. This means that the present writer's prudent political judgment differs from that voiced by the so-called pro-life movement, which has generally opposed such legislation in the several states. Amendments to come could readily prove my tactical judgment to be incorrect. Still, I do not know a better way than through our representatives in the state legislatures for a people to make known and

than life in the dying." And "decisions about the means and treatment of dying patients are above all quality-of-life judgments—judgments about how a patient will live while dying. . . ." The reader should note the adoption of Arthur Dyck's language, which, I argued in chap. 4 above, is compatible with a medical indications policy. One of the authors of the present article elsewhere affirms that Dyck's "otherwise fine presentation" does not "enlarge our understanding of the moral relevance . . . of the descriptive difference between commission and omission, direct and indirect" (McCormick, "Notes on Moral Theology," *Theological Studies* 14, no. 1 (March 1973) : 70. In that place, McCormick was moving to replace the distinction between letting die and directly dispatching patients with an estimation of the greater or lesser evil or burden to them.

effective its moral purpose in regard to the protection of life in the first and last of it. Legislation is our last resort if I am correct in believing that the common law's ancient protection of life—against any private decision makers and against any consensus—is eroding.

Many factors or influences conspire today to weaken our moral abhorrence of voluntary and of involuntary euthanasia. Doubtless many cultural forces are needed to complete the picture; but the reasons I summarize below come within the purview of an ethical analysis, even if these are only proximate causes or signs of more ultimate grounds for our increasing willingness to do perhaps the ultimate violation to a human life, our own or another's. The irony is that some of the reasons tempting to the embrace of euthanasia are reasons believed to be right-making or wrong-making in past religious ethics pertaining to medical practice.

The chapters in part 2 of this volume have cumulatively shown, I believe, that wrong-making is now one of the consequences of continued appeal to the distinction between ordinary and extraordinary means as mere classifications, as class names for certain procedures—that is, appeal to what I have called the "categorical" meaning of that ancient medical-moral distinction. This is most certainly the case when the class meaning of extraordinary (or morally dispensable) means is used by someone who fails to distinguish (1) between (a) conscious decision to refuse treatment in one's own case and (b) withholding treatment in the case of another; (2) between (a) "terminal" patients who are dying and (b) "terminal" patients who are simply incurable; (3) between (a) medical help and (b) prolonging dying; (4) between (a) biological indices for medical help and (b) socioeconomic measures of burden or advantage to come for the primary patient; or (5) between (a) medical help for a primary patient and (b) relieving the burden or serving the advantage of others.[17]

17. The following tabulation might be made of some of the conclusions suggested by the foregoing chapters. If 3a and 4a are the case, 1b is not morally permissible for 2b, 4b, or 5b reasons; 1a may be morally permissible or even praiseworthy for 2b, 4b, or 5b reasons even if 3a and 4a are the case; 1b is morally permissible if 2a; 2b patients, given that 1a is not the case, should be evaluated for treatment in terms of 4a and 5a and the availability of 3a; 1b is morally permissible even if 4a is the case, if there is no 3a or if to attempt 3a would likely do more harm; 1a is morally permissible if 2a. The last two formulations describe the two sorts of cases in which Dr. R. B. Zachary withholds treatment from defective babies: he does not "treat" the untreatable and he does not treat those whose death is impending. See chap. 4 above.

In 1957 Francis J. Connell, then professor of moral theology in the School of Sacred Theology at the Catholic University of America, stressed that Pius XII's address on prolonged artificial respiration meant that procedures that "only give a few days more of life to a dying person" are "extraordinary," and hence not obligatory.[18] That same address is now used in support of a notable shift of Catholic moral thought over to a minimum quality-of-life judgment—because the pope also drew attention to the fact that earthly life is not everything.[19] The *contemporary* history of the class concepts *ordinary* and *extraordinary* bids to become a movement away from decisive application to the dying to decisive application also to the nondying who are incompetent to speak for themselves. Thus, the Most Reverend John F. Wheaton, Roman Catholic archbishop of Hartford, pronounced that "no one is obliged to prolong his or her life or the life of another by using extraordinary or very difficult means." [20] That was a routinized categorical response to the announced practice of refusing treatment to defective infants, and moreover one that compresses its analytical failure in the expression "prolong life." That implies yet does not claim that all those babies were dying soon. Where this is not the case, continued use of this classificatory language *must* stretch to encompass a *kind* of life to be prolonged and a *kind* of life that ought not to be sustained.

This then is coupled with a doctrine of "substituted judgment" according to which treatment may be refused for another by appeal to the minimum quality of life we deem the primary patient would not want, or indeed would not want because he ought not. Given minimum sociability as a human being, a low-grade mongoloid would not want its life saved because of the great suffering his life would impose on the family; assuming minimum human decency, he ought not to want a life of such impairment at such cost to others. Some people come to favor the practice of benign neglect on simple utilitarian grounds. I suspect that religious people will work their way to this conclusion in a fashion similar to that just suggested. In all such reasoning, a categorical meaning of *ordinary* / *extraordinary* remains the constant

18. National Catholic Welfare Conference News Service, December 9, 1957.

19. See chap. 4 above, n. 33 and related text, for the current debate about the pontiff's meaning.

20. *The New York Times,* November 8, 1973.

factor, with its permissions embracing quality-of-life judgments never before a part of our religious and moral heritage.

Meantime, similar developments have taken place in the doctrine of substituted judgment in American legal cases. That used to mean a genuine search for some reasonable, uniquely individual basis for construing what an incompetent would consent to do. Realistic limits upon substituted judgment have now suffered "death by a thousand qualifications." That doctrine is now used "not to deny" incompetent subjects the "right" to do almost anything the courts want them to want to do.[21]

Therefore, it seems to me that if, as a consequence of the California law, current and future medical practice were braced to live up to its standards, then substituted judgments negligently bringing death to incurables would be ruled out. Such judgments made by familial or physician proxies, or by courts, need to be anchored in a determination that death is imminent (where there is the greatest possible clarity that medical treatment to sustain only purposelessly prolongs dying).[22] This needs to be so with rare "exceptions" (if there are any) or in cases to which indeed a medical indications policy itself may lead. In any case, physicians ought not to allow, as a professional rule of practice, the neglect of the incurable because they are incurable or because they have a terminal illness or because they were born that way. Moreover, it does seem evident that crying classes of ordinary / extraordinary means works in the opposite direction—namely, in the direction of substituted judgment favoring involuntary euthanasia (or, if someone prefers to say it euphemistically, nonvoluntary euthanasia) by omission or by action. The next logical step beyond choosing death by negligence for patients who are not dying is to choose these deaths by affirmative action. One can expect the logic of moral reasoning to "work" in the real world, too.

21. See John A. Robertson, "Organ Donation by Incompetents and the Substituted Judgment Doctrine," *Columbia Law Review* 76, no. 1 (January 1976) : 48–78; and chap. 7, n. 19 above.

22. Too late for analysis in this volume I obtained a manuscript copy of an alternative to "death with dignity" legislation, by Joseph M. Boyle, Jr., and Germain Grisez. Their model bill would simply make the tort (battery) of treating a patient against his express refusal survive the subsequent incompetence and death of the person wronged.

Endpiece

And after such training in common together, then at last, if we think fit, we may enter public life, or we may take counsel together on whatever course suggests itself, when we are better able to take counsel than now. For it seems to me shameful that, being what apparently at this moment we are, we should consider ourselves to be fine fellows, when we can never hold the same views about the same question—and those too the most vital of all—so deplorably uneducated are we! Then let us follow the guidance of the argument now made manifest, which reveals to us that this is the best way of life—to live and die in the pursuit of righteousness and all other virtues.

Plato, *Gorgias*

For discussing words with words is as entangled as interlocking and rubbing the fingers with the fingers, in which case it may scarcely be distinguished, except by the one himself who does it, which fingers itch and which give aid to the itching.

You as well as other men who judge matters suitably would reply to a garrulous word-lover who said: "I teach in order to talk" with "Man, why not rather speak in order to teach?" For if these things are true, as you know they are, you truly see how much less words are to be esteemed than that for the sake of which we use words, since the use of words is superior to the words. For words exist in order that they may be used, and in addition we use them in order to teach. As teaching is superior to talking, in like degree speech is better than words. So of course doctrine is far superior to words.

St. Augustine, *Concerning the Teacher*

I think I have now, by God's help, discharged my obligation in writing this large work. Let those who think I have said too little, or those who think I have said too much, forgive me; and let those who think I have said just enough give thanks, not to me, but rather join me in giving thanks to God. Amen.

St. Augustine, *The City of God*

The Final Decision in the Saikewicz Case

Almost six months after its ruling, the Supreme Judicial Court of Massachusetts issued its delayed 41-page opinion (November 30, 1977). Speaking for a unanimous court, Justice Liacos held that the probate court had full and the *sole* authority to make such a determination; and, for an undisclosed numerical majority, held that the judge made a proper decision in this particular case. The court (1) rejected *Quinlan's* privatizing of such decisions, its giving death decisions over to a concurrence of family, physicians, and ethics committees; (2) jettisoned Judge Jekanowiski's reference to "the quality of life possible to him even if the treatment does bring about remission" among his reasons against treatment ("To the extent that this formulation equates the value of life with any measure of the quality of life, we firmly reject it"); and (3) turned thumbs down on any need to ask whether many or most competent patients choose treatment ("Nor do statistical factors indicating that a majority of competent persons similarly situated choose treatment resolve the issue"). In summary, where Judge Muir in *Quinlan* held that "there is no constitutional right to die that can be asserted by a parent for his incompetent adult child," the Massachusetts court asserted that there *is* a constitutional right to die that can be asserted for an incompetent by an impartial court. That such a determination must be judiciable is a glory of American law. However, we may ask whether the court's reach did not exceed its grasp. In substituting judgment for this never-competent patient, it set aside the standard of a normal child patient, who also cannot understand the pain, would have to be restrained during prolonged treatment, etc. Attempting to get at Saikewicz's "subjective" standard, the court treated him *as if* he were a competent patient who, then, would "reasonably" take into account the fact that he was incompetent. Background quality of life was, thus, brought into the foreground.

Index